The Law School of University College Dublin

A History

The Law School of University College Dublin

A HISTORY

W.N. Osborough

FOUR COURTS PRESS

This book was set in 10.5 on 13 point Ehrhardt by
Mark Heslington, Scarborough, North Yorkshire for
FOUR COURTS PRESS
7 Malpas Street, Dublin 8, Ireland
www.fourcourtspress.ie
and in North America for
FOUR COURTS PRESS
c/o ISBS, 920 N.E. 58th Avenue, Suite 300, Portland, OR 97213.

A catalogue record for this title
is available from the British Library.

ISBN 978-1-84682-542-2

SPECIAL ACKNOWLEDGEMENT

The publication of this book was supported by the UCD Sutherland School of Law.

Printed in Great Britain
by Antony Rowe Ltd, Chippenham, Wilts.

Contents

Illustrations

Abbreviations

AC	Appeal Cases
App Cas	Appeal Cases
Atk	Atkyns (reports)
Barn	Barnewall (reports)
Bl Com	Blackstone, *Commentaries*
Burr	Burrow's (reports)
Cal. S.P. Ire.	*Calendar of State Papers, Ireland*
Camb LJ	*Cambridge Law Journal*
Car & K	Carrington & Kirwan (reports)
CLR	Commonwealth Law Reports (Australia)
Co. *Inst*	Coke, *Institutes*
Dears	Dearsley (reports)
DIAS	Dublin Institute for Advanced Studies
DIB	*Dictionary of Irish Biography*
Dick	Dickens (reports)
DNB	*Dictionary of National Biography*
Dublin Univ LJ	*Dublin University Law Journal*
DULJ	*Dublin University Law Journal*
El & Bl	Ellis & Blackburn (reports)
Eng Rep	English Reports
H. Bl	Henry Blackstone (reports)
ICLR	Irish Common Law Reports
IFS	Irish Free State
IHS	*Irish Historical Studies*
ILR	Irish Law Reports
ILRM	Irish Law Reports Monthly
ILT & SJ	*Irish Law Times and Solicitors' Journal*
ILTR	Irish Law Times Reports
IR	Irish Reports
Ir Eq Rep	Irish Equity Reports
Ir Jur	*Irish Jurist*
JRSAI	*Journal of the Royal Society of Antiquaries of Ireland*
JSPTL	*Journal of the Society of Public Teachers of Law*
L & H	Literary and Historical (Society)
LLB	Bachelor of Laws

LLM	Master of Laws
LQR	*Law Quarterly Review*
LR Ir	Law Reports, Ireland
Mod	Modern (reports)
MRIA	Member, Royal Irish Academy
NILQ	*Northern Ireland Legal Quarterly*
NUI	National University of Ireland
P Wms	Peere Williams (reports)
PROI	Public Record Office of Ireland
QCG	Queen's College, Galway
RR	Revised Reports
RUI	Royal University of Ireland
Salk	Salkeld (reports)
SDLP	Social Democratic and Labour Party
S.I.	Statutory Instrument
SIPTU	Services Industrial Professional and Technical Union
S.R. & O.	Statutory Rule and Order
TCD	Trinity College, Dublin
T.R.	Term Reports
UCC	University College Cork
UCD	University College Dublin
UCG	University College Galway
US	United States Supreme Court reports
Valletta memoir	Lois Valletta, 'Memoir of the Westby family'
Ves Sen	Vesey Senior (reports)

Preface

Histories of university law schools compose a small but select library. In 1908 Harvard saw the appearance of a three-volume history of its school: Charles Warren, *History of the Harvard Law School* (New York, 1908). Lawson followed suit for Oxford in a single volume produced sixty years later: F.H. Lawson, *The Oxford Law School, 1850–1965* (Oxford, 1968).

Ireland can scarcely compete. The Law School of Trinity College, Dublin, aside, where Delany and others have tackled facets of that institution's law school – see, for example, V.T.H. Delany, 'Legal studies in Trinity College, Dublin, since the Foundation', *Hermathena*, 89 (1957), 3 – there has been little enough to record. It thus has to be faced that accounts of the other university law schools, whether in the State or in Northern Ireland, have been unresearched, and their contribution and achievements, accordingly, unsung. Until recently that is, for NUI Galway, the former Queen's College, Galway, then redesignated University College, Galway, has now had the story of its law school rehearsed by O'Malley in an impressive 108-page essay, included as a chapter in a book devoted to the entire university itself: Liam O'Malley, 'Law' in Tadhg Foley (ed.), *From Queen's College to National University: Essays towards an Academic History of QCG, UCG, NUI Galway* (Dublin, 1999), p. 16. For UCD, the focus of the present volume, I myself have written a piece on 'The law school's early professoriate' (*Irish Jurist*, 46 (2011), 1), which is now superseded by the discussion of that professoriate in chapters 2 and 3 below.

The Law School of University College Dublin: a History, in tandem with O'Malley's essay, capitalizes upon the sense that surveys of one species of a third-level department – the law school at university on the island of Ireland – were long overdue for an airing. An additional warrant for such an undertaking was suggested by the publication of a recent collection of essays, supported by the Irish Association of Law Teachers, which has highlighted the very considerable contribution to legal scholarship which has been made by the personnel serving on the staffs of the various university law schools: Thomas Mohr and Jennifer Schweppe (eds), *Thirty Years of Legal Scholarship* (Dublin, 2011).

How exactly the airing that is proposed should proceed – what topics to cover, how to arrange the pertinent data, the balance between the treatment of personalities and that of the educational programmes for which they were responsible, any kind of bias to impart – all this can give rise to endless debate. And the success or otherwise of what *The Law School of University College Dublin: a*

History has set out to accomplish, it must be left to the individual reader to decide for himself or herself. The plan, nevertheless, may be briefly set down here. After a historical chapter which is designed to set the scene prior to the adoption of the Irish Universities Act of 1908 (chapter 1), the fortunes of the new law school are examined in a series of chapters, chronologically ordered, which trace the story down to the year 2000 (chapters 2, 3, 4 and 5). Separate chapters then address the subjects of the Law collection in the College Library and the arrangements for housing the law school itself (chapters 6 and 7). A final chapter, or epilogue (chapter 8), provides a bird's-eye view of developments occurring after the year 2000.

Among the Appendices the reader will find transcribed and published for the first time an undelivered judgment of Chief Baron Palles that came to light from an examination of Palles manuscript material in the College Library (Appendix III), as well as a revisiting of a well-known mid-nineteenth-century law case, in which John Henry Newman, the future cardinal, and at the time the first rector of the Catholic University, from which UCD traces its beginnings, was unfortunate enough to become embroiled (Appendix II).

A large number of people have assisted in various ways in bringing the project to fruition. I am grateful to them all. For information, sundry advice or for permission to quote from material in their possession, I should like to thank the Brothers at the Oratory of St Philip Neri, Birmingham, Edward Valletta and the late Lois Valletta, Hugh Geoghegan, Tom O'Higgins, Christine Casey, Charles Lysaght and Colum Kenny. For assistance with illustrations, I am endebted to Naoise Bermingham at the Italian Cultural Institute Dublin, Thomas Watkin, Mary Ryan, John R. Holohan, Roger Kenny, Averil Henchy, Colum Kenny, Kevin Costello, Sister Evelyn Cardoz at the Park Place Pastoral Centre, Wickham in Hampshire, Victor Hoban of the Audio-Visual Centre, UCD, and the Board of Trinity College, Dublin as well as the Library there. Thanks, too, to Renate Ní Uigín of the King's Inns Library.

In today's UCD Law School, I should like to thank the following for their assistance of various kinds: the present Dean, Colin Scott, Imelda Maher, Paul O'Connor, John O'Dowd, and Barry Kelly, our IT Specialist. I should also like to express my appreciation to the staff in the NUI headquarters, and in the UCD President's Office, also the staff in the Archives Department, in the Library proper and in Special Collections in that Library, in addition to the Law School secretariat. Miriam Walsh, who typed everything, faced the challenge of my handwriting. Last, but by no means least, I am very grateful to her.

Nial Osborough
July 2014

I

Legal Education and the University: the Historical Context

The intellectual revival of cities in the north of Italy in the twelfth century occasioned the birth of the European university in which provision for the study of Law was, from the outset, a key element. Rashdall describes the development in the following language. 'Just', he wrote,[1]

> as the demand of the cloisters north of the Alps for speculative knowledge – for knowledge for its own sake, knowledge apart from all relating to social life, manifested itself in a revival of metaphysical and theological speculation and was ultimately met by the discovery of Aristotle; so in the commercial and political society of the Italian cities there arose a demand for fruitful knowledge, for science applied to the regulation of social life – for *civilisation* in the strictest sense of the word. And this demand was met by a revived study of the long-neglected, but never wholly forgotten, monuments of Roman jurisprudence. It is only in such communities that in the heart of the Middle Ages the purely mundane science of law could have awakened the enthusiasm – the genuine intellectual enthusiasm – which attended its study in the early days of the School of Bologna: it is only in such communities that so democratic, so unhierarchial an institution as an autonomous university of students could have sprung into existence.

Rashdall goes on to recall one early explanation for the revival of the study of Roman law – that the citizens of Pisa, on the capture of Amalfi in 1135, discovered a manuscript of Justinian's *Digest*, whereupon the Emperor Lothair II, with an intuitive recognition of the value of the 'find', forthwith directed its contents to be taught in the schools and enforced in the tribunals – before pronouncing this a fabrication.[2] Since the days of Savigny it had been accepted that it was quite erroneous to assume that prior to the taking of Amalfi a knowledge of Roman law was as rare as that of the laws of Manu. It is also accepted that, whatever about Pisa, it was at Bologna that epoch-making strides were made, and that that was the accomplishment of one teacher who stands out – Irnerius, whose statue still graces the environs of the University of Bologna.[3]

On the periphery of Europe the linkage of law with the fortunes of the university down the centuries – something taken for granted on the Continent itself – was to be far from assured. The divorce puzzled a neophyte Prince of Wales in a conversation recalled by J.B. Ames, a towering figure in the history of American legal education, in his *Lectures on Legal History.* Sir John Fortescue, nominal Lord Chancellor to the Lancastrian government in exile, sought to explain to the Prince why the laws of England were not taught at the universities. 'In the universities of England', Fortescue asserted,[4]

> Sciences are not taught but in the Latin tongue, and the laws of the land are to be learned in the three several tongues, to witte, in the English tongue, the French tongue and the Latin tongue.

There was, of course, much more to it than this. In England, the role of the Inns of Court in controlling access to the profession and Henry VIII's diktat against canon law being taught in the universities both contributed to a state of affairs where the university was divorced from anything approaching an active role in the promotion of legal instruction. In Scotland matters were to be different, as recalled in the major House of Lords appeal from Scotland, *Burmah Oil Co.* v. *Lord Advocate,* back in 1965.[5] In Ireland, under the Gaelic social order, the university was unknown, provision being made for instruction in law in an array of Brehon Law schools, such as that known to have been kept at Cahermacnaghten in the Burren of Co. Clare. In areas of Ireland, where the king's writ held sway, English practice governed, a rule confirmed by a statute of Henry VIII in 1542, the Statute of Jeofailles,[6] which made it incumbent on those aspiring to practise law in Ireland to keep a stipulated number of terms common at one of the London Inns of Court – an arrangement which entailed, certainly by the end of the seventeenth century, that, in Barnard's words,[7] entry to the Irish Bar was 'very much the preserve of the well-to-do in local society of *arrivistes* from England.'

That perhaps for a minority of aspiring lawyers some form of instruction in the law of the Common Law dispensation became possible in a setting neither of any university nor of any inn of court as indicated by a record relating to the youth of Sir William Darcy for the years 1482–3, which Kenny's researches conducted into the background to the establishment of King's Inns were to bring to light.[8] An extract from the memoranda rolls of 9 & 10 Henry VIII (1517–18)[9] suggests, Kenny claims,[10]

> that at least some of the preparatory functions of the Inns of Chancery in London were discharged personally in Dublin by leading lawyers who individually tutored a small number of students of the law.

The memorandum in question from the king's attorney contains a report of how Darcy spent his formative years in Dublin ('Divelyng'). The king's attorney wrote that

> the which Sir Wyllim showed me that he and his cousin Sir Thomas Kent, being learning their Tenuors and Natura Brevium with Mr John Stret at Divelyng, was tabled at Hugh Talbott's, the said Hugh then dwelling there as John Dyllon now dwelleth; And that Phyllip Bermingham, then chief justice of the King's bench, at that time dwelled there as Ann White dwellith now, having one John Harper in his service. Unto the which John Harper the said Sir Wyllim and Sir Thomas with other their companions on holydays resorted to learn to harp and to dance at the said justice's place.

The two texts that Darcy and Kent are said to have studied in Dublin 'were considered to be central to the training of such members of the Inns of Chancery in London as intended to proceed to the Inns of Court'.[11]

How widespread may have been this pattern of informal instruction in the law of the Common Law dispensation is impossible to say. What is undeniable is that the contrast between the arrangements for learning the law on the Continent and those for learning the law in England and Ireland remained very marked indeed. There is a lacuna in historical source-material of a particular kind for the two Common Law jurisdictions that may be viewed as a matter of regret. A German law student, Johann Wilhelm von Botzheim, was to leave us an invaluable account of the fate of Huguenot law professors in the course of the massacre at Orleans in 1572 inspired by the preceding massacre of St Bartholomew's Day in Paris.[12] As a German, and not generally known to be a Protestant, von Botzheim managed to escape the fate of his Huguenot friends, but he witnessed, and was forced to appear to applaud, the most revolting exhibitions both of cruelty and of selfishness. Baird tells us,[13] from reliance on von Botzheim's reminiscences, that the latter's favourite professor, one François Taillebois,

> after having been twice plundered by bands of marauders, was treacherously conducted by the second band to the Loire, despatched with the dagger, and thrown into the river.

'The last lecture, which he gave on Monday at nine o'clock', von Botzheim's memoir continues,[14] 'was on the Lex Cornelia [de sicariis] of which he made the demonstration by the sacrifice of his own life'.

'It is pitiful to read', Baird's précis concludes,[15]

> that even professors in the university were not ashamed to enrich their libraries by the plunder of the law-books of their colleagues, or of their scholars. The writer traced his own copies of Alciat, of Mynsinger and 'Speculator' to the shelves of Laurent Godefroid, Professor of the

> Pandects, and the entire library of his brother Bernhard to those of his neighbor, Dr Beaupied, Professor of Canon Law.

This was not perhaps the finest hour in the history of the Law Faculty in the University of Orleans.

Twenty years later, the establishment in Ireland of its first university, set to endure and to prosper and not to be dismissed as another blip in the night, augured well. This was Trinity College in Dublin, which came into existence once the mortmain licence had been procured to buttress the conveyance to it from Dublin Corporation of the lands to the east of the City, the erstwhile property of the dissolved religious House of All Hallows. Early Trinity College statutes prescribed the election of a law fellow ('*jurista*') and in 1668 there came the appointment of Henry Stiles, the first regius professor,[16] but together these developments constituted nothing other than a false dawn so far as the embryo Law Faculty was concerned. What Provost William Bedell (1627–9) wrote then was prescient, and it was only from the middle of the nineteenth century that Trinity was to make any kind of significant contribution to legal education in a university setting.

'I suppose', wrote Bedell of his short provostship in the 1620s,[17]

> it hath been an error all this while, to neglect the Faculties of law and physic, and to attend only to the ordering of one poor College of divines; whereas, with a little more labour and a few priviledges attained, a great many more good wits might have been allured to study, and seasoned with piety, and made instruments for the bringing in learning, civility and religion, into that country.

The first serious effort to promote instruction in law at Trinity, as we have remarked, only came in 1850, with an agreement between the Board of Trinity College and the Benchers of King's Inns. They announced their cooperation in a programme of instruction in which Trinity's two professors would be assisted by two King's Inns professors that the Benchers would be appointing. Of Trinity's duo, the Regius Professor of Civil Law became responsible for instruction in Civil Law (i.e., Roman Law) and General Jurisprudence, and the Regius Professor of Feudal and English Law for Equity and Real Property. The first of the new King's Inns professors was made responsible for Constitutional Law and Criminal Law, and the second for Personal Property, Pleading, Practice and Evidence. Overlapping of instruction would be avoided.[18]

McDowell and Webb say in their history of Trinity College that the initiative, that led to this key agreement of 1850, came from the Benchers.[19] A memorial had been forwarded which suggested that the College and the Inns should collaborate in the setting up of an effective school of law. In addition, however, there had been unease within Trinity itself over the miserable fate meted out to its chairs in law. As regards the Regius Professor of Civil Law, they were to write that since the death of Arthur Browne in 1805, it had reverted to being 'a near-sinecure' held by 'a Senior Fellow' and usually by one of the dimmer ones.[20] It was only right that it should be 'transformed into an effective teaching post.' There was another factor that they say weighed with Trinity's Board: 'the need to meet at least in part, the unfriendly comment which in that year was widespread … on the excessive salaries of the Senior Fellows.'[21]

In Trinity in the eighteenth century and in the early days of the nineteenth, only two individuals named to Regius Chairs had left any kind of legacy. Both were remarkable individuals – F.S. Sullivan (d.1766), the author of *An Historical Treatise on the Feudal Law* (1772),[22] and the Arthur Browne mentioned above, who died in 1805, the author of works on civil law, embracing admiralty, and marriage law as well as ecclesiastical law.[23]

Aside from the important agreement of 1850, linking Trinity College and King's Inns, specific provision had been made for law faculties at the several Queen's Colleges, at Belfast, Cork and Galway, set up under legislation in 1845,[24] and which admitted their first students four years later. Here graduating students obtained their degrees from the Queen's University of Ireland with its headquarters in Dublin, which received its first charter in 1850. The Colleges, as is well known, experienced 'a baptism of fire', for as Moody and Beckett were to write, in their official history of Queen's, Belfast:[25]

> The completion of the university system [with the charter for the Queen's University of Ireland] coincided with the final and decisive condemnation of the Queen's Colleges by the Catholic Church.

The antipathy of the Catholic Church, most resoundingly expressed by the Synod at Thurles in 1850, was based on its opposition to mixed education. One sweetener, to be found in a section of the Queen's Colleges Act, made no earthly difference. This section, section 14, provided:

> and for the better enrolling every student in the said Colleges to receive religious instruction according to the Creed which he professes to hold, be it enacted, that it shall be lawful for the President and Professor or other governing Body of each of the said Colleges … to assign Lecture Rooms within the Precincts of such College, wholly or in part, for the use of such religious teachers as shall be recognised by such governing Body, subject in each case to the Approval of Her Majesty, Her Heirs and Successors … Provided always, that no Student shall be compelled by any Rule of the College to attend any theological Lecture or religious Instruction other than is approved by his Parents or Guardians, and that

> no religious Test shall be administered to any person in order to entitle him to be admitted a Student of any such College.

There had been other straws in the wind. In 1838, for instance, the Dublin Law Institute, the brainchild of one Tristram Kennedy, was established. It was designed to impart instruction in law, and had a short but remarkable history, which is now the focus of a full-length study.[26] When it collapsed, as a result of the withholding of financial backing, that collapse triggered the appointment of a parliamentary select committee at Westminster, whose remit, as finally agreed, was to survey provision for legal education throughout the United Kingdom.[27] The committee finally reported in 1846. Initiatives already taken at Oxford and in London were now set to be replicated elsewhere.

Another contemporaneous departure, not, naturally enough, unconnected with the growing distaste for what were to be dubbed 'Godless Colleges', which heralded the prospect in Ireland of legal education again within a university environment, was the establishment of the Catholic University on a restricted site bordering St Stephen's Green in the centre of Dublin. The Catholic University remained throughout its existence a small-scale operation, but since today's UCD can trace its origins back to 1854 when the Catholic University admitted its first students, the part that that university institution might, or could have played in the fortunes of Irish university legal education is deserving of consideration.

The plans for the university included provision for a law school, but this, as we shall see, came to nought. J.H. (later, 1879, Cardinal) Newman, the University's first Rector – he served in that capacity from 1851 until his resignation in 1858 – lists a Law Faculty, along with Faculties of Theology, Medicine, Philosophy and Letters and Science in a letter presented to Benjamin Disraeli, the Chancellor of the Exchequer and Leader of the House of Commons in Lord Derby's Conservative administration, in July 1858, at the start of the ultimately forlorn endeavour to secure a charter for the University.[28] The letter includes the key admission that only four of these faculties were in active operation at the time, an admission from which the influence to be drawn is that the Law Faculty was but a phantom.[29] As it happens, an essay Newman had written in January 1858 furnishes confirmation that no real progress had actually been made in regard to Law. In this piece in the *Weekly Reporter*, Newman invited his readership to accept the unpalatable truth that universities could not be 'carried out all at once'.[30] There was bound to be much 'incompleteness', 'many a desideratum', 'many a hiatus' in its provisions 'for a long time to come'. 'For a long time to come', Newman continues,

> it will be easy enough to find fault with it, and ask a multitude of questions which it will be very difficult to answer. It will be easy to say:

> Where is your recognition by the State? How do you mean to get it? Where are your degrees? Where are your theological students? Where are your lectures in law? Where are your collegiate buildings?

It is likely, however, that at the outset Newman would have dearly wished to inaugurate a properly functioning Law Faculty. So much is clear from surviving correspondence dating from as early as the spring of 1854, in which Newman as rector canvassed support for just such a plan. In May 1854, one B.A. Murray replied to Newman's offer to him of a choice between a professorship of Law and one of Political Economy.[31] In the process, he expressed his thoughts on Newman's project for a Law School. Murray was not optimistic. The reason he principally advanced was that the number of Catholics who would have aspirations to practise at the Bar would be too small. He estimated a figure of 15 to 16 as the number of Catholics who at the time annually went to the Bar. In addition, Murray adverted to the disinclination, as he saw it, of many to be associated with what he described as the ultra-Catholic character of the new institution. A further reason for Murray's scepticism as regards creating a law school was that, under the existing scheme of things, students would be obliged to attend law lectures elsewhere (i.e., Trinity) and, as a consequence, attendance at law lectures in the Catholic University could only be on a voluntary basis. The object of a law school, as Murray envisaged it, was 'the professional education of young men going to the Bar'. All things considered, he added, 'the chance of having any pupils in the law school of the University, would at least for a long time be very small'. The difficulties Murray outlined he reckoned

> could only be overcome by recognised ability and standing on the part of the professor, together with a large amount of perseverance and devotion to that special object and a capacity for organisation and arrangement.

In all such 'qualities and qualifications' he confessed he was personally deficient. Murray in his letter was then to turn to the offer Newman had extended to him of the professorship of Political Economy where he sounded much more enthusiastic, averring that there was 'nothing more needed at present than a candid investigation & exposition of the principles of political economy from a Catholic point of view'. But he had one last thought to convey to Newman on the functions a law professor might discharge in any projected law school for the University, 'There is', Murray wrote,

> another species of duty, and I think a very useful one which a professor of Law might perform. I mean giving instruction to the general students of the university in the principles of constitutional law and of some of the other more important branches of our law.

Murray offered to help out here with such 'very good work'. As it was to transpire, however, Murray was not to be added to Newman's team of professors, neither in political economy nor in law.

Other correspondence that has survived shows that from an early date, some thought was being given to the number of law professors it would be incumbent to appoint, together with the subjects they might teach – Constitutional and Criminal Law; Real Property; Principles and Practice of Equity. None of this came to pass. Yet, coverage of law in the day-to-day running of the Catholic University once it opened its doors was not, as it happened, a complete dead letter. One should perhaps leave to one side the case of the Revd Lawrence Forde, who, at Archbishop Paul Cullen's insistence, was in 1856 made Professor of Canon Law. Newman thought the appointment 'premature' and found Forde 'unsympathetic', going so far as to label him 'intolerable' in a letter to one of his friends – 'coarse, vulgar, unreal and solitary'.[32] John O'Hagan, made Lecturer in Political Economy in 1854, later had duties in Jurisprudence assigned to him when by 1858 he was ranked as a professor. In a summary of university accounts prepared by Newman in the autumn of 1858, O'Hagan was scheduled to be paid £200 a year, £100 by virtue of his membership of the Faculty of Law and £100 by virtue of that of the Faculty of Philosophy and Letters.[33]

Despite Murray's discouraging observations on the establishment of a proper law school, the next year – 1855 – it was quite plain that Newman had by no means relinquished the vision that he should do just that. That is obvious from his continuing interest in inaugurating what he described as a professorship of Practical Law. Rebuffed by Murray and, seemingly, a number of others, he now sought to appoint to this post John Edward Pigot, the son of Chief Baron Pigot. Pigot was in his thirties. A barrister, as well as a writer and musician, he was a 'charismatic and handsome figure', who did much to win support for Young Ireland among fashionable society in Dublin.[34] He had been a close associate and friend of Thomas Davis.[35] He was elected a member of the Royal Irish Academy in 1851.

Newman had met Pigot in 1854, and they had corresponded over a purchase of theological manuscripts by Trinity College, which the two of them agreed was inappropriate and regrettable.[36] A tentative offer of this chair of Practical Law appears to have been extended to Pigot in March 1855. It was not to be taken up, though whether this was due to scruples on Pigot's part or Newman's reluctance to have another battle on his hands with Archbishop Cullen should the appointment be mooted is not altogether clear. Newman liked Pigot. He 'talked like a republican – but he was full of views and a clever man'.[37] Bishop David Moriarty of Kerry whom Newman consulted agreed: Pigot was a 'truly estimable young man, working quietly at his profession'. Cullen, however, was aghast: Pigot, as we have recalled, had been a Young Irelander, and that was enough to damn him. Moriarty told Newman that, in obedience to his father, Pigot had withdrawn from his political party in 1847 and had never, in his recall, taken part in politics since.[38] In Cullen's mind, however, Young Ireland was as bad as Young Italy: as for Young Irelanders 'they never came right – never'.[39]

Newman was especially keen to have Pigot teach the law of Real Property. Pigot, in response, acknowledged his willingness to do so, unless, as he phrased it, 'his political opinions would be compromised by connection with the university'.[40] Newman then sought to offer assurance. Politics, he wrote, did not enter into the academical body, and for his own part, he 'would not have any quarrel with an Irishman holding opinions which his patriotism dictated'.[41] Pigot, however, remained reluctant to make a move, while accepting that 'politics did not belong to the university.' He feared, he wrote to Newman in another letter which, I believe, may have signalled his wish to be *hors de combat*,[42]

> that some of the law professorships might be made the vehicles of the inculcation of opinions which I hold to be not only false but so peculiarly criminal in Ireland, and that he would thus be compromised in conscience.

Pigot concluded by alluding to

> that class of exaggerated opinion touching the British 'Constitution' on the one hand and the necessary 'allegiance' of my country to the laws and government of that particular English nation on the other, with which most English law books teem.

Even if, as Newman, sensing defeat, told Moriarty in April that the law of Real Property was not a subject 'which admits politics',[43] Pigot was to decline to take up the offer. Pigot had been called to the Irish Bar in 1844.[44] In 1865 he was to emigrate to India, and in Bombay, as Gwynn was to phrase it, 'he quickly obtained a large and very profitable practice'. He was to die back in Ireland in 1871, not yet 50.[45]

Barr, it has to be said, in revisiting the entire episode, implies that Newman back in 1855, stood his ground, and that Pigot was in fact appointed.[46] If so, it was indeed, a Pyrrhic victory, for, as Barr goes on to say, Pigot did no teaching for there were no law students to teach.[47] Whether Pigot was ever formally entered up 'in the books' must remain doubtful. He is certainly not listed as a drain on the University's meagre resources in the statement of accounts furnished by Newman later in 1858.[48] There remains one bonus from Barr's account of these matters: Cullen's attitude to the Young Irelanders seems to have been more flexible than has customarily been supposed. This is made clear from what Barr writes of the relationship between the archbishop and another ex-Young Irelander who secured a definite appointment from Newman, John

O'Hagan, the Professor of Political Economy and Jurisprudence.[49] Barr also makes it plain that Moriarty was mistaken in his belief that the Pigot of 1855 had ceased to be politically engaged.[50]

On 4 November 1858 Newman faced the sea crossing back to Britain for the last time; he was never to return to Ireland. By his own calculation, Newman had crossed St George's Channel 56 times during the period of his rectorship of the Catholic University. Amongst those last to hear of his resignation and departure were his colleagues in Dublin – the professors and lecturers of the Catholic University. The news was greeted with dismay. There was the risk, 24 of them wrote to Newman,[51] that after his departure

> the institution, in some important functions very unformed and unsteady, will just when there is a chance of its becoming firmly knit, be exposed to the danger of a rickety growth, if not of failure.

Responding to this missive a few days later,[52] Newman insisted he had had no alternative. The Birmingham Oratory where he was the Father Superior sought his undivided attention. In Ireland, Archbishop Cullen required the services of a rector who was more permanently in post. Cullen had a point: seemingly in the entire year of 1858, prior to his return to Britain on 4 November, Newman had spent but a mere ten days in Dublin.

In the autumn of 1859, Newman turned down an invitation to allow himself to be nominated Chancellor of the University he had done so much to establish.[53] As the most distinguished of Victorian theoreticians of higher education, however, his legacy endures. The direction that a university law school, when faced with a particular challenge, is invited to take is commonly followed by the sort of discussion that Newman in his classic work *The Idea of a University Defined and Illustrated* (1873) would have anticipated. The primary end of a university was a training of the mind. Room was to be found for an acknowledgement of the love of knowledge for its own sake, a love transmitted through 'a "liberal education" in the true sense of "liberal" as the free work of a free man other than the servile work of a slave'.[54] 'This training in a "habit of mind", a "philosophical habit", in an enlargement of mind', Sheridan Gilley has written in explanation of Newman's approach,[55]

> like the intellectual contemplation which Aristotle considered the highest good, is an ultimate value, and requires no religious or moral defence, as it is an end in itself regardless of any use it might possess for the learned professions and religion.

Newman, in his essay in the *Weekly Reporter* for 30 January 1858,[56] focused on an amount of unfinished third-level business that would dominate the university question in Ireland in the second half of the nineteenth century and for a smattering of years beyond: the inability of Catholic University students to procure degrees, and the lack of a charter for the institution itself. In contrast, the failure of the University to develop a Law Faculty did not appear nearly as significant; but as we shall soon discover, this specific lack was in the end to become for many a festering sore.

Nothing was directly accomplished as a result of Newman's letter to Disraeli of July 1858, apart from placing the future of the Catholic University on the political agenda. The Conservatives lost the general election in June the following year. But it was to be six more years before any kind of progress could be reported – and again this was to lead nowhere.

A life-line of sorts for the students of the Catholic University on the face of it did, however, appear to be assured for them in June 1865 when Palmerston's administration announced a new policy for Irish higher education:[57]

> On 20 June, in response to a motion from Mr O'Donoghue, the Home Secretary, Sir George Grey, promised in the House of Commons that steps would be taken to enable Catholics to obtain the degrees of the Queen's University without having attended any of the Queen's Colleges.

The resultant detailed scheme involved Newman's institution being chartered but only as a College and the Queen's University receiving a supplementary charter enabling it to confer degrees on all who passed its examinations. 'Privately apprised of this scheme', Moody and Beckett were to write,[58] 'the Catholic prelates were at pains to show how small an instalment it was of the justice they demanded'. Protestant opinion was equally dissatisfied, but for very different reasons. The so-called 'Provost's House declaration', issued from Trinity College in the spring of 1866, 'over the signatures of 3,000 members of the established church', made their position pellucidly clear: 'We … desire', they announced,[59]

> to express our earnest hope that the principle of united secular education, as opposed to the denominational system, may be maintained in Ireland.

The auspices were decidedly unfavourable when the government of Earl Russell, which had succeeded Palmerston's, decided to press ahead with one part of the scheme – to issue the supplementary charter to the Queen's University.[60] This charter, which issued in June 1866,

> empowered the Queen's University to hold a matriculation examination different from that of the Queen's Colleges, and to grant degrees to any

> persons who had thus matriculated and were deemed by the Senate to be qualified, though they had not matriculated, or pursued their studies in one of the Queen's Colleges.

Matters now moved with remarkable speed. The government appointed six new members to the University Senate who were known to be supporters of the scheme, and on 6 October that Senate voted by a majority of two (11 – 9) to accept the supplementary charter. All of the Queen's College presidents voted against. Six days later, the first meeting of the Convocation of the University resolved without a division that the acceptance of the supplemental charter was inexpedient.[61] If the message was clear enough, this was a more timid response than that which had emanated from a special meeting held by graduates of the Queen's University in Belfast in December 1865, a meeting later branded by Chichester Fortescue as 'a somewhat noisy and tumultuous assemblage of high-spirited young men'.[62]

Later in the autumn, three graduates of the University, William McCormack, Andrew Cummins and Charles Hooper, moved in the courts in Dublin to secure, in effect, the nullification of the new charter. Pressed to act by the decision of the Senate to set the first examinations authorised by the charter for January 1867, Dr McCormack and his two colleagues sought in their cause petition to have Chancery uphold the following two propositions:[63]

(i) that the charter of 1866 was inconsistent with the University charter of 1854;
(ii) that the resolution of the Senate accepting the 1866 charter was void, it being maintained that acceptance had to be by the entire corporate body.

In addition they pressed

(iii) their entitlement for the issuance of an injunction against the Senate carrying out any act in compliance with their impugned acceptance of the charter and particularly against their conferring of any degrees consequent on that.

On 16 April 1867, the Master of the Rolls, John Edward Walsh[64] gave judgement against the petitioners, but this was no victory for the University Senate or the government's plan. The subject-matter of the petitioners' complaint, Walsh held, was not properly justiciable by means of a cause petition; the correct procedure was to invite the Attorney General to proceed by information. In any event, the Master of the Rolls continued, there was a second reason why the petitioners lacked locus standi: their complaint that the standing of the degrees they possessed would be diminished by the changes that were under contemplation was not a matter of which the law took cognisance, that interest being dismissed as 'shadowy, uncertain and indefinite'.[65] In the circumstances of this curious judgement, Walsh's foray into one matter that, arguably now, would not fall for consideration by him, was nonetheless of equal significance: it had not been competent, Walsh averred, for the Senate, acting alone, validly to accept the supplementary charter. It can certainly be argued that such a conclusion was plainly *obiter*, but, although from the post mortems that punctuate the columns of Hansard for the next several months,[66] it looked as if all was not lost, the practical effect of what Walsh had decided was, indeed, as Moody and Beckett phrased it, 'to render the charter ineffective'.[67]

The establishment of the Royal University in succession to the Queen's University in 1880, did at long last provide the life-line that the students of the old Catholic University had regularly sought – the prospect of securing a degree from a fully-fledged university. On this occasion, there was the added bonus of an indirect endowment for Newman's institution, renamed University College Dublin in 1882, the administration of which was transferred to the Jesuits the following year. This was through the medium of fellowships awarded by the new Royal University, as anticipated by a section in the enabling legislation of 1879, the University Education (Ireland) Act of that year,[68] and further explained by the Royal University of Ireland Act of 1881,[69] which arranged for funds accruing from the disestablishment of the Church of Ireland under the Irish Church Act of 1869[70] to be expanded in defraying the several expenses of the Royal University, including the charge of these fellowships. As it turned out, the old UCD was to receive the lion's share of these teaching fellowships.

That students of the old UCD enjoyed an advantage over the students from the Queen's Colleges at Cork, Galway and Belfast in the matter of obtaining degrees and honours was an aspect of the new dispensation aired but infrequently, but real enough, it appeared, for all that. The advantage was said to accrue from the circumstance that the dominance of UCD teaching staff among those given Royal University Fellowships was mirrored in their dominance as examiners at the Royal's degree examinations,[71] one which the appointment of truly external additional examiners could hardly be expected fully to curtail. But this is not the complaint most commonly voiced regarding the deficiencies in the pattern of Irish higher education between the founding of the Royal University and the passing of the Irish Universities Act in 1908. Moody and Beckett's verdict on these 27 odd years is distinctly gloomy:[72] those years were 'marked by chronic unsettlement and embittered controversy'.

Certain elements among the politicians in Britain and within Irish society took their cue from the Provost's House declaration of 1866 and sought a non-denominational solution to the undoubted problem posed by the failure of the Queen's Colleges to attract Catholic students in sufficient numbers and by the diminished standing of Newman's institution. Not everyone was convinced of the worth of the latter, or of its offspring – the same institution re-designated University College Dublin (the 'old' UCD) in 1882. As late as 1901, Dr O'Dwyer, the Catholic bishop of Limerick, dismissed this institution – the old UCD as 'a burlesque' – 'a house on the side of the street'.[73] Matthias Bodkin, who was made the County Court Judge for Co. Clare in 1907, had been a student of the Catholic University (he had been prevented by his family from applying for Trinity). Bodkin's recollections of his time spent there were scarcely favourable. He had entered, he was to write,[74]

> the so-called Catholic University, which had neither charter or endowment, and even obtained an exhibition on matriculation, but the business was so wholly futile that I abandoned it before six months were over, sacrificing my exhibition. A smattering of Terence was the only asset derived from that wasted six months.

Barr's verdict on the Catholic University after Newman's departure in 1858 is not markedly different.[75] It 'stuttered on', ceasing 'to exist as a university in any meaningful sense by the mid-1860s'. 'It is ironic', Barr continues,[76]

> that the institution for which an acknowledged classic of educational philosophy was written proved a failure.

The disappointing uptake by Catholic students of places in the Queen's Colleges led some critics to mount an assault on the Roman Catholic hierarchy as the entity principally to blame. Back in 1867, one MP, Mr Lowe, the member for Calne, described the denunciation of the 'Godless Colleges' as having been orchestrated by the Roman Catholic Church 'with all its terrors and thunders'.[77] The laity, Lowe assured the House of Commons,[78] had been 'driven into antagonism by the coercion of spiritual terror'. The non-denominational solution was ardently canvassed by William Whitla, the Professor of Materia Medica at the Queen's College in Belfast in a pamphlet he brought out in 1899.[79] 'In the distracted state of Ireland', Whitla wrote,[80]

> rent asunder by fierce sectarian discords, and even by the bitter contentions of racial and party strife, the one thing which above all others is needed is the training of the youth of the country side by side under the softening and ameliorating influences of a higher education.

Reflecting the views of the Catholic hierarchy back in 1867, Mr O'Reilly, an MP for Co. Longford, maintained that 'the great mass of Roman Catholics would not accept an un- denominational system of education'.[81] Trinity College, viewed as a bastion of irredeemable Anglicanism, had already breached that principle: why could not the same be done for Irish Catholicism? In evidence to the Robertson Commission in 1901, Dr McKeown, a Belfast doctor and a Member of the Senate of the Royal University, drew attention to the charters granted third-level institutions of higher education that were denominational in nature in both Australia and Canada (the University of Laval in 1854). There was thus no inseparable barrier to this being done, and he urged that it should.[82] For the Catholic hierarchy, the snag inseparable from the non-denominational solution was that it placed a premium on a 'mixed system', which represented a challenge to the faith. It was a challenge that the church was right to seek to avoid, as William Walsh the Catholic Archbishop of Dublin since 1885 – and, as it chanced, a later benefactor of the new UCD's Law School[83] – forcefully pointed out in another pamphlet on the Irish University question equally prescient with that of William Whitla.[84] Walsh doubted whether Catholics would survive unscathed when forced to experience the perilous encounter with any mixed system. 'I may be told', Walsh declared in an inspired piece of prose,[85]

> that individuals have passed, not only in safety, but in honourable fidelity to every Catholic principle, through Trinity College, and other Colleges of mixed education in the country. Yes. And there were survivors of the charge of the six hundred at Balaklava. And men have passed with their lives through the rapids of Niagara.[86]

Even if it was the case that the system of the award of Royal University fellowships undoubtedly signalled the abandonment 'though not openly or explicitly' of the principle that public money was not to be used to subsidise sectarian colleges,[87] the great question itself – how to procure a satisfactory settlement of full Catholic demands – had still not been resolved when Queen Victoria paid her last visit to Ireland in April 1900. From an entry in her journal for the end of that month, it is painstakingly plain where she stood on the issue. 'I regretted', she wrote in her journal,[88]

> that the proposal for a Roman Catholic University had not been agreed to in Pt … Ld. Salisbury said that many of their supporters in the Hse of Commons were much against it, which I could not understand.

More especially now, however, we need to turn to the plight of the old UCD's students with their Royal University BA degrees who aspired to join the Irish Bar, and examine how the failure in the nineteenth century to make adjustments to the Irish University system, in the opinion of the students, aggravated their position. The problem, we shall see, writes a minor but not totally insignificant chapter in the continuing sense of injustice.

That Catholics could be hard done-by when it came to the matter of qualifying for possible admission to the Irish Bar was a focus of complaint in the last years of the nineteenth century and the early days of the twentieth. Following the key agreement between the Benchers of King's Inns and the Board of Trinity College in 1850 that ushered in a new era in provision for legal education, the Benchers in 1852 introduced fresh regulations governing entrance to the Irish Bar, which provoked the sort of grievance of which much more was heard in later years.

The rules of Hilary Term 1852, in regard to those seeking admission to the Irish Bar, distinguished between graduates of certain recognised universities and all non-graduates. Graduates of the University of Dublin (i.e., Trinity College), Oxford, Cambridge, London and the Queen's University of Ireland would henceforth be required to attend six terms commons at King's Inns as well as six terms commons at the appropriate Inn of Court in London – this last being the stated requirement prescribed by the Statute of Jeofailles of 1542.[89] The non-graduates, on the other hand, would be obliged to keep nine terms commons at King's Inns and eight terms commons at a London Inn of Court.

The author of an anonymous article in the *Dublin Review* in 1856 objected to the privilege accorded graduates of Trinity College by these regulations.[90] 'There is no sound reason', this author insisted,[91]

> why great establishments, with immense resources, and all the favour and patronage of the State at their back, should require the additional protection of the privilege which we have just enumerated.

'The continuance of such privileges', the writer continued,[92]

> is a gross injustice to the Catholics of Ireland. Why should Irish Catholics, who do not choose to go to Trinity College or the Queen's University, be obliged to spend two years more in the pursuit of a profession than their Protestant competitors who have no scruples in seeking knowledge in such places? Or why should such Irish Catholics be in a worse position than their brethren in England who, so far as the Bar is concerned, are now precisely on an equality with their Protestant competitors?

The *Dublin Review,* the writer concluded, was in favour of 'free trade in education', And all the Catholic University wanted was 'fair play and no favours'.

Another bone of contention, possibly even more immediately germane, was the lack of provision for instruction in law at the Catholic University, despite provision for this to occur in Newman's blueprint. This lacuna, one that persisted in its successor, the pre-1909 'old' University College, can be counted among the deficiencies in the structure of the Irish University system, and recognised as such in the last decades of the nineteenth century and even into the early years of the twentieth. In 1870, and again in 1897, a large number of members of the Roman Catholic laity put their names to a petition making the case for university reform on a more general basis.[93] The petition does not deal expressly with law, but this clearly was one of the disciplines that the signatories will have had in mind. The wording of the two petitions is identical. That the later one of 1897 is a simple reissue of what was said in 1870 speaks volumes. In the interim, in 1880, the Royal University of Ireland had been established. It functioned, as we have seen, exclusively as an examining and degree-conferring institution, a restriction that came increasingly under attack. There is no allusion to it at all in the Catholic laity's reissue of the 1870 petition in 1897.

The wording of the petitions furnishes very well evidence for the mood of one significant section of Irish opinion pressing for change:

1. That it is the constitutional right of all British subjects to adopt whatever system of collegiate or university education they prefer.
2. That perfect religious equality involves equality in all educational advantages afforded by the State.
3. That a large number of Irishmen are at present precluded from the enjoyment of university education, honours and emoluments, on account of conscientious religious opinions regarding the existing systems of education.
4. That we therefore demand such a change in the system of collegiate and university education as will place those who entertain these conscientious objections on a footing of equality with the rest of their fellow-countrymen as regards colleges, university honours and emoluments, university examinations, government and representation.

Christopher Palles, who was to play a key role in the establishment of the post-1908 'new' University College Law Faculty, and whose law library was to be acquired by the College after his death, was among the signatories of both petitions, the first of 1879, as a QC and thus four years before Gladstone appointed him Chief Baron of the Irish Exchequer, and the second, of 1897, actually as Chief Baron. Swift McNeill, one of the new Law School's first professors, identified himself as a supporter of the 1897 petition, along with twelve other Protestant MPs representing Irish constituencies.[94]

In July 1901, the British government established a royal commission with a membership of twelve[95] under the chairmanship of Lord Robertson, a Scots Lord of Appeal in Ordinary, to inquire into all aspects of the Irish University question. This was – to give it its formal designation – the Royal Commission on

University Education in Ireland. Along with the Fry Commission of 1906 that dealt specifically with the future of Trinity College, the reports of the Robertson Commission[96] contain a great deal of useful information on the circumstances out of which the scheme laid out in the Irish Universities legislation of 1908 was to take shape.

The announcement of the setting up of the Robertson Commission in July 1901 concentrated the minds of half-a-dozen law students of the Royal University who had been receiving their instructions in Arts in the 'old' UCD. 'We desire', they stated in their memorial to the members of the Robertson Commission, writing from 'University College, Stephen's Green, Dublin' and dated 19 September 1901,[97]

> to draw your attention to a grievance affecting certain Catholic students of the Faculty of Law in the Royal University.
>
> By Rules xv and xvii of the 'Rules of the Honourable Society of King's Inns', one of the conditions for admission to the Irish Bar is attendance for a year at the Law School of a University. For this purpose the Law School of Trinity College, Dublin, is recognised for all students. For graduates of the University of London, University College London is similarly recognised. Graduates of the Royal University, attending Cork, Galway or Belfast Queen's College, are allowed to keep this year in the Law Schools of their respective Colleges.
>
> All efforts, however, which have been made to secure similar privileges for the Catholic Law Students attending University College, Dublin have failed. A projected Law School was refused recognition on the ground of the unofficial character of the College. Hence all Catholic Law students residing in Dublin are obliged to attend lectures at Trinity College, though they are not members of it. This necessity of attending is, naturally, objected to by students, who do not feel themselves justified in otherwise attending the College.

'We beg, therefore, to suggest', the six memorialists concluded, 'this is a matter worthy of the consideration of the Commission'. The six signatories were (i) 'Arthur E. Clery, Sch., B.A., R.U.I.' – later one of the new UCD's first professors; (ii) 'Hugh Kennedy, BA, RUI' – later (from 1924) Chief Justice; (iii) 'James A. Murnaghan, BA, RUI' – also one of the new UCD's first professors and later a High Court and Supreme Court judge; (iv) 'Cornelius Lehane'; (v) 'William Barrett' – later a reporter for the Council of Law Reporting; and (vi) 'Vincent Rice, BA' – made a senior counsel in 1924 and later a TD.

There was to be no specific allusion to this 'grievance' in the *Final Report* of the Robertson Commission. That the 'old' UCD had not been operating as well as it might have, the Commission did concede, noting that it was 'crippled on the side of the practical sciences'.[98] The College had high standards in Arts, but Catholics, in the Commission's view, had failed to obtain through the Royal University and the College that 'combination of general education with technical knowledge which is required by the social conditions now prevailing in Ireland'.[99] The result: 'a dearth of trained capacity for professional posts in the several departments of applied science'.[100] That this was deemed the principal shortcoming was underscored by a final observation that attacked the RUI Arts degree obtained by UCD students as too cheap an attraction. 'Of the successful candidates in Arts', the commission wrote,[101]

> some of the abler men go to the Bar; many, we are told, find their way into the lower grades of the Civil Service, others whose natural fluency has been added by practice in examinations, become journalists; but this profession, by common agreement, is overstocked.

'The kind of literary education which the Royal University promotes', the commission concluded,[102] 'has been pushed beyond the due limits, and has become a source of weakness rather than of strength to the country'.

The bigger picture – the neglect of Science and Engineering – was possibly correctly emphasised by the Robertson Commission. This, naturally, was no comfort for the Catholic Law graduates of the Royal University intending, hopefully, to enter the Irish Bar. In the UCD student magazine, *St. Stephen's*, the grievance highlighted in the petition of September 1901 was to be regularly reiterated.[103] This was no surprise, for in the magazine's early issues, three of the six signatories of the memorial served on the *St. Stephen's* editorial team – Kennedy (as editor), Clery and Murnaghan. In December 1903, when clearly, once again, no remedy was in sight, *St. Stephen's* termed obligatory attendance for intending Bar students at Trinity 'a most unpleasant and inconvenient arrangement'. The students themselves attended 'as a species of outlanders'.[104] By now the editorial team at *St. Stephen's* were in a position to highlight a further drawback: the fact that, under an agreement between King's Inns and the authorities at Trinity College, King's Inns let TCD law students one year off the King's Inns course. 'The practice', it was pointed out in *St. Stephen's,* 'gives a clever student of Trinity a year's start as compared with a Catholic University man [*sic*].' The 'irregularity', it was predictably urged, 'should be remedied'.[105] A remedy, it is worth pointing out, was to be promptly secured after the Law School at the new UCD was born.[106]

There may well have been several contemporaries besides members of the Robertson Commission who, against the bigger picture, refused to treat compulsory attendance at TCD for intending RUI Catholic Bar students as anything approaching the bitter pill that they were obliged to swallow. By the early years of the new century, Trinity, of course, continued to be viewed in certain quarters as not only irredeemably Protestant but also anti-national. A 'psychological sketch' of the typical University College man that appeared in the December 1903 issue of *St. Stephen's* and written by 'Chanel' (Arthur Clery) attempted to broaden the grounds for complaint over enforced attendance at Trinity. 'To go from the society of University College men', 'Chanel' wrote,[107]

> into the company of the students of a certain other distinguished college is about like passing from heaven to its alternative ... There is also a simplicity, a confidence in each other, and an open-heartedness about our men that makes life in the college particularly pleasant ... True friends, joyous hours, and noble characters; is not this more to look back to than the massive buildings or splendid endowments?

One complaint remarkable for its absence in such pieces in *St. Stephen's* was the history of disabilities visited on Catholic students who had sought their higher education in Trinity, disabilities the last vestiges of which were removed by Fawcett's Act in 1873 – An Act to abolish tests in Trinity College and the University of Dublin.[108] The preamble to this major ameliorative statute had explained its business with admirable lucidity.

'Whereas it is expedient', the preamble ran,

> that the benefits of Trinity College and the University of Dublin and the schools in the said University as places of religion and learning should be rendered freely accessible to the nation, and whereas by means of divers restrictions, tests and disabilities, many of Her Majesty's subjects are debarred from the full enjoyment of the same ...

Historical recollection could even have taken us back to Trinity thirty years earlier, and the controverted failure of Denis Caulfield Heron to be elected one of the College's Scholars for 1843. That year 16 vacancies fell to be filled. Heron came fifth in the examination held on 1 June, but he was excluded from the final list of those to be dubbed Scholars. Eleven who were inferior to him in merit were in consequence preferred. Heron had been rejected as he would not receive the sacrament according to the rites of the established Church of Ireland and because he was a Roman Catholic. Heron succeeded in obtaining from the Queen's Bench an order of mandamus compelling the College Visitors – the Church of Ireland Archbishops of Armagh and of Dublin – to hear his appeal complaining of what he termed the undue elections of Scholars.[109] He fell at the next hurdle, however, for the judgement of the Visitors prepared by their assessor, Mr Justice Keatinge, the judge of the Prerogative Court, held that, on a true interpretation of the College's charters and statutes, election as a Scholar was not available to those who professed the Roman Catholic faith.[110] Heron went on to have a not undistinguished career as a barrister and professor at Queen's College, Galway; and, ironically, a text of his on Jurisprudence was destined to feature in a list of recommended reading for Trinity's Law School.[111] It merits notice that shortly after Heron experienced his final defeat, the Board of Trinity College took steps to provide for the election of Catholics to Scholarships through the establishment of so-called Non-Foundation Scholarships.[112]

The grievance drawn up by the six students in September 1901, and presented then to the Robertson Commission, was fated to be revisited by the Revd Dr Delany, the President of the old UCD, in evidence to the Fry Commission on Trinity College[113] in November 1906.[114] The matter arose as a result of a probing question directed at Delany by Christopher Palles, a member of the Commission. Palles had asked Delany what would be the likely enrolment in any proposed new university satisfactory from the Catholic point of view.[115] Delany furnished an estimate, and then added that, of course, numbers would be swollen if there was provision for a law school. Delany seized his opportunity. 'We are under a grave grievance' he went on,[116]

> which we and our students feel very seriously – namely, that our students, no matter how distinguished they are, if they want to study for law are obliged to go, and take courses at Trinity College. That, we hold, is unworthy of any University; and we sent in a unanimous vote to the Government from the Senate [of the Royal University] that we did not consider it consonant with our dignity to be obliged to follow courses of Law in another University, and that we were ready to provide lectureships of our own out of our own funds. We sent a representation to that effect, and it was put into the waste-paper in the Castle.

Two years earlier *St. Stephen's* had announced its frustration at the lack of progress in the university question generally. But there were implications in its observations, that were absent in any remarks of Delany's. There was 'nothing fresh to chronicle or criticise,' this editorial offering confided:[117]

> It is the old story, the story that comes from every country whose affairs are managed by foreigners – a minority pampered, like that donkey celebrated by Charles Lamb, into insolence and rapacity, a Government employing all the machinery of State to perpetuate injustice, and a people so schooled in slavery that they think it quite a blessing to turn the left side as soon as the right has been sufficiently roasted. This last is the worst symptom of all, this apathy and indifference.

The Fry Commission was furnished with statistics on the proportion of King's Inns-registered students who were not Trinity College students who attended Law classes at Trinity under the terms of the King's Inns/ Trinity College arrangement[118] – the obligation to do so (for those intending to proceed to the Bar) that had attracted the ire of the memorialists of 1901 and the criticism in the pages of *St. Stephen's*. It is a reasonable assumption that most of such students were from UCD. In the year 1903–4 the number was 29 out of a total class of 69, and the proportion changed little over the next two years: 27 out of 64 in 1904–5, and 22 out of 66 in 1905–6.

Though plainly invited to follow up on what had been trumpeted over a number of years as a 'grievance', the Fry Commission declined to do anything of the sort, choosing instead to describe these arrangements as 'resonate and advantageous to the students of law',[119] whether or not they were members of Trinity College. Further criticisms directed at the then-existing arrangements governing education at and for the Inns, criticisms likely to have been shared by all students, brought no promise of action from the Commission either. 'The complaints', they wrote in their *Final Report*,[120]

> which have been laid before us as to the overlapping of courses in the College and the King's Inns, as to the hours of lectures and as to the division of fees, are subjects on which it is not needful for us to enter.

Further evidence on matters germane to legal education, aside from Delany's reference to the grievance of Royal University Catholic law students that was aired before the Fry Commission, merits more than a brief note. The first is linked to what appears to have been a throwaway remark from Delany after pointing out to Palles that a UCD Law School would, of course, swell any new institution's student intake. This led another member of the Commission, Sir Thomas Raleigh, to pose another equally searching question. Raleigh, a Fellow of All Souls, who had been Reader of English Law at Oxford between 1884 and 1896 before moving to India to serve on the Viceroy's Council and who had published an *Outline of the Law of Property*,[121] must have startled all those in attendance at the hearings of the Commission in London on 12 November when, quite out of the blue, he asked Delany 'Why have two Law Schools in Dublin?'[122] – a question that was to be repeated very much later on in an independent Ireland towards the end of the twentieth century. This is what Delany is recorded as having replied; it touched again on the role of King's Inns:[123]

> Let it be a Law School attached to no University, and we have no objection at all, if all the law teaching is done at King's Inns. We have no objection to that, but why we should go from one University, which is supposed to have all the privileges of any University, to another University is what we have a strong objection to. But we should have no

> objection if the Benchers of King's Inns had the whole thing in their own hands.

'Chanel's' views on the educational credentials of King's Inns, given in *St. Stephen's* four years earlier, suggest that he, for one, would by no means have been enamoured of Delany's abdication of interest. 'The King's Inns', 'Chanel' wrote,[124]

> is a strange survival. Its main function has ever been the supply of dinners. After three hundred years, lectures and examinations were added to the culinary curriculum of the old legal university. But they have been slow to take root. In the three years' course, a student attends about as many lectures, and does about as much work as he would do in six months in University College, or Cecilia Street. Even now, in some of the examinations, no one is allowed to be plucked [i.e., to fail]. In the others, no one was ever stuck during the nineteenth century, and the evil practice is only being gradually introduced in the twentieth. Dining is unquestionably still the forte of the Honourable Society.

Criticisms of this ilk were not new. Six months or so earlier, in the very first issue of *St. Stephen's*, it was bluntly asserted that increasing the difficulty of King's Inns examinations was both desirable and overdue[125] – not too frequent a grievance aired by any student body. 'Surely', an editorial expressed it,

> some improvement might have been looked for in the courses preparatory to these [King's Inns] examinations, which are at present ill-arranged, indefinite, and, though we intend no slight upon the learning of the lecturers – inefficiently imparted.

To return to the Fry Commission and its hearings in London in November 1906, it is requisite that we take note of the evidence given to the Commission on 8 November by no less a figure than H. Brougham Leech, the Regius Professor of Laws at Trinity.[126] Whether he can be viewed as a steady hand on the tiller may be doubted, for in 1902 Leech had objected vehemently to the introduction of a Moderatorship in Legal and Political Science in Trinity and the manner in which this and other changes to the pattern of legal education in Trinity had been brought about. The Board of Trinity had in 1901 set up a high-powered committee to report on the Law School; its conclusions had been damning – 'the teaching was too restricted and elementary' – 'the school trained lawyers, not jurists'.[127] In addition, Leech was on the brink of resigning and moving to England, as he was to do in 1908.[128] It is difficult to say whether, in the circumstances, this extraordinary background, revisited as it was by other witnesses appearing before the Fry Commission,[129] had any bearing at all on the answers to the questions put to him, as it happens by Dr Denis Coffey, a commission member and soon enough to be installed as first president of the new UCD. Dr Coffey first asked Leech would it not be the case that if a new university structure replacing the Royal University emerged, containing a Law School recognised by the Benchers of King's Inn, Trinity's Law School would lose many of the students who currently attended. Leech replied:[130]

> I should take the chance of that, and rest upon the value of the teaching given. It would certainly act as a stimulus, and that would be a very good thing perhaps for the College [TCD]. I believe in competition. I should not object in the least to any of the Universities having the same privileges as we have, and then let us each stand upon our own merits.

Having acknowledged to Coffey that he might have been aware of the protest the six Royal University Catholic students had sent the Robertson Commission,[131] Leech commented on these supposed privileges. Trinity's privileges, he went on,[132] were 'not by any means so great as we ought to enjoy. They consist at present in doing a large amount of work for a small amount of pay'. Coffey then returned to the key question. 'But if your view as to legal education were adopted', he began,[133]

> would you have any objection to the Royal University or a future University such as that you have described, being equally privileged with Trinity College?

To which Leech replied, quite unequivocally,[134] 'None whatsoever; I should like it.'

2

Fresh Beginnings: the UCD Law School, 1909–25

The Irish Universities Act of 1908[1] radically reshaped the pattern of the Irish university system. Trinity College, Dublin was left untouched; the Queen's College, Belfast was dissolved but transformed by charter to become Queen's University Belfast;[2] and Dublin's UCD, freshly chartered, joined the former Queen's Colleges of Cork and Galway as constituent colleges of the new federal National University of Ireland, like the new university in Belfast also acquiring a charter.[3] The old Royal University disappeared.[4] Cork and Galway already possessed functioning faculties of law (though numbers were small). One of the foundation faculties in the newly constituted College of UCD was a faculty of law.[5]

This new faculty in the first months of existence moved swiftly to arrange and to publicise its teaching and examining programme for the three degrees that were its principal business: the BA in Legal and Political Science; the LLB; and the LLD. For good measure, in cooperation with the College's Governing Body, it sought due recognition of the BA and the LLB from the Benchers of King's Inns for professional purposes. As regards the solicitors' profession no such action was required, the Universities Act itself achieving that limited reform.[6]

The BA was a three-year course, all the subjects of the first two years being 'Arts' subjects. Four of the five subjects in the final year were 'Law' subjects, viz. Jurisprudence; Roman Law; Constitutional History, Law and Evidence; and Law of Property and Law of Contract. Success in this final year of the BA was treated as success in the first year of the LLB, the examinable topics being identical. The second and third years of the LLB obliged the student to revisit Jurisprudence and Roman Law, doubtless at a more elevated level. In addition, they were introduced to the Law of Public and Private Wrongs, i.e., Criminal Law and the Law of Torts, Legal History, the Law of Real Property and Equity, the Law of Landlord and Tenant in Ireland, and the Law of Specific Performance.[7] In 1914, in the first of the minor modifications that were to be approved, Equity was dropped from the course on the Law of Property and Equity.

These rubrics remained in place with but few alterations until the major changes introduced in the 1950s.

UCD was to inherit the role of the Royal University acting as an exclusively examining body, but this was a role it was by no means anxious to retain. This explains the decision from 1913 onwards not to hold examinations in the LLB for the so-called 'extern students'. (Three of these had been among the first of those awarded the UCD LLB in 1911.)

Regulations of the former Royal University dealt with the LLD, another degree UCD's Law School was empowered to award. Following the establishment of the Royal University, a student could present for the LLD one year after obtaining the Royal's LLB. This period was later extended to a three-year minimum interval.[8] To acquire the degree the student was 'required to answer in a further course to be from time to time prescribed from the subjects fixed for the LLB examination'. The authorities in the new UCD were not enamoured of these arrangements, and the ability to secure the LLB by examination was soon jettisoned; by 1919 it had gone altogether. Henceforth it could only be obtained on the basis of published work. But for a few years at least the old dispensation held sway, and thus early in 1913 we read what was planned for that year's autumn examination for the LLD. There would be two examination papers apiece for Roman Law, International Law, English Constitutional Law and History; and two further single examination papers from this group of three – the Law of Limitations as to Real Property, the Law of Principal and Agent, and Specific Performance. In 1919, as it happens the year the old LLD finally disappeared, the Law School was to award its first new LLD on published work. For many years thereafter, it is only right to point out, this remained a lonely statistic.

Securing from King's Inns due recognition of the BA in Legal and Political Science and of the LLB – the LLB being the particular concern – had been high on the College's agenda – a reflection of the frustration articulated so forcefully in the past by a generation of students in the old UCD. The College's Governing Body moved quickly to secure the concession. The President Dr Coffey's letter to the Inns in April 1911[9] furnished the details to which the Benchers were to be expected to pay heed: details as to the 'professorial staff, the subjects of study, the syllabuses of courses of lectures, the number and duration of lectures and also the examinations and attendances required from students in order to get credit for the courses'. Coffey's accompanying memorandum identified eleven designated 'law' subjects from both the BA and the LLB in respect of which recognition was sought. The Benchers referred the question to their Education Committee who reported favourably, as confirmed by the Under-Treasurer to Dr Coffey the following June.[10] The upshot was that the new UCD was placed in the same position as Trinity College with reference to qualifications for call to the Irish Bar.

The Education Committee report which accompanied the Under-Treasurer's letter set out the reasoning behind their recommendation and dealt with some matters of implementation. 'Hitherto', the committee argued,

> Trinity College has been the only College in Dublin with a Law School connected therewith; and as the Bench has always held that the proper

> place for conducting legal education is in the City where the Law Courts and the Inns of Court with its splendid library are situated, an arrangement such as has been described, could only have been made with Trinity College. Now that there is another College having a Law School with three Professors attached the Committee is of opinion that the two ought to be placed as far as possible in the same position in the course of legal education prescribed by the Bench.

UCD would be expected to cooperate with the Education Committee 'in setting the course and subjects of its lectures' and adopting a rule similar to that in force in Trinity College 'as to the percentage of marks necessary to obtain certificates required by the Benchers'. Previously, the Trinity law professors had been individually paid a certain fee for teaching subjects required under King's Inns regulations. The financial arrangements to be made following approval of the UCD courses were to be radically refashioned. The governing authorities at both Trinity and UCD were to be paid a fixed amount of £75 a year each, to be applied by such authorities at their discretion for the benefit of the two separate law schools.

This report was sent to Trinity College for consideration by the Law School and Board there. Approval was given 'on the assumption that the stringency which exists at present in Trinity College as regards the percentages required in passing the Law Examinations shall be maintained in University College'.

At the end of June 1911 the Governing Body of UCD accepted the proposals relayed to it from the Benchers with the conditions attached.[11] They also passed a resolution to thank the Benchers for what was described as 'the handsome manner' in which they had met the wishes of the College. From Michaelmas Term 1911 it was envisaged that the new dispensation would apply.

The major responsibility for ensuring success for the new law school in Dublin necessarily devolved on the early professoriate. But before making the acquaintance of the sundry individuals concerned, it will not be amiss to record something of the state of play with regard to legal education at the three erstwhile Queen's Colleges – at Cork, Galway and Belfast respectively – and also at Trinity College in Dublin, on the eve of the inauguration in the autumn of 1909 of the new law school at UCD.

The Robertson Commission, in its final report of 1903, was grim in its assessment of the then existing law schools at Cork and Galway. It announced bluntly that in its view both should be abandoned.[12] In the session 1901–2 Cork boasted a total of seven law students: the commission was to conclude that in the Munster capital, while the Medical School could be viewed as a useful and substantial institution, the Law School could not be so regarded. In the same session there were three registered law students at Galway. The position of the Law School there was even more precarious, and the commission concluded that it should be given up.

Both Law Schools continued to exist even so but, to judge from the figures returned for the session immediately prior to the two Colleges being reborn as constituent Colleges of the new National University, they continued to struggle. Of Cork's 266 students on the books in 1908–9, 9 were law students;[13] of Galway's 131 students, 9 again, as it happens, were law students.[14] The Cork students were under the tutelage of George C. Green, KC, Professor of English Law; their counterparts at Galway under that of James M. Sweetman, also denominated Professor of English Law. Green was paid an annual salary of £157 and was about to sever his ties with Cork, being appointed a County Court Judge for Armagh and Louth in 1909 – altered to Armagh and Fermanagh after Partition.[15] Sweetman was paid £165 and he, too, was soon to sever his connection with his College and, indeed, with the practice of the law, at the start of a successful career in business.[16] In both these cases the standard stipend was fixed at £150. The variations – £7 more for Green and £15 for Sweetman – were attributable to extra earnings from what were designated 'class fees'.

In Belfast the situation was a good deal more encouraging. The Queen's College there, in the last year of its existence, claimed it had 456 students on its books, of which 14 were law students.[17] The Law School boasted two lecturers in 'Medical Jurisprudence', but the responsibility for the mainstream law subjects devolved on two men – James A. Strahan, Professor of Jurisprudence and Roman Law, and James Sinclair Baxter, Professor of English Law.[18] In both cases class fees generated greater earnings than at either Cork or Galway: Baxter, for instance, was paid £172 in the year 1908–9. It is worth noting that Baxter served as an examiner for the Royal University for some years after 1901, and that Strahan served concurrently as Reader in Equity at the Inns of Court in London. The two men collaborated on *A General View of the Law of Property*, brought out in 1895. They had other publications as well, again on strictly legal topics such as equity, wills and conveyancing.

The numbers of law students at the only other Irish university law school of the period can be briefly set down as well. In Trinity College, Dublin, ten LLB degrees (and ten LLD degrees) were conferred in the session 1905–6, figures extrapolated from the Fry Commission reporting in 1906.[19] While by contemporary standards, ten primary undergraduate degrees in a single year appears miniscule, when in the case of Queen's College, Belfast for 1908–1909, there are seen to have been 14 students in total over all years, Trinity's school must have bustled as a hive of activity. This, as it happens, is reflected in the details the Fry Commission furnishes for us of the five teachers in the Law School and of their annual earnings – again for the session 1905–6.[20] Two of the professors, G.V. Hart and C.F. Bastable had income well in excess of their Queen's Colleges counterparts, at £356.9*s* and £503.16*s*, respectively. Noteworthy, too in the data for Trinity, is the appearance again of the name J.S. Baxter, also listed as a professor at Queen's College, Belfast. Baxter served as a law professor at Belfast from 1900 to 1933 and at Trinity College from 1899 to 1904[21] and again from 1908 to 1933 – a notorious double job, which prompted McDowell and Webb in their history of Trinity College to observe, a mite unkindly perhaps, 'that the Great Northern Railway must have seen almost as much of him as either of the universities, at which he taught between train journeys'.[22]

The picture is completed by taking note of degrees awarded by the Royal University in the last year of its existence – a statistical count of relevance in the context of students of the old UCD availing of the Royal University's function as an examining body alone. In this last year nine LLB degrees were conferred. There were also three LLDs – one of which was bestowed on Arthur Clery, soon to achieve appointment as a professor at the new UCD.[23]

The parliamentary papers from which these data for 1908–09 have been extrapolated do not ignore the magnitude of the changes being introduced by the Irish Universities Act. In his report for 1908–9, Dr Alex Anderson, the President of Queen's College, Galway, greeted the fresh legislative dispensation as bringing with it 'hope for new life and vigour'.[24] The Revd Thomas Hamilton, the President of Queen's College, Belfast, and about to become the first Vice-Chancellor of the new Queen's University of Belfast, in his final report as President, was similarly effusive in his expression of faith in the future. 'As we prepare for an important new chapter in the history of the higher education of the North of Ireland', Hamilton wrote,[25]

> we earnestly pray that the Almighty Disposer of all events, who has prospered us hitherto, and without whose aid we labour in vain, may continue to bless our labours, and that the latter house, which we have now built, may far exceed the former in glory, in beauty, and in usefulness.

The challenge that faced the entirely new Law School at the regenerated UCD in Dublin was, if anything, even greater. Invoking the aid of the Almighty to bless the fresh enterprise about to be undertaken in the Irish capital possibly even more of a necessity.

Under the terms of the Universities Act of 1908[26] two sets of commissioners were appointed to handle the arrangements that needed to be made before the formal inauguration could take place of the Queen's University in Belfast and that of the National University (with its constituent colleges in Cork, Galway and Dublin) at its base in Dublin.[27] Among the major tasks that befell the ten Dublin commissioners, presided over by Christopher Palles, the Chief Baron of the Exchequer, was to make the initial appointments for the new University College in Dublin.[28] In the case of the College's Law Faculty, three professorships were planned: Roman Law and Jurisprudence; the Law of Property and the Law of Contracts; and Constitutional Law and the Law of Public and Private Wrongs. In the course of 1909, applications for appointment to these three chairs were invited by advertisements appearing in the public press.[29] The posts were to be remunerated at the rate of £250 per annum.[30] By the terms of the legislation each appointee would hold office only on a temporary basis – for seven years; but such seven-year contracts were made renewable.[31] When in 1916, UCD's Governing Body took steps to renew all the original seven-year appointments of professors and statutory lecturers, a remarkable distinction was again drawn between the treatment of the three law professorships and that of all the other professors, a distinction that had its origins in Statute I of the NUI in 1911. Whereas the latter group of professors, provided favourable reports were returned by the Academic Council, were renewed up until the retirement age of 65 (with a possibility of a further five years service provided certain conditions were fulfilled), this was not done in the case of the three law professorships. The latter were simply made eligible for reappointment for a further seven years, subject to favourable reports on all three being returned by the Academic Council.[32] All appointees at the same time held their posts subject to good conduct and the due fulfilment of their duties. The distinction here drawn by the College – set out in NUI's Statute of 1911 and in UCD's Statute IV of 1916 – plainly requires some kind of explanation. None is forthcoming in official sources, but it seems probable that since the likeliest source of appointees in law was considered at the time the practising profession – and in particular the Bar – and that such individuals were likely to continue to practise as well as to lecture, they would enjoy two sources of income and were rightly relegated to the status of part-time professor and with a reduced stipend. Difficulties for the development of the Law School may have lain hidden in the mindset of those responsible for a distinction that today sounds invidious. But, in fairness to both the Commissioners who drew up NUI's Statute I and to the Governing Body responsible for UCD's Statute IV, it is worth recalling that at this juncture the professorships at King's Inns, of which there were always at least two, were tenable for a mere three years, the holders not necessarily being eligible for reappointment.[33] A recent development within the Council of Legal Education in London could also furnish a part-explanation. In 1898, ten of the Council's lecturers were all replaced – a somewhat drastic turnover in the staff. The Lord Chief Justice, Lord Russell of Killowen, pondered the wisdom of the move, only to be told that the Council

> thought if they did not effect frequent changes, and thus permitted the idea to grow up that teachers should be continued in office so long as they did their work well, it would be interfering with them in the pursuit of their profession, and it would be unfair to remove them later.[34]

(Ames, who recalls the episode, also repeats Lord Russell's comment to the effect that the policy rendered it impossible to look at the creation of an experienced professional class of teachers.)[35]

Encouragement to return to full-time practice in Ireland at the Bar might naturally have lain behind a rule that ensured the prospect of a fresh competition at least every seven years. The corollary here, of course, was the establishment of an arrangement under which all aspiring practitioners – almost certainly, exclusively barristers – were guaranteed the possibility of a bite at the proverbial cherry – and at not too infrequent an interval.

That this last explanation could have lain at the heart of the matter is suggested by a comparable controversy over tenure for two new lectureships in the College's Faculty of Medicine late in 1925. In regard to these planned lectureships – in Gynaecology and Obstetrics – the Medical Faculty passed the following resolution, which was accepted by the Governing Body: that the posts in question were not to be renewable after seven years at the behest of the first holders of the lectureships,

> so as to provide in those part-time offices for fresh appointments being made after that period. The College would thus have an opportunity of giving teaching experience in the subject to as many graduates of the College as possible.[36]

Considerations that prevailed with both the Medical Faculty and the Governing Body in 1925 did not, however, dictate the final outcome when early in 1933 the question of the future of the two incumbent lecturers in Gynaecology and Obstetrics fell to be decided. There would appear to have been no difficulty when at the January 1933 meeting of the Governing Body, the President, Dr Coffey, argued that the earlier resolution endorsed by the Governing Body on 22 December 1925 was a mistake, and moved successfully – and, it would seem, uncontroversially – for it to be rescinded.[37] As things turned out, there were to be second thoughts over the restricted tenure for the UCD law professors as well, but this belongs to developments which will be recorded in the next chapter.

The Act of 1908 provided that the powers of the two sets of commissioners would lapse at the end of 1910.[38] It was additionally provided, however, that such powers could be extended by no more than one further year. Early in 1911, an order in council was made extending the powers of both sets of commissioners until 31 July 1911.[39] In the case of the new UCD Law Faculty this had the perhaps unintended consequence that all five of the early appointments were made by the Dublin Commissioners presided over by Christopher Palles. The number was five, because two of the earliest of the commissioners' choices were to resign shortly after taking up their appointments, creating in both 1909 and 1910 vacancies that needed straightaway to be filled.

The first three appointments made by the Commissioners in 1909 were Daniel F. Browne, KC, Professor of the Law of Property and Law of Contracts; Charles F. Doyle, KC, Professor of Roman Law and Jurisprudence; and J.G.

Swift MacNeill, KC, MP, Professor of Constitutional Law and the Law of Public and Private Wrongs.

We turn now to each of these individuals.

DANIEL F. BROWNE (1858–1913)

Browne had been called to the Irish Bar in 1881, serving in the ensuing year as auditor of the Law Students' Debating Society.[40] He secured a reputation as an excellent chancery conveyancer and was to act as standing counsel to the Dublin Port and Docks Board (now the Dublin Port Company). He took silk in 1902. In November 1906, he gave evidence to the Fry Commission on Trinity College, Dublin, acting as a representative of an Association of Catholic Laity which he had helped to establish.[41] At an early meeting of the new NUI Senate in April 1909, Chief Baron Palles, a member of the Senate, was to recommend the choice of Browne – soon to be appointed professor – to act as legal adviser in the drafting of regulations.[42] His obituarist described Browne as possessed of 'refined literary tastes' with a marked interest in yacht racing.[43]

Browne was nominated to serve as the new Faculty of Law's representative on the General Board of Studies in November 1909,[44] but his association with UCD in that or any other capacity was destined to be short-lived, for in the following month, he was named the county court judge for Kerry and resigned his UCD chair on 13 December.[45] Browne's tenure of his post in Kerry, described by Maurice Healy as 'at least scholarly, if not very practical',[46] was not fated to last much longer than his time with UCD, for Browne was to die of pneumonia while conducting his sessions at Tralee in 1913 at the young age of 53.[47]

A little curiously, Browne had not been among the individuals recommended for this particular professorship (Property and Contracts) in the list that the Governing Body had forwarded to the Dublin Commissioners on 7 October 1909.[48] Two names had then received the Governing Body's approbation:- Charles F. Doyle, KC and Charles Maturin, LLD. With Browne now *hors de combat*, the Governing Body repeated its previously expressed preference that Doyle, recently announced as the Professor of Roman Law and Jurisprudence, should be switched to Property and the Law of Contracts. The replacement of Doyle at Roman Law and Jurisprudence – James Murnaghan – had also been anticipated in the list the Governing Body sent to the commissioners on 7 October.

The Commissioners adopted both of these suggestions, so that by early in 1910, the new team, with altered responsibilities, was in place: Doyle, Property and Contracts; MacNeill, Constitutional Law and Public and Private Wrongs; and Murnaghan, Roman Law and Jurisprudence.

CHARLES F. DOYLE (1863–1928)

Doyle, as we have just shown, was originally appointed to the professorship of Roman Law and Jurisprudence, but, following Browne's elevation to a county court judgeship, in what the College's Governing Body viewed as bordering on an emergency, he was promptly switched to Property and Contracts, somewhat ironically it would seem, since this had been the post earmarked for him by the Governing Body in its recommendation of 7 October 1909.[49] Charles Maturin, the second candidate for the job mentioned on the Governing Body's list of 7 October, was passed over without comment. As it happens, Maturin was already a professor of law at Trinity College, a post to which he was appointed in 1909 and which he continued to fill until his death in 1915.[50] The McDowell and Webb verdict on Maturin makes it difficult to be certain whether UCD lost much by the preference being shown to Doyle rather than Maturin. They wrote of Maturin that 'he was esteemed for his good conversation and his great knowledge of international law. But he had apparently no desire to put this knowledge to any use, either in the courts or in publications'.[51] Evidence to enable any kind of comparison to be drawn was not, as it turned out, to come to hand, for Doyle, like Browne, was not destined to leave his mark for any length of time on the new UCD Law School. By November 1910, he, too, like Browne, was gone – to another county court judgeship.

Doyle had been named a member of the first Governing Body of the new UCD. He had also had close links with the old Royal University. He had acted as an examiner in law there,[52] and had also served as clerk to its Convocation. He was to continue as clerk to the Convocation of the new NUI before resigning on his appointment to the Bench, when he was to be succeeded in that post by his colleague in the Law School, J.G. Swift MacNeill.[53]

After the student disturbances at the Royal University conferring ceremony in October 1905, which prevented the playing of 'God save the King', the Senate of the University pondered the launching of disciplinary proceedings against the students concerned but, finding itself unsure of the legal grounds to take any initiative, called upon Doyle to tender legal advice. To the fury of one element on the Senate, Doyle was to argue that the University had no power to punish or try its students – its functions were entirely 'academical' – though, of course, it could take steps to prevent disorderly behaviour on any future occasion.[54] Further guidance on the matter was sought, and this came from Chief Baron Palles. He agreed with Doyle's analysis: there was nothing the Senate could do by way of proceeding against the assorted culprits.[55]

Like Browne, Charles Doyle, as we have already remarked, was not destined to grace the new UCD Law Faculty for long; in November 1910 he was named county court judge for Mayo. Doyle was a graduate of both Trinity College and the Royal University. At Trinity he became auditor of the College Historical

Society in 1889, the year after he had been called to the Bar; there he had also won prizes in both Greek and Latin. He took silk in 1906. In 1924 he left his post in Mayo when he was made the Circuit Court judge, under the new dispensation, for the Eastern Counties – Louth, Meath, Kildare, Wicklow and Wexford. Doyle died in 1928.[56] For a short while in 1909–10 he had served as the Law Faculty's first dean.[57]

The gap in coverage for property law and contract law resulting from Doyle's resignation led the Governing Body, faced with another crisis not of its making, to ask Murnaghan, now appointed to the Roman Law and Jurisprudence professorship, to shoulder, albeit temporarily, an additional burden. Remuneration followed: in February 1911 the Governing Body approved the award of £39 18*s*. to Murnaghan, for his services as temporary professor of property and contracts from 3 November to 31 December 1910.[58]

By early in 1911 a permanent replacement had been found in the person of Arthur Clery. But it is first necessary to consider the contribution to the new Law School of the two individuals who provided a degree of continuity during the difficult birth of the School – J.G. Swift Mac Neill, one of the three original appointees; and James Murnaghan, Doyle's replacement in Roman Law and Jurisprudence.

JOHN GORDON SWIFT MACNEILL (1849–1926)

Only one of the three first appointments to a chair in the new UCD Law School had experience both of teaching and of publishing. This was John Gordon Swift MacNeill, appointed to teach 'Constitutional Law and Public and Private Wrongs'.[59] The oldest of the three original appointees – MacNeill was born in 1849, D.F. Browne in 1858 and Charles Francis Doyle in 1863 – MacNeill's background was also very different. He was the son of a Church of Ireland clergyman of the exact same name who served as a curate in two successive Dublin parishes, St James' and St Catherine's, before becoming chaplain to the Richmond Bridewell.

Swift MacNeill, MacLysaght tells us, belonged to the MacNeills of Antrim and Derry who themselves were descendants of Scottish Gaels from the Western Isles who had settled in the north of Ireland before the Plantation of Ulster.[60] Arguably, the rather-more celebrated Eoin MacNeill – no relation – who also was appointed to a chair at the new UCD, and who hailed from the Glens of Antrim, was of Catholic stock, but most of the MacNeills at some point had become Protestant. MacLysaght lists among the more celebrated Protestant MacNeills Dean Hugh MacNeill (1795–1879), a noted Antrim-born anti-Catholic preacher in England, and Sir John Benjamin MacNeill (1749–1880), the builder of Irish railways, as well as J.G. Swift MacNeill himself.

MacNeill himself adds a little bit more. His paternal grandfather, a Gordon MacNeill, is described in *What I Have Seen and Heard,* MacNeill's memoirs, as a descendant of the last John MacNeill, Laird of Barra in the Outer Hebrides.[61] This grandfather had served in the Walcheren expedition[62] as an officer in the 77th Regiment, and was reputed to have known both Henry Grattan and John Philpot Curran. He had written plays too, and was particularly known for his *Changes and Chances*, in which drama the celebrated actor W.C. Macready had played the part of Major Forrester.

The clan MacNeil, usually spelt with a single 'l', is still prominent in the Outer Hebrides, Barra in particular. An intriguing detail is that in 1970 one Iain Roderick MacNeil was elected the 46th Chief of the MacNeils.[63] This MacNeil was at the time a professor of law at Cornell University in New York State, but went on to hold chairs in law, successively, at the University of Virginia (1972) and Northwestern University (1980). In 1966, while a Visiting Professor at the University of East Africa at Dar-es-Salaam, he brought out his first book, *Bankruptcy Law in East Africa*.[64] While at Cornell this MacNeil found himself embroiled in a controversy on student involvement in decision-making, a controversy most unlikely to have occasioned sleepless nights for his Irish namesake with the double 'l'.[65] Iain Roderick MacNeil died at Castlebay on the Isle of Barra in 2010.

Swift MacNeill's recollections of his early years growing up in Dublin made him a link with what, by the time he gained his appointment to UCD in his sixtieth year, was a past that had long since vanished. He claims to have recalled the Scots Greys leaving King's Bridge Station (today's Heuston Station) on their way to Cork for embarkation to the Crimea;[66] also to have witnessed the Dublin riot of 12 March 1858 on the occasion of the entry into Dublin of the new Lord Lieutenant, the earl of Eglinton and Winton. The future Lord Justice FitzGibbon and the future Church of Ireland bishop of Derry, Dr Chadwick, were both spotted, as students of Trinity College, assaulting members of the Dublin Metropolitan Police on the occasion.[67] Of E.H. Caulfield, one of the last governors of the Dublin Marshalsea, he recalls the criticism levelled at him, for permitting debtors, his charges, out to vote in the general election of 1868.[68] He tells the story, too, of the response of Master Litton, a Master in Chancery who had been promised support for a judgeship by Lord Chancellor Napier, only to discover that, when it came to the crunch, Napier had blocked any such move. Litton apparently told Napier to his face: 'Lord Chancellor, though you are, you are nonetheless a damned liar, a damned blackguard. Good morning!'.[69]

MacNeill spent one year as an undergraduate at Trinity College. Unfairly, as he would have us believe, deprived of Scholarship at Trinity, MacNeill spent the remainder of his undergraduate years in Oxford at Christ Church College.[70] In *What I Have Seen and Heard,* MacNeill leaves us pen portraits of a number of personalities of his day. The eulogies of H.G. Liddell, Dean of Christ Church (of Liddell & Scott fame), and of Benjamin Jowett at Balliol conclude with the bestowal of similar praise on Dr Coffey, the new UCD's first president[71] – sadly, the single reference to UCD in MacNeill's volume. MacNeill knew the Revd C.L. Dodgson ('Lewis Carroll'), who lectured in mathematics. 'The teaching of Euclid', MacNeill writes,[72]

> seemed more in keeping with his manner as a somewhat serious and austere divine than indulgence in the revelations of an unrivalled imagination.

There is a cameo, too, of Bishop Stubbs who, according to MacNeill, talked to himself, and invariably referred to Henry VIII as that 'impure felon'.[73] MacNeill went to the lectures of E.S. Talbot (1844–1934), later Bishop of Winchester, on real property law and to those of Mountague Bernard (1820–82), the holder of the Chichele Chair of International Law and Diplomacy, 'a very distinguished authority', as Lawson phrases it, 'who took an important part in the settlement of the Alabama Claims'.[74] These related to the Confederate cruiser that had been built in Liverpool during the American Civil War.

MacNeill, in his memoirs, is most fulsome in his praise of another of his mentors, Charles Neate (1806–79), a fellow of Oriel. 'I may ascribe to his teaching as a practical politician', MacNeill writes,[75]

> my first introduction to the close study of constitutional law and history, and the trend of my reading and taste in that direction.

In Lawson's study of the Oxford Law School, Charles Neate receives something of a mixed notice.[76] Neate's views on the respective responsibilities in the Oxford context of college tutors and university professors are dismissed as being 'now so out of date as to appear almost ridiculous'. At the same time Lawson labels him an 'interesting character who lectured regularly … sometimes on rather abstruse topics'.

MacNeill left Oxford in 1873. Two years before he had unsuccessfully proposed a motion in favour of a parliament for Ireland at the Oxford Union. In 1873 he addressed the Cambridge Union on the same subject.[77] MacNeill had now decided to read for the Bar. He was admitted a student of King's Inns in Dublin, and under the rules that still existed, he also joined a London inn of court: he chose the Inner Temple. The educational value of the relevant arrangements he begged leave to doubt, the pertinent visits over to London being dubbed 'completely devoted to amusement and holiday-making'.[78]

What I Have Seen and Heard livens up as a volume of reminiscences as MacNeill recalls his period as a young Bar student and later barrister. As auditor of the Law Students' Debating Society – this was in 1875–6 – he made the acquaintance of Mr Justice Keogh. Having replied to Keogh's inquiry whether MacNeill was related to Jonathan Swift, 'I am only collaterally related to him', Keogh apparently responded: 'Only collaterally? I wish to God I were even his bastard'.[79] The verdict on Jonathan Christian is extraordinary. Christian himself, MacNeill writes, was 'sour-visaged, acrimonious and unamiable'. Yet his promotion to a law officership, a puisne judgeship and the Court of Appeal was

> a wonderful tribute to an ability heavily handicapped by a lack of sympathy, a poverty in friendships and a great power of making enemies.[80]

Very different was a man with whom he was accustomed to stroll arm-in-arm, a man reckoned by him to be the 'most sagacious and far-seeing': the future lord chief justice, Lord O'Brien of Kilfenora.[81]

In 1882, following the death of Charles Henry Tandy, MacNeill was appointed Professor of Constitutional and Criminal Law at King's Inns, and was reappointed for another three-year term in 1885, four years before the Benchers responded to a motion in the names of Serjeant Jellett and Vice-Chancellor Chatterton to proscribe all such reappointments.[82] Shortly before his appointment in 1882, he had started to write for the *Dublin Daily Express* and, ignoring what he perceived as his past humiliation, served as a 'public examiner' for the law school at Trinity College.[83] Inspired by Charles Neate at Oxford, he had already reached certain conclusions as regards the constitutional history of Ireland, conclusions that would be repeated in his published *oeuvre*. The essential preservatives of the British Constitution and the fundamental laws of Great Britain', he was to record,[84]

> were in some cases not extended to Ireland for centuries after their enactment in England; that in other cases they were not extended to Ireland at all; and that even those that were so extended came only after long intervals and in mutilated form.

It is a passage he was regularly to reproduce in his writings.

In 1887 MacNeill's career took an unusual turn when he was elected an MP for the constituency of South Donegal, a constituency he continued to represent until 1918. Earlier the same year ill-health had prompted MacNeill to seek to recuperate by making the first of his visits to South Africa. He returned there in 1891.[85] Meeting Cecil Rhodes on board the RMS *Garth Castle* on the first of these voyages, he kept an appointment to see him later at Port Elizabeth. The outcome was a donation of £11,000 plus for the cause of Home Rule from Rhodes. In South Africa, MacNeill also met Dr Jameson, of the celebrated, later, Jameson Reid and Olive Schreiner, the author of *Story of an African Farm.*

MacNeill was made a QC in 1899. The same year he was reported to have assaulted the *Punch* cartoonist, Henry Furness, for depicting him as a chimpanzee.

The only one of the three original professorial appointments to leave any kind of mark on the future of the new UCD Law School in its early years, MacNeill was scarcely a surprising choice. An MP at Westminster from the late 1880s (as we have noted), and an established author and authority on constitutional matters, it is hard at this remove in time to visualise who else could have been so well placed to cover questions of constitutional law in lectures – one half of MacNeill's formal responsibilities. The other half required MacNeill to teach criminal law. There was an additional consideration that must surely have weighed with the Dublin commissioners who gave MacNeill the job – he had served as a King's Inns professor in the 1880s, even though that experience was twenty years in the past when MacNeill was appointed to UCD in 1909. It is, of course, possible that the commissioners hesitated even so. MacNeill continued to serve as an MP at Westminster – and did so until 1918, when he was deselected in favour of J.T. Donovan, an associate of Joseph Devlin. That move rankled with MacNeill, who earlier in the decade when Home Rule seemed imminent had been tipped as the first speaker of an Irish House of Commons on account of the extensive knowledge of parliamentary procedure he had gained at Westminster. Hesitation there could well have been, as we have said, for on paper at least, it did not appear entirely satisfactory if at the same time a man represented South Donegal as an MP in London and held down the job of a UCD professor in Dublin. We know, thanks to George O'Brien, one of his students at the time, how exactly MacNeill accomplished this particular feat. During parliamentary sessions, MacNeill would lecture in Dublin on Saturdays and Mondays. The rest of the week he would spend at Westminster. O'Brien, in his reminiscences drew attention to one advantage he claimed accrued to students such as himself, as a result. 'We used to hear', he recalled,[86]

> a good deal of the latest political gossip during our lectures on Constitutional Law. This gave us a feeling of being in touch with real constitutional problems.

On the appointment itself, another aspect to it can scarcely be ignored. W.E.H. Lecky, the historian, took a dim view of MacNeill's publications in the field of constitutional law and history – which we will be reviewing shortly – dubbing him a 'propagandist'. Lecky's distaste for the man and his *oeuvre* he pushed so far, it has been argued, that he went out of his way to support official refusals to let MacNeill research state papers.[87] This, if true, did little to dissuade MacNeill from continuing to dabble in constitutional history, even, as we shall see, an activity he continued into his last years.

As previously mentioned, there is but a single mention of UCD in MacNeill's memoirs. Other sources fortunately enable gaps in his precise contribution to be filled. Aside from George O'Brien's recollections, those of Dermot F. Gleeson, also preserved in Meenan's history of the College's L & H, help a little. Gleeson recalled a meeting of the Society held on 4 February 1916, i.e., shortly before the Easter Rising, which was chaired by MacNeill, and where one Kevin O'Higgins proposed the motion, 'That constitutional agitation has been a failure in Ireland'.[88] O'Higgins' 'quiet, intense and inspiring words', Gleeson would have us believe, 'brought rounds of applause from his youthful audience'. At the end of the debate MacNeill seemingly 'spoke with great kindliness and feeling of O'Higgins' speech'.[89] But, as a stalwart of the Irish Parliamentary Party, MacNeill was not going to leave it at that. MacNeill said, Gleeson reported,[90]

> that when he also was young, he had felt and spoken as the speaker but, as the years advanced, his fire had declined and he had come to see that violence even in a good cause had brought evil in its train.

It remains remarkable that *What I Have Seen and Heard* has so little to say about MacNeill's tenure of his chair at UCD. His silence on his double-jobbing is eloquent too, and it is possible that he would have preferred to keep it that way. As it happens, *What I Have Seen and Heard* does mention the matter of double-jobbing but at a different time (1887–8) and in a different context.[91] In 1882, as we have seen, MacNeill became a King's Inns professor and in 1887 we know he entered parliament. Plainly he could not be in both places – Dublin and London – at the same time, and, predictably, it would occur that he sensed he needed to be present in Parliament for political reasons on a day he was scheduled to lecture at King's Inns. From the autumn of 1887, under a temporary arrangement between the two men, Dunbar Plunket Barton, the other King's Inns professor, who had been appointed to the professorship of Personal Property and other subjects in 1885, would 'take' MacNeill's lecture days when MacNeill was in London. The Benchers of King's Inns, not unsurprisingly, were unhappy with this arrangement and pressed MacNeill into giving more time to his duties at King's Inns. Interpreting this as pressure on him to resign his King's Inns chair, MacNeill turned up the records to try to find a precedent in his favour. He was in luck. Apparently, Baron Rathmore of Shanganagh, as plain David Robert Plunket, had represented Dublin University at Westminster while holding the chair at King's Inns to which he had been appointed in 1868, the same year he became a QC and served as Law Advisor to the Irish government. He was to go on to serve a stint as Irish solicitor-general from 1875 to 1877, before being elevated to the peerage in 1895. A keen Unionist and opponent of Gladstone, Plunket belonged to a somewhat different camp from that of MacNeill.[92] Turning to his personal difficulties with King's Inns, MacNeill relates that in some instances Plunket had not delivered a single lecture during an entire term. Relaying that precedent to the Benchers, MacNeill somewhat unconvincingly asserts, caused all complaints against him to cease.[93] That, indeed, may be so, but we know that in 1888 MacNeill's occupancy of the most prestigious of the King's Inns professorships was to come to an end, for in the middle of that year the Benchers adopted a rule proposed by Vice-Chancellor Hedges Eyre Chatterton and seconded by Chief Baron Christopher Palles that for the future, King's Inns professorships were not to be tenable by any MP.[94] Whether a serving professor who during the tenure of his chair was elected an MP was obliged to resign his post at the Inns as a consequence was not immediately explicit.

MacNeill published his first book in 1885 whilst still the King's Inns Professor of Constitutional and Criminal Law. *The Irish Parliament – What it Was and What it Did* was brought out in London.[95] The constitutional history of Ireland prior to the Act of Union of 1800 – a preoccupation of MacNeill throughout his career – was covered in a series of chapters that dealt successively with the composition of the Irish House of Lords and that of the Irish House of Commons; the relationship of Ireland to the English Crown; the relationship of the two parliaments, the English and the Irish; constitutional relationships before 1782; such relationships after 1782; the Irish executive; and, finally, differences between the constitutions of England and Ireland. A primer that MacNeill's King's Inns students must have found invaluable was enlivened, first, by MacNeill's regular employment of remarks from sundry generations of politicians: liberal use is made, for example, of speeches recorded in the late eighteenth-century volumes of the *Irish Parliamentary Register*. MacNeill went out of his way to justify the approach. 'In this inquiry', he wrote,[96]

> I will, as far as possible, quote the remarks of contemporary statesmen in the workings of a Constitution with which they were familiar. Such remarks are always interesting; addressed to popular audiences they are not likely to be misunderstood; spoken in the presence of persons well acquainted with the facts, and without fear of contradiction, they are presumably correct.

But, secondly, MacNeill did not hesitate to convey his own point of view. Noticing the opposition of the bishops of the Church of Ireland – who, of course, sat in the Lords – to repeal of the Test Act, MacNeill then trots out Swift's yarn concerning the highwaymen who murdered on Hounslow Heath the gentlemen appointed to the Irish sees, stole their letters patent, came to Dublin and were consecrated in their place. MacNeill then adds his own wry comment. 'A visitor to the Universities of Oxford and Cambridge', he writes,[97]

> would be easily led, by the number of portraits of Anglo-Irish bishops in 'artful folds of sacred lawn', which adorn the college halls, to conclude that the special mission of England during the eighteenth century was to evangelise ungrateful Ireland.

The final chapter in which MacNeill focuses on differences between the constitutional dispensation in England and that in Ireland covers ground that is now very well known: differences in regard to the duration of parliament (differences reduced with the adoption of the Octennial Act in 1768), the adoption of Mutiny Acts, habeas corpus, judicial tenure, money bills, the law of treason, the appropriation of supply and laws affecting religious liberty.

The volume was to earn praise from Gladstone. 'The book contains', the latter wrote,[98] 'within a wonderfully narrow compass, the heart and pith of a large as well as a sad chapter of Irish history'.

MacNeill followed up his primer on Irish constitutional history with another on the history of the regulation of Irish trade.[99] In the preface MacNeill quoted the observation of the English attorney-general of the day, Sir Charles Russell (later Lord Russell of Killowen) on the 'evil marks' left on Ireland by the adoption of 'the direct legislation avowedly contrived to hinder the development of Irish commerce and manufactures'.[100] Different chapters examine laws adopted by the English, and later the British, parliament to restrain Irish trade; the opposition of governments in London to efforts made by the Irish parliament, to promote Irish trade; and the effects of English/British legislation on Irish trade. The three final chapters tackle the tendency towards fair trade and the actual arrangements in place between 1782 and 1800 and those introduced by the Act of Union (see Article 6 of the Treaty of Union). Source material utilised was similar to that employed in *The Irish Parliament*. 'In this inquiry', MacNeill writes,[101]

> I will, as far as possible, confine myself to an examination of the statutes, which will speak for themselves; to the journals of the Parliaments of England and Ireland; and to the statements of contemporary speakers and writers whose accuracy has not, so far as I am aware, been impeached.

What are now known to be the usual subjects were intelligently surveyed – the Navigation Acts and their impact on shipping; the proscription of the woollen trade; the encouragement of linen manufacture, etc. Less well known are the restrictions on glass manufacture and even the ban on the export of Irish beer. Temporary embargoes are also discussed. Froude's acceptance[102] that the various prohibitions had turned the Irish as a whole into being idle, and comparable observations from others, are answered by a quotation MacNeill furnishes for us from O'Connell. 'Idle?', the latter asks, disbelievingly: 'They are to be found making roads in Scotland and digging canals in the poisonous marshes of New Orleans'.[103] A number of other details retrieved from the exclusively printed sources MacNeill surveyed embellish the finished product. One thinks of pressure sometimes exacted in England to tighten the screw even further – the abortive effort of the fisher folk of Folkstone and Aldborough to ban imports of herring from Waterford and Wexford (1698)[104] – and the welcome it is claimed Louis XIV gave Irish Protestant exiles who set up woollen manufacture in France.[105] Molyneux, Swift, Edmund Burke and Chief Justice Whiteside all make an appearance, and at one point MacNeill introduces a forcefully expressed personal opinion. 'Speaking as a Protestant', he writes,[106]

> I have no hesitation in saying that the injuries inflicted in Ireland by the Penal Code exceeded the injuries inflicted on her by the trade regulations.

In his book on *The Irish Parliament*, MacNeill, when dealing with the pre-Union House of Lords, had alluded to the practice of the ennoblement of commoners to secure the passage of the Act of Union in 1800. The allusion is capped by a quotation from John Philpot Curran, destined to become Master of the Rolls after the Union. 'The sale of peerages', Curran noted,

> is as notorious as the sale of cart-horses in the Castle Yard, the publicity the same, the terms not very different, the horses not warranted sound, the other animals warranted rotten.

The entire episode involving the creation of new peers at the time in question provided the focus for another volume brought out by MacNeill, in 1894, one with the scarcely neutral title of *Titled Corruption*.[107]

The timing was no coincidence: the vote in the House of Lords against the Second Home Rule Bill gave MacNeill an opportunity he was not prepared to let slip – to highlight the peers who voted against Home Rule who were the descendants of individuals who secured their peerages in the years mainly of 1799 and 1800 or were advanced in the peerage at that time. The title page of the volume is enhanced by an apposite quotation from Juvenal:[108] *nobilitas*[109] *sola est atque unica virtus* (the one and only nobility is personal excellence).[110] And on the page facing we are supplied with another apt quotation, this time from none other than Lecky – no admirer of MacNeill as we have seen:[111] 'The majority of Irish titles are historically connected with memories, not of honour, but of shame'.[112] MacNeill makes most use of Lord Cornwallis' correspondence with the duke of Portland and Jonah Barrington's so-called 'Black Book'. He also acknowledges his indebtedness to Lecky, whom he commends for his 'majestic impartiality', and also to W.J. Fitzpatrick. MacNeill deals with all the peerages concerned, from Lord Ashtown (Frederick Trench as was) down to Lord Avonmore (Barry Yelverton). There is a gossipy tone to certain of the entries, reminiscent in a few instances of the style of today's tabloid press. Indeed, as MacNeill himself freely points out, the various entries in his inventory had originally appeared as articles in the press.

No one should presume to open *Titled Corruption* without first digesting the preface, which has important things to say. 'It must not be supposed', MacNeill frankly concedes,[113]

> that I have taken pains in the selection of the peerages whose origin I have attempted to describe. They are largely taken up haphazard, and are not cases of exceptional corruption but are rather types of the character of the ordinary Irish Peerage. I am confident that I could have placed before the public many peerages whose creation was due to circumstances quite as discreditable if not transcending in iniquity the origins of the titles I have endeavoured to trace.

In a further passage in the preface, MacNeill alludes to the political context in which he had set about his task. 'It seems a somewhat ungracious task', he begins,[114]

> to revive the memory of the discreditable transactions of bygone days. The holders of the Irish Peerages are not, it may be said, responsible for the conduct of their predecessors. It should, however, be borne in mind that the chief argument in support of hereditary legislators is the services rendered to the country by their ancestors. It will be difficult to argue with a serious countenance that a gentleman is entitled to obstruct and thwart the wishes of the House of Commons, from the fact of his holding a Peerage which is in some instances the reward of shame and dishonour, and in some even of crime, and thus being ennobled to sit in the House of Lords, or to vote for the election of Representative Peers in that assembly.

W.E. Gladstone: Anecdotes and Reminiscences, brought out by MacNeill when made aware of Gladstone's impending demise – he had resigned in March 1894 and died in May 1898 – is a slender enough volume that does MacNeill no favours.[115] A modern critic would dismiss it as sycophancy and pass on. He would have cause. One detail that MacNeill preserves might perhaps merit notice. During his speech on the second Home Rule Bill in the Commons in February 1893, Gladstone after one hour, we are told,[116] took a sip from a little glass jar containing a preparation of eggs beaten up with sherry, as a prevention to hoarseness and throat irritation. Also arresting is W.H. Margetson's picture cover with colour in green and purple, which shows Gladstone on his deathbed. In the bottom left hand corner lines from Walter Scott's poem, 'Marmion', à propos of the death of the younger Pitt, are reproduced:[117]

> Now is the stately column broke
> The beacon light is quench'd in smoke
> The trumpet's silver sound is still
> The warder silent on the hill.

In a pamphlet brought out in 1912 MacNeill was to pay further tribute to Gladstone by recalling a speech that the latter had given in Truro in Cornwall in June 1889, a speech that touched on what had become a vexed question in the Ireland of the 1910s: would Home Rule mean Rome Rule? The specific issue was the fear that with the grant of devolved government to Ireland the Catholic majority would seek to persecute the Protestant minority. The notion was preposterous, Mac Neill claimed, and he sought at some length to refute it in his pamphlet, *Home Rule and Religious Intolerance*.[118]

Gladstone in his Truro speech had alluded to the protection accorded Bishop Bedell, the Church of Ireland bishop of Kilmore in 1641, and in the previous century the refuge that had been given in Ireland to English Protestants fleeing the Marian persecution and the fires of Smithfield.

In this overtly political offering, MacNeill made use as well of the expressed views of Daniel O'Connell and Isaac Butt. In 1873, the latter, in his discussion of the question, had seized on the example of Canada. 'Sectarian hatred in Canada', MacNeill assured his readers,[119]

> is as dead as Queen Anne, and sectarian hatred in Ireland will die when in Ireland the conditions are the same as in Canada today.

Addressing himself in particular to an English audience,[120] MacNeill went on to assure the inhabitants of the larger British Isle that

> these Roman Catholic people [in Ireland] will be found fighting breast to breast with you the battles of religious liberty. They will set an example to the other Roman Catholic peoples of the world; they will show the sincerity of their attachment both to the Throne and to the law.

The preparedness of Dublin Corporation to elect Protestants to the position of lord mayor; the willingness of the same corporation to repair damage inflicted on the statue of William III in College Green; the addresses of the welcome given to prelates of the former established church:[121] all of this is cited as proof of the friendliest of intentions of the Catholic majority vis-à-vis their Protestant fellow citizens.

MacNeill employs, too, his own impressions of the true state of affairs, by way of rejecting the calumnies heaped on Catholics by their critics. His triumph in the election for the South Donegal constituency in February 1887, when he beat his Catholic Unionist opponent by some thousands of votes; his election to a chair in the National University of Ireland,[122]

> an institution mainly established for the purpose of enabling the young people holding the faith of the great mass of the Irish race to receive the advantages of University education without any violation of conscience or danger to faith or morals;

his election in 1910, in succession to Charles Doyle, to the position of clerk of Convocation of the National University.[123] MacNeill makes no bones about it. 'I have received', he adds[124] 'super-abounding kindness, affection and sympathy from my fellow Catholic countrymen'.

It was to be in his capacity as clerk of Convocation that MacNeill late in 1914 wrote formally to Dr Coffey, the President of UCD, conveying the wishes of Convocation that UCD might re-establish evening courses 'similar to those so successfully carried on in the old University College in connection with the Royal University'. To no avail; the Governing Body responding in February 1915 that they would 'find it impossible to establish a separate course of evening lectures for degrees'.[125] As Clerk of Convocation, MacNeill was involved in the ceremony attending the installation of Eamon de Valera as the National University's new Chancellor in December 1921. A luncheon ensued, the bill for which, the Comptroller and Auditor-General was later to argue, was not a proper charge on the University's finances.[126]

Some note deserves to be taken of MacNeill's career in politics. A Protestant nationalist Home Ruler, who represented South Donegal from 1887 to 1918, he came to the fore in the obstruction tactics adopted by Irish nationalists at Westminster. In the Parnell split, he sided with T.M. Healy, whom as it chanced, along with both Redmonds, John and William, he had taught as a King's Inns professor.[127] MacNeill caught the attention of the public on a number of occasions during his parliamentary career. In 1890, he vehemently opposed the return of Heligoland to Germany.[128] Two years later he successfully moved to prohibit three fellow MPs from being allowed to vote on a motion to give a grant to the British East Africa Company to enable a preliminary survey to be carried out for a railway from the Indian Ocean to Lake Victoria. Two of the MPs were directors in the company, and the third was a shareholder.[129] Maintaining his interest in African affairs, he resolutely opposed the Boer War, and it was to be claimed that he had even cheered in the House of Commons when news was received of a British defeat.[130] He supported the abolition of flogging in the Royal Navy, something finally achieved in 1906.[131]

MacNeill's expertise in constitutional law enabled him to display his talents in the area in an unusual context, not long after his appointment to UCD in 1909. This was when Asquith's government introduced a measure to alter the wording of the declaration of attachment to Protestantism to be demanded of the sovereign on their accession. The death of Edward VII on 6 May 1910 created an obvious moment for such a change to be implemented, and it was done very quickly indeed, the change being introduced in legislation that received the royal assent from the new King, George V, on 3 August.[132]

The old declaration drawn up at the time of Titus Oates, the 'Popish Plot' and the Exclusion Crisis (the movement to deny the throne to Charles II's Catholic brother, James II) was to be found in an act of the thirtieth regnal year of Charles II, 'An Act for the more effectuall preserving the King's person and government by disabling papists from sitting in either House of Parliament'.[133] The Bill of Rights[134] and the Act of Settlement[135] together ensured that the declaration (which continued to be mandatory) retained its constitutional legitimacy. The declaration read as follows:

> I A. B. doe solemnly and sincerely in the presence of God professe testifie and declare that I do believe that in the sacrament of the Lord's Supper there is not any transubstantiation of the elements of bread and wine into the body and blood of Christ at or after the consecration itself by any person whatsoever; and that the invocation of adoration of the Virgin Mary or any other saint and the sacrifice of the masse as they are now used in the Church of Rome are superstitious and idolatrous, and I doe solemnely in the presence of God professe testifie and declare that I doe make this declaration and every part thereof in the plaine and ordinary sence of the words read unto me as they are commonly understood by English Protestants without any evasion, equivocation or mentall reservation whatsoever and without any dispensation already granted me for this purpose by the Pope or any other authority or person whatsoever or without any hope of any such dispensation from any person or authority whatsoever or without thinking that I am or can be acquitted before God or man or absolved of this declaration or any part thereof although the Pope or any other person or persons or power whatsoever should dispence with or annull the same, or declare that it was null and void from the begining.

The replacement declaration introduced by the Accession Declaration Act of 1910 was very much shorter, but blunt enough (without going into detail).[136] This is the declaration that remains in force today. It reads:

> I [here insert the name of the sovereign] do solemnly and sincerely in the presence of God profess, testify, and declare that I am a faithful Protestant, and that I will, according to the true interest of the enactments which secure the Protestant succession to the Throne of my Realm, uphold and maintain the said enactments to the best of my powers according to law.

The Accession Declaration Bill, despite the forceful case in favour of it presented by Asquith, the prime minister, during its second reading in the Commons on 27 July 1910,[137] did not have an entirely smooth passage through parliament, but in the end it enjoyed a comfortable enough majority. MacNeill, as a participant both in the second reading debate in the Commons and at the later committee stage, made two important contributions. First, he traced the historical origins of the old declaration before adducing evidence to indicate that two sovereigns, Victoria and Edward VII, had not been exactly enthusiasts when making it.[138] In the case of Edward, he reported the views of Lord Herries in the House of Lords who was close to the new King in 1901 when he made the declaration that 'he never saw anyone so embarrassed or so confused'.[139] As regards Victoria, MacNeill added, it was striking indeed that although other oaths would have been required of Prince Albert under the terms of the Regency Act of 1840, mention of the declaration was studiously omitted.[140] MacNeill's second contribution came at the committee stage when controversy broke out as to the precise moment after an accession to the throne when any new sovereign would be obliged to make the declaration. Asquith indicated that one view prevalent at the time was that the monarch could give the royal assent to legislation even before he had made the declaration. This, however, argued for an early date rather than a later one. Asquith paused at this point, having noticed that MacNeill, who was present in the chamber at the time, had shaken his head. He continued:[141] 'I confess I speak with some trepidation in his presence'. MacNeill's argument, however sound he may have reckoned it was, was not especially realistic. In his view, the pressure that was put on Edward VII to make the declaration on 14 February 1901 had been wrong. The correct moment would have been at the first new parliament convened under his authority in 1906.[142]

What anyone in the House made of this particular intervention it is not easy to say. That MacNeill's general approach can only have been welcome to the Liberal administration was his early countering of 'loyalist' opposition to any change being made with evidence of a Protestant petition circulating in Dublin at least that supported the government's initiative,[143] and what he had uttered in the peroration of his speech on the second reading[144] that he was glad to be able to support by his vote 'the advance of the great cause of human liberty, freedom of conscience and equal rights between man and man'.

The next year, 1911, MacNeill sought unsuccessfully to have the UCD

Library added to the list of British legal deposit libraries. 'Is Trinity College', he demanded unavailingly,[145] 'to have an advantage from which the National University is excluded?'

MacNeill was prominent in another piece of business that dominated discussion at Westminster shortly before MacNeill ceased to be an MP. During the First World War, MacNeill, like a number of others, considered it nothing short of scandalous that sundry German princes continued to hold British titles of honour. Pressure mounted, and in 1917 the Titles Deprivation Act,[146] a measure to deprive enemy peers and princes of British dignities and titles, entered the statute-book.[147]

In these war years and later MacNeill continued to visit some of the more obscure corners of constitutional history. In 1914, for instance, the passage of the Third Home Rule Bill prompted a piece from MacNeill which queried the validity of the Act of Union of 1800 on grounds not too frequently advanced.[148] No express mandate that an Union between the two kingdoms would be sought, MacNeill argued, had been placed before the electorate at the general election of 1797. Did this then nullify what was afterwards attempted? Howsoever that intriguing question was answered, there is no doubt at all – and here MacNeill quotes chapter and verse (from episodes recalled from 1759, 1776, 1785 and even as late as 10 October 1798) – that the Union had not been regarded 'officially' as on the cards.

Two years later the failure of the Irish government to prevent the Easter Rising provoked an extraordinary outpouring of bile, in which MacNeill lambasted the 'disastrous incompetence of the Irish executive'.[149] Targeted here was a triumvirate upbraided as not fit for purpose – Lord Wimborne, the lord lieutenant; Augustine Birrell, the chief secretary; and Sir Matthew Nathan, the under-secretary. MacNeill's thesis quickly calls history in aid. What had occurred was entirely predictable. 'The friction', he wrote,[150]

> inevitably arising between a lord lieutenant, a chief secretary and an under-secretary, by reason of the lack of a distinct and administrative definition of their relations to each other in the administration of Irish affairs, is no new thing.

Deficiencies in the Dublin Castle executive over the years, as set forth by a succession of witnesses, MacNeill then rehearses: the duke of Wellington in 1850, Earl Cowper in 1882 and Morley in 1905. The unflattering views of Dr Whateley, the Church of Ireland archbishop of Dublin, on the lord lieutenant's job as relayed to an acquaintance in 1852, bear repetition here. 'The Lord Lieutenant's days and nights', Whateley confided,[151]

> are wasted in intrigue and petty squabbles – on the management of the Press and the management of fêtes, on deciding what ruined gambler is

> to have this stipendiary magistracy, and which Repealer is to be conciliated by asking his wife and daughter to that concert – in short, on things nine-tenths of which cannot be so well treated as by being left alone.

Benign neglect was very far from being the approach adopted by MacNeill in regard to something entirely different – the Royal Marriages Act of 1772.[152] This measure, which gave the holder of the crown a limited veto on marriages within the royal family, MacNeill argued, in a forceful piece in the *Law Quarterly Review*, was overdue for repeal.[153] Forced through a reluctant and venal parliament, by the personal will of the Sovereign [George III]', MacNeill wrote,[154] it was

> a wanton violation of the liberty of the individual, subversive of the principle of equal rights for all, [which] aimed to secure the establishment of a royal caste system borrowed from the German Courts and repellent to the genius of the people of the British Empire, who desire their Royal Family to be closely associated and identified with them by community of wants and wishes, of sentiment and of blood.

George III had been aggrieved at the marriages of two of the royal dukes – of Cumberland to a Mrs Horton and of Gloucester to the Dowager Lady Waldegrave – and the strength of his feelings was revealed in his note to Lord North with its implied threat to any parliamentary opposition:[155] 'I have a right to expect a hearty support from everyone in my service, and I shall remember defaulters'.

Smuts' contribution to the discussion of the question in 1917 MacNeill had earlier recorded; Smuts' gift of prophecy may have proved inadequate.

'Our Royal Princes', Smuts opined,[156]

> instead of getting their consorts from the princelings of Central Europe, will go for them to the Dominions and other portions of the British Empire.

Kate Middleton, who married Prince William in 2011, did not fit into either of Smuts' 'catchment areas'. Queen Elizabeth II's consent to the marriage under the terms of the legislation so bitterly attacked by the MacNeill was forthcoming nevertheless:[157]

> NOW KNOW YE that WE have consented and do by these Presents signify Our Consent to the contracting of Matrimony between Our Most Dearly Beloved Grandson Prince William Arthur Phillip Louis of Wales, K.G., and Our Trusty and Well-beloved Catherine Elizabeth Middleton.

Towards the end of the tenure of his UCD chair MacNeill plainly sensed the need to say something about the new constitutional dispensation following the establishment of the Irish Free State. The drift to affairs had clearly not been to his taste no more than it had been for Clery, his younger colleague, though for very different reasons. But, in the end, he seems to have become reconciled to the new Ireland, and one result was his *Studies in the Constitution of the Irish Free State* brought out in 1925.[158] It had been preceded by his 'Thoughts on the Constitution of the Irish Free State', which had appeared two years before.[159]

MacNeill's approach here was to examine the Constitution article by article, and, where appropriate, explain their origin in earlier constitutional development. Article 6 on the liberty of the person is followed by a long excursus on habeas corpus,[160] which touches on Article 69, regarding the independence of the judiciary. The latter, for its part, is graced by a not untypical entry, based on MacNeill's considerable knowledge of the eighteenth-century dispensation – the content of a letter from a lord lieutenant of the period, Lord Harcourt, opposing the plan in 1776 to make the change that only came in Ireland in 1782 (An Act for securing the Independency of Judges, and the impartial Administration of Justice: 21 & 22 George III, c.50). Harcourt had written six years earlier:[161]

> The state of the country duly considered, I am persuaded it would be undesirable to make the commission of judges during good behaviour, so many inconveniences would result from such a Bill that I think it will not be deemed proper to return it to Ireland.

MacNeill's note on the prohibition of the conferment of titles of honour (Article 5), afforded him the opportunity to repeat in a much briefer compass the message of his book *Title Corruption*. What in certain quarters was seen as controversial at the time, the location of sovereignty in the people (Article 2), produced the historical detail that Charles James Fox had been removed from the privy council for claiming as much.[162]

MacNeill's general tactic throughout was to assert that many of the conventions of the British constitution had been made into explicit constitutional norms by the Constitution of 1922.[163] But there was more to it than that, and here MacNeill struck a note that can only have been regarded as welcome by the new Free State administration. 'The new Irish Constitution', he wrote,[164]

> in poignant contrast with its predecessor, contains provisions and capacities for development calculated to excite the envy and admiration of the lovers of the British Constitution.

Despite the wealth of historical precedent and anecdote – and there is a very great deal of both – incorporated by MacNeill into his text, these *Studies* somehow fall short of what might have been anticipated.[165] MacNeill's swansong thus disappoints, certainly by comparison with Leo Kohn's study that came out some seven years later.[166]

Stephen Gwynn's entry on MacNeill for one of the *DNB*'s supplementary volumes,[167] offers a contemporary assessment of this intriguing member of UCD's original law professoriate. 'Whether in public speech or private conversation', Gwynn wrote,[168]

> MacNeill was an exuberant and untidy talker; enthusiasms, information, and gossip tumbled pell-mell from a loose-hung mouth set between a ragged beard and prominent, excited light-blue eyes. But his good nature, his courtesy, and his out-flowing humanity made him widely beloved. Nobody delighted more to do the honours of parliament; and his erudition there and elsewhere, though not always exact, was generously available. Few figures in the House of Commons were better known or better liked than this eccentric, warm-hearted Irish Protestant gentleman.

Maume's summation is a good deal shorter. MacNeill, he writes,[169] was 'a Buttite, a nostalgic antiquarian throwback to eighteenth-century colonial nationalism'.

It is overstating the mark for any biographer to have described MacNeill's memoirs as 'amusing'. One final parliamentary recollection of MacNeill's might just warrant the verdict. Towards the end of *What I Have Seen and Heard,* MacNeill makes an impassioned plea for improved bathing facilities in Westminster Palace.[170] The time one spent, our erstwhile MP wrote, waiting to take a bath was indefensible. There follows a pretty allusion to conditions at the pool of Siloam,[171] best recalled, as aficionados of hymnals will be aware, by Bishop Heber's lines:

> By cool Siloam's shady rill,
> How sweet the lily grows!

MacNeill never married, and his last years were spent at his home in Dublin in the society of his sister, his life-long companion, and their cats and dogs. The Senate of the National University had brought before them in July 1926 a proposal that MacNeill should be given an honorary degree.[172] Matters had not progressed very far however when all discussion of this suggestion ceased when MacNeill died on 24 August. The Senate conveyed its formal condolences to Miss MacNeill the following month, and, on account of his [MacNeill's] exceptional services, also arranged for her to receive a gratuity based on half of MacNeill's annual salary.[173]

JAMES AUGUSTINE MURNAGHAN (1881–1973)

Doyle's successor as Professor of Roman Law and Jurisprudence was a considerably younger man, James Murnaghan, who was fated to enjoy close on a thirty-year tenure on the Bench following his translation there in 1924 – first to the High Court, and a year later to the Supreme Court. The choice of Murnaghan to occupy the post vacated by Doyle may not have been a complete surprise. Murnaghan had been prominent in student life in the pre-1908 University College. He was defeated in the election for auditor of the Literary and Historical Society in 1901,[174] but both then and over the next couple of years he played a not-insignificant role in the affairs of this most celebrated of the old College's student societies. William Dawson was to recall in the pages of the L & H's centenary history that Murnaghan was a skilled shorthand writer and was thus in a position to embarrass Monsignor Molloy, rector of the Catholic University, by publishing the ipsissima verba of the rector's anti-English rant, on an occasion when it was made demonstrably clear that he had thus dropped his mask as a 'Cawstle Catholic'.[175] In the L & H's session of 1902–3, Murnaghan was to share in the award of the Society's gold medal for oratory.[176] That same year he was called to the Irish Bar, winning the John Brooke scholarship. Two years later, in 1905, he gained an LLD from the Royal University. Around this time, he also appears to have lectured in the pre-1909 University College, the student journal, *St. Stephen's,* for which he also wrote, describing him as 'the youngest man ever attached to the College staff'.[177]

An article Murnaghan published in *St. Stephen's* in December 1901 was a thoughtful contribution to discussion then being engaged in on the inadequacies of the Royal University *qua* university. A Hannah Moylan had addressed herself to the issues that arose in an essay entitled 'A plea for specialization', which had appeared in *St. Stephen's* the preceding November.[178] Murnaghan, in his response, 'The Royal University and research',[179] endorsed Ms Moylan's general line of attack. Under the Royal University dispensation, specialisation, Murnaghan argued, 'was not sufficiently encouraged'. Indeed, sadly, what we had was a fostering of mediocrity. The practical politician in the making then essays to have the last word. 'If a University is ever to establish a School of Research', Murnaghan concluded,[180]

> it must be able to grant Research Fellowships, continued as long as good work is done, or, at least, Fellowships with such an amount of teaching attached to them that the holder would have time to devote to research work. This the Royal University cannot do.

The problem – the deficiency – that Moylan and Murnaghan described with startling accuracy back in 1901 was fated to haunt the new University College even after it opened its doors in 1909.

George O'Brien, in his reminiscences, lauded Murnaghan's appointment, describing him as an 'academic lawyer of the highest calibre'.[181] The tribute was deserved. Not long after his appointment in 1911, Murnaghan had two articles on Irish legal history published in the new quarterly journal, *Studies*. Both are fine pieces of work, even if limited by the range of sources consulted during their composition. 'The development of supreme judicature in Ireland'[182] is exactly that – a voyage through the centuries to chart key features of the system of final appeals. Telling use is made of the *Justiciary Rolls*, the *Year Books*, the medieval statute-book, the *Lords'* and *Commons' Journals of Ireland* and the controversies generated in the eighteenth century by such cases as *Annesley* v. *Sherlock* and *Murray* v. *Bateman*, to flesh out the details of what, on any view, is a remarkable story, and certainly worth revisiting by some modern researcher. Murnaghan's second article, 'The Lordship of Ireland and the counties palatine',[183] is another impressive piece of work, for the time that was in it: we have Henry II's grant of Meath to Hugh de Lacy and Sir John Davies' sentiments on the wisdom of any grants of palatinates at all. Murnaghan also tackles the difficult problem of the manner of the extinction of each palatinate. Both these pieces compare very well with the better-known offerings of the time on medieval Irish history that came from the pen of William Johnston,[184] also destined, incongruously, for high judicial office in the country as well.

It ought not, perhaps, to pass without notice that in the 1930s Murnaghan and Johnston found themselves on opposite sides in two celebrated legal historical controversies. In the litigation over the Erne several fishery, Johnston J. in the High Court upheld Moore's title to the fishery: *Moore* v. *A.G.*.[185] The Supreme Court, by a majority, reversed.[186] Though the judgment of the majority was delivered by Kennedy C.J. on behalf of himself and Murnaghan J., the chief justice acknowledged[187] that 'the great labour of putting it together' had been Murnaghan's.

Johnston was promoted temporarily to the Supreme Court to hear the appeal – against a judgment of Meredith J. – in the Erasmus Smith Schools case.[188] The Supreme Court on this special occasion thus consisted of Kennedy C.J., Murnaghan J. and Johnston J. Kennedy died before judgment was delivered and then, early in 1937, it was disclosed that the two remaining judges – Murnaghan and Johnston – had prepared judgments but had disagreed. These judgments were then suppressed, and the controversy between the parties over the schools – it touched on religion and eligibility for attendance – was resolved through government intervention and the passing of a private Act of the Oireachtas.[189]

For his two articles in *Studies* in 1912 and 1913, preceded as they were by papers on the same subjects delivered to the College's Legal and Economic Society, Murnaghan can plainly lay claim to being the begetter of the tradition in which the UCD law professoriate has sought down the years in their published writings to shed light on Ireland's complex legal past.[190] Murnaghan's historic sense is evidenced at this juncture in a very different manner. In the L & H centenary volume the well-known Dublin solicitor, the late Arthur Cox, recalled an utterance of Murnaghan's on the occasion of the Labour troubles of the period. 'The time may come', Murnaghan, the young professor, is reported to have confided in Cox,[191] 'when you will look back on this as a golden age'.

In the summer of 1924 Murnaghan was made a judge of the High Court. The appointment was announced on 5 June. His stay in the High Court was short-lived, following his translation to the Supreme Court on 1 May 1925, a court in which he continued to sit for 28 more years. He announced his resignation from his chair in UCD in a letter to Dr Coffey shortly after his appointment to the High Court.[192] He relinquished his chair, he told Coffey,

> with great feelings of regret. Fourteen years ago the College founded a teaching school of Law and it has been my privilege to have cooperated in the work of the school. The Professorship had become part of my life, but I have no option left.

'Please accept', he continued,[193]

> my thanks for the great help and encouragement which you have always shown to the work of the law school. I shall follow its future with deep interest as I know that it serves an important and necessary purpose in the life of our nation.

With MacNeill, until 1918 at least, regularly absent at Westminster, Murnaghan had been the obvious choice to succeed Doyle as Dean, and so it had turned out. MacNeill, however, was not to be exempted from other possible responsibilities. In November 1912, as reported to the NUI Senate the following February, a meeting of the NUI's Faculty of Law – about which little is otherwise known – was held; and at this MacNeill was elected the NUI Faculty of Law dean[194] – a post of uncertain scope.

From an early date, Murnaghan had found himself constrained to teach International Law as well as Roman Law and Jurisprudence.[195] He had also, from 1913 onwards, along with Charles Oldham, the Professor of Commerce, who subsequently became Professor of National Economics on the death of Tom Kettle, collaborated in the giving of a regular course of lectures on Commercial Law, for which the Governing Body paid each of them an additional honorarium.[196]

Murnaghan even before this had found there were to be even other calls on his services. We have already noticed, for example, that the vacancy resulting from Doyle's resignation in the late autumn of 1910 had been filled by Murnaghan offering lectures as a stand-in, in both property and contracts.[197]

News of his talents had spread elsewhere, for NUI records show that for a period in 1910 he had lectured in jurisprudence and political economy at University College Galway as an 'acting professor'.[198]

Nor were the calls on his talents limited to lectures in the classroom. In December, 1909, following Browne's resignation of his chair, Murnaghan was picked to succeed Browne as the NUI Senate's legal advisor in regard to the drafting of regulations.[199] The proffering of advice to the Senate on sundry matters followed, for example, on the rights of engineering students under the Act of 1908;[200] on whether the Senate could hold meetings at St Patrick's College, Maynooth to confer degrees;[201] and – a crucial question this – on the validity of arrangements for the conducting of examinations under the NUI's aegis.[202] The advice on this last matter was a joint opinion of Stephen Ronan, KC and himself. But Murnaghan seems to have been commissioned alone to represent the NUI Senate at an Irish Privy Council appeal lodged under the 1908 Act.[203] How long transitional arrangements to facilitate Royal University matriculated students had to be kept in place by the National University formed the subject of yet another legal advisory opinion furnished by Murnaghan to the NUI Senate in 1911, and reconsidered by the Senate in 1913.[204] In the intervening year – 1912 – he was also asked to pronounce on the legitimate use of the term 'University of Dublin' employed by the authorities of Trinity College when communicating with the National University.[205] The rights of honorary graduates in regard to Convocation and the question of the liability of holders of travelling studentships to pay income tax – a problem that was to prove a running sore for many years – were in due course also referred to Murnaghan for his professional opinion, in 1914 and 1915, respectively – the income tax conundrum, perhaps predictably, also requiring a second opinion that was to be furnished by Herbert Wilson, KC.[206] The problem generated by conflict between College and University Statutes – which involved University College Galway battling with NUI – a problem that reached a peak in 1916, was also forwarded the same year to Murnaghan for consideration, who on this occasion, was able to call on the assistance of another leading counsel, Denis Henry, KC,[207] who, after Partition, would become the Lord Chief Justice of Northern Ireland.[208]

Pressure eased over the next couple of years, but by 1919, Murnaghan was again in demand. The NUI Senate saw to it that Murnaghan should serve on the special committee set up to draft regulations for the new degree of PhD,[209] a task that Murnaghan must surely have welcomed, given his interest in university-backed research, as expressed in his fine *St. Stephen's* article of December 1901.[210] The same year he was asked to advise on a question thrown up by the interregnum at University College Cork – the period between the retirement of one President, Sir Bertram Windle, and the election of his successor as President, Dr Patrick Merriman. Could the acting President of UCC, C. Yelverton Pearson, attend as of right meetings of the NUI Senate and exercise a vote there? Murnaghan said 'no'.[211]

The year 1920 saw no let-up in the Senate's demands on Murnaghan. In May he told the Senate that he did not consider it lawful for any member of the Senate or any member of a constituent College's Governing Body to act as an NUI Extern Examiner.[212] He was to be dismissive too – as again not being allowed – of an application by a student with a Bachelor of Engineering degree to present himself again for the degree, pursuing a different B Eng course.[213] A second query, doubtless raised by another student, received another dusty response. In Murnaghan's view, the NUI could extend no credit to courses attended elsewhere by any student prior to an NUI matriculation.[214] In December 1920, he dealt with a further problem brought about by the phenomenon of the gaelicising of students' surnames. When a student sought to change the spelling of his surname by placing an 'O' or a 'Mac' in front of it, was the University correct to demand formal evidence of the change having been brought about by deed poll? Murnaghan answered 'Yes'.[215]

Whether the University Chancellor, the University's Vice-chancellor and the President and Registrar of UCD could properly serve as executors of the will of a William Lalor, deceased, reached Murnaghan's desk in 1921.[216] So, too, two years later, the tricky question of the pension rights of the then recently deceased NUI Registrar, Sir Joseph McGrath, whose career went back to the time of the old Royal University. Here Murnaghan was satisfied that, in the circumstances of the case, part of the pension due Sir Joseph's widow should quite properly be borne by the Queen's University, Belfast.[217] It is not clear whether Murnaghan was ever asked to advise the Senate on its power to tackle personation, a question that featured on its agenda in the autumn of 1921.[218]

The records of NUI's Senate furnish us with details of the earnings Murnaghan derived from drafting work for the Senate – Statutes in the main, but work on the Supplementary Charter was a heavy burden, and for the furnishing of his many legal advisory opinions. These are shown below:

1911–13	150 guineas[219]
1913–15	£80[220]
1915–17	£80[221]
1917–18	£75[222]
1918–19	75 guineas[223]
1919–1920	75 guineas[224]
1920–21	£40[225]
1921–2	£42[226]
1922–3	£25[227]
1923–4	60 guineas[228]

Once the Governing Body of the new UCD got into its stride, it too was to call on the services of its Professor of Roman Law and Jurisprudence, particularly as regards the drafting of a sequence of UCD's own Statutes. The Governing Body's records testify to the following payments for each of the purposes as stated:

1912	£50 – Statute III (new posts in College)[229]
1917	£36 15*s*. – Statutes IV and V[230]
1924	15 guineas – 4 College Statutes[231]

In Murnaghan's case, one jurisprudential flourish stands out in the many judicial opinions he was to write as a judge of the Supreme Court. In *Mulhern* v. *Clery*,[232] a problem in the area of succession law was caused by uncertainty as to whether a couple – one Philip Harding and a Margaret Sweeney – had ever been married. One piece of evidence tendered in the case as tending to show that the two had not been married was the smallness of the annuity left Ms Sweeney. Murnaghan leaves us in no doubt that he was personally far from impressed. 'We were asked', he wrote in dissent,[233]

> to draw an unfavourable inference from the smallness of the annuity given to Margaret Sweeney by the will. But do we know that she had not got other provision made for her outside the will? There is no evidence that she was known in the neighbourhood as the Widow Sweeney, as she is described in the will – in the baptismal records she is called Margaret Regan – but even if this was proved it would not be conclusive. Was it not more strange that Madame de Maintenon, after her recent marriage to Louis XIV of France, resigned herself to a position which was misunderstood by the whole world?

Murnaghan aligned himself with the views of Mr Justice FitzGibbon rather than with those of his old comrade-in-arms at UCD, Chief Justice Kennedy, in the critical Supreme Court decision in *The State (Ryan)* v. *Lennon* in 1934.[234] Here the two judges of the majority, affirming the High Court, held that the period during which the Constitution of the Irish Free State could be amended by ordinary legislation had been validly extended from eight years to sixteen. In Murnaghan's estimation, the argument that was to appeal to Kennedy that constitutional fundamentals could not be set aside in so cavalier a fashion cut no ice at all.

The appellants in the case contended that they were in unlawful custody and averred that they were about to be brought to trial before a tribunal which had no legal authority to try them. They accordingly had sought from the court orders of habeas corpus and prohibition. The majority decision of the Supreme

Court entailed that the measure[235] under which amendments could be made to the Constitution for as much as 16 years was valid and the key legislation under which the appellants had been arrested was one such constitutionally valid amendment. The legislation, the Constitution (Amendment No. 17) Act of 1931,[236] nevertheless did not receive a favourable notice from Murnaghan. 'The extreme rigour of the Act in question', he observed,[237]

> is such that its provisions pass far beyond anything having the semblance of legal procedure, and the judicial mind is staggered at the very complete departure from legal methods in use in these Courts [where the appellants were to be tried].

Murnaghan had previously served on the committee set up by the Provisional Government in January 1922 to draft the Constitution for what became known as the Irish Free State, a role recalled by George O'Brien in his posthumous tribute.[238] A little light on Murnaghan's contribution to the enterprise is shown in Farrell's four-part article on the drafting of that document which appeared in the *Irish Jurist* in 1970 and 1971.[239] Murnaghan was ill at certain stages of the committee's work, but it appears that he shared with John O'Byrne responsibility for drafting articles dealing with the judiciary[240] and, together with O'Byrne and Darrell Figgis, an article suggesting disqualifications for membership of Dáil Eireann.[241] Most remarkably of all, was Murnaghan's support for the so-called Draft C, the brainchild of Alfred O'Rahilly, which in its treatment of fundamental rights and matters of social policy – marriage, family life, education and public morality – came very close indeed to what was prescribed on such topics in de Valera's Constitution of 1937.[242] Draft C, it is only proper to remark – to avoid any possible misapprehension – did not, however, prosper at the time.[243]

Another task discharged at this point by Murnaghan was to serve as secretary to the Law Reporting Council. In that capacity he was to report to the Council in November 1923 that the Council's minute book starting from 1904, though charred at the edges, had been recovered from the ruins of the Four Courts and rebound.[244] Earlier, in 1920, he had predicted a gloomy picture of the Council's financial situation.[245]

James Murnaghan's appointment to the High Court Bench in 1924 was, on one view, remarkable, given his relatively modest professional status. A future chief justice, Ronan Keane, remarks on Murnaghan's early judgments, that they 'covered many topics with which his practice could hardly have made him familiar'.[246] With a lifelong interest in art, he was appointed to the Board of Governors of the National Gallery of Ireland in 1925, becoming chairman in 1962. He was also to serve on the Board of Visitors to both the National Museum and the Botanic Gardens at Glasnevin. Retiring from the Supreme Court in

1953, he died in 1973 at the age of 92. His widow, Alice Murnaghan, was to establish a memorial prize at King's Inns in his name. This is awarded to the student who obtains the third-highest aggregate marks in the examinations conducted by the Inns, including marks for assessments, throughout the year.

Murnaghan, on his retirement from UCD's Law School in 1924, was far from severing his ties with his *alma mater*, continuing to serve as a government nominee on the Governing Body for a number of years.

ARTHUR EDWARD CLERY (1879–1932)

The vacancy in the professorship of the Law of Property and the Law of Contracts which Arthur Clery was to fill arose from the resignation of Charles Doyle on his elevation to the county court judgeship of Mayo, a resignation of which the Governing Body took note on 2 November 1910. James Murnaghan, as we have recounted, was drafted in for the next two months – in addition to his other duties – to cover for the lecture courses, now abruptly deprived of the lecturer allocated to them.[247] In the meantime, too, the Governing Body moved with extraordinary speed, as indeed did the Dublin commissioners, to find a permanent replacement. On this occasion, no less than eight individuals threw their hat in the ring and, amazingly, by 10 December the Governing Body in its meeting that day was in a position to vote on all eight and make their recommendations for the appointment to the commissioners. A vacancy in the professorship of architecture had also arisen, and the Governing Body held a ballot as regards the filling of that chair as well on the same day.

The votes for the eight candidates for the Law chair were as follows:

Arthur Clery	20	Christopher Roche	3
Richard I. Sheehy	19	Dr Charles Murray	2
Hugh Kennedy	15	L. O'Brien Kelly	2
John McGonigal	10	J.I. Sutherland	2

The Governing Body thus forwarded the names of the three candidates who had received the most votes: Clery, Sheehy and Kennedy.[248] Clery was appointed by the Dublin Commissioners on the same day that Swift MacNeill was preferred to him by them as the new clerk of NUI's Convocation.[249]

A word on the unsuccessful candidates will not be out of place. Kennedy, of course, was destined to become the first Chief Justice in the new Irish Free State. McGonigal received a consolation prize of sorts. He was made a KC in 1911 and acted as a professor at King's Inns from 1911 to 1914. After Partition he served at the new Northern Ireland Bar where he became a Bencher (he had already been a Bencher of King's Inns) and where he was elevated to the county court judgeship of Tyrone in 1939.[250] Maurice Healy recalled McGonigal in practice at the Bar, where he dubbed him 'a very formidable opponent'.[251] Christopher Roche (three votes) has been identified as 'Nasty Roche' in James Joyce's *A Portrait of the Artist as a Young Man*. In this connection it is worth mentioning that, despite the soubriquet, Roche in the novel made a point of commiserating with Stephen Daedalus over the grotesquely unfair punishment – pandying – meted out to Stephen by the prefect of Studies, Father Dolan, for breaking his glasses and his inability in consequence to complete written work.[252] As we will shortly be discovering, an identification of the inspiration behind the character Whelan in Joyce's *Stephen Hero* has also been made.[253] Lastly, Laurence O'Brien Kelly, who, like McGonigal, also receives a mention in *The Old Munster Circuit*. Healy relates two stories regarding Larry, as he was apparently known.[254] 'Larry', Healy wrote,[255]

> always did his best to conceal a learning which had been sufficient to win him the Brooke Scholarship; he had a rich brogue and a cheerful disposition, and he rather encouraged jokes at his own expense. He liked the pleasures of the table and of the turf.

Arthur Edward Clery, a former student of the old University College and a graduate of the Royal University, was also a qualified barrister. As Doyle's successor as professor of Property and Contract, he was to occupy the position until his death in 1932. In the course of the movement for Irish independence, Clery was also to serve as a judge of the Dáil Supreme Court, an office, it can safely be conjectured, he was reluctant to relinquish.

MacLysaght has an instructive entry on the family name in his *Irish Families, Their Names, Arms and Origins* – an entry to which it is not inappropriate to allude, given the assertion on the part of the author of the entry on Clery in the *Dictionary of Irish Biography*, that he entertained 'fantasies of aristocratic descent'.[256] 'Clery, often spelt "Cleary"', we read in MacLysaght,[257]

> is one of the Gaelic Irish surnames which has kept the prefix O to some extent in modern times. O'Clery is Ó Cleirigh in Irish, probably derived from the word *cleireach* meaning a clerk or cleric.

'The name itself', MacLysaght continues,

> means descendant of Cleireach, who was of the line of the famous Guaire the Hospitable, King of Connacht.

For good measure, he adds the detail that O'Clery was 'one of the earliest recorded surnames, dating from the tenth century'. The family's arms shown in the colour in plate IV of the MacLysaght volume are given as 'Or three nettle leaves vert'.

Arthur Clery's own historical interests, reflected above all in the historical novel he published in 1909 under the pseudonym of Arthur Synan, were in line with those of his father, Arthur Patrick Clery (usually spelt Cleary), who a few years before the son was appointed to his chair at the new UCD had published an extraordinary ground-breaking volume on Irish history prior to the coming of Henry II.[258] Arthur Clery senior, born in 1840 in Limerick, was called to the Irish Bar in 1864 and was later made a King's Counsel.[259] His Irish nationalist credentials were on conspicuous display in his *History of Ireland*, in effect a trawl through the difficult evidence for Ireland's history before the twelfth century. The final chapter, bearing the possibly tendentious title, 'The Cymro-Frankish Adventurers', has this to say of the Bull *Laudabiliter* and the supposed donation of Ireland to Henry II by Pope Adrian IV:[260]

> Rome distracted with internal troubles was misinformed and ill-advised and the Gael, who deserved a better fate, were delivered into the hands of ruthless and rapacious adventurers.

Clery senior's preface to his *History* makes interesting reading, concluding, as it does, with a gracious apology that the son could well have taken to heart. 'This volume', Clery senior writes,[261]

> is the fruit of many years' labour. I have to the best of my ability made every point the subject of independent inquiry and written in great part *ex messibus meis*. I have not worked in the expectation of literary fame or pecuniary profit, but because I had been convinced from early manhood that no greater service could be due to the Irish race at home and abroad than to tell them the naked truth as far as it can be ascertained about their early history.

'This will, no doubt', he continues,[262]

> dispel many illusions which they will be loathe to part with; but on the other hand, unless I greatly deceive myself, it will convey lessons of high political import which they may take hopefully to heart. The early history of Ireland is a story of arrested evolution.[263]

Clery senior, it needs to be added, also published rather more pedestrian fare – a commentary on laws regulating the parliamentary franchise,[264] as well as his ideas on reforming the High and County Courts in Ireland.[265]

Our UCD professor was born in 1879, and entered the old University College in 1896, at a time when it was in no position to award degrees, so young Arthur sat for his degree at the Royal University. Graduating with an LLB in 1902, he was also to be conferred with an LLD by the Royal University in 1908/9. It has been established that the character of Whelan in James Joyce's *Stephen Hero*, described there as 'the College Orator',[266] was based on Clery, and it is not, therefore, altogether fanciful to view Joyce's admittedly sparse allusions to Whelan in his narrative as telling us something of how one fellow student at the old University College regarded his contemporary.

A central episode in *Stephen Hero* revolved around the preparation by Stephen Daedalus of a paper on aesthetics originally entitled 'Drama and life', but later changed to 'Art and life', which Daedalus was scheduled to read at the customary Saturday meeting of the Literary and Historical Society. It is in this paper that Daedalus was to praise the dramatic *oeuvre* of Ibsen, praise, as we shall see, which was to get him into trouble. Maume has argued that this specific idea to eulogise Ibsen came to Joyce by way of responding to a paper that Clery had read to the UCD Literary and Historical Society as its auditor in 1899, in which he maintained that all Irish drama should be religious.[267] Writing some eight years later, after the rioting that greeted Synge's *The Playboy of the Western World*, Clery had scarcely shifted his ground. 'In much of contemporary French literature', he was to write under the pseudonym of Chanel,[268] the author's mind

> dwells with a morose satisfaction on the diseases of life. Such an attitude of mind was in great measure exhibited in *In the Shadow of the Glen*, and it was this rather than any moral it taught that made one turn away from it. And *The Playboy of the Western World* merely showed the same tendencies in a more exaggerated form.

Earlier, warming to this theme, Clery made no secret as to where he stood. The Irish nation, the future law professor contended,[269] had 'a right to protest if they find their National theatre tending towards immoral, anti-Christian or anti-human propaganda'.

Leaving aside Maume's views on Clery's impact on Joyce, and to return to Daedalus and the fictional development in *Stephen Hero*, College practice at the time obliged the auditor of the Literary and Historical Society to procure an advance copy of any paper scheduled for formal delivery, and pass it on to the College's President – in this case, the Revd Dr Dillon – for vetting. [The portrayal of Dillon was loosely based on that of the real-life president of University College of the period – the Revd Dr William Delaney, SJ.][270] This arrangement, involving possible censorship as it did, was not, predictably enough, to Daedalus' taste at all. It is Whelan, who breaks the news to Daedalus, that the President had turned the paper down. 'The suave rotund young man', Joyce writes,[271]

> who was the Secretary of the Society, was reading for the Bar. His eyes regarded Stephen now with mild, envious horror and he forgot all his baggage from Attica.
>
> 'Your essay is tabu, Daedalus'.

Whelan, in response to Daedalus' inquiry as to who said so, having identified Dr Dillon as the person responsible, temporarily remains mute:[272]

> The delivery of this news was followed by a silence during which Whelan slowly moistened his lower lip with saliva from his tongue.

Daedalus immediately waylays Dr Dillon and there follows the most celebrated passage in *Stephen Hero*, where professor and student set out their stalls on the subject of art in the modern world. The upshot is that the prohibition on Daedalus' reading his paper is reversed, and Daedalus does in fact deliver his paper to a somewhat bewildered audience on the Saturday as previously announced.[273] Here Whelan makes another appearance, for the task that falls upon him on the occasion is the formal one of proposing the vote of thanks.[274] The thoughts that pass through Daedalus' head as he listens are not, perhaps, the impression that Whelan /Clery would have wished. Daedalus noted that Whelan would wag his head in time to his ornate phrases. He asked himself if anyone else had observed 'the infantile movements of the orator's mouth'. He then expressed the hope that Whelan would shut his mouth with a clap so as 'to reveal the presence of solid teeth'. Whelan rattled on. 'The mere sound of the speech', Joyce makes Daedalus reflect,[275]

> reminded him of the noise Nurse Sarah used to make when she mashed Isabel's [Daedalus' sister, soon to die] bread-and-milk in the blue bowl which his mother now used to hold starch.

Of the substance of Whelan's admiring oration, we are given just a few *soupçons*.[276] During the reading by Daedalus of his paper, he, Whelan, had felt 'as though he had been listening to the discourse of angels and did not know the language that they spoke'. He went on to charge Daedalus with no true understanding of 'Attic theatre': Aeschylus was 'imperishable'. The possible peroration follows: 'Great art is not for a time, but for all times. It stands aloof, alone. It is imperial, imperious and imperative'. The next year we are told Whelan is awarded a gold medal for oratory.[277] There are no further references, and he does not reappear among the *dramatis personae* in the completed novel, for which the fragment that is *Stephen Hero* is the trial run, *A Portrait of the Artist as a Young Man*.

In real life, it is worthy of notice that Clery was active in the revival of the

Literary and Historical Society, which occurred in 1897. It had been dormant since 1891. In 1897 he was elected on to the Society's committee, becoming, in turn, in 1898, Junior Secretary and in 1899, as we have seen, Auditor. His inaugural address was entitled 'Irish genius in English prose'.[278] Here Clery boldly asserted that the Anglo-Irish writers, Swift, Burke and Berkeley, were 'the true representatives of our genius, in so far as it has taken form in English'. The President of the College, Dr Delany, who responded to Clery's inaugural address, was not apparently convinced. The writers Clery had listed, who included Goldsmith and Steele as well, could not, Delany insisted, be considered adequately representative of Irish genius. They were, rather, 'exceptional children of a class' and not of the race.[279] The occasion of Clery's inaugural was remarkable for a very different reason, as Felix Hackett, the future Professor of Physics, was to recall in his reminiscences:[280] 'With this address the dignified formality of holding a public inaugural meeting in the *Aula Maxima* was resumed'. As late as 1907, Clery was still in a position to cause ripples at meetings of the L and H. That year's inaugural was delivered by the new auditor Maurice Healy on the subject 'The Irish exodus'. The Chief Secretary for Ireland, Augustine Birrell, was among these listed to respond.[281] So, too, was Clery, who, however, extended no quarter, as Morrissey relates:[282]

> Arthur Clery, noted for his graceful, suave manner and polished speech during his student days, but now in the words of C. P. Curran, bitten by 'the Gaelic bug', gone 'Irish-Ireland' and sporting a shaggy beard, led the attack on the Chief Secretary's speech, ridiculing his promises, and deriding his nonconformist conscience and all his liberal gods.

Like Swift MacNeill, who became a colleague on his appointment to his chair, Arthur Clery junior had a number of publications under his belt, when he sought and gained his appointment in 1911, and he continued to be reasonably productive in his writings, if not a tad sadly, in the sphere of the law. This lacuna, or deficit, in a professor who, after all, held a chair in law had not been unanticipated by William Dawson, his friend and early obituarist. Clery's choice of career, Dawson was to write soon after Clery's death, had not been 'the happiest'. It was indeed a distinct pity, Dawson added, that Clery's chair had not been in 'a more liberal subject – English literature, let us say'.[283] Clery's interests certainly lay in that direction and help to explain his unsuccessful bid to be appointed an assistant librarian at the National Library of Ireland,[284] some time before the vacancy occurred at UCD arising from Doyle's translation to the bench.

Two of Clery's early publications did deal with the law unlike virtually everything else that followed. These were detailed commentaries on recent acts of parliament – not ordinarily reckoned the most attractive of literature. Both were written with co-authors. Of the two, the commentary on the Public Health Acts Amendment Act 1907, published in 1908, is perhaps the most rewarding.[285] The subject-matter of the legislation is a good deal broader than the title of the measure might suggest. Predictably enough, topics such as sanitary provisions, urinals and infectious diseases all merit attention, but so too do streets and buildings, common lodging-houses, recreation grounds, fire-brigades, sky-signs, beaches and bathing-places, life-saving apparatuses and licences for pleasure boats.

It is impossible to tell how much of the detailed comments on the provisions of this Act of 1907 are to be ascribed to Clery rather than his co-author, fellow barrister James McWalter, who gives as his qualifications an MA, an MD, and a DPH as well as that of a member of the Bar. Individual comments, even so, can be arresting. On the authority given to change the name of a street, the two authors comment:[286]

> The naming of streets may often be a matter of no little public interest in this country, and changes of name [from English to Gaelic] are likely to be increasingly common in future.

An attempt to be similarly prescient with regard to new rules regarding bye-laws for seashores and promenades produces the following remark:[287]

> The seaside visitor is not such a nuisance with us as in England, nor have we anything in Ireland even faintly resembling Southend or Blackpool. We take our pleasures respectably, if not sadly.

Sky-signs were advertisements sustained by systems of support erected over buildings. The two authors append a lengthy note on a novel regulatory provision, which enables them to attack a recent English decision that had favoured Madame Tussaud's in London.[288] 'The proprietors of Madame Tussaud's', Clery and McWalter write,[289]

> were permitted to add a new eye-sore to London by a trellis work advertisement,[290] whilst, on the other hand, where a merchant had a windmill erected over his premises which, in addition to catching the breezes and working his machinery thereby, was also intended to attract custom by having the merchant's name inscribed upon it in open work, the court refused to yield to this evasion of the law, and anathematised it as a sky-sign.[291]

An Irish footnote, as it were, is then appealed. 'No doubt', the two authors assure us,[292]

> sky-signs are not among the most urgent of Irish evils. In most parts of Ireland one can see sky enough, and to spare, and in many places a sky-sign might be rather welcome as diversifying the landscape.

The wind-farm with its multitude of turbines, it could be claimed from this, would have found a least two supporters in 1908.

Clery, with, on this occasion, two co-authors, Hugh Kennedy, the future chief justice, and Michael Dawson, brought out a second practitioners' manual – one devoted to the Town Tenants (Ireland) Act of 1906.[293] The assistance of others including Arthur C.J. Cox, John A. Costello (the future Taoiseach) and Ambrose Davoren (who was to die in the First World War), in checking references and the like, is specifically acknowledged by the three co-authors. The volume itself was originally published in 1907; six years after the Act in question was passed, and to take account of the 40 or so judicial decisions on the Act that had occurred in the interim, and, mainly reported in the Irish Law Times Reports, a second edition saw the light of day in 1913,[294] two years or so into Clery's holding of the chair in UCD. The pressure of multiple authors ensures *Town Tenants (Ireland) Act 1906 and the Rules and Forms made Thereunder* is both more comprehensive and authoritative, but, unlike Clery's earlier co-authored volume on the Public Health Acts Amendment Act, there seems to be lacking a freshness of approach, even a touch of individuality. The stodginess of the format as presaged in the preface scarcely serves as the harbinger of a palatable read. 'As is the case of most Irish text-books of recent years', we are told there, 'it has been thought best to add the new matter [of the second edition] in the form of a Supplement to the original work'. On that, even at the time, people must surely have taken leave to doubt.

The Act of 1906 signalled a major improvement in the legal position of tenants holding property in an urban environment, and the social impact of the legislation and of certain of the key judicial rulings on its interpretation is brought out well enough by the three joint authors when the reader knows where to look. In fact, we have here a novel source for our understanding of changes in the urban landscape from the early years of the twentieth century. Section 17 of the measure explained that the 'holding' to which the provisions of the Act regarding compensation for improvement related applied only to 'houses, shops, and other buildings situate in urban districts, towns, or villages'. What was a village, and whether a particular holding could be said to be situated in one, prompted a number of lawsuits as intriguing as any on the meaning of demesne lands under the Land Acts: cases from Drumahoe, Co. Derry; Whitegate, Co. Cork; Dundrum, Co. Dublin; and Cushendun, Co. Antrim are all carefully summarised. Section 2 (5) posed an altogether different conundrum: what was a 'permanent building?' This is because the subsection provided that a tenant should not be 'entitled to claim compensation for any improvement made before the passing of this Act, except permanent buildings, unless made within ten years before the date of such claim.' The body of precedent that here too began to be assembled and expertly summarised in the manual before us, ought certainly to instruct the social historian.

If these practitioners' manuals on public health and tenants helped to secure Clery the job he held from 1911 until his death – which seems likely – it is striking that we know little enough about his role as a teacher in UCD. Maume repeats the report that he was 'inefficient', yet beloved by his students.[295] There were several aspects to this. Of wide general culture himself, he taught his students much besides the law. It is to George O'Brien, later the Professor of Political Economy, that we owe the insight that Clery was more able and willing to bridge the gap between teacher and student than his colleagues, who were either elderly or busy.[296] O'Brien too tells us that Clery used to entertain his students by hosting very pleasant dinner parties in Dublin restaurants and larger parties in his own rooms.[297] Maume adds the final detail – perhaps not apocryphal – that it was claimed Clery never failed a student in his examinations.

In the early days of the twentieth century Clery was a frequent contributor not only to the student journal, *St. Stephen's*, where he served for a while on the editorial team, but also to *The Leader*, founded in 1902, and edited by D.P. Moran (1869–1936), which soon established itself as a vehicle for Catholic nationalist opinion. In 1933, William Dawson left his readers in no doubt that in the early 1900s Moran's influence on the undergraduates of the old University College 'cannot be exaggerated'.[298] This was certainly true of Clery who had a high regard for Moran and shared a number of the latter's views. Moran, for instance, took issue with the nineteenth-century nationalists who laid stress on the Protestant Anglo-Irish patriot tradition, which it was his inclination to dismiss as an ephemeral colonial phenomenon. (In view of Clery's praise for Swift, Burke and Berkeley that we have already encountered,[299] it is possible that here pupil and mentor may not have seen eye to eye.) Moran, very clearly, as Maume was to explain,[300] was unsympathetic to the Irish literary revival and particularly disliked Yeats whom he dismissed as a snob seeking self-advancement and Protestant supremacy through cultured mystification. Yeats, for his part, it is only right to point out – as Maume records – viewed Moran as symbolising demagogic philistinism. In light of Arthur Clery's involvement in the early 1900s in moves for the reform of the Irish university system, it is very likely indeed that, in addition to sharing Moran's views on the literary revival at this juncture at any rate, he would have supported Moran's campaigns to expose Protestant domination in certain professions and in the higher echelons of the Irish civil service. Confirmation is to hand in Maume's verdict that Clery's 'radical temperament' derived as much from resentment of Protestant influence networks as from resentment of opportunistic Catholic whigs.[301]

In 1907 Arthur Clery brought together a number of his essays that had first appeared in *The Leader*, publishing these under the title *The Idea of a Nation*[302] and employing another pseudonym – Chanel – also used by him when writing in *St. Stephen's*, and explained by Maume as a name he took at his confirmation.[303] Clery had gone to school at the Catholic University School in Dublin before being sent to Clongowes Wood College in Co. Kildare. The Marists at CUS encouraged devotion to the Marist martyr Pierre Chanel, and, significantly, the Revd Dr Delany, in 1890, between his two stints as head of the old University College had delivered a sermon on the beatification of Blessed Peter Chanel:[304] hence Clery's adoption of his confirmation name, later his first pen-name.[305]

For insight into the ramifications of what was understood by nationalism in Ireland at this key point, Clery's collection of essays under this evocative title could be reckoned obligatory reading. A character in an imaginary dialogue reproduced early in the collection expatiates on the meaning of 'a nation'. 'A nation', he is made to say,[306]

> is a body that, as the result of continued existence, has collected and retains a sufficient sum total of such qualities and characteristics, say for instance, common language, history, manners, tradition, music and so on. You might even consider rudeness as a part of English nationhood.

A nationalist, Clery had early asserted, was a man driven by a desire for 'the welfare and spiritual integrity' of his nation,

> though the means he may approve for promoting that welfare and integrity may vary infinitely, from presenting petitions to the Lord Lieutenant to arranging for dynamite explosions.[307]

If this is predictable, though contentious enough fodder, given the spirit of the times, Clery's assertion that the co-operative movement in Ireland, land purchase too and even the Dublin tram system were all inspired by continental models[308] might raise a few eyebrows. The allusion is followed up with this after-thought. These posit, Clery avers,[309]

> a few examples of the value of not confining ourselves to England when we are obliged to go outside of Ireland. I do not advocate undue cosmopolitanism. We should develop our own lines as far as possible.

Clery has interesting things to say concerning cultural matters (even where one does not agree with him). The comparative neglect of art, summarised by Clery in the dictum that 'Valasquez has fewer admirers amongst us than Beethoven'[310] and followed by praise for Hugh Lane,[311] leads the author to argue for Irish development of religious art. 'Why should we not,' he demands to know,[312]

> as at Bruges, have Madonnas and Apostles, whose features were the idealisation of Irish faces, a loveliness fresh with the breath of our own life, and not a halting copy of some dead foreign imagining?

The comparative neglect of philosophy and hard thinking presages another assault. 'If', Clery hypothesises,[313]

> a Royal University Fellow or one of the professors of Maynooth were to produce a work on literature or philosophy to-morrow, it would probably, in most cases, have a sale of about twenty copies in his own country.

Worse was to follow. 'Rich Catholics', Clery would have us believe,[314] are

> the worst offenders. To be able to hunt, or to keep a carriage, or a motor-car, is the be-all and end-all of their desires. And, if this be impossible, they find a consolation in frequent race-meetings. A work of literature they never think of buying, and even the sixpenny magazine and the four shillings and sixpence novels, which form their chief mental pabulum, are imported from England. There are a large number of wealthy people in Ireland whose intellectual condition is precisely on a par with that of their coachman.

Two moderately successful pastiches are included in *The Idea of a Nation*. One is an imaginary dialogue between two Catholic parents who disagree over whether to send their son to Trinity College.[315] The other, a discussion in the style of a dialogue penned by J.M. Synge, between, on the one hand, Lady Gregory and, on the other, W.B. Yeats, on the topic of a philosophy for an Irish theatre.[316] Here and in allied pieces in the collection, Clery, more perhaps than elsewhere, nails his colours very firmly to the mast. It will be twenty years later that he was to preside at a debate over the riots at the Abbey Theatre that accompanied Sean O' Casey's *The Plough and the Stars*[317] in February 1926. It is unlikely that to some at least Clery will have appeared even-handed in his chairmanship.

We have already drawn attention to certain of Clery's other views on matters theatrical – his distaste for *In the Shadow of the Glen*, and *The Playboy of the Western World*.[318] Long before either of these plays was performed, Clery in a paper delivered to the Literary and Historical Society in March 1899, and included in his *Dublin Essays* of 1919, expounded his views at considerable length. This was his remarkable paper, 'The Theatre: its Educational Value'. Described by Felix Hackett as 'a tantalising document', it read 'as if it had been sub-edited with an attenuation of all references to the contemporaneous theatrical activities of Dublin'.[319] Farces are 'out' so, too, is Ibsen. Shakespeare and 'the classical Irish comedies', are allowed; singled out for praise, too, are, 'these plays that produce elevation through the Christian virtues of humility and kindness, virtues which ancient critics would have despised, and to which Christianity may be said to have first accorded that rank'.[320]

A final essay finds Clery supporting the prospect of a partition solution to the problem of Ulster – a perceptive glimpse into the future from the standpoint of 1907.[321] A lighter note is struck in a somewhat earlier contribution (which, if it reflected anything at all of the nature of his lecturing technique as a UCD professor, would help to explain his reputation among his students). 'Love-making', Clery confides,[322]

> is proverbially expensive for the male participant in the transaction. Even an afternoon devoted to adoration on one side and the consumption of chocolate creams (let us hope of Irish confection) on the other, results in a financial deficit to the admirer.

Newman, the first rector of the Catholic University, had many strings to his bow. Today it is perhaps forgotten that the author of the *Apologia pro Vita Sua* and *The Idea of a University* was also the author of two novels. These cannot compare with the *Sybil* or *Coningsby* of Disraeli; but *Loss and Gain, the Story of a Convert* (1848), and *Clarissa, a Tale of the Third Century* (1856) are interesting even so – *Clarissa* especially, given the attempt to imagine and express from a Catholic point of view the feelings and mutual relations of Christians and heathens at the period to which it belongs.

In this singular respect, as a writer of fiction, Clery was to follow in Newman's footsteps. In doing so, he was to become the first of two members of the UCD faculty's professoriate to publish a novel. Employing the nom de plume Arthur Synan – Catherine Synan was the name of his paternal grandmother[323] – Clery brought out in 1909, a few years before his appointment to the UCD Faculty, an historical novel, *The Coming of the King: a Jacobite Romance*.[324] Set in the 1720s, it tells of an abortive mission on the part of the Old Pretender, James III in the calculations of English and Irish Jacobites, James IX in those of their Scots confrères, to recapture the thrones of the three kingdoms by seizing power in Dublin. The novel divides neatly into two parts. The first treats of the journey of the man called Righ Seamus from Bantry Bay, where he had landed, to Celbridge in Co. Kildare, where he takes refuge in a safe house and finalises his plans for the onslaught on Dublin Castle with a motley band of supporters, both Catholic and Protestant. Accompanied by the principal female protagonist in the story, the devout Cathleen, one Sir Denis' ward, the soi-disant king, travelling under a succession of aliases, M. de St.Germain and then M. de la Rue, a Huguenot weaver, and often with difficulty, when, for instance, crossing Ceiman-Fhiaidh, escapes capture and betrayal as he makes his way to the north, via Inchigeela Lake, where his horse is lamed, Macroom and Mallow. Hospitality is extended by two Catholic priests, a Fr McSweeney and a Fr Jeremiah, the first of whom was to pay the penalty for so doing. At Macroom, a Revd Dr Pratt, chaplain to the Protestant bishop of Waterford (both of whom are identified as closet Jacobite sympathisers), makes available to James and Cathleen, the bishop's carriage for the continuation of the journey north. It was a splendid chariot with the bishop's mitre embossed on the outside panels. James is delighted for this relief from the saddle (Tour de France cyclists would have been envious), and the rest of the journey to Celbridge is accomplished without any untoward incident.

At Celbridge there are moments of relaxation. A female songstress entertains the company with renditions of an air by Mynheer Handel,[325] but James soon turns his attention to the exact plans for seizing power. There was to be a march by supporters to Cork Hill, the unguarded Castle would then be seized and James would be placed on the throne. The principal architect of James' restoration on the Protestant side turns out to be none other than Jonathan Swift, the dean of the Church of Ireland St Patrick's Cathedral. While Swift is supportive of James and his right to practise his own Catholic faith, he objects to the command of the march on Dublin being given to a Papist and any future legislative reversal of the laws against Dissenters and Catholics: the Protestant, Anglican, ascendancy was to be maintained. On the Catholic side, any talk of James being forced to do the reverse of Henri IV in France, and convert to Protestantism, as a condition of his continuing to receive Protestant support – talk that now goes the rounds – is immediately pronounced unacceptable, most forcefully by the devout Cathleen, James' fellow traveller on the long and anxious journey from Bantry. 'Are we to fight only to remain outlaws?' she taunts the would-be king.[326] Swift and James go into conclave and reach a compact, but the details prove attractive to neither side, and amidst mutual recriminations, the plot unfolds, the conspirators split up, James returns to France and Swift retires to his deanery.

Clery adds at the end of the final chapter, a quite extraordinary coda. 'And perhaps some critic', he writes,[327]

> if he have read thus afar [sic], will object, that not all the things in this book are written in our histories; that, for instance, Swift never admitted himself a Jacobite, though oft accused of it. Let him that puts forth such objections resolve me first this question: is all that is true written in history, is all that is in history true?

Contrast this with the poetic flourish with which the tale begins:[328]

> A fine morning at last. For weeks the dull, brown mists had drifted up from the sea, gathered sadly round the hills and lain upon the pass. The winter had dragged slowly along in the Old Castle by the shores of Bantry Bay. Old Sir Denis was growing feebler every day, his rheumatism becoming more acute. Cathleen, his ward, was all alone with him in the great stone house. She had a dreary time.

According to Dawson, Clery prepared a dramatised version of *The Coming of the King* for stage performance, but no such performance ever took place.[329]

Clery continued to write a number of essays – on diverse themes in politics, the arts and letters – in such publications as *The Leader*, *Studies*, *Irish Educational Review*, and the *New Irish Review* – and in 1919, ten years after he, writing as Arthur Synan, had brought out *The Coming of the King*, and twelve, as Chanel, *The Idea of a Nation,* he published a collection of these essays under the anodyne title *Dublin Essays*.[330] The timing was no coincidence. For Clery the times in which he lived and served as a UCD law professor were indeed extraordinary. There had occurred a 'revival of art and of national life', 'a native theatre, a native literature and a new courage of nationhood' being 'its manifestations'.[331] A sweeping claim then follows – one dismissed by William Dawson as 'characteristically extravagant':[332] 'Unless the judgment of living men upon themselves is wholly wrong, the age of Pearse will, in after time, have a glory like the age of Pericles'.[333] Within a page or two of this bold assertion, Clery appears to backtrack. Ireland comprised 'a public much inclined to book-making, but steadily averse from book-buying'.[334] 'The Irishman', he adds, 'who would write for posterity, must write for export, as Lecky discovered'.[335]

The quality of the material reprinted in *Dublin Essays* is uneven, and certain of the essays, especially those in the area of politics are curiously dated. There is an attack on the Latin author Horace, on the emphasis still being given the classics,[336] and praise for Newman in introducing night classes (which could be reinstituted to help with the revival of Irish).[337] There is a tribute to Tom Kettle, who had been a fellow professor, of National Economics, at the new UCD,[338] and an implicit attack on the GAA for its attack on 'foreign' games.[339] British rule in Ireland is predictably assailed especially over the delay there had been in settling the university question. It was truly shocking, Clery writes, that it was only recently possible 'for an Irish Catholic to possess a University degree and a conscience at the same time'.[340] His other thoughts on matters educational – linked to his own experiences – are best related elsewhere. While a place for drama was to be found in the universities, Clery, as we have already discovered, seriously doubted the value of much of what was performed.[341]

One essay in the collection, I believe, is outstanding. This is his 'Votes for children',[342] which Clery would have us accept is not a satirical attack on women's suffrage – a plea that the reader him or herself must decide whether or not to accept. The right to vote could be given at the age of 12 or 14. The suffering of those in that group only needed to be itemised: underfeeding; bad housing; want of medical attendance; being obliged to learn their £.s.d.; and the English system of spelling; child labour; blind-alley jobs; flogging. The scout movement had succeeded beyond all measure, and the young, unlike adult members of the community, 'read serious books for pleasure'; only one adult in 100 did likewise.[343] Clery perhaps spoils the effect of all of this with a concluding remark, of a sort that Swift studiously eschewed when he gave us his 'A modest proposal'. 'I cannot, of course', Clery concludes his essay,[344]

> hope for an immediate acceptance of these proposals. I shall be satisfied if I awake some faint stirring in the political conscience of the community, even though that stirring should have its beginning in the risible faculty.

The versatility of Clery the essayist is demonstrated in a number of pieces published after the last selection was brought together to form his *Dublin Essays* of 1919. None, once again, tackle legal themes. Of four pieces that appear in *Studies* in 1921 and 1922, 'The politics of "*Macbeth*"',[345] 'Shakspere and Christianity',[346] 'Accents: Dublin and otherwise',[347] and 'The philosophy of sanity: Chesterton and Belloc',[348] and thus at a time when he was also acting as a judge of the Dáil Supreme Court, the first and the last perhaps deserve more than a passing mention. In the Macbeth essay Banquo, of course, is identified as the progenitor of James VI and I. Who then were Macbeth and his consort meant to represent? Controversially – fantastically? – Clery opts for the character of Elizabeth I as viewed by some deadly enemy: a history of barrenness, jealousy and treacherous bloodshed. In 'The philosophy of sanity' there are sketches of Oscar Wilde and George Bernard Shaw as well as of Chesterton and Belloc. Clery's colleague, Swift MaNeill, would have been unlikely to have approved Clery's posthumous award to Gladstone of a trophy for platitudinous speeches. Equally arresting was Clery's firmly held belief, expressed in the same essay, that 'only in fully Christian countries like Spain and Italy and the old-time France, do we find the use of alcohol without its abuse'.

Following his appointment to UCD, Clery continued his work as a barrister. He had been named a reporter for the Irish Reports in 1910, but resigned in 1916 when his performance in that role was adjudged unsatisfactory.[349] The same year he was to defend his fellow UCD Professor Eoin MacNeill at the latter's court-martial relating to the Easter Rising. However, briefs neither before nor after were plentiful. Dawson, in his memoir, offered the explanation that the calling of an advocate was not suited to Clery's specific temperament.[350] C.P. Curran agreed. Clery had, he recalled,[351]

> a discursive intellectual interest in law, but nothing of the forceful concentration, the absorbing relentless fanaticism of its votaries.

Clery over the years did in fact do a little advisory work and also some conveyancing.[352] He was to be posthumously upbraided by Maurice Healy for confessing his ignorance of the meaning of a *que* estate in the law on easements.[353] When Murnaghan resigned in 1924, the NUI Senate lost thereby the services of its regular legal advisor and draughtsman. These were roles seemingly intended for Clery subsequently to discharge. And to an extent he did, but by no means on the scale or to the degree expected of Murnaghan. As before, the evidence furnished by the records of the NUI Senate provide us with the essential information.[354]

In the years 1917–18, Clery's extra-curricular activities included campaigning on behalf of Sinn Féin. Later, the £200,000 capital of the Sinn Féin Land Bank was to be deposited under his name – to prevent it from seizure.[355]

In the summer of 1920 an entirely novel task was to be thrust upon Arthur Clery when he was made a member of the Supreme Court, under the regime of republican courts set up under the authority of the First Dáil.[356] On 16 January 1920, Austin Stack was confirmed as Minister for Home Affairs in the underground Dáil administration. It fell to him, following months and further consultations, to establish a set of courts that would sit in opposition to the official crown courts and which might, indeed, totally supersede the latter. Eventually, on 29 June 1920 a decree was adopted providing for this to be done. A little later a committee of lawyers in sympathy with Sinn Féin drew up rules for these new courts, which were published under the sub-title 'Judiciary'.[357]

At the apex of this new structure was a Supreme Court. It was planned that this would be a court of three members, but, in fact, only two were to be appointed: James Creed Meredith (1875–1942), who had been called to the Bar in 1901 and was to be recognised as the chairman[358] (he later became a High Court judge (1924) in the Free State dispensation, eventually moving to the Supreme Court (1936)), and Arthur Clery. Two other barristers, Cahir Davitt and Diarmuid Crowley, were appointed to the lower tier of a Circuit Court. There were, in addition, innumerable District Courts. The four men mentioned were appointed for life and at a salary of £750 per annum. The courts were abruptly terminated in the summer of 1922, to the disgust most certainly of Crowley and almost certainly as well of Clery. Clery thus refused to have anything to do with the Winding-up Commission that settled all outstanding court business from the moment the courts themselves were abolished;[359] and, although legislation was enacted in 1925 to deal with one other matter of outstanding business – Dáil Supreme Court pensions – Clery resolutely refused to apply for the pension to which he would have been entitled.[360] (Crowley, it is worth noting, sought to secure his £750 per year after the courts shut, pressing his claim through litigation in the 1930s, which ultimately proved abortive.)[361]

It is significant that Clery as well as Crowley appears to have been 'left out of the loop', when the crucial letter telling the judges to suspend their sittings was sent out in July 1922 by Hugh Kennedy, the Provisional Government's law adviser and, of course, one of Clery's co-authors of the commentary on the Town Tenants (Ireland) Act 1906.[362] Indeed, there is evidence that Clery continued to hold court sittings at a time when he must have appreciated that this was not supposed to be occurring. (He was based in Cork at the time.) On the rapport between Meredith and Clery there is little enough evidence. They did, however, disagree on a possible role for juries on the introduction of a system of criminal prosecutions: Meredith supported juries; Clery was in favour of lay justices sitting with the judge.[363] Kotsonouris, in her review of the work of the Winding-up Commissioners,[364] tells us that the Commissioners (headed by Meredith who had become the Chief Commissioner under the winding-up scheme) allowed two appeals against decisions by Clery: *Lady Arnott* v. *Trustees of Sir John Arnott* and *Corbett* v. *Cork Electric Tramways Lighting Company*.[365]

Late in 1922 the anti-Treaty Republicans entrusted Clery with a diplomatic mission. In December Dr Con Murphy, a dismissed civil servant, and Clery were sent by the Republicans as representatives to Rome to protest against the hostility of the Irish Catholic hierarchy towards Republicans. They made sufficient of an impression for a Vatican envoy, Monsignor Luzio, to be sent to Ireland. Clery was later to speak of his mission to Rome 'as his greatest achievement'.[366] This was not to be the last time a UCD law professor undertook a diplomatic task.

In June 1927, Clery was elected to the Dáil as a member for the NUI constituency, but refused to take the oath, which he was to deride as 'the Devil's sacrament';[367] and at a later election the same year he declined to offer himself again.[368] Clery's intense hostility to the Treaty – he had become a convinced Republican – Dawson was to categorise as 'quite unreasonable'.[369] The year before he had chaired a meeting of the UCD Republican Club at which Sean O'Casey was invited to explain his motives in writing *The Plough and the Stars,* the performance of which at the Abbey Theatre in March of that year had generated a riot.[370] O'Casey walked into a veritable lion's den, for Clery, as would be shown from a brief foray into his essays, was not at all likely to be sympathetic to O'Casey.

In the autumn of 1932 Clery attended the Pan-Celt get-together at Truro in Cornwall. A few weeks later, he caught a chill; this developed into the pneumonia of which Clery died on 20 November.[371]

An enthusiastic rower, an accomplished swimmer, a rabid teetotaller, an eccentric who, after the Treaty, would insist on calling Dun Laoghaire and Cobh by their old names of Kingstown and Queenstown,[372] this versatile essayist, clearly beloved by his students, Clery was, as Dawson plainly saw it, a mass of contradictions. The character of Whelan, in James Joyce's *Stephen Hero,* as we have seen, was said to be based on Clery. But the essence of the man, as discerned by Dawson, is even more complex. 'A curious mixture,' Dawson wrote,[373]

> combining temerity with timidity, generosity with parsimony, breadth of view with lack of perspective or sense of proportion, and – strangest of all – sound democratic Republican sentiments with a distinct respect for rank and the claims of long descent.

Dawson's conclusion nevertheless was essentially positive:[374]

> A high sense of honour, a strict sense of duty, a delicate sense of humour, joined with a fervent faith, combined to make up the kindly, able, upright man that was Arthur Clery.

Not long after Clery's death the fine portrait in oils of Clery by Leo Whelan RHA came on the market. Pressing the Governing Body successfully to pay the 100 guineas demanded, Dr Coffey argued that it was 'desirable the College should possess such a memento of one who had taken so great an interest in its progress and welfare'.[375] The tribute he paid to Clery's memory in his *President's Report for 1931–1932* is equally generous.[376] 'The Law Faculty', Coffey claimed,

> has lost a Professor unexcelled in legal learning, and the students of that Faculty at once a guide and a personal friend of unceasing devotion to all their interests. Throughout his life unselfish and unworldly, deeply religious, living simply, his actions were guided by the highest dictates, and his loyalties were deep and abiding. One of the first of those loyalties was to his own College and with its outlook and spirit he was in perfect agreement. Whether in the joy with which he entered in his under-graduate days into the encouragement of a high tone amongst his fellow students in their conduct, their literary work and their sports, or in later life the devotion and constancy of purpose with which he aided the progressive development of the College, as well as the special advancement of the School of Law, it may be truly said that the well-being of the College and its faithfulness to its mission formed one of the supreme interests of his career.

Coffey does not here record what soon enough became public knowledge: that Clery, a bachelor, had bequeathed to the College a not-insubstantial sum of money that was utilised principally to improve the College's sporting facilities –

tennis courts and for athletics, for instance.[377] A special interest was the Rowing Club and the development of the boathouse at Islandbridge on the Liffey: as early as 1909, Clery had bemoaned the fact that in the old UCD on the Green there had been 'no facilities for boating'.[378] Not long before Clery's death, as it turned out, the College had managed to secure a lease of the site on the Liffey where it was proposed to erect the boathouse, on foundations partly completed by excess soil removed from Earlsfort Terrace.[379]

A tender for the erection of the boathouse at a cost of £1,090 had been accepted in January 1932,[380] but, as became immediately clear, extra finance would be needed for a landing stage, furniture and the installation of electric light. Money to hire a boat man was also required, which does seem finally to have been forthcoming from the College. The challenge presented by finance for the entire initiative seems certainly to have registered with Clery – and the money did finally come through. However, Dr Coffey was undoubtedly on secure ground when, in the spring of 1933, he urged the Governing Body to turn down the request from the Rowing Club that a preliminary advance of £1,400 for the benefit of the boat club under the terms of Clery's will should be authorised.[381] Long after Clery's death the Rowing Club continued to benefit from this munificent bequest.[382]

Patrick Maume's verdict on Clery the thinker – not the professor, the UCD alumnus, nor the man – is undeniably severe. 'Influenced by post-war conditions and the writings of Chesterton and Belloc', he writes in the entry for him in the *Dictionary of Irish Biography*,[383] Clery's

> anti-liberalism hardened into contempt for democracy as a self-serving middle-class sham, and dreams of a Catholic civilisation instituting social justice on what he foolishly and idealistically imagined to be the principles of Mussolini and Lenin.

There is an even harsher tone in Maume's concluding thoughts on the man in his *Irish Historical Studies* article. Fianna Fáil came to power shortly before Clery's death. Maume pondered the implications for Clery: would he have become reconciled with Fianna Fáil, or remained among the diehard Republicans? The answer supplied by Maume was to be that the question really did not arise:[384]

> By the end of his life Clery was so immersed in fantasy, paranoia and self-pity that it was hard to see him making any significant further contribution to public life.

Curran's verdict, at this remove in time, sounds more balanced. In Clery, he wrote,[385] there was

> a quiet contrariness that teased, tantalised and fascinated his friends and for a middling element in his make-up that turned him aside from well trodden ways into private retreats of his own.

It is to Curran that we are indebted for a rare assessment of the man *qua* professor:[386]

> His law lectures covered conscientiously the Law of Property but they were informal and conversational. He defined a contingent remainder as the chance to a dispensary doctor's son to inherit the dispensary.

Clery's failure to publish much in the areas of expertise where he lectured ought not to pass without comment. An observation of Donal McCartney's, provoked by criticism directed at William Magennis, the early Professor of Metaphysics at UCD, should not, however, be left out of the reckoning. 'The occupants of the foundation chairs at UCD', McCartney wrote,[387] 'published a great deal, especially in the scholarly journals and reviews – but not, it has to be conceded, in what might be looked upon as their own narrowly specialist fields'.

There was to be considerable discussion after Clery's death as to how best he might be remembered. A stage in one of the opinions examined was reached in November 1940 when the College's Governing Body expressed its approval of the wording for an inscription to be placed on a plaque scheduled for erection at 86, St Stephen's Green.[388] The wording had been drawn up by the Revd. Professor Timothy Corcoran, the Professor of Education at the time. It read as follows:

ART O CLEIRIG (1879–1932)

("CHANEL")

UNIVERSITY CLASSICAL SCHOLAR, 1898–1901;

B.A. (with Classical Honours), 1900, LL.B., 1902; LL.D 1908

PROFESSOR OF LAW, U.C.D. and N.U.I., 1911–1932

CHAIRMAN OF CONVOCATION, 1924–32

Author of "The Idea of a Nation" (1907); "Dublin Essays" (1919)

MUNIFICENT BENEFACTOR OF OUR COLLEGE ROWING CLUB,

TENNIS CLUB, AND UNION CENTRE

EARLY LAW STUDENTS

A number of the law school's early students gravitated towards such student societies as the L & H – the Literary and Historical Society – celebrated for its debates. There was one society that had a more obvious legal focus – the Legal and Economic Society. It can hardly be said to have flourished, for by the mid-1920s it appears to have faded out altogether. From certain details concerning it that are extant, it would seem to have aspired to be an intellectual power-house. Professor Murnaghan in 1912 and again in 1913 read papers at meetings of the society, which were chaired by members of the judiciary, on high-sounding jurisprudential and legal historical problems – 'The appellate jurisdiction of the House of Lords in Ireland' (1912)[389] and 'The King's Court and the counties palatine' (1913).[390] Both of these papers found their way into print.

A few cameos of the law school's first students will help to flesh out the story of the law school's early days. Three of the five to be introduced here, it will be noticed, all died young, well before their time.

Thomas Arkins

An amount of invaluable information is to hand in the case of one of the early auditors of the new Legal and Economic Society. This was Thomas Arkins, one of the first graduates of the UCD Law School, obtaining his LLB in 1912. Arkins was a candidate for the chair of English Law at University College Galway, which was due to be filled at the end of 1913. Testimonials produced on behalf of all four candidates applying for the post were forwarded to the NUI Senate and these are reproduced in the Senate minutes.[391] The Governing Body at UCG had strongly supported the candidacy of Arkins, the latter receiving at the customary ballot 11 votes, Richard J. Sheehy 5, William H. Brown, KC 3, and Conor A. Maguire 2. Arkins' testimonials came from all three of his professors at UCD – MacNeill, Murnaghan and Clery – as well as from Dr Coffey, the President, one of the external examiners, Thomas Molony, and Richard Davoren, Solicitor, who, alluding to Arkins' role as auditor of the Legal and Economic Society, pronounced him a fluent and effective speaker. MacNeill went into rather more detail. He praised Arkins for his 'quickness of apprehension, grasp of principle, power of generalisation, and faculty of bringing the resources of a hugely gifted and richly stored mind to our subject of study'. Arkins had obtained his BA in 1909, an MA in 1911 with a thesis on 'The protective system in Ireland in the eighteenth century', and his LLB, as we have said, in 1912. Both the BA and the LLB were obtained with 1st class honours. Arkins was reputed to have had published in *Studies* a text on 'The labour problem', based on an inaugural address he had given to the Solicitors' Apprentices Debating Society, but this attribution seems to have been based on a misapprehension, the only articles under his name appearing in *Studies* concentrating rather on the penal laws against Catholics.[392]

The UCG Governing Body had voted on the vacancy on 6 November 1913, and the NUI Senate was due to act on their recommendation on 11 December 1913. When the Senate assembled on that date, and this item on the agenda was reached, the Registrar, Joseph McGrath, broke the news that could not have been anticipated. Arkins had died on 28 November.

Richard Sheehy who had come second in the UCG Governing Body vote was then appointed. Half-a-dozen or so years earlier he had come first in the Bar finals, winning the John Brooke Scholarship. Members of the Bench had strongly supported his bid.

Ambrose Davoren

Ambrose Davoren, another early graduate, was reckoned a brilliant student. A product of Clongowes, he was reported to have regularly engaged in discussions about the law with a neighbour of his in Dundrum, Co. Dublin – no less majestic a figure than another Clongownian, Christopher Palles, the Chief Baron. War had broken out around the time Davoren obtained his LLB and this dissuaded him from proceeding immediately to the Bar. He joined up instead, being commissioned into the Royal Field Artillery. He was killed at the young age of 27, near Poperinge, in Flanders, on 18 July 1917. Delany recalled Davoren's links with Palles,[393] and Maurice Healy, in his reminiscences, recalled Davoren's reading of John Buchan's *A History of the War* and his desire, classical scholar that he was, to translate into Greek one key historical reference there to heroes and professions of loyalty to king and country – the speech of King Peter of Serbia on the eve of the Battle of the Ridges.[394]

Kevin O'Higgins

The assassination of Kevin O'Higgins, Minister for Home Affairs in the new Free State government, on 10 July 1927, at the age of 35 was quickly followed by the Senate of the National University at its meeting five days later, with the Chancellor, Eamon de Valera in the chair, adopting a vote of condolences to O'Higgins' widow, the former Brigid Cole.[395] The Senate expressed

> its deep sympathy to Mrs Kevin O'Higgins, B.A., H.Dip. Ed., on the murder of her distinguished husband, himself a graduate of our University in the Faculties of Arts and of Law; and desire to place on record its reverent appreciation of the noble and Christian spirit so splendidly evinced by him in those hours of supreme trial and suffering.

The vote had been proposed by Denis Coffey, the President of UCD and seconded by Patrick Merriman, the President of UCC.

It was an ironic twist of fate, for O'Higgins' earlier life as a student first in Arts and then in Law had straddled both campuses – at UCD and in Cork – and had presented acute difficulties, which on more than one occasion had been brought to the attention of the self-same Senate. O'Higgins' career at university came to an end with the award to him at UCD of the degree of LLB in December 1919,[396] but controversy continued to dog both him and the institutions of the Irish Bar when, in 1925, technical rules, arguably, were broken to facilitate his admission to the Irish Bar. His murder two years later meant that this 'victory over bureaucracy' was not one from which ultimately he was to derive any personal benefit at all. That the episode should have provoked a split in the Irish Bar – the Northern Benchers objecting to O'Higgins' rushed admission without their consent – and should have led to the establishment of a separate Inn of Court for Northern Ireland could even have caused O'Higgins himself a degree of remorse. He had, after all, clear-headed views on the North–South relationship, which were by no means popular with mainstream political thinking in the South.

O'Higgins' passage through the National University was certainly to be unusual. In 1915, he obtained his BA in Legal and Political Science from UCD.[397] The following year he passed Part I of the UCD LLB.[398] The ensuing year, enrolled as a student at UCC, he envisaged, doubtless, sitting Part II there, and thus completing the requirements for the LLB degree. He then discovered that the Law Faculty at UCC did not break up the LLB into two parts. Though the necessary detailed information is not to hand, it seems probable that O'Higgins was then informed he would have to sit all the subjects of UCC's LLB degree exam (what in Dublin would have been all the subjects of year 2, together with all the subjects of year 3). This must surely have seemed unfair, so scarcely unexpectedly, O'Higgins pressed for himself to be exempted from sitting examinations in the subjects of UCC's Final LLB degree examination, which he had already taken in Part I of UCD's LLB degree examination. The manoeuvre received the endorsement of the NUI Senate in March 1917.[399]

Things, so far as O'Higgins was concerned, did not yet go according to plan. In the autumn of 1917, we find he is again writing letters – on this occasion appealing the award of the examiners. This sounds to me as if he did not pass the remaining subjects of the LLB degree examination which he sat at UCC. The Standing Committee of the NUI Senate considered both O'Higgins' letter of 5 October 1917 and a letter which Sir Bertram Windle, the President of UCC had written on the 8th. Windle urged the special circumstances of the case, leaving it open to infer from the report of the examiners that O'Higgins might be adjudged to have passed the LLB. The Senate, however, when it debated the entire question at its meeting on the 26th, finally decided to secure the views of the examiners in Law.[400] The latter, when consulted, were unmoved, and dug in their heels. There were no grounds they said for varying the award[401] – which again, it sounds to me, as if they were confirming a fail. This report from the examiners was considered by the Senate on 7 December, when it chose to endorse it. O'Higgins returned to UCD where in the autumn of 1919, he presented himself for the examination in Part II of UCD's LLB.

There were to be further reports from O'Higgins that were to be processed before the NUI Senate.[402] Two letters from him, penned in September 1919, dealt with the contingency – which did in fact come to pass[403] – of his being awarded the LLB at UCD. He asked, first, whether, in that case, he could graduate *in absentia*. The explanation for the request was simple and straightforward. Being a marked man, O'Higgins, if he had turned up in person, was bound to have been arrested, and thus facing another spell in prison, such as he had undergone for 5 months in the middle of 1918. (The same problem arose in connection with O'Higgins presenting himself for the Solicitors' Final examination in 1920.)[404] The answer to this request was 'yes'. But, secondly, he enquired whether his name as a forthcoming graduate might be withheld from the list sent to the Press prior to the conferring ceremony. Here, the response of the Senate can scarcely have given O'Higgins complete satisfaction. 'In all other respects', he was told, 'the case should go through the ordinary procedure'. O'Higgins graduated LLB *in absentia* on 16 December 1919.[405] It was not with first-class honours, as stated by de Vere White.[406] Three other UCD law students graduated at the same time – Francis Gallagher, BA, with first-class honours, John J. Hearne with second-class honours. Joseph P. Walshe, MA, like O'Higgins, received a Pass degree.[407]

In 2012 a plaque was unveiled on Cross Avenue in Booterstown, Co. Dublin, at the very spot where in July 1927 O'Higgins had been shot. It has since disappeared.

John J. Webb

John J. Webb, MA, LLB was to be the first recipient of an LLD on published work processed through UCD. This was in respect of his book *Municipal Government in Ireland* published in 1918.[408] The LLD under the Royal University dispensation had been obtainable by written examination alone, and although the new UCD after 1909 accepted that arrangement for a year or two, by the end of the decade, as we have recalled, a critical change had been introduced preventing the obtaining of the degree in that fashion. It was still the case however that one could not present for the degree until a prescribed period of time – 15 terms – had elapsed since the obtaining of the LLB degree. Webb's application came before the General Board of Studies in November 1918. The Board resolved that the two Law external examiners, Serjeant Sullivan and Patrick Lynch, should be appointed to read Webb's book, and recommend accordingly. A favourable report was received from the examiners in mid-February, 1919, and the award of the degree was sanctioned by the NUI Senate a fortnight later. Webb was later conferred with the degree on 28 April 1919.[409] Over half a century was to elapse before the next LLD on published work was to be processed through UCD's Law Faculty.

Webb subsequently discharged the role of Lecturer in Municipal Government in UCD, a post that was funded for a number of years by Dublin Corporation. In this capacity, Webb, in October 1924, delivered the first of a series of lectures under the auspices of the Civics Institute of Ireland. His theme was the manner in which Irish towns had been governed in the medieval period.[410]

A linked topic was that of the municipal trading guilds, and on these Webb, in 1929, published a further volume.[411]

Webb was made a Senior Counsel in 1953, and served as the Registrar of Wards of Court.[412]

Brian (Bernard) MacKenna

MacKenna, who was to go on to become a judge of the Queen's Bench Division in London and receive a knighthood, included a short piece of autobiography in a paper read at the Law Faculty in 1973.[413] From this, it would seem, he merely studied Arts in the new UCD. 'My father having died young, and left me a little money', the future judge was to recall,

> I was by this time a ward of chancery. 1917 came, when the Irish Lord Chancellors Department discovering that some of the 1916 rebels had been old Belvederians, sent me in haste to Clongowes, where it was hoped their ward might breathe a less infected air. Clongowes was a pleasant school where Chief Baron Palles was still commemorated by a fearsome photograph showing us what we might yet hope to become by prayer and study. Leaving Clongowes in 1922, I came to Earlsfort Terrace where Coffey was then President. Michael Tierney taught me Greek and Semple Latin.

He was to continue his education in Berlin and Oxford before determining on law as choice of career.

> I was interested in the meaning of words, had no ability as a writer, lacked the stamina to be a professor, and even so was fond of the sound of my own voice. There was nothing for it but the Bar.

MacKenna's memoir concludes with a few wry observations on why he had chosen to make his career in London rather than Dublin.

3

New Brooms: the Law School, 1925–45

James Murnaghan, the Professor of Roman Law and Jurisprudence, was made a judge in the summer of 1924, and consequently resigned. Swift MacNeill, the Professor of Constitutional Law and Public and Private Wrongs, died in harness in August 1926. The vacancies thus arising were filled in due course by the appointments of D.A. Binchy and M.J. Ryan, respectively.

An element of folklore, as we will be discovering, has entered into consideration of the circumstances surrounding the appointment of Binchy – paradoxically, as it turned out, this being one of the more imaginative appointments the Governing Body and the NUI Senate were to sanction. It is as well then that we say a little about the cultural environment in which UCD at this point in its history sought to attract the best of candidates to fill new or vacant positions.

In the autumn of 1914, when many people's thoughts may have been directed elsewhere, the Governing Body was successfully pressured into setting up an Appointments Committee, consisting of the President, the Registrar, the Secretary and others with this specific remit: the members were to maintain a record of vacant posts 'for which distinguished and eligible graduates may be recommended'.[1] Pressure again to appoint graduates of the College when filling vacant chairs came from a specific group of lobbyists in 1926. This was the Women's Graduates Association who saw nothing wrong at all in arguing for the College to become, in effect, an employment bureau, at a time when jobs in the market were few and far between.[2]

One further plan, hatched in late 1932 and early 1933, following the death of the erstwhile colleague of both Murnaghan and MacNeill, that of Arthur Clery, had it succeeded, could have had a major impact on the fortunes of the Law School, though the proof of that, naturally, is not there to be had. A vacancy having arisen at this time on account of Clery's death, the Gaelic League sought to employ the occasion to further its own agenda. In a letter to the President, the League urged the College to accept that 'a knowledge of Irish should be made an essential qualification for the [vacant] professorship, and that this condition should be inserted in the advertisement of the vacant office'. The matter was aired at the January 1933 meeting of the Governing Body. At the end of the discussion, the President, Dr Coffey, proposed, and the Registrar, Dr Conway, seconded, that no action should be taken. A motion to this effect was then passed; there were three dissenters.[3]

It is not clear if Murnaghan's departure for the High Court or MacNeill's death caused the College to look again at the different arrangements on tenure for professors in the Law School, but the matter was now taken on board even so, a move that could have been inspired in part by the controversy surrounding lectureships in the Medical School which was recounted in the last chapter.[4]

Whatever the explanation, it is instructive that at its meeting in December 1926, the Senate of the NUI sought the advice of the Academic Councils of the three constituent Colleges on a proposed change in tenure for the three UCD chairs so that, as it was put, in the request for advice,[5]

> The first period of seven years' appointment should be probationary and if reappointed at the end of that period they shall hold office without further reappointment until they shall have reached the age of 65 years.

The responses of the three Councils were considered the following March.[6] Both Dublin and Galway approved the proposed alteration, Galway pointing out that this was the standard rule in the sections on tenure in its Statutes. Cork for some reason argued for no change.

The following November the Senate considered the question again,[7] but a decision was postponed until 9 December when the views of Dublin and Galway were adopted, and the drawing up of a fresh Statute to alter the existing position was approved.[8] All this was made known to the Governing Body at UCD when at its January meeting in 1928 it performed what, seen in retrospect, was a remarkable volte-face. This was when the following motion was adopted:[9]

> That the tenure of Professorships in the Faculty of Law in University College, Dublin, shall in the event of a Statute to the same effect being made by the National University of Ireland be the same as the tenure of the other Professorships of the College, namely to hold office subject to good conduct up to the age of 65 years, and such tenure shall apply to the present holders of the offices of the Professorships of Roman Law and Jurisprudence, of Constitutional Law and History and the Law of Public and Private Wrongs, and of the Law of Property and Law of Contracts.

The UCD Statute XIV that came into force later in 1928 effected the necessary change, a change that was in compliance with Chapter II of NUI's Statute XXXVIII, which sanctioned this particular modification in the tenure arrangements for the UCD Law chairs.[10]

In the years from 1925 to 1945 there were no major changes to the pattern of instruction for law students following the BA in Legal and Political Science and following the LLB.

Changes in the professoriate have already been signalled; and in the wake of

Clery's death yet another newcomer – Patrick Mc Gilligan – was welcomed on to the Faculty. These years of consolidation were unusual in a number of respects: McGilligan was a former government minister and Binchy was granted leave of absence to serve a turn as Ireland's envoy to Germany. After Clery's death it was this team of Binchy, Ryan and McGilligan that was to guide the Law School through the years of the Emergency – known elsewhere as the Second World War.

DANIEL ANTHONY BINCHY (1899–1989)

The appointment of Murnaghan to the High Court in 1924 created a vacancy in the chair of Roman Law and Jurisprudence. The post was to be offered to a young barrister who had been admitted to the Irish Bar in 1920, and was only in his mid-20s. This was Daniel Anthony Binchy, originally from Charleville in Co. Cork,[11] who, more perhaps than any other of UCD's early appointments in the Law School, was destined to shine very considerable lustre upon it indeed. Binchy attended Clongowes Wood College from 1910 to 1916, then proceeded to UCD where he graduated with a BA in Legal and Political Science in 1920, following this up with an MA in Modern Irish History the next year. During his time in UCD Binchy was auditor of the Literary and Historical Society, where, in the estimation of one of his contemporaries,[12] he 'must rank very high among the very best of auditors'. Having joined King's Inns as a student in 1917, he was admitted to the Bar three years later,[13] but his time as a student was not thereby brought to an end, for from 1921 to 1924 he attended the University of Munich, graduating from the latter in 1924 with a doctorate. The thesis he had produced as part of the course requirements touched on ecclesiastical history: 'Die irischen Benediktiner-klöster in Regensburg'.[14] And among the lectures Binchy attended was a series entitled 'Das Fortleben der heidnischen Ideenwelt im christlichen Mittelalter', which dealt with the survival of pre-Christian customs and primitive superstitions, a series he recalled with gratitude many years later.[15] Binchy was already in print, and was thus early marked out as someone from whom much might be expected in the years ahead. But what at this stage had attracted his attention was very different from the story of Irish Benedictines abroad. His focus rather was on links between Ireland and Spain during the reign of Elizabeth I. This was his 'An Irish Ambassador at the Spanish Court, 1569–1574', an essay in six parts, which appeared in Dublin between 1920 and 1923.[16] On leaving Munich, Binchy signed on for a year's attendance at the Ecole des Chartes in Paris.

The circumstances of Binchy's appointment were unusual. The story circulated that the President at the time, Denis Coffey, offered the job to Binchy when he encountered the latter strolling through Dublin's St Stephen's Green.[17] (One might compare this story with the supposed appointment of Thomas Cranmer as archbishop of Canterbury by Henry VIII in 1533 when they met at a bear-baiting,[18] or that of Christopher Palles as Chief Baron of the Irish Exchequer by Gladstone in 1874 on the railway platform of Paddington station, when the latter was on his way to see Queen Victoria at Windsor Castle to resign.)[19] Doubt must attach to this story that Coffey did any such thing. Donal Cregan accepted that the two men did in fact meet in St Stephen's Green, but maintained that Coffey employed the occasion to apprise Binchy of the fact that the vacancy in the chair of Roman Law and Jurisprudence had arisen and to encourage Binchy to apply for it.[20] There is a further possible explanation: that this encounter occurred after the prescribed formal procedures had concluded, with Senate approval following the Academic Council assessment and a vote in the Governing Body.[21] Five applications had been received for the chair so recently vacated by Murnaghan, one of them in the name of Conor Maguire, the future Chief Justice (1946–61).[22] All five were adjudged qualified, but only Binchy possessed a doctorate, and he scored 16 votes as opposed to the 6 for Maguire who came second when the Governing Body held its second ballot. By the time the offer of the job was made to Binchy,[23] he was of course fully committed to his year's study at the Ecole des Chartes and was anxious not to have his sojourn in Paris interrupted. Coffey and the Governing Body were to go out of their way to accommodate him by granting him leave of absence until, in effect, the start of the session 1925–6 in the autumn.[24] In the meantime, the two existing professors, Clery and MacNeill, were deputed to cover the courses that Binchy would in the normal course of events have been obliged to offer.[25]

Of his appointment Binchy said at the time that he reckoned his qualifications for the job somewhat scanty. But this show of modesty naturally could not conceal the fact that he had acquired qualifications in both Law and History, had a postgraduate qualification, had published, and had attained fluency in German – all accomplishments that no formal board of assessors today could possibly have ignored and which were destined to stand him in very great stead indeed. Many years later, viewing the matter dispassionately, Binchy added, intriguingly, as regards his joining the UCD staff,[26] that 'the appointment of a non-practising barrister to a post hitherto monopolised by practising members of the profession caused widespread dismay among their ranks'.

Binchy was not long installed in his chair at Earlsfort Terrace when the prospect of a career very different from the one upon which he had embarked lay open before him. In 1929, the new Free State government took the first steps to establish a diplomatic presence abroad. London had had its High Commissioner since the foundation of the State – the designation changing to Ambassador in 1950 following the declaration of a republic and secession from the Commonwealth. But elsewhere no independent voices for the new Irish State had been accredited. In 1929, this changed, with Irish ministers being appointed to the United States, France, the Holy See and Germany. In July

Binchy was named Minister Plenipotentiary and Envoy Extraordinary to Germany, a post he retained until March 1932.

Binchy's unusual appointment was almost certainly due to his knowledge of, and proficiency in, German. On his return to Dublin he was to translate into English a classic work by his mentor and fellow Celticist Rudolf Thurneysen, the latter's *Handbuch des Alt-Irischen* (1909). Binchy's translation *A Grammar of Old Irish* came out in 1946. Binchy, in Michael Kennedy's estimation,[27] proved a conscientious and highly professional diplomat. His main achievement was 'in setting up the Irish Legation in Berlin and in reporting on a troubled time in German history in an astute manner'.

Documents now in the public domain make it possible independently to evaluate such a conclusion. It would indeed appear correct. Barely a few months in office, Binchy gave it as his view to Dublin[28] that the Foreign Office in Berlin

> is not really interested in us any more than it is in any small unimportant state situated a considerable distance from its frontiers. It thinks of us in precisely the same terms as it thinks, say of Bulgaria, or a small Central American Republic.

By March 1931, his assessment of the true state of affairs was different but not perhaps by very much. 'Our chief significance in German eyes', Binchy reported back to Dublin,[29] 'is whatever influence we can exert on the policy of the Commonwealth as a whole'.

On matters German, particular interest attaches to his longer reports. One of August 1931 on the plebiscite to secure the dissolution of the Prussian parliament makes compelling reading.[30] On 1 March 1932, shortly before his own recall, Binchy furnishes exhaustive detail on the moves to procure German citizenship for a potential candidate – Adolf Hitler – in the forthcoming presidential election (which Hindenburg was to win).[31] Officials in the service of any German State government received German nationality automatically. Efforts by Hitler himself, or his associates, to secure appointment as a teacher of art, as head constable in an obscure Thuringian village, or as Professor of Education in the State University in Brunswick, and thus satisfy the necessary requirements, all failed, due, as Binchy expresses it, to 'the excusable opposition of future colleagues'. Eventually, however, the government of Brunswick saw fit to make Hitler an attaché to the state's Legation to the Reich.

Binchy had personal interviews with Hindenburg when presenting his letters of credence and those of his recall, and leaves us his account of both.[32] He was proud of the flat he occupied in the embassy on Tiergartenstrasse. It was, he wrote to his UCD colleague, Michael Tierney,[33] 'a dream of beauty'. People – and this would have included Micheál MacLiammóir and members of his theatre company who performed in Berlin in the summer of 1931[34] – Binchy insisted, spent most of their time admiring it:[35]

> Germans think it is 'eine typischen irische Wohnung'; whereas I doubt if there is anything like it in the whole of Dublin, with its Dun Emer carpets, Hicks furniture, Carrickmacross lace, and pictures (mostly lent by friends) by Lamb, Paul Henry, Jack Yeats, AE and Nathaniel Hone.

For all his professionalism, Binchy frankly admitted to Tierney, at the time UCD's Professor of Greek, but soon enough in 1947 to become the College's President, that the diplomatic life did not appeal. His counterpart in Paris, Count O'Kelly, he suggested probably felt very differently:[36]

> I am temperamentally a complete misfit for my job, really nothing like as good as Gerald O'Kelly,[37] for example, who feels at his happiest in a morning suit or a frock. For me the round of social activities is an unceasing torment, I dodge them with increasing unscrupulousness when at all possible, and while I flatter myself that I manage to keep up a brave appearance, my heart is all the time wrung, thinking of the number of [Charles] Plummer's[38] slips I could have verified and checked, during those wasted hours.

Binchy was not the first diplomat, nor was he to be the last, who felt the urge to decry what Lawrence Durrell would later describe as 'the tiresome treadmill of protocol and entertainment – so like a surrealist nightmare',[39] but the forcefulness of the distaste for his official life expressed in this letter to Tierney should occasion for us no surprise that Binchy would in 1932 leave the Department of External Affairs, as Foreign Affairs was then known, and return to academic life in Dublin. The allusion Binchy makes to the philological endeavours of Charles Plummer (which he had found less time to peruse then he would have wished) naturally suggests a second reason for his decision to return to UCD – based there, he would enjoy the opportunity to disentangle linguistically some at least of the many mysteries posed by early Irish law, in the study of which, as we now know, his star was destined to shine.

The Berlin Binchy was to leave was described by MacLiammóir on the occasion of his visit in 1931 as 'very gay and friendly'. 'The marching', he continued,[40]

> and saluting and shouting, the self-conscious jamboree, the bloodcurdling boy-scoutishness of later years showed no sign of ever becoming popular. It just shows how deceptive things are.

The Berlin years left their mark on Binchy too. If we think of him today as the leading scholar of his generation in early Irish law, he himself at this critical juncture in his career sensed the allurement of seeking to understand the drift to contemporary European history. That he had no truck with National Socialism is clear from his reports to his boss Joseph Walshe in Dublin. That is plain from a series of sketches of German personalities – Heinrich Brüning, Paul von Hindenburg and Adolf Hitler himself – he penned for *Studies* and published there in the 1930s. Binchy in his piece on Brüning, the chancellor who preceded Papen and Schleicher, the last of whom, in turn, in January 1933, was succeeded by Hitler, makes clear his admiration for the man and his policies.[41] Writing in 1932, Binchy regretted that Brüning's steady hand had been forced from the steering-wheel, adding, however – though this we now know was overly optimistic – 'But the end is not yet'.[42] Binchy returns to his appreciation of the man in his 1937 sketch of President von Hindenburg, written after the latter's death,[43] a piece provoked, it would appear, by Wheeler-Bennett's biography of Hindenburg published in 1936,[44] which Binchy reckoned was overly critical. Binchy yet blamed Hindenburg for the dismissal of Brüning, who represented 'the only possible dam against the threatened Nazi inundation',[45] elsewhere described by him as 'the madness of Hitlerism'.[46] Hindenburg had admittedly had to put up with the 'shrill obscenities' of Joseph Goebbels during the 1932 presidential election,[47] but even so, the circumstances of the invitation to Hitler to accept the chancellorship on 28 January 1933 in succession to Schleicher betrayed a naivété which was hard to credit. Hindenburg had sought to impose conditions on the new chancellor. Binchy was incredulous:[48]

> Impose conditions on a river in full spate after he himself had removed the dam [seemingly a further reference to the dismissal of Brüning]! Hitler accepted all the conditions and broke them all in turn. The President had not read *Mein Kampf.*

Binchy published his piece on Hitler in 1933, the same year as the latter came to power.[49] It was a damning essay well worth revisiting, not least because it rankled with the German government at the time, as Charles Bewley, Binchy's eventual successor as Irish minister in Berlin, who proved much more understanding of what Hitler and company were at – he was to publish a biography of Hermann Göring in 1962[50] – was not slow to point out, protesting that it had compromised his own position as an Irish minister.[51]

Binchy's first sight of Hitler was in Munich in November 1921. 'Would it be possible' he was to inquire, 'to find a more common-place-looking man?' His account continues:[52]

> His countenance was opaque, his complexion pasty, his hair plastered down with some glistening unguent, and – as if to accentuate the impression of insignificance – he wore a carefully docked 'toothbrush' moustache. I felt willing to bet that in private life he was a plumber: a

> whispered query to my friend brought the information that he was a house painter.

Giving credit where credit was due, Binchy conceded that behind an 'insignificant exterior' there was to be found even so 'a born natural orator'. Not everyone, of course, would have relished the 'traces of foam' when Hitler was in full flight, that materialised 'at the corners of his mouth'.[53]

This and other meetings in Munich were advertised by 'flaming red posters designed by Hitler' displaying a swastika in each corner and bearing the legend –

JEWS NOT ADMITTED
JUDEN IST DER ZUTRITT VERBOTEN.[54]

On *Mein Kampf*, brought out in 1925, Binchy was again critical:[55]

> Written in a maddeningly wooden style, in which hackneyed clichés alternate with windy rhetoric, full of rambling digressions and hysterical denunciations, it affords no insight whatever into Hitler's own life and development.

Singled out for special attack was Hitler's rant regarding the Jews in Russia.[56] The leaders of international capital, they were at the same time the leaders of the Bolsheviks who sought to destroy it – an apparent inconsistency. An anonymous reader of Binchy's article in the UCD Library's copy of volume 22 of *Studies* at some point in the past elected to take umbrage with Binchy's argument at this juncture, for at page 39 you will find this note in the margin:

Binchy: you should read Fr Fahy's book Rulers of Russia
(Jews are the real rulers of Russia).

The passage in Binchy's critique likely to have given most offence is the one where Binchy again emphasises matters personal. 'There are', Binchy was to report,[57]

> only two barriers to megalomania in public life: intelligence and a sense of humour. Either of these qualities would suffice to prevent it, but I believe Hitler to be lacking in both … It is not merely the right sort of faith which is capable of moving mountains.

In 1937, Binchy was invited by the Royal Institute of International Affairs in London to produce a report on contemporary Italy, an invitation inspired by the Lateran agreements of 11 February 1929. The outcome, *Church and State in*

Fascist Italy, was published four years later, in the midst of war.[58] Arthur Conway, who became UCD's president in 1940, was to alter the format of the annual *President's Report*, by including for the first time information regarding the College's staff – appointments, resignations, deaths, publications, etc. It tells us something about the seemingly precarious standing of the College's Law Faculty at this juncture that in the whole of the 1940s only one staff member from the Law School – Binchy – has publications credited to him. This occurs in 1940–1 when *Church and State in Fascist Italy* is listed along with Binchy's edition of *Crith Gablach*, an old Irish tract on the law of persons.[59]

In *Church and State in Fascist Italy* Binchy's point of departure, in relation to the key issue of the Roman Question, is well illustrated by this acerbic passage on the Risorgimento:[60]

> Now that the British Empire has discovered united Italy to be a dangerous and unfriendly neighbour, perhaps we may expect some mitigation of the uncritical enthusiasm for the Risorgimento which has been the fashion for so long. It is about time that the whole movement should be viewed in its proper perspective, as a mixture of heroism and baseness, valour and cowardice, high patriotism and squalid intrigue, disinterested service and craven selfishness – in short, no better and no worse than most national revolutions.

In his preface, addressing himself to more recent occurrences, Binchy, as he had done in the case of Germany and Nazism, put his cards on the table for all to see. 'Fascism, both in its theory and its practice', he wrote,[61]

> has always been abhorrent to me, and thus I have been singularly immune from a temptation which, up to recently, at least, used to trouble some of my coreligionists in Great Britain, the temptation 'to gaze on prosperous tyrants with a dazzled eye'.[62]

'At the same time', Binchy continued,[63]

> I do not believe that my dislike of the totalitarian machine has led me to minimise any of its practical achievements, or to deal unfairly with the remarkable man who for twenty years has dictated the tortuous courses of Italian Fascism. True, Mussolini has ridden by me in the Villa Borghese without ever conveying to me the least impression of 'the world spirit on horseback'; on the other hand, I find it difficult to be patient with those who affect to see in him nothing more than a glorified Al Capone.

A later passage in *Church and State* effectively, if quietly, conveys the most compelling reason why the Fascist state under Mussolini merited no general encomium. 'The ordinary Italian', Binchy wrote,[64]

> who reads on every dead wall and public building that he passes the mystic formula *Credere, Ubbidere*, *Combattare* must feel that of these three imperatives only the second is a constant: he knows not what he is to believe tomorrow, for that depends on what the Duce may think, nor whom he is to fight, for the enemies of Fascism have a habit of changing from time to time; but he has no doubts about whom he is to obey.

Binchy maintained an interest in Italian politics after the Second World War, contributing his thoughts on the general election of April 1948 in *Studies* that year.[65] An acerbic note was to be struck immediately after confirming the defeat of the Communists. 'The complacent satisfaction', Binchy observed,

> with which the results of the Italian election has been hailed (notably in the Irish Catholic press) as a 'smashing defeat of the Reds' only shows how far removed from the realities of post-war Europe the (to my mind) disastrous policy of neutrality and isolation has left us. To these jubilant scribes I can only repeat Wallenstein's warning:-
>
> Frohlocke nicht!
> Denn eifersüchtig sind des Schicksals Mächte.[66]

His *Church and State in Fascist Italy* was to be reprinted in 1970, Binchy declining to undertake anything in the nature of revision. In the preface he wrote for his new impression, he did make the point that the Catholic Church had weathered 'the stormy period of transition' far more successfully than he had anticipated: 'the post-Fascist era began with both the Papacy and the Italian Church in a much stronger position than seemed likely in 1941'.[67] But difficulties, of course, lay ahead. The book itself in the main thus remains what Binchy himself termed a 'period piece' – 'the record of one observer's impressions and conclusions, all too often mistaken, but at least contemporary'. A bonus for Irish readers remains Binchy's discussions of Fascism in the Irish Free State and why, ultimately, it did not prosper there.[68]

Nowhere is the versatility of Binchy, the professor, best evidenced than in the pages of *Studies* in the 1930s. In the interval between his sketches of Brüning and Hitler, 1932–3, and of Hindenburg, 1937, he contributes his thoughts on proposals for a new Irish Seanad[69] and on Partition.[70] On this last he made clear his support for an 'integral acceptance of the Dominion position' and his distaste for the declaration of a Republic, which he was certain would copperfasten Partition. No less remarkable is the fact that in 1934 he produced for *Studies* critical reviews of two classic works from the Blasket Islands, off the coast of Co. Kerry: Tomás Ó Criomhthain's *An t-Óileanach* and Muiris Ó Suileabhain's *Fiche Blian ag Fas*, in both the original Irish and in their English translations.[71] Binchy's 'Two Blasket autobiographies'[72] transports us a fair distance from the Berlin of diplomatic protocol and Tiergartenstrasse, but it is an excellent indicator of where his interests truly lay. 'When I first came to the district in quest of modern Irish', Binchy writes,[73]

> my intention was to make the island [Great Blasket] my headquarters; but fear of the treacherous Sound whose quick changes of mood are agony to a bad sailor, kept me in Coumeenole on the extreme point of the mainland, a place that I have since grown to regard as my second home.

A thumbnail sketch of Ó Criomhthain follows. 'I can still see him', Binchy writes,[74]

> as he stood by the hearth in his own kitchen, a trim lithe figure with finely chiselled features, and keen bright eyes that seemed to survey the world with friendly and somewhat ironic detachment.

It is not without interest that 'Beginish', the name of one of the smaller Blasket Islands, was given to the house that Binchy lived in for many years in Crosthwaite Park West in Dun Laoghaire.

Binchy resumed his career as a professor at UCD in March 1932, the same month that he had signalled his resignation from the civil service. J.P. Walshe, the secretary at the Department of External Affairs, broke the news that Binchy would be returning to his *alma mater* in a letter to Dr Coffey that was to find its way into the Governing Body minute book.[75] Walshe confided in Coffey 'the very highest appreciation' of the work Binchy had done as the Irish envoy in Berlin. 'The Minister', Walshe continued,

> knows what valuable service the Professor has already rendered, and will continue to render, to the community, through his University work, and he believes that his experience as a State servant will give a new value to Dr Binchy's work in the University.

Following Arthur Clery's death in November 1932, Binchy was to be elected dean, an office he was to hold for the next four years. Until a replacement for Clery could be found, what had become the conventional practice was followed – the remaining two professors one of whom was Binchy – were obliged to cover for the courses thus left without their prescribed teacher. On this occasion, we know the financial implications. For each of the three terms (Michaelmas, Hilary and Trinity) to the end of the 1932–3 session, the two professors – Binchy and M.J. Ryan – were to be paid £75 each extra, a grand total for the year of £225.[76]

Binchy was almost certainly the architect behind a major paper of recommendations from the Faculty of Law that went to the Academic Council early in 1933 that presaged major changes for the Faculty, from which Binchy himself was destined to derive the principal benefit.[77] The paper began somewhat portentously: 'To ensure that the large and constantly increasing number of Law students may receive comprehensive grounding in legal studies, the Faculty recommends reorganisation of Law Chairs in the College with consequential modification in the courses'. On the professorship of Constitutional Law and the Law of Public and Private Wrongs, with which the teaching of International Law had come to be linked, the paper argued for a change of name to Constitutional, International and Criminal Law – all, effectively, Public Law topics – sharing the same teacher, for, in the modern world, Constitutional and International Law were supposedly inexorably connected. On the professorship that Clery had held, the paper recommended that the title should be changed to Professorship of Property, Common Law and Equity, in effect bringing together 'all the main departments of Private Law, the subjects of which form a natural group, and would secure a corresponding logical order in the courses'.

His own chair, Roman Law and Jurisprudence, Binchy in the Faculty of Law's paper argued should be made full-time – a move first urged for adoption by the Academic Council in 1929.[78] It was thus to be brought for the first time within the scope of section 2 in Chapter xxvi, 'The duties of Professors and Lecturers', in Statute I of the National University introduced by the Dublin Commissioners in April 1911:[79]

> Every Full-Time Professor shall, so far as it is compatible with the other duties of his Chair, devote himself to research and the advancement of knowledge.

Binchy was far from disappointing in his compliance with this rubric.

The Faculty's paper, in accordance with Binchy's plans for his future in UCD, also proposed a change in the title for his Chair. It was to become the professorship of Roman Law, Jurisprudence and Legal History (including Ancient Irish Law). In justification of the change, the paper argued as follows:[80]

> These are essentially academic subjects[81] – for which students (while compelled to take them for their final professional examinations) receive no tuition outside the universities. Up to the present time there has been no course in Legal History, and students have been compelled to make up this subject from English textbooks, which take little or no account of the special circumstances regarding the introduction and development of

> English law in Ireland, still less of the native legal system which preceded it. The study of the latter has advanced so much in recent years that it is now possible to teach it on scientific lines.[82]

The Academic Council went on to approve this document, as did the Governing Body. In due course, a new Statute, Statute XIX was adopted, which besides altering the titles of the three Law chairs, made changes to the annual stipends payable. Roman Law, Jurisprudence, etc. was to be paid £800, Law of Property, etc. £450, and Constitutional Law, etc. £350. The new Statute came into force in 1934.

Binchy was immediately involved in working up new teaching in the area of Legal History. The course itself we learn from the *Calendar* was divided in two.[83] The first part was devoted to a general history of the common law and equity with special reference to Ireland; the second was described as 'Outlines of the old Irish legal system', classic works by Sir Henry Maine and Eoin MacNeill's two books, *Early Irish Law and Institutions* and *Celtic Ireland* here being listed as recommended reading. There was another aspect to this innovation, for Binchy announced that 'a special course in translation and exposition of selected Irish legal tracts will be arranged for advanced students of Old and Middle Irish'.[84] For the next ten or so years this was the heavy work load that our returned diplomat set himself. Over his stint of teaching Roman Law for the duration, he was later to confess a degree of embarrassment: it was something about which he was 'least proud'.[85]

How Binchy came to concentrate his interests on Early Irish Law, the area where he would achieve his renown, is not altogether clear. But he himself has left us a number of clues. In his retrospective memoir published in *Studia Hibernica* in 1975, Binchy recalls that in Paris, in what would have been 1925, he was introduced to Sir Paul Vinogradoff, Corpus Professor of Jurisprudence at Oxford (Vinogradoff was to die in December that year in Paris). Binchy, in his memoir, continues,[86]

> On learning of my nationality and the post that awaited me in Dublin, Vinogradoff urged me strongly to take up the study of early Irish law, a subject which he hoped would throw fresh light on the political and social evolution of Western Europe during the Dark Ages. What he had written about the 'Brehon laws' in the first volume of his *Outlines of Historical Jurisprudence* [(1920)] was, he had now come to believe, in need of drastic revision.

Vinogradoff's conviction, bolstered by the views of his colleague in Corpus Christi College, Charles Plummer, based on the writings of Eoin MacNeill and Rudolf Thurneysen, that a thorough investigation of the sources for early Irish law would be productive of important results 'gave me', Binchy wrote,[87] 'the first impulse towards a new subject which would reconcile my previous lines of research with the terms of my future appointment'.

The introduction he wrote for the first volume of the *Corpus Iuris Hibernici* furnishes another clue.[88] His enthusiasm for a possible major work on the law of early Ireland he tells us was fired by the precedent of Felix Liebermann's four-volume *Die Gesetze der Angelsachsen*,[89] one of the classic works from a distinguished band of German legal historians, which he had doubtlessly been introduced to during his three student years in Munich. What was needed in the case of the Irish material would be an authoritative text, translation, notes, a vocabulary and a glossary. In 1943, in his celebrated Rhys lecture,[90] Binchy was to give a felicitous title – *Corpus Iuris Hibernici* – to the work which at that point had reached no more than the planning stage,[91] but which was clearly inspired by the works of scholars such as Liebermann and Wasserschleben.[92]

The major difficulty that Binchy faced, as he set about his self-appointed task, was the nature of the written sources he would be handling. Thurneysen had written that they had bequeathed 'das Bild einer Ruine, um nicht zu sagen eines Trümmerheufens' (the picture of a ruin, not to say a mound of rubble).[93] But, in addition, there was the challenge of the language in which they were expressed. Here Binchy found his guide in another mentor, Eoin MacNeill. In *Celtic Ireland*, the latter had written:[94] 'The great need of historical studies in Irish antiquity is now a sound equipment in knowledge of the Irish language in its successive stages of development'. Binchy entirely agreed, and thus it came about that with the support of his UCD colleague, Osborn Bergin, from 1926 to 1931 Binchy, so he tells us,[95] spent every summer in Kerry, at Coumeenole, beside Dunquin and overlooking Blasket Sound,

> among a small community of monoglot native speakers, all of whom I have cause to remember with deep affection and gratitude, for they gave me far more than a writer's knowledge of West Munster Irish, though in the interval, alas, much of it has evaporated, *cheal taithí* 'for want of practice', as those good friends would have said.

Hence, of course, Binchy's appreciative remarks, when reviewing the two Blasket Island autobiographies in his *Studies* article of 1934.[96] It will occasion no surprise either that when he was the Irish minister in Berlin Binchy found time and made the effort to attend a number of courses on Comparative Linguistics at the University of Berlin.[97]

Binchy contributed his thoughts on the intellectual politics of Irish cultural nationalism in a symposium published in *Studies* in 1938.[98] We also learn from *President's Reports* in the early 1940s – under the revamped style of these reports attributable to Coffey's successor as President, Arthur Conway – that he participated in at least two programmes of public lectures in the College, or public extension lectures as they were then dubbed, in both 1942 and 1945. Binchy's lecture on 'Ancient Irish Law' delivered on 25 February 1942 was one of nine public lectures organised by the College on the theme of Irish history and literature and given between November 1941 and February 1942. A second talk by Binchy on the topic of 'Social life in early Ireland' followed in a second series of such lectures given over the winter of 1944–5.[99]

We can glimpse something of Binchy at this juncture in his career in a vignette penned many years later by Thomas Finlay, the future Chief Justice. Finlay entered UCD in 1940, graduating with a BA in Legal and Political Science three years later. Binchy, as a lecturer, Finlay recalled,[100]

> was clear, wide-ranging and strongly intellectual. He successfully conveyed to his students his conviction of the importance of both his subjects, but particularly of Roman Law, to the interpretation and development of the common law.

An intriguing detail was appended.[101] Binchy apparently

> was a keen follower of the Ward Hunt and, at the appropriate time of the year, it was most reassuring at his Saturday morning lecture to see a pair of hunting boots peeping out below his gown as a guarantee of the punctual end of the lecture.

Binchy served on a committee of the UCD Academic Council which in the spring of 1943, at the request of Dr Conway, elected President in 1940, pondered the question of the employment of Irish as the medium of instruction in the College. In high dudgeon, a parent had written to Conway (in English) lambasting the fact that his progeny who were fluent in Irish would not be catered for linguistically – as they had a right, he argued, to require – at third level. Thus did the language question, which had been the focus of the earlier controversy over matriculation,[102] come back to haunt the College. At a special meeting of the Academic Council held to consider the entire question, Conway sought to bring matters to a swift conclusion by proposing that Irish should be the medium of instruction for courses in Mathematics, Latin, Greek, French and History, probably in addition to courses in Irish itself. This dramatic proposal was shot down, 10 members of the Council voting for and 17 against. The upshot was a decision to set up a committee, on which Binchy was to serve, which a little later brought forward a set of suggestions much more limited than those Conway had embraced. Courses through Irish would be mounted in Modern Irish, First Year French and some elements in the H Dip Ed. Liaison with the other constituent Colleges of the NUI followed, and this and other developments resulted in demands for yet another report on the entire question

– tackling its motivation and setting forth detailed proposals – to be redrafted. At this point, the Professor of Roman Law, Jurisprudence and Legal History bows out. Whether out of pique or otherwise, Binchy was to let it be known that he would refuse to return to the Academic Council's committee to redraft any report.[103]

In 1946, Binchy resigned from UCD on being elected to a Senior Research Fellowship at Corpus Christi College in Oxford. The formal letter of resignation, addressed to the President Dr Conway, strikes a note of graciousness which recalls to mind that of Murnaghan in 1924. 'I have been a Professor in University College for over 20 years', Binchy wrote,[104]

> and throughout that time I have been treated with the utmost kindness and consideration by my superiors and my colleagues.

'May I', he went on, 'be permitted, then to tender to you, Sir, and to the authorities of the College the assurance of my deep gratitude?'

Conway, in response, extended his warmest congratulations, tingeing that with an expression of regret that the College was losing 'one of its most distinguished professors' and being deprived 'of the counsel of one who has given outstanding service to the well-being of the College'.[105] Conway repeated the sentiments in his *Report for 1945–46*.[106] Conway, a mathematician, had spent part of his student years in Corpus Christi, as it chanced, and it was this college that was linked to both Vinogradoff and Plummer. It was at Corpus Christi that by 1948 the seemingly thankless task of transcription of source material for the *Corpus Iuris* began in earnest. Two years later that work was to be continued in Dublin when Binchy was made Senior Professor in the School of Celtic Studies at the new Dublin Institute for Advanced Studies. The institute had been set up by statute in 1940 'to supplement work that cannot under the pressure of modern conditions be given full attention in the universities'.[107] Though the enabling legislation envisaged a number of research schools being attached to the institute, only one has been added (for Cosmic Physics) to the two, for Celtic Studies and for Theoretical Physics, recognised by the original Act of the Oireachtas.[108] Binchy was to serve as Senior Professor in the School of Celtic Studies until retirement in 1975.

Binchy's first major foray into print in areas that are germane here came in 1936, with an essay on the legal capacity of women in early Irish law.[109] Two years later he published the text of *Bretha Crólige*, the tract on sick maintenance (*orthrus*), accompanying this with his own commentary.[110] *Bretha Crólige* was found in the Phillipps MSS, then recently acquired by the National Library of Ireland and buried among this collection with its focus on medical matters. Allusions to the tortfeasor's obligation to provide sick maintenance were to be found in the *Táin Bó Cúailnge,* where Cuchulainn, addressing Tuachell mac

Nechtan, told him, 'He shall never have house of healing from me; I'll kill him outright'; and, equally suggestively, in chapter 21 of *Exodus*:[111]

> If people quarrel and one strikes the other a blow with stone or fist so that the injured party, though not dead, is confined to bed, but later recovers and can go about, even with a stick, the one who struck the blow will have no liability, other than to compensate the injured party for the enforced inactivity and to take care of the injured party until the cure is complete.

The first paragraph in Binchy's Sir John Rhys memorial lecture of 1943, read before the British Academy in the midst of war on 24 November 1943,[112] began provocatively – the provocation being entirely warranted – before its author got down to the nitty gritty. 'It is a moot point', Binchy began,[113]

> whether the reputation of native Irish law has suffered more at the hands of its enemies or its admirers … On the one hand, those who directed the policy of forcibly incorporating Ireland in the English legal and political system – from Edward I, 'the English Justinian', in the thirteenth century to Sir John Davies in the seventeenth – maintained a continuous barrage of abuse against the 'lewd customs hateful to God', which were 'so contrary to all law that they ought not to be deemed laws'. On the other hand, the reaction of nationalist writers in a later age, though in some degree justified, has been pushed to equally fantastic extremes.

At which point Binchy goes on to castigate the author of *The Ancient Land Tenures of Ireland*[114] for speaking of the laws of early Ireland as ones

> which for their justice and humanity have been a source of wonder to modern research students in the province of legal and social science.[115]

The piece of scholarship produced by Binchy over his long career which has had the widest circulation and is, therefore, perhaps, the best known, is his essay on the secular institutions of early Irish society, which began life as a radio broadcast in 1953.[116] Here Binchy commenced with an apposite quotation from J.B. Bury, 'There are', Bury claimed in his inaugural lecture of 1903 in Cambridge,[117] and which Binchy repeats,

> few fields where more work is to be done or where labourers are more needed than the Celtic civilisation of Western Europe. In tracing from its origins the course of Western history in the Middle Ages, we are pulled up on the threshold by the uncertainties and obscurities that brood over the Celtic world.

'Fortunately', Binchy interrupts,[118]

> we are now able to offer more concrete evidence at least about the institutions that obtained in the extreme North-West corner of the Celtic-speaking world. This evidence survives in the old Irish law tracts, whose archaic and difficult language has at last begun to yield up its secrets.

There then follows a masterly synopsis of up-to-date thinking on quotidian life in early Irish society as reflected in the legal sources. It is a classic statement. 'It was', Binchy averred,

> a pattern of life that differed in almost every essential point from Irish society as we know it today. If you asked me to define its main characteristics, I should say that it was tribal, rural, hierarchical and familiar (using this word in its oldest sense, to mean a society in which the family, not the individual, is the unit) – a complete contrast to the unitary, urbanised, egalitarian and individualist society of our time.

The claim, asserted here, that the law tracts, once properly understood, would yield a flood of new knowledge was not accepted by everyone. A.P. Smyth's rejection of the argument, a rejection which clearly merited an airing, significantly was to serve as the opening target in Binchy's two-part retrospective memoir of 1975–6.[119] The broadcast of 1953 on secular institutions itself on no account deserves to be cavalierly dismissed. The quality of the research that informs it and the succinctness of the author's exposition puts it on a par with those other classic discussions of early Irish law and indeed of Celtic legalities generally – the Welsh as well as the Irish – from the likes of Thurneysen and MacNeill that you will find brought together in *Celtic Law Papers*.[120]

In these years Binchy had also earned attention and courted controversy by discussing at considerable length the problem of the historical St Patrick, an exercise which drew a detailed response and certain criticism from Francis Shaw.[121] One could hardly of course expect this particular cobbler to stick to his last.

The year 1970 saw not only the reprint of *Church and State in Fascist Italy* but also the publication of Binchy's O'Donnell lecture of 1967–8 on *Celtic and Anglo-Saxon Kingship*.[122] Binchy's career at the Dublin Institute was now approaching its end: it terminated with his retirement in 1975. He is to be glimpsed at work in this appreciative paragraph in the entry for him in the *Dictionary of Irish Biography*:[123]

> When conducting seminars at the Institute he was able to sustain a demanding level of seriousness. They were occasions that required

> extreme intellectual effort from participants and that promised significant discoveries about material of the highest difficulty. They attracted the best Irish scholars, professors as much as students, and the Institute scholars, who were called upon to translate, did so in front of an audience that would intimidate the most brash.

Binchy was a visiting professor at both Harvard University and the University of Wales. He received honorary doctorates from Wales, Rennes, Queen's Belfast and Dublin University.[124] His honorary doctorate from the National University of Ireland – an honorary D Celt Lit conferred in 1973 – meant he was the second professor of the UCD Law Faculty to be honoured in this fashion. Patrick McGilligan had been previously conferred with his honorary D Econ Sc in 1940. There is a list of his published work in volume 5 of the journal *Peritia* (1986), a volume named in his honour. It was to be three years after his retirement that the culmination of Binchy's life's work, the *Corpus Iuris Hibernici* was published under the aegis of the Dublin Institute. The six volumes, unlike the six of the old and oft-criticised *Ancient Laws of Ireland* (1868–1901), are accompanied by no English translations. Liam Breatnach now has produced an invaluable companion volume or guide.[125] The introduction to the first volume of the *Corpus* is written in English – all else throughout the six volumes is in Irish – and here in the introduction, towards the conclusion, Binchy takes leave of his subject by addressing a series of key questions to his readers. 'How far', Binchy asks,[126] 'do these legal records reflect existing conditions?' Again:

> How can the tribal society mirrored in them be reconciled with the testimony of the Annals or more or less contemporary literary works, in which powerful rulers and their kingdoms play such a leading role?

And this:

> Were the early jurists, too, like their successors 'backward-looking' …, their gaze still fixed on a dead past?

Again:

> How and why was the text of the tracts, with its different linguistic strata, definitely empanelled about the end of the seventh century?

These questions, Binchy concedes, would not be easily or quickly answered, going on to quote remarks of F.W. Maitland apropos Anglo-Saxon legal sources, remarks, which were, if anything, even more appropriate in relation to native

Irish law.[127] 'Many an investigator will leave his bones to bleach in that desert before it is accurately mapped'.

The place that Binchy occupied in Celtic studies is best exemplified perhaps by the list of the obituaries he wrote between 1940 and 1980. These encompassed a startlingly impressive roll-call. Rudolf Thurneysen, Osborn Bergin, R. I. Best, Gerard Murphy, Carl Mastrander, Myles Dillon, Eleanor Knott and Cecile O'Rahilly. He also furnished the entry on Eoin MacNeill for the *Dictionary of National Biography*,[128] as well as contributing to a collection of essays devoted to this 'scholar revolutionary'.[129]

Breatnach, in his companion to the *Corpus Iuris* expresses a few criticisms.[130] Not escaping unscathed either has been his essay on the so-called passing of the old order on the occasion of the Viking invasions.[131] Miscellaneous contributions to the journal linked to the UCD Law School, the *Irish Jurist* deserve a final mention.[132] As it happens, there was another service Binchy rendered his old *alma mater* from his redoubt at Corpus Christi College in Oxford in the late 1940s just prior to his appointment to the Dublin Institute for Advanced Studies. He was asked to offer his thoughts on the way forward for legal studies in the UCD Law Faculty at a time when a new president, Michael Tierney, was being installed, and the entire question of the direction any structural changes for the Law School might take was being seriously canvassed probably for the first time since the College opened its doors in 1909. Binchy, as we have seen, was no novice in regard to matters of legal education.[133] On this occasion he responded with a paper which is printed in the volume of *Studies* for 1949.[134] The arguments presented by Binchy and by those who responded to his paper[135] – whose views are also to be found in the same volume of *Studies* – are best dealt with in a separate chapter.[136] It will suffice here to note that Binchy was critical of the calibre of the existing so-called Honours BA Degree in Legal and Political Science, and argued strongly for a more pronounced division between theoretical legal training and the practical, leaving it to a professional body such as King's Inns, to concern itself exclusively with the practical, run-of-the-mill subjects such as Contract, Tort, Real and Personal Property and Evidence. The President of the High Court, Mr Justice Gavan Duffy, disagreed. So, too, from a later generation of law teachers did Binchy's nephew, William Binchy, regius professor at Trinity College, Dublin. In a piece published in 2011,[137] William Binchy took particular exception to this passage in 'The law and the universities', where the author had stigmatised torts as a

> so-called 'practical subjec[t] which clutters up the [law degree] course [and which] of [its] very nature [is] quite unsuitable for conditioning the youthful mind … [N]ot even the most stimulating lecturer can make bricks without water. The subject-matter … simply does not provide the necessary instrumentum pedagogicum'.[138]

The side of the argument that, back in 1949, Gavan Duffy represented was the one which over time was to prevail, as is clear from an examination of the structure of the College's new Bachelor of Civil Law course which was introduced in the mid-1950s. It is just possible that Daniel Binchy interpreted this reverse – undoubtedly a personal defeat – as evidence for the university, possibly the universities, having lost their way. A throwaway remark in the Introduction he penned for the *Corpus Iuris Hibernici* could be seen perhaps to constitute the views not only of a disappointed scholar but also of a pessimist. Straightaway in that introduction, Binchy intrudes the problem of reconstructing individual law tracts 'from isolated brocards scattered at random' throughout the pages of his new 6-volume *Corpus Iuris.*[139] There then follows this thought, enclosed in parentheses. 'Here', Binchy avers,[140] 'is a task for future students of Irish law, should there be any room for such specialised research in the Ireland of tomorrow'.

Mercifully, Binchy's penchant for straight talking could on occasion have its humorous or mischievous side. Take this passage, for instance, on the contrasting styles of annalists over the centuries when marking the obit or death notice of some ecclesiastical celebrity:[141]

> At any time down to the twelfth century the *obit* … of an ecclesiastic would read simply: 'The rest of A. B.', or 'A. B. rested in Christ'. Now listen to the *obit* of … Cathal MacManus Maguire, the compiler of the *Annals of Ulster*, who died in 1498:[142]
>
> Grievous news throughout all Ireland this year: the death of MacManus Maguire, Cathal son of Cathal, etc., tenant of (the castle of) Seanad, canon choral in Armagh and in Clogher, dean of Loch Erne, parson of Inis Cáin, and diocesan vicar for fifteen years before his death: the precious stone, the glowing gem, the shining star, treasure-store of wisdom, clustered branch of Scripture, fount of charity, meekness and leniency; a dove in purity of heart, a turtle in chastity; one who most deserved thanks from the poetic schools, the strangers and the needy orphans of Ireland; one who to the day of his death was full of grace and learning in every subject, law and divinity, science and philosophy', etc.

Binchy comments: 'You may well think that this is carrying rather too far the principle *De mortuis nil nisi bonum'*. It is not an inappropriate point at which to take leave of the man correctly hailed by Morfydd E. Owen as 'one of the giants of Celtic scholarship'.[143]

MICHAEL JOSEPH RYAN (1890–1952)

The death of Swift MacNeill in August 1926 created the vacancy that, eventually, Michael Joseph Ryan was to fill, thus beginning an association with the Law School and its professoriate which was remarkable on any count. Ryan remained in office until his death in the autumn of 1952, having held in succession two different chairs in the school – Constitutional Law and the Law of Public and Private Wrongs, 1927–34; and Law of Property, Common Law and Equity, 1934–52.

On MacNeill's death the Academic Council advised that no changes needed to be made in the terms of the vacant chair[144] and the Governing Body moved swiftly to arrange for the lectures MacNeill might have been expected to deliver to be shared between the two surviving professors, Clery and Binchy, each of whom was to be given an honorarium of £41 13*s.* 4*d.*, for their labours as stand-ins for Michaelmas term 1926 and again another honorarium for the period from 1 April to 12 May 1927 (£19 4*s.* 7*d.* each).[145]

The advertisement for the vacancy attracted two candidates: Conor Maguire, who was to become, successively, attorney-general, judge and later President of the High Court, and Chief Justice; and Ryan. The Academic Council, having reviewed the credentials of both candidates, pronounced that both were qualified, but that Ryan was 'better qualified academically'[146] – a verdict that was both understandable and unremarkable for, whereas Maguire could boast only an MA and an LLB, Ryan was the proud holder of a Bachelor's degree in Arts, in Science and in Engineering as well as the possessor of an LLB. At the vote in the Governing Body, Ryan received 20 ballots, Maguire but 2. The Governing Body thus recommended the appointment of Ryan, a recommendation the NUI Senate was happy to endorse.[147]

As we have seen, the death of Arthur Clery in November 1932 occasioned a rethink by the two remaining professors, Binchy and Ryan, on the division of teaching responsibilities among Law's professoriate and for changes in the titles of the chairs.[148] We have already discussed the implications for Binchy of the changes signalled by Statute XIX which came into force in the spring of 1934.[149] Ryan had succeeded MacNeill as Professor of Constitutional Law and the Law of Public and Private Wrongs. Under the new dispensation, introduced in 1934, changes had been made in the terms of the chair held by Clery, that of the Law of Property and the Law of Contracts. That chair was now to be designated the professorship of Property, Common Law and Equity, and it was this chair to which Ryan sought to be appointed in the spring of 1934, switching thus from Constitutional Law and the sundry other legal subjects to which that topic was attached.

Precisely why Ryan opted to volunteer his services in notably different areas of expertise is not easy to fathom. Under Statute XIX, both the Constitutional

Law chair and the Law of Property chair, unlike Binchy's chair of Roman Law, Jurisprudence and Legal History, remained part-time, but between the two of them Statute XIX drew a remarkable distinction. The stipend was fixed at £350 for the Constitutional Law chair (Constitutional Law, International Law and Criminal Law), but it was set £100 higher at £450 for the chair of Property, Common Law and Equity.[150] That Ryan, understandably, could have been attracted by a higher level of remuneration is almost certainly the case: would he have been human if he hadn't been? To what extent, if at all, the two professors in the Law School had been in cahoots to secure an outcome favourable to Ryan when the terms of Statute XIX were first projected, again must remain a mystery.

For Ryan to have been attracted by the prospect of a higher level of pay (if, indeed, that was the explanation for his decision to apply for the chair of the Law of Property, etc.) was at the time thoroughly understandable, for, as it happens, the vacancy occasioned by Clery's death coincided with a period of government cutbacks, which was to result in a reduction of three per cent in a fair number of salaries paid by the College in the year 1933–4.[151] The early summer of 1933 caused ructions in all three Colleges of the NUI when, under the terms of the new Fianna Fáil government's Public Services (Temporary Economies) Bill, it was sought to interfere directly with the autonomy of each College by forcing reductions in the pay of all office-holders. The authorities in the three Colleges protested, drew up a memorandum of opposition and lobbied the then Minister for Finance, Sean MacEntee.[152] The government backtracked and proposed instead that there would be a reduction in each College's block grant, thus leaving it to the individual Colleges to decide how to effect the necessary economies.[153] The Colleges' victory, therefore, has to be adjudged, unequivocally, a Pyrrhic one. A few quotations from the Memorandum drawn up at the behest of the three Colleges by Professors O'Rahilly and Tierney will serve here to demonstrate the strength of feeling over the entire issue that this plan, hatched in 1933, was to arouse. Their detailed protest was prefaced, O'Rahilly and Tierney argued,[154]

> by an emphatic expression of our amazement that before entering upon an enterprise of such far-reaching importance for Irish Catholic education, a Government composed of Irishmen, and having at its head the Chancellor of the National University,[155] has not seen fit to invite even the briefest discussion with the authorities of the Colleges concerned.
>
> ...
>
> We brand as despotic and dangerous the principle of this innovation which, had it been enacted by the British Government, would have been denounced with ferocity by the whole country.[156]
>
> ...

> We reiterate our fixed conviction that to attempt to reduce University salaries by any form of Government action is at once an unwarrantable interference with that autonomy which is our most precious attribute, a reactionary infringement of the principle upon which Irish Catholic higher education rests, and must continue to rest if it is to exist, and a flagrant injustice to a profession which least deserves and can least easily bear such unlooked-for treatment.[157]

As already explained, the Government withdrew its original plans, but proposed instead, as the Department of Finance explained to Dr Coffey in March 1934 would take place, a reduction in the block grant.[158] There was to be a sting in the tail, however, for quite independently, the government proposed, as a condition of an increase in the grant to fund new posts in the Department of Irish, that a qualification in Irish would be mandatory for students presenting for any degrees in the future. The Government decision, relayed to Coffey in January 1934,[159] led the latter to send the draft bill containing this precise proposal to Ryan, still just the Professor of Constitutional Law and the Law of Public and Private Wrongs, for his legal advice. With talk of the invasion of autonomy being so much in the air because of the conflict over the original proposals contained in the Public Services (Temporary Economies) Bill, it was predictable that Ryan, in his considered opinion, should tackle that point head-on. 'There is not anything in the draft Bill', Ryan advised,[160]

> which directly or indirectly limits the autonomy of the College as granted by the said Act of 1908 and the said Charter and Statutes.
>
> ...
>
> It appears to me, however, that in the event of the College failing to make provision by regulation or otherwise to secure that no person should, with certain exceptions, unless he has previously passed an oral examination in the Irish language, be permitted to present himself for any degree examination in the College the grant would not be payable. The function of the Minister for Education appears to me to be limited merely to an advisory function and does not extend to any interference with the College as to the standard of the oral examination in Irish, or the competency of the Professors, Lecturers or Assistants in the teaching of the language.

The University College Dublin Act, introducing the special grant for posts in the Irish Department, and attaching the requirement that students presenting for their degree should have passed an oral examination in the language, became law on 19 July 1934.[161] Intriguingly, the Governing Body was made to accept that no deductions were to be made in the salaries funded out of this increase in the grant.[162]

With Statute XIX in force, UCD sought to fill Clery's old chair which was now designated Property, Common Law and Equity, the chair to which Ryan sought the appointment. Five candidates applied, in addition to Ryan himself: Kevin Dixon, who became attorney-general in 1942, and served as a judge of the High Court from 1946 to 1959; Joseph S. Geraghty, who had previously applied, unsuccessfully, for the chair Binchy was appointed to in 1924; P.J. McEnery, who was to practise at the English Bar from 1940; Frederick J. Mangan; and Ashley Powell, at the time Reid Professor in Trinity College and joint author of *A Manual of Egyptian Arabic*, published in Cairo in 1926.

At the meeting of the Academic Council in June 1934 where the question of the candidate to fill the post was debated, Binchy, still himself just the Professor of Roman Law and Jurisprudence, proposed and Professor Magennis, the Professor of Metaphysics, seconded, that Ryan should get the job as 'the candidate who was outstanding in teaching and practical legal experience'.[163] In compliance with custom the Governing Body held two votes. At the first vote the following result was declared: Ryan 20; Mangan 7; Dixon 1; McEnery 1. No one voted for the Trinity man and Arabic scholar. At the second vote, Ryan received 22 ballots and Mangan six. The Governing Body resolved to send all the names recorded in the first vote and the result of the second vote.[164] At its July meeting the NUI Senate approved the appointment of Ryan.[165]

Ryan would appear to have been the effective successor to Murnaghan in the matter of advising the NUI Senate on legal matters and, on occasion, of drafting University Statutes. He was to join forces with Gavan Duffy, SC, in offering an opinion on the operation of section 3 of the University College Galway Act 1929,[166] which obliged that College to appoint to posts in the College, among candidates adjudged suitable, the candidate best able to lecture through the medium of Irish.[167] The question had arisen on the occasion of a vacancy in the chair of English Language and English Literature. The planned establishment of an NUI Appointments Bureau – to assist graduates to obtain employment – was queried on the basis that it might not have been allowed under the Charter. This problem winged its way to Ryan in 1935.[168] The following year another matter of in-house business was sent to Ryan for his advice – the question of the salary of the NUI Registrar, following the death of McGrath's successor, Dr F.H. Wiber.[169] In 1937 Ryan was asked to pronounce on the legality of a grant to St Patrick's College, Maynooth, via a union of students, to support publication of their work.[170] The same year and at the same time the issue began to be canvassed as to whether a new Statute would be required to prescribe the qualifications for the appointment of the new NUI Registrar. This was another question on which Ryan was invited to pronounce.[171]

In 1938, Ryan was able to confirm to the Senate that the question of gratuities in favour of the widows of two recently deceased professors was effectively covered in the appropriate Statute,[172] and in the following year, in regard to the

Visitorship to the University, that it would be worthwhile to make it abundantly clear that the relevant functions attaching to the Visitor were now exercisable by or on the authority of the Government, quoting Article 49 of the new Constitution.[173] Here it is worth noting that Ryan had liaised with Philip O'Donoghue in the office of the Attorney-General. Some uncertainty was to attach to the holding of a meeting of the Senate in April 1940 to proceed to the appointment of a successor to Dr Coffey as President of UCD – the meeting that was to anoint Dr Conway – and legal advice was sought. In a joint opinion, Ryan and Cecil Lavery, SC, advised that the Senate was competent to proceed to make the appointment on the chosen day.[174]

In his history of UCD Donal McCartney was to draw attention to at least one further occasion, besides that on which Ryan had advised Dr Coffey on the legality of what became the University College Dublin Act 1934,[175] where Ryan proffered advice to the College authorities. This was in 1947 when it became clear, following the retirement of Dr Conway as President, that there would be a contest for the succession.[176] This was unprecedented so far as the short history of the College was concerned, for the transition in 1940 from Coffey to Conway had been comparatively, if not completely, smooth. How exactly the Governing Body, who would be obliged to forward the names of suitable candidates to the NUI Senate, should go about its business was the problem. James N. Meenan, the Acting President during the Interregnum, consulted Ryan, and his advice on the procedure to be followed was then adopted.[177]

This was a role that Ryan, much more than any of the law professors, with the possible exception of Murnaghan, was regularly asked to discharge. And neither in Murnaghan's case, nor in his own, ought this role to be downplayed. Taking matters in chronological order, Ryan early in 1938 acted as the legal assessor at the election of graduates to serve on the Governing Body: for this he earned £5.[178] Later the same year he was asked to advise on the legality of a payment it was proposed to make out of Arthur Clery's residuary estate. A Robert Kirby, the surviving executor of Arthur Clery's will, had gone to considerable trouble to wind up Clery's estate in the United States. What was intended as an *ex gratia* payment, it was nonetheless felt by the Governing Body, should receive Ryan's acquiescence, which was duly signalled.[179] What appears to have caused much more trouble was the question of whether the College should join the University of Salamanca in Spain to match funds provided under the Cunningham Trusts so as to promote student exchanges. There had been hostility on the Governing Body at the outset to the College getting involved at all – because of the drain on sparse enough College resources; and it seems probable that when Salamanca announced in the summer of 1940 that it was withdrawing from involvement on account of the difficulty it was encountering in acquiring the necessary foreign currency, an announcement that led to UCD withdrawing as well, a number of persons on the Governing Body will have heaved a collective sigh of relief.

Ryan's advice and correspondence during a series of protracted exchanges will doubtless have been found of considerable assistance.[180]

The transition from Coffey to Conway in 1940, as explained above, may have been relatively smooth, for Coffey, as retiring President, had left little to chance by calling in aid Ryan to advise on managing the procedure for the choice of his successor[181] – a precedent, doubtless, that James N. Meenan was happy to repeat in the much more difficult circumstances in 1947, when the successor to Conway had to be identified.[182] Back in 1940, doubtless to avoid personal embarrassment, Coffey made use of Ryan to handle the explanation to the Governing Body of the pension and gratuity entitlements of a retiring President.[183] There was to be a single occasion when a considered legal opinion tendered to the College authorities by Ryan generated controversy. This occurred in the spring of 1940 at the first meeting of the Governing Body being chaired by Dr Conway as Acting President.[184] At this meeting Professor O'Kiely had sought to move the following motion: 'Eolas oilte ar an nGaedhilg d'áireamh ar cháilíochtaibh riachtanais Uactaráin an Choláiste Ollscoile, Baile Átha Cliath', or, in the second official language: 'That a skilled knowledge of the Irish language be deemed one of the qualifications necessary for the President of University College, Dublin'. Conway, however, ruled the motion out of order, relying expressly, so he told the Governing Body, on advice furnished by Ryan. Ryan, the note of what transpired in the record of the Governing Body proceedings tells us, had relied on the Charter and Statutes,[185] but that modest amount of enlightenment did not satisfy a vociferous faction on the Governing Body who then proposed a motion that Ryan's legal advice should be circulated. This motion, however, was lost, those voting for it 9 and against 12. O'Kiely's original proposal was then put to the vote as well, but it, too, was lost on a vote of 8 for, and 12 against.[186] A few weeks later, as it chanced, a proposal to enact a Statute to the effect that the College's Registrar should also have Irish was also narrowly defeated: those voting 'for' 10 and 'against' 11. On this occasion the Governing Body did, however, adopt a rubric to the effect that it was desirable that the Registrar should be competent in Irish.[187] This had become a live issue, for, following Conway's accession to be President, the office of Registrar had naturally become vacant.

The NUI Senate continued likewise to seek advice from Ryan. In 1942, for instance, he was called to explain and advise on the functions of the Irish Universities Committee recognised by section 18(1) in the 1908 Irish Universities Act.[188]

Aside from his toil as an unpaid legal advisor, Ryan, like Murnaghan and Clery before him, was to supplement his income from the College for his work in the drafting of College Statutes; for work on Statutes XXIV and XXV he earned 12 guineas; for that on Statute XXVI, 7 guineas.[189]

Ryan continued to act as legal advisor to Coffey's successors as President and to the Governing Body. In 1944 he was asked to draft a clause for inclusion in a forthcoming College Statute empowering a President approaching retirement to appoint a Deputy or Acting President to make arrangements for the succession;[190] the contested succession in 1947 demonstrated that this was a prudent move. In 1945 advice was tendered on what was by no means a rare occurrence – a problem of pension entitlement.[191] Two years later Ryan found himself appointed to a Governing Body sub-committee pondering whether the College had the power to introduce a scheme of compulsory mass X-rays for students in the battle against tuberculosis, and to exclude students from the College who suffered from an infectious disease. The outcome here was the introduction of a voluntary scheme of mass X-rays.[192] In 1949, Ryan tussled with a problem of the wording in part of a draft Statute contemplating the inauguration of a chair in Medieval History.[193] Discussions the same year of the implications for the College of the slander action brought against the President Dr Tierney by the student Kirkwood Hackett[194] found Ryan urging that, for purposes of indemnifying the President, a Statute might be required.[195] Ryan was to be proved correct in one opinion he expressed at the time: Tierney would win any appeal to the Supreme Court.[196] Ryan was of counsel for Tierney[197] when the case came before the Supreme Court in February and March 1950. The majority decision allowing Tierney's appeal was announced on 18 May 1950. The last occasion upon which Ryan tendered legal advice to UCD came a year later when he argued that, if the College desired to provide pensions for its retired porters, attendants and cleaners, a new Statute would be necessary.[198]

Alfred O'Rahilly served as President of University College Cork from 1943 to 1954. In a piece he contributed to *Studies* in the early 1960s O'Rahilly revealed that he, too, had sought legal advice from Ryan.[199] This concerned a plan hatched in Cork during his presidency to introduce a new course in Catholic apologetics. Would this be legal, given the language of section 3(1) of the 1908 Irish Universities Act? O'Rahilly tells us Ryan thought not. 'A preference on the ground of religious belief', which the sub-section proscribed, would have been involved. O'Rahilly was disenchanted with this advice, and went on to obtain an opinion at complete odds with that of Ryan, from another Senior Counsel, Richard McGonigal, and this he sets out *in extenso*.[200]

Serving, along with Clery, as a stand-in for Binchy while the latter acted as Irish envoy in Berlin, earned extra money for Ryan.[201] So too, did the period from late 1932, when with Binchy now returned, the two delivered the lectures that it would have fallen to the now-deceased Clery to deliver.[202] Ryan was again to 'stand in' for Binchy from late 1946, following the latter's move to Oxford and his resignation. Dr Conway, as President, was to report to the Governing Body that Binchy's workload had been split in two, Ryan being deputed to cover lectures in Jurisprudence and Legal History at a rate of £300 per annum, until a successor was in post.[203] The next year 1947, saw an increase in Ryan's salary as a part-time professor from £450 per annum to £540 per annum.[204]

Ryan died on 24 October 1952. Tierney, in his *President's Report for 1951–1952*,[205] paid tribute to what had been a remarkable career: graduating with a Bachelor's degree from no less than four different faculties – Science, Engineering, Arts and Law; an auditor and gold medallist at the L & H; John Brooke scholar at King's Inns; a teacher of mathematics at Knockbeg College; a temporary Circuit Court judge and Land Settlement Commissioner; secretary to the Compensation (Ireland) Commission; and, finally, Reid professor at Trinity College between 1921 and 1925 before joining the Law professoriate at UCD in 1927. From 1944 to 1948, too, he was also to represent the NUI Constituency on Seánad Éireann. 'An indefatigable worker especially in legal research', Tierney added, 'Ryan was also one of the kindest and most unassuming of men'.

For many years Ryan kept in touch with student affairs by virtue of his role as treasurer to the Literary and Historical Society, a role he discharged until his death. Ryan's style in the lecture theatre, it needs to be recorded, did not, however, apparently earn universal plaudits from the generations of law students under his charge. Thomas Finlay, the future Chief Justice, discerned merit in Ryan's approach even so. Ryan's lecturing method, Finlay later recalled,[206]

> was simple and unvaried. He slowly read paragraphs from a recognised and reputable textbook, spelling some of the more difficult words and almost all words occurring in a foreign language. He never commented on the text nor developed its content by example or otherwise … but fortunately he set his exams by it.

PATRICK MCGILLIGAN (1889–1979)

Patrick McGilligan, appointed to the freshly designated chair of Constitutional Law, International Law and Criminal Law in 1934, had had a long association with both the College and the National University. Born in 1889, he had matriculated in the old Royal University before graduating BA in Classics in UCD in 1910. He obtained an MA, in which he had concentrated on the theory and practice of education. A further qualification earned was an H Dip Ed. He won the gold medal in oratory at the Literary and Historical Society in 1912, and served as chairman of the Classical Society too at this time. In 1918, he became an Assistant to the Professor of Latin, thus acquiring some experience as a university lecturer. In 1921, he was called to the Bar, emerging the same year as a Victoria Prizeman. Elected in 1919 by Convocation to sit on the NUI Senate,[207] McGilligan pressed for, and secured, a re-ordering of the format of the *NUI Calendar*.[208] He served on the Senate until 1934.

In a number of other respects McGilligan was no neophyte. In 1922 he worked as a secretary to Kevin O'Higgins, following that up the ensuing year as a secretary to James McNeill, the recently appointed Irish Free State High Commissioner in London. In November 1923 he was elected a TD, and served in Dáil Éireann until 1965. In 1924, he became the Minister for Industry and Commerce, combining the portfolio with that of External Affairs, until going out of office in 1932. He was the Minister responsible for the Shannon Hydro-electric Scheme and played a key role in the establishment of the ESB (Electricity Supply Board).

McGilligan's hands-on approach to matters falling within his ministerial responsibilities in these years is best demonstrated in his level-headed response to a cry for help from the railway lobbyists seeking government assistance in the continuing battle with road transport. McGilligan's reaction to Edward MacLysaght's plea on behalf of the financially threatened railways amounted to a detailed rebuttal of certain of the claims pressed on him as Minister on behalf of the railways, of the Great Southern Railway Company (with its pay roll of 14,000) in particular. These exchanges saw it into print in 1932[209] at the end of McGilligan's first period in office (1927–32), a period, some would have it, that represented the apogee of his political career. It is of this period that Harkness was to write, heaping praise on McGilligan:[210]

> At home, power and light were brought to factory and cottage as the country emerged from the neglect of centuries and the ravages of recent civil war; abroad, at the League of Nations, and within the comity of an emerging Commonwealth of Nations, Ireland's status and international identity was assured and enhanced.

The referees who supported McGilligan's application for the UCD chair in 1934 included, predictably perhaps, both Coffey the College's President and Hugh Kennedy, the Chief Justice. Less predictable, perhaps, were letters of support from two Commonwealth premiers, R.B. Bennett from Canada and J.P.M. Herzog from South Africa.

The two law professors already in post in 1934, and who were to make their recommendation on filling the vacancy – Binchy and Ryan – left the Academic Council in no doubt as to who was the right person to choose, among a total of five candidates. They did so in a report carefully preserved in the College muniments. 'The School of Law', Binchy and Ryan write,[211]

> growing as it is, needs at this stage the best trained ability in its Professional Chairs. The students of the Faculty of Law require all the assistance which their Professors can give to enable them to reach the highest possible attainment in the several subjects of the Faculty, and consequently no person who is not a master of his subject in every sense

of the word is worthy of appointment to a Chair of Law in University College.

They continue:[212]

> We have considered carefully the Applications of the five candidates for the vacant Professorship, and we have no doubt that Mr McGilligan stands out from the other candidates in his proved ability, his special qualifications and great experience, an experience which has brought him into contact in public life with Statesmen and Jurists of many countries in the practical handling of questions of Constitutional and International Law and their development. He is a practising Barrister; he had had a distinguished University career; he has been a Victoria Prizeman at King's Inns and has had experience of University teaching. His great energy and industry and his brilliancy of mind have long been known in University College. We have no hesitation in recommending Mr. McGilligan for appointment to the vacant Professorship.

Thomas Finlay, the future Chief Justice, writing in 1999 and describing his sojourn in the Law Faculty when taught by McGilligan, leaves one in no doubt that the decision to appoint McGilligan in 1934, tempered as it was to the needs of the Faculty at the time, had been well-deserved. Politics in McGilligan's case, Finlay reflected,[213]

> may have remained his first love, but he brought to the study of law a lively and extremely sharp mind and a splendid capacity for critical analysis.

Finlay's encomium continued. McGilligan's lectures, he went on,[214]

> speedily delivered in the strong accent which he never lost, were arresting and highly informative. In 1936 and 1937, he had been opposed to a great number of the proposed provisions of the Constitution almost line by line in Dáil Éireann. He carried this critical analysis into his constitutional law lectures and whether you agreed with him or not, this made his lectures vivid and interesting.

McGilligan had shone as a classicist in his undergraduate days, going on, as we have seen, to become an Assistant to the Professor of Latin. It was hardly unexpected then, when, on the occurrence of Binchy's resignation in 1946 and of the need to cover for Binchy's lectures until a successor was appointed, that McGilligan should have been asked to assume responsibility for Roman Law. Dr

Conway, as President, made the announcement in the autumn of 1946, indicating that McGilligan, like Ryan – who would be discharging the other half of Binchy's duties – would receive extra payment at the rate of £230 per annum until an appointed successor was in post – something that finally took place late in 1948. A Statute, adopted by the College in the intervening year of 1947, signalled an increase in his ordinary stipend from £350 *per annum* to £420 *per annum*.[215]

Like Ryan, Clery and Murnaghan before him, McGilligan was asked to tender legal advice to the Governing Body on a number of questions, but this occurred with nothing like the frequency that had previously obtained – a development that would appear, with the benefit of hindsight, to presage a change in the perception of what the Law professoriate was for. He was asked in 1957 to advise on the acceptability of a proposed endowed chair in Industrial Microbiology,[216] and, a few months later, on another problem linked to a pension entitlement.[217] He also served as an assessor at a Governing Body election in 1956. From 1955 onwards his tenure as Professor of Constitutional Law was regularly annually extended until retirement age was finally reached. In 1959, Tierney made him an Acting Professor in his seventy-first year, which entailed he continued to hold office – at that advanced age, if only for one more year.[218] Later the same year he was asked to represent the College's position along with H.J. Moloney, SC, at the Visitation obtained, at the instigation of John Kenny, in protest at the College's appointments strategy. The year before, the NUI Senate availed of his legal services in the case of the earlier Visitation procured by Séamus Henchy, McGilligan's professorial colleague.[219]

A curious incident occurring much earlier in McGilligan's career sheds light on that career so far as the understanding of modern Irish constitutional law is concerned. Many years before, Patrick McGilligan had been scheduled to give a lecture in the Physics Theatre, Earlsfort Terrace, as part of the programme of public lectures open to the public in the session 1947–8. The lecture sanctioned by the Governing Body and as advertised in the Dublin press late in 1947, was scheduled for 10 March 1948.[220] However, the lecture was destined never to be delivered. The de Valera Government fell in the interval. A Coalition administration was formed, and McGilligan went off to become Minister for Finance in the First Inter-Party Government. Postponement of the lecture, which became, in effect, a cancellation, was announced on 23 February.[221]

This non-event was to be recalled by Mr Justice Barrington in his contribution to a special issue of the journal *Administration* to mark fifty years of the adoption of the 1937 Constitution.[222] McGilligan had chosen as the title for his lecture a phrase taken from a letter of Lord Macaulay written in 1857 to Henry S. Randall, author of a biography of Thomas Jefferson, that made disparaging remarks about the United States Constitution: 'Your Constitution: All Sail and No Anchor'.[223]

Barrington found the title for a talk that was never delivered true enough in an Irish context, for it effectively captured the attitude towards the Constitution at the time. 'To change the metaphor', Barrington wrote in his piece in *Administration*, 'there was a general feeling that the Constitution was a broken reed'. He offered this explanation:[224]

> This feeling resulted in part from the decision of the Supreme Court on the reference to it of the Offences against the State (Amendment) Bill 1940.[225] The Supreme Court in that case had, in effect, held that a person was deprived of his personal liberty 'in accordance with law' if he was deprived of it in accordance with an Act of the Oireachtas not otherwise repugnant to the Constitution. It also held that the guarantee of personal rights contained in Article 40.3 was a general guarantee extending to all the citizens and that the task of deciding how the rights of the individual citizen were to be reconciled with the rights of the community at large was a matter for the Oireachtas rather than for the courts.

From the approach that the Supreme Court had embraced, Barrington drew this sombre inference. 'On this line of interpretation', he contended,

> it is difficult to see how the Constitution was going to protect the citizen against abuse of power by the legislature.[226]

McGilligan's political adversaries drew the inference from his choice of title that he was intent on attacking the Constitution of 1937, no venial transgression in the Fianna Fáil rule book.[227] It would seem more probable however, that his plan, rather, was to press for a robust invigoration of the document. That is certainly how John Kelly would have viewed it. Consider this passage, for instance, from Kelly's preface to *The Irish Constitution*. 'Of the twenty-one judges' sitting in the High and Supreme Courts – Kelly is writing in 1980:

> seventeen learned constitutional law from Patrick McGilligan (Professor at University College, Dublin, from 1934 to 1959 simultaneously with a brilliant political career) who believed strongly in vigorous judicial review.[228] Thus the judicial arm of the Irish State contained within the short stretch of sixty years both judges who were willing to assent to the doctrine of automatic implicit amendment of the Constitution by ordinary legislation; and judges who, a few years ago, evoked from a Taoiseach (Mr Jack Lynch) the comment that 'it would be a brave man who would predict, these days, what was or was not contrary to the Constitution', so adventurous have the courts become.[229]

McGilligan was involved as counsel in one key constitutional adjudication – in 1961. He was on the team representing Senator John O'Donovan in the latter's successful challenge to legislation which had allowed for an uneven spread of seats for Dáil Éireann among the population.[230] The contention that the Electoral (Amendment) Act of 1959[231] had failed to respect the requirement of Article 16.2.3 of the Constitution that the ratio of members to population should 'so far as it is practicable be the same throughout the country' certainly seemed to be conclusively established:[232]

> While the national average ratio was one Deputy per 20,197 people, the constituency of Dublin South (West) contained 23,128 people per Deputy, while the constituency of Galway South contained only 16,575 people per Deputy.

The two constituencies in question represented the two extremes.

Mr Justice Budd, whose task it became in the High Court to resolve this particular conundrum, had been invited to accept the principle of 'western tolerance':[233]

> It was pointed out that on the western seaboard particularly the indented coastline, large sparsely-populated areas, mountains and other geographical considerations gave rise to difficulties of communication and thus made it hard for constituents to see their deputies and for deputies to serve their constituents properly.

He was not persuaded:[234]

> Dublin deputies have different problems to attend to from those in the West, but I remain unconvinced that by and large they have not as great calls on their time as at least some of their western colleagues.

McGilligan is unusual among the Law School's serving professoriate in having been given an honorary degree by the National University.[235] It had been projected to bestow a similar honour on Swift MacNeill but, as we have seen,[236] death supervened and the project was never carried out.

Early in 1940 it was mooted before the NUI Senate that McGilligan might be thus honoured for his 'pre-eminent services in the promotion and development of the Shannon Hydro-electric scheme',[237] a reference to the key role McGilligan had played in the realisation of this major infrastructural project as Minister for Industry and Commerce. McGilligan indicated his acceptance, and in March he was given the option of being conferred with an LLD or a D Econ Sc.[238] Honorary LLDs being two-a-penny, McGilligan, unsurprisingly, opted to become a D Econ Sc,[239] and that was the honorary degree with which he was conferred in July 1940.[240]

On Ryan's death in 1952, McGilligan and Henchy, Binchy's eventual successor, had been retained as stand-in lecturers for the areas left uncovered, at a rate of £270 *per annum*.[241] For his advisory and other work a number of other small payments were made.[242] Travel and subsistence costs were defrayed too, when, in 1951 – in what appears to be the first such claim presented by any of the Law staff – McGilligan attended the 3rd International Congress of Social Defence in San Marino (though not before an explanation was tendered to the Governing Body by Tierney – and accepted – as to what 'social defence' was about).[243] McGilligan himself served for a while on the Governing Body, being elected to it in 1944.[244] He sat in Dáil Éireann, as previously rehearsed, until 1965. His recollections of Eoin MacNeill, as regards the latter's role in the Irish Boundary Commission, were relayed by him to a successor on the Law School's professoriate, Geoffrey Hand, as Hand was to explain in a key essay on MacNeill and the Commission.[245]

McGilligan died in 1979. Thirteen years earlier, the first volume of the relaunched *Irish Jurist* was dedicated to him.[246]

PATRICIO MCGILLIGAN
MVLTOS PER ANNOS APUD COLLEGIVM
VNIVERSITATIS DUBLINENSE IVRVM PROFESSORI INTERQVE
IVRISCONSVLTOS HIBERNICOS
PAN INGENIO QVAM VIGORE PRAECLARO
NECNON REIPVBLICAE NOSTRAE
EX QUO TEMPORE CONDITA EST FIRMISSIMO PRAESIDIO
HVNC FASCICVLUM
NVPER COLLEGAE ATQVE VSQUE AMICI
LIBENTISSIME DEDICANT

* * * *

Cameos of three students who graced the Law Faculty in these years of consolidation help once again to put flesh on the bones. Also meriting a mention is the re-establishment in the mid-1930s of a society for law students, designated on this occasion simply the Law Society. This Society has enjoyed a continuous presence in the Law School from that date.

Timothy Forbes

Timothy Forbes perpetrated an offence against discipline in late 1928 which earned him a certain notoriety. In the Law section of the Library in Earlsfort Terrace most books could be borrowed on filling out, and presenting, the appropriate docket. But books most frequently in demand were placed in a reserved collection and these could not be borrowed – only consulted in the Library. The regulation irked Forbes, a student studying for the LLB, and in the autumn of 1928 he embarked on a tactic which got him into hot water. Forbes approached the issue desk, seeking to borrow – to take home – the Library's copies of Snell's *Principles of Equity* and Anson's *Law of Contract*. The attendant advised Forbes that both were part of the reserved collection and thus could not be borrowed. Rebuffed by this news and not at all pleased, Forbes then forced his way behind the issue desk, took the two books and stormed out. The matter was brought straightaway to the attention of the Librarian, Mr James O'Neill, who reported the matter as a breach of Library regulations – and thus of student discipline – to the Registrar for consideration by the Academic Council. He also, off his own bat, sought the return of the books from Forbes, together with an expression of apology from the latter for his conduct. Forbes cooperated, returned the books, and, signing himself in the Irish version of his name, tendered his apology. 'I trust', he wrote to Mr O'Neill,[247] 'your understanding will obviate long-windedness in this my unreserved apology', ending with 'Your sincere friend'. In his own report on the matter to the Registrar, Dr Conway, the Librarian acknowledged that Forbes 'did not give me any personal annoyance or inconvenience in my official capacity'.[248] When the matter came formally before the Academic Council on 5 November, the sanction was a modest one: Forbes was to be reprimanded and told not to do anything of the kind again.[249] This was not quite the last we were to hear of Mr Forbes' activities. In the autumn of 1929 Forbes was suspended directly by the President for what is termed 'breach of order', no details however being forthcoming. Sadly, therefore, it is not clear whether flouting of Library regulations was again an issue. It had been planned to deal with Forbes' subsequent actions at an Academic Council meeting on 12 December, but the matter for some unknown reason was held over. The affair was brought to an end at a meeting of the Council on 6 February 1930, when the President's recommendations that the suspension order on Forbes should be terminated was accepted.[250]

Thomas F. O'Higgins

Thomas O'Higgins, the future Chief Justice, had this to say about the BA degree course in Legal and Political Science, upon which he embarked in 1934. The extract that follows is taken from his autobiography published in 1996:[251]

> The BA degree in Legal and Political Science covered economics, politics, logic and certain legal subjects. It has now been replaced by the BCL, a degree of a much more specialised legal nature. I think this is a pity, but admittedly I am prejudiced because I particularly enjoyed the legal and political course and the lectures. Following this course brought me into contact with the Revd Denis O'Keeffe, who lectured with deep

wisdom and caustic wit on political philosophy, and with Dr George O'Brien, who had initiated informed discussion on economic policies in modern Ireland. I remember also with pleasure Professor Dan Binchy, who introduced us to the complexities of Roman law and jurisprudence, and Professor McGilligan, who grounded us in the basic principles of constitutional law. We had other lecturers also, but of these, in charity, I will say nothing.

Fernand E.J. Justice

The first recorded award of a PhD to any student researching under the aegis of the UCD Law Faculty occurred in the early 1940s, when the recipient was one Fernand E. Jean Justice, then the Belgian vice-consul in Dublin. Late in 1937 Justice sought to develop his legal know-how and applied to UCD to have the academic qualifications he had acquired in Belgium accepted as the equivalent of a BA, thus enabling him to proceed to UCD's LLB course. Justice had acquired a Licence en science commerciale with honours at the University of Ghent and UCD's Academic Council recommended that this Licence should be treated as equivalent to a BA. The Standing Committee of the Senate, acting on that recommendation, then voted that Justice should be accepted for the BA degree *ad eundem* with a view to his proceeding to the First Law examination and thus to the LLB degree.[252]

The UCD Registrar reported further on Justice's academic progress in December 1941. By then Justice had gained both an MA degree for a thesis entitled 'Du droit urbain de la Ville d'Ypres (XIIe – XVIe)' (1940) and the coveted LLB (1939). He now sought admission as a PhD student. The Senate obliged, admitting him on to a course of study and research on 'Aspects of the theory of abuse of rights (l'abus des droits) and the theoretical and practical attitude of some continental legislation and English jurisprudence'. Professor Binchy was named as Justice's supervisor and Justice's registration – to cover six terms – was backdated to 1 October 1940.[253] This rubber-stamped the earlier recommendation of UCD's Academic Council.[254] Justice was in due course awarded his PhD, being conferred with the degree in December 1943.[255]

Justice was an established playwright and poet. In November 1936, he gave a radio talk on 'Literature in bi-lingual Belgium', where he drew particular attention to the circumstance that many of the most celebrated French-language authors from Belgium were, in fact, of Flemish origin. Egypt was the focus of two of Justice's earliest pieces of writing – 'L'Egypte de 1914–1925' that appeared in *Le Flambeau: Revue Belge des Questions Politiques et Littéraires* in 1925[256] and 'Les premières relations entre la Belgique indépendante et l' Egypte, 1837–8' in the *Revue Belge de Philologie et Histoire* in 1928.[257] This article appeared around the time when he was initially appointed to his consular post in Dublin.

After serving some twenty years as vice-consul in Dublin, Fernand, in 1946, was transferred to Alexandria in Egypt as consul-general.[258] Promotion to the level of deputy ambassador came in 1950 when he was moved to Warsaw in Poland. Here he served for four further years before his final transfer to Budapest in Hungary in the spring of 1954. Justice died of a heart attack in Budapest on Christmas Eve 1954.

Justice's son Jean, born in Dublin in 1930, was prominent in the campaign, unsuccessful as it turned out, to save James Hanratty, convicted in 1962 of the A6 murder in England, from the gallows. So much was to be recalled in obituaries of Jean, who died in July 1990[259] and also of Jeremy Fox, Jean's erstwhile partner, who died in May 1999.[260]

To return to Fernand Justice and to his PhD from UCD, it will not be thought amiss to furnish statistics regarding the different branches of study where PhDs were awarded throughout the entire NUI system around the time – 1941 – that Fernand was admitted to the PhD register. Over the years 1919 to 1941: 28 in Arts; one in Engineering; 24 in Science; 5 in Agriculture; 4 in Celtic Studies; and one in Dairy Science.[261]

Thomas Finlay

The future Chief Justice entered the College in 1940, graduating with a BA in Legal and Political Science in 1943. His reflections on the three Law Professors who taught him – Binchy, Ryan and McGilligan have been introduced to the reader on earlier pages. A few of his other ruminations merit a mention here. Of the student Law Society, Finlay was to recall[262] that it

> was an active and pleasant group. It met in the Palles Library and its proceedings were, in general, calmer and more restrained than those of its main rival, the L & H. Outside debating competitions or inter-university debates were unheard of at that time.

A further paragraph of reminiscence emphasised yet another difference between the early 1940s and today:[263]

> In those war years, travel outside Ireland was out of the question. So, we lacked the broadening influence of travel and, in particular, acquaintance with other legal systems. Basically, a law graduate at that time had limited outlets consisting of practice in either of the two professions in Ireland; appointment to the Civil Service or, to a limited extent, legal employment in the private sector. I do not recollect the narrowness of this horizon to have been a source of worry or to have impaired our enjoyment of life.

4

Challenges and a Major Reform: the Law School, 1945–67

The reform of the pattern for undergraduate legal education in the UCD Law School that was inaugurated in 1954 was preceded by a period of discussion and debate over the direction any reform might take. There had been little of such discussion since the opening of the Law School in 1909, and the devotion of an issue of the journal *Studies* to the topic must have occasioned some surprise at the time. 'The law and the universities', containing one major paper addressing the theme and four short replies from sundry contributors, did not take up the whole of the September 1949 issue.[1] Nevertheless, it is not impossible that some individual subscriber might well have pondered why the topic was receiving any kind of airing at all. Might not *Studies* have been better advised to concentrate on some subject – any subject – that would have been rather different?

If the initiative was bound therefore to antagonise a few, the fact that it was taken at this particular juncture is naturally of immense value for any historian of the Law Faculty. The principal paper, to which Michael Tierney, the recently appointed President of UCD, Mr Justice Gavan Duffy, the then President of the High Court, the Very Revd Denis Canon O'Keeffe, Professor of Ethics and Politics in the College, and Mr Richard O'Sullivan, KC, in turn were to respond, was delivered by Professor Daniel Binchy.[2] Binchy had been appointed to the chair of Roman Law and Jurisprudence in the College in 1924 in circumstances that are detailed elsewhere.[3] Between 1929 and 1932 he had served as Irish minister in Berlin. He had resigned from UCD in 1945 on his election as Senior Research Fellow at Corpus Christi College in Oxford. He was to leave Oxford in 1950 to return to Dublin, not to UCD but to the School of Celtic Studies at the new Dublin Institute of Advanced Studies. He had served as dean in the UCD Law Faculty from 1933 to 1937.

Binchy commences his paper by asserting his claim to be heard on the question he had been invited to address. His personal educational formation had taken in Classics, Law, Medieval History and Literature, and Celtic Languages, Binchy adding that, as he phrased it, 'one of the few advantages of having been a "jack of all trades" in the academic world' was that it had furnished him with 'a broad-based standard of comparison with which to measure the educational value of particular University courses'.[4]

Binchy's verdict on UCD's BA in Legal and Political Science was harsh in the extreme: 'Long experience of teaching and examining for this Degree', he asserted, 'has left me profoundly sceptical of its worth as an intellectual discipline'.[5] Three subjects alone encountered in the course of three years study – Roman Law, Jurisprudence and Constitutional Law – had, in his estimation, 'any claims to figure in an academic Honours programme'.[6] He went on with his devastating critique:[7]

> All the so-called 'practical' subjects which clutter up the course – Contracts, Tort, Real and Personal Property, Evidence, etc. – are of their very nature quite unsuitable instruments for conditioning the youthful mind.

And he refuted the argument that everything depended on how well or otherwise the 'practical subjects' so-called were taught.[8] 'Not even the most stimulating lecturer can make bricks without straw'.

The gradual penetration of what today would be termed 'hard law' subjects into the curriculum of a three-year undergraduate programme Binchy attributed to 'pressure from prophets of "specialisation" and "utility"', which he dubbed 'those twin idols on whose altar so much of what was precious in our educational system has been sacrificed'.[9] The rot had started in Oxford eighty years before when the so-called Honours School of History and Jurisprudence had been inaugurated, the History element soon going the way of all flesh. Cambridge had followed suit with its Law Tripos, an equally disastrous change of direction.[10] UCD thankfully had retained two non-legal subjects in its BA in Legal and Political Science – (i) History or Political Economy; and (ii) Politics. This was applauded:[11]

> In so far as this course adds a certain amount of ballast to weight the hopelessly light cargo of legal subjects, it represents an improvement upon such educational abortions as the Honours School of Jurisprudence [at Oxford].

But his major complaint remained. The undergraduate was now enabled to specialise in legal subjects from his first day in College, 'to the grievous detriment not merely of his own education but of the great profession to which he aspires'.[12]

History conveyed a lesson it was folly to ignore. 'The more talented students', Binchy averred,[13] 'and the law has always claimed a high proportion of these – won their academic spurs in subjects which had no "vocational" significance whatever'. Study of the profession down the years told a lot. A very large percentage of eminent lawyers and judges had read Classics at university; others had excelled in Philosophy, History, Mathematics and Economics. Society had been the beneficiary:

> The success of our 'case law' is in great part due to the fact that throughout its formative period, it was moulded by men with a wide background of general culture, judges who were also 'learned' in far more important things than the law. The great figures in its history were no narrow professionalists.

In brief, there had been in place a 'broad-based intellectual formation that enabled the great judges to avoid the pitfalls of a petty legalism'.[14] 'There could be', Binchy added, for good measure, 'no more triumphant vindication of Newman's views on the relative merits of a "liberal" and a "professional" education'.[15]

The 'hard law' subjects, which were properly examinable for professional purposes, in Binchy's estimation, tended 'to restrict rather than to enlarge the student's mental horizon'.[16] What he proposed therefore was an abandonment of the present BA in Legal and Political Science or a drastic remodelling of it which would involve the jettisoning of all the practical subjects – Contracts, Tort, etc. – and the regrouping of the remainder round their true centre of gravity.[17]

This leads Binchy on to say rather more on three key components of a reformed curriculum – Roman Law, Constitutional Law and Jurisprudence. On Roman Law, 'the embodiment of judicial wisdom', as it had been termed, it was otiose to say more.[18] The problem of the status of Latin in secondary schools – clearly a consideration today – had not raised its head in 1948, and is not even mentioned: *o tempora, o mores*! As to Constitutional Law, Binchy allows himself to remark that the more concentration there was on any existing local constitution, the less valuable was the instruction. 'On the other hand', he added,[19] 'to hear it expounded (as it is expounded, for example, by the great French masters of the subject) against its proper background of history and political theory is a most stimulating experience for any student'.

Binchy has most to say regarding Jurisprudence, 'the lynch-pin of all higher legal studies'.[20] Its true function, Binchy boldly asserted, was 'to provide a *trait d'union* between the profession of law and the philosophical and ethical principles from which alone legal systems derive their ultimate validity'.[21] It was a matter of regret that Jurisprudence in England had travelled down a blind alley. In the United States, too, matters were little better. 'One cannot help feeling', Binchy wrote with some passion in a footnote,[22] 'that most American works on the philosophy of law would have gained considerably if their writers had condescended to learn a little philosophy first'. A sound theory of law was indispensable, and the writings of François Gény, Léon Duguit and Giorgio del Vecchio all cried out for consideration.[23] On Natural Law Binchy, not unexpectedly, proved eloquent:[24]

> The traditional theory of the Natural Law was asserted as firmly by Blackstone and Lord Mansfield as by their medieval predecessors and St. Germain. All of them were equally convinced that the legal system they helped to fashion was not an independent constellation but a planet following in the wake of a star.

To do justice to the subject of Jurisprudence the College would be obliged to recruit a full-time professor, who was trained in Philosophy as much as in Law.[25]

In the course Binchy would recommend for adoption, he envisaged much expanded instruction in Ethics and Jurisprudence as well as instruction in Roman Law, Politics and Constitutional Law. He was aware that the jettisoning of the 'hard law' subjects from the programme might be unpopular. He dealt with this objection in the following manner:[26]

> To those successful men of affairs who ask what practical help a course of this kind can give to the future lawyer, I need only reply in Newman's words:[27]
>
>> The man who has learned to think and to reason and to compare and to discriminate and to analyse, who has refined his taste, and formed his judgment, and sharpened his mental vision, will not indeed at once be a lawyer, or a pleader, or an orator, or a statesman, or a physician; but he will be placed in that state of intellect in which he can take up any one of these sciences … I have referred to … with an ease, a grace, a versatility, and a success, to which another is a stranger.

Such an educational formation would prove a life-long possession;[28] in Menander's words:[29] 'ἀναφαίρετον κτῆμ' ἐστὶ παιδεία βροτοῖς'.

In their responses to Binchy's paper, Mr O'Sullivan and Canon O'Keeffe add little to the debate. O'Sullivan supported the re-arrangement of legal studies along the lines suggested by Binchy: the emphasis on Natural Law was very much to his taste.[30] O'Keeffe, for his part, disclosed that even then a remodelling of law studies was under consideration by a College committee.[31] Tierney acknowledged this as well,[32] after adding that the so-called practical subjects would be looming large in any planned restructuring[33] – not something Binchy would have relished hearing. Tierney sensed he had no option other than to dampen expectations on this particular front. 'The salaries which University College at least can afford', he began,[34]

> have rarely been such as to induce any man to abandon the practice of a remunerative profession and devote himself wholly to the kind of schol-

> arship that must be looked for in a full-time Professor of, say, Jurisprudence.

Mr Justice Gavan Duffy's response was probably the most enlightening. He broadly welcomed Binchy's views on Jurisprudence, the role of the universities, and the place in them of the humanities,[35] but he disagreed vehemently with the suggestion that the 'practical subjects' should be squeezed out of the curriculum. Tierney, as we have seen, appears to have held a comparable view. In the light of this stiff opposition to Binchy's ideas, Gavan Duffy's arguments deserve to be set down in such detail as he furnishes. The President of the High Court opts to clash head-on with Binchy. The first principal point he makes is this. 'I favour', he says,[36]

> an early introduction of the talented student to the realm of law, because he is entering an unknown territory, which he must find so strange, with an atmosphere so esoteric, that he can penetrate the enclave only by slow and laborious stages.

The second principal point was to assert the educational value of coming to grips with the content of 'hard law' subjects:[37]

> Those practical subjects 'which clutter up the course' are brimful of interest to stimulate the adolescent mind, when treated by such masters as Holmes, or a Wigmore, a Cheshire, a Winfield or a Hanbury.

Gavan Duffy goes on to urge the creation of a statutory committee representative of the professions and the universities who would together settle outstanding issues on curriculum and on examinations.[38] For good measure, he appends a suggestion that a School of Jurisprudence might be added to the School of Celtic Studies and that of Theoretical Physics at the Dublin Institute for Advanced Studies[39] – the very institute where Binchy would soon be taking up appointment as a Senior Professor.

This rare in-house survey published in *Studies* in 1949 on the needs of the College's Law Faculty merits a little further consideration. That there was an acute difference of opinion between Binchy, on the one hand, and Gavan Duffy, on the other, was glaringly obvious. For Binchy to have contended that it should be left to the professional bodies exclusively to impart instruction in the so-called practical or 'hard law' subjects appears, with the benefit of hindsight, to have been not just unwise but unrealistic. Whatever the merits of such a proposal, did Binchy convincingly dismiss the alternative of teaching some at least of the practical subjects in the undergraduate university programme on the grounds, as he expressed it, that 'not even the most stimulating lecturer can make bricks without straw'?

For Delany, writing a few years later, a criticism such as Binchy had expressed that law schools had become 'too vocational' was, in his view, 'a condemnation not of the value of a degree in law, but rather of the prevailing methods of teaching legal subjects'.[40] This explanation, as we have seen, Binchy, for his part, was not prepared to accept: no straw, no bricks.

It is possible that such divergent views had their origin in contemporary perceptions of poor quality lecturing – reading non-stop from pages in textbooks, for instance – and an allied appreciation of the Sisyphean task that any effective remedy presented. As it happens, Lord Denning in an essay also published in 1949 sought to square the circle.[41] There was, in Denning's opinion, a threefold purpose for legal education:

(i) To show how legal rules had developed, the reasons underlying them, and the connection between legal and social history;
(ii) To extract the principles underlying the existing rules; and
(iii) To point the right way forward for legal development.

Four more years were to pass before, in the autumn of 1953, the first steps were actually taken to overhaul the pattern of legal education in the College. The regulations for the higher degrees of the LLD and of the PhD were unaffected. By a curious coincidence, two applications to be admitted as PhD students – to deal exhaustively with the law of copyright and with aspects of administrative law – were processed through the Academic Council at the same time as replacement courses for the old BA in Legal and Political Science and the old LLB were proposed. These PhD applications represented the third and fourth such applications in the history of the Law Faculty.[42]

Binchy, as we have seen, had expressed dissatisfaction with the old BA and argued for something different. By 1953, Tierney, too, was made to feel a degree of unease, which, in his case, precipitated the need for action. He was later to explain that his stance and that of the Faculty had not been unaffected by the approach adopted by a deputation from the Incorporated Law Society in reference to the education and training of solicitors' apprentices.[43] In discussions held with the Faculty, it was apparently to be generally agreed that

> it would be desirable for all solicitors' apprentices to take a degree in the University on a more general and philosophic Law course, which would provide a suitable training for future lawyers, the Society itself to provide the more technical side of their training.

Four subsequent meetings of the Law Faculty were held on the challenge that the introduction of this major change involved. Finally, in February 1954, the Law Faculty recommended to the Academic Council the introduction of the new 3-year Bachelor of Civil Law (BCL) to replace the old BA. The proposal was forwarded to the General Board of Studies who attached its imprimatur the same month, and the change was approved by the NUI Senate on 8 April 1954, the institution of the degree itself being sanctioned by Statute XCVIII, made on 28 October 1954. Entrants into the Law Faculty in the autumn of the same year thus registered for the new degree.[44]

At the same time, the old LLB was altered. Six terms had previously to elapse between the obtaining of a BA and presenting oneself for the LLB examination. The period that had to intervene was now reduced to three terms. In effect, the old LLB was being phased out, to be replaced, first of all, by a one year's multi-subject course. (It would later be designated an LLM.) The content of the LLB meanwhile was drastically reshaped.

In the case of the new BCL, the major change affected the programme for the First Year. That programme now consisted of the following subjects: Introduction to Legal System; Modern History; Introduction to Philosophy; and one from among the following subjects of the First Arts curriculum – Irish, English, Latin, Greek, French, German and Economics.

The introduction to Legal System course was stated to embrace 'Development of Courts of Law and of the main Legal Institutions (Property, Contract, Tort, Criminal Law and Procedure)'. Modern History was split in two, one half dealing with 'Ireland and Great Britain, 1800–1914', the other half with 'Europe, 1815–1914'. 'Particular regard' here was to be paid to the constitutional history of Ireland and Great Britain. (No excuse, therefore, for ignorance of the series of Home Rule Bills!) The description of the 'Introduction to Philosophy' course was unusually detailed. It was divided into four components:

1. Principles of Philosophy – Outline of main problems with a critical presentation of the suggested answers.
2. History of Philosophy – Broad lines of development in Greek, Medieval and Modern Philosophy.
3. Moral Philosophy.
4. Special Ethics – Moral principles of individual and family life. Moral principles in legal practice.

For details on the outstanding seven optional subjects from the First Arts course, one of which had to be taken, students reading the *Calendar* would be diverted to what was stated for these subjects in the section of the *Calendar* dealing with the Arts Faculty.

The plan for 1954–5 envisaged this distribution of BCL subjects between the Second and Third or Final Years (effectively scheduled for the sessions 1955–6 and 1956–7 respectively):

Year 2	Year 3
Politics (Moral Principles governing political life).	Roman Law
	Common Law (Contract and Tort)
Jurisprudence	Constitutional Law
International Law	Equity
Common Law (Real and Personal Property)	Criminal Law

Even though all these arrangements were approved for introduction as from 1954–5, there were second thoughts over the distribution of subjects between the second and third years. (The arrangements for First Year were left untouched.) The *Calendar for 1955–1956* had altered the distribution quite drastically. The revised distribution was as follows:-

Year 2	Year 3
Roman Law	Politics
Constitutional Law	Common Law (Contract and Tort)
Criminal Law	Jurisprudence
Real and Personal Property	Equity
	International Law

A decade or so after what in the case of the Law Faculty has to be viewed as a momentous change, and somewhat incongruously, a post mortem was pronounced on the new BCL that was hardly enthusiastic.[45] In evidence to the Commission on Higher Education, Michael Tierney made no secret of his disappointment. 'Until 1955', the Commission reported, summarising Tierney's opening observations on the matter,[46]

> the degree taken by law students was normally the BA degree in legal and political science, in which, however, the emphasis was heavily on legal subjects of a practical nature; as a result, 'the standard of this degree bore only a slight relation to that required for the honours BA' in other arts departments.

The degree of BCL had been introduced, we are then assured, to remedy this situation, but continuing the account given by Tierney,[47]

> the practical requirements of both the legal professions have rendered it difficult to give the courses for this degree anything other than a severely practical, professional bias or to provide for the kind of theoretical, historical and philosophical training which is associated with university law courses in America and on the continent.

Tierney went on to call for 'a sharper distinction' between study of the theory of law and training in the practice of law.

J.J. Hogan, in his evidence to the Commission,[48] saw the implications of this in terms of the policy that should inform recruitment of staff. Full-time professors were necessary, and it was UCD's intention to secure their appointment: they might be counted on to deal 'with the theoretical and historical side of the law better than could ever be expected of legal practitioners in their spare time'. But it would always be necessary, Hogan added, to have part-time professors 'who know not only their legal theory but who are in touch with the work of the courts'.

Mr Justice Henchy shared Hogan's belief in the need for a much expanded staff.[49] It would be a little while yet (though not overlong) before that call, and, indeed, Hogan's balanced assessment of the situation would lead to action being taken.

The changes signalled for the start of the academic year 1954–5 also encompassed the old LLB. Formerly a two-year course, with Jurisprudence, Roman Law, Constitutional Law with International Law, and Common Law all being taken in Year One, and Jurisprudence, Roman Law, Legal History, Criminal Law and Evidence, Torts, and Property and Equity, all being taken in Year Two (the Final Year), the LLB now became, in effect, a one year course in Jurisprudence, Roman Law, Canon Law, Real and Personal Property, Criminal Law, Evidence and Equity.[50]

A major innovation of this newfangled LLB, it can immediately be seen, was the introduction of a course in Canon Law, which continued to be taught and examined in until 1970. The course was taught by the Revd John Gerard Sheehy, whose career and publications are dealt with below.[51]

With the changes of 1954–5, the shape of the basic educational programme in the Law Faculty for a generation and more had been laid down. The multi-subject LLB was, of course, soon enough, in 1970, as we have seen, to be replaced by a short-lived multi-subject LLM. And more so-called 'hard law' subjects were to be introduced into the BCL, but both staff and students in the Law School of today would perceive elements in the programmes they are familiar with that can trace back their origins to the major overhauling of 1954–5.

These various changes necessitated the introduction of the inevitable transitional arrangements. Students who in 1954 entered the second or third year of the old BA in Legal and Political Science remained entitled to enter the old LLB programme.[52] To make matters crystal-clear it was thus laid down that the first examination under the new LLB degree and syllabus would be held in 1958.

One consequence of the revamping of the primary degree offered by the Law Faculty – a consequence not generally understood to have occurred – was the launching of a Visitation into the conduct of affairs by the National University Senate[53] at the instigation of Séamus Henchy, whose appointment in 1949 as the professor of Roman Law, Jurisprudence and Legal History we will shortly be considering. Henchy had taken exception to the two Statutes (Statute CV and Statute CVII) adopted by the Senate in 1957 to add to the composition of the Faculty of Law in the University as well as in all three constituent Colleges such Professors and Lecturers responsible for the clutch of non-law subjects introduced into the BCL, especially in the First Year. The two Statutes in question which had made this change, in Henchy's view, had altered 'the constitution' of the several Faculties, and could only be valid if the procedure requiring prior consultation with the existing Faculties had been followed, as mandated by Chapter XI of the Charter of 2 December 1908.

The considered view of the Board of Visitors[54] was that designating fresh subjects for subjects of any Faculty and associating with that change additions of the relevant statutory personnel to the membership of the respective Faculties had not violated 'the constitution' of each. Henchy's petition was thus refused, and the conduct of the NUI Senate in the matter vindicated.

Final remarks by the Board of Visitors are important, however, and merit being recorded. 'The Petitioner and those members of the University who supported the Petition',[55] the Board recites,[56]

> are obviously apprehensive of the possible consequence of having in the Faculty of Law a majority of members who are not Professors or Lecturers in legal subjects. This could result in the Dean of the Faculty being a Professor in a non-legal subject, and also in the direction and guidance of the Faculty resting in the hands of persons unfamiliar with the academic or professional requirements of students of the Faculty.[57] We consider that these apprehensions are not unreasonable, and are deserving of close and sympathetic consideration by the Senate of the University and the Government.

The Board of Visitors continues:

> The remedy for this situation, if thought desirable, might lie in either a re-definition of the constitution of a Faculty or a definition of the subjects of a Faculty so as to ensure that the mere addition to a prescribed course of study of a subject or subjects not characteristic of the particular Faculty would not have the effect of adding to the personnel of the Faculty the Professors and Lecturers in such subject or subjects.

The Professor of German at University College Galway, Professor Margaret M. Shea, had implicitly supported this addendum when writing to the Secretary to the Board of Visitors[58] that, in her opinion,

> every Faculty in the National University – and, indeed, in every University, should at all times and in all circumstances do everything in its power, to retain and preserve its essential character.

The resignation of Binchy from the chair of Roman Law, Jurisprudence and Legal History, effective from the autumn of 1946, was followed by a lengthy intermission before his eventual successor, Séamus Henchy was picked. Henchy was to assume office early in 1949. In that interval there was, of course, to be a change of President, with Michael Tierney succeeding Dr Conway (October 1947) and the holding of the seminar, possibly convened at the instigation of Tierney, to chart the future course for the law school, when Binchy made a return visit to express his view on that portentous topic (1948).[59]

Under a new Statute adopted in March 1947[60] increases had been sanctioned in the salaries for the two Law chairs then occupied – Ryan's Law of Property, Common Law and Equity and McGilligan's Constitutional Law, International Law and Criminal Law and Procedure. In the succeeding June it was also resolved by the Governing Body that the stipend for Binchy's vacant chair should be raised to £1,100[61] – in other words, it was to remain a full-time chair, payable at the conventional rate for a full-time Professor, with the now-customary perk of the post being pensionable. But this was not to happen, and it was not long after Binchy's resignation took effect in the autumn of 1946 that events began to unfold that represented a reverse. As reported to the Academic Council in mid-December, the Law Faculty had already concluded that there 'might be some difficulty in obtaining a successor to Binchy with the like qualifications'.[62] The Faculty was adamant, however, that the chairs in the Faculty 'should include a full-time professorship of theoretical legal subjects'. What the Faculty proposed – and this meant Ryan and McGilligan plus the President, Dr Conway – was (i) that the obligation to teach 'ancient Irish law' should no longer be the responsibility of the holder of the Roman Law, Jurisprudence and Legal History chair; (ii) that the chair itself, with this modification, should nonetheless remain full-time, and (iii) that a lectureship in Ancient Irish Law should be established.[63]

The Academic Council considered the question of what was to be done at this mid-December meeting and decided to support recommendations (i) and (ii) of the Faculty of Law in its report to the Governing Body. Recommendation (iii) was forwarded to the Faculty of Celtic Studies in the interim.[64] A few days later, when the Governing Body met, that part of the recommendation (i) that involved the dropping of the subject 'Ancient Irish Law', was, like the creation of the alternative lectureship in that specific subject, again referred to the Faculty of Celtic Studies.[65] What occurred there, however, is nowhere recorded, and there does not in fact appear to have been any follow-up. A change in the occupant of the Presidency takes place before any further development is mentioned in the records – though whether Michael Tierney's succession to Conway in October 1947 is in any way significant as regards the future trend to events remains problematic. What is a matter of record is that the Law Faculty was forced to admit defeat. Though 'Ancient Irish Law' was to be dropped from the title of Binchy's old chair, none of the other suggestions of the Faculty were in the end to be implemented. Nothing further is heard of a separate lectureship in Ancient Irish Law, but what must surely have been regarded as even more demoralising, Binchy's chair was to cease to be full-time, and was to revert to what it had been before 1934 and in the time of James Murnaghan: part-time. A brand new Statute, Statute XXXIX, announced in January 1948, introduced the new dispensation.[66] Binchy's full-time chair was abolished and was replaced with a new part-time one, paying £500 a year. A competition for this now somewhat downgraded chair was then publicised with a closing date set for the end of June 1948.[67]

Five candidates threw their hats in the ring – Thomas F. Donnelly,[68] James (Séamus) A. Henchy, John J. Kenny,[69] Gerard A. Lee[70] and Margaret O'Toole.[71] All were members of the Irish Bar. A majority of the Law Faculty, which at the time comprised the President and Professors Ryan and McGilligan, backed Donnelly, asserting that he had the requisite qualifications for the job, and in successive votes at the Academic Council and Governing Body, he again came top, followed by Kenny and O'Toole, who at the Governing Body were to muster equal ballots. Henchy came after them both in the Academic Council vote and again fourth in the two Governing Body votes.[72] All five names including that of O'Toole, the lone female candidate, were forwarded to the Senate for consideration, where, perhaps surprisingly and against the odds, Henchy was appointed, a choice communicated to the Governing Body and recorded there on 1 February 1949.[73] Henchy was 31. He acted as Professor of Roman Law, Jurisprudence and Legal History until 1962, when he resigned on his appointment to the High Court Bench.

Up until the 1950s, all teaching of the 'law' subjects in the two relevant degree programmes – the BA in Legal and Political Science and the LLB – was the responsibility of the three statutory professors. Whenever a vacancy had arisen, for whatever reason, the other two professors rallied round and gave the covering lectures, attending to any examinations as well. The speed with which the vacancy was filled was naturally of concern to the students but perhaps of equal concern to the two remaining professors who found themselves saddled with the obligation to undertake an amount of extra lecturing. As practising barristers, this must at times surely have seemed more than a mere inconvenience. The circumstance that they received additional remuneration may have been little enough consolation.

With the dawn of the 1950s, this pattern was about to change, as expansion in law teaching in the Faculty and in law staff there was set to take off.

Presaging the future course of events, ironically enough, was an appointment not in the Law Faculty at all but in the Faculty of Arts. This was the appointment to the History Department from the start of the Michaelmas Term in 1950, retrospectively validated by the Governing Body, of a new Assistant.[74]

The Assistant in question was a Czech refugee and the holder of a law degree (Dr Jur) from the University of Prague, Zdeněk Sydney Ehler. Recruited at a rate of £400 per annum, an arrangement that was annually renewed,[75] Ehler soon indicated that his talents in International and Comparative Law could equally be availed of in the Law Faculty. From the session 1952–3, he began lecturing both in History and in the Law School, and that was reflected in changes in his remuneration: for his work in Law he was to receive £200 per annum and his services as an Assistant in History were reimbursed at a rate of £500 per annum. A responsibility for a course of evening lectures appears to have been part of the new deal.[76] Ehler's total emoluments were raised to £750 in 1954, by which date even more dramatic infusions of fresh blood into the Law School were scheduled to occur. This development was not, of course, unconnected with the introduction of the new BCL degree and the revamping of the old LLB. Ryan's death at the end of 1952 also appears to have concentrated peoples' minds on the imperative of attending in a more radical fashion with the staffing needs of the Law School.

Ryan's death was followed by the new traditional expedient of inviting the two surviving professors, McGilligan and Henchy, to assume responsibility for the courses that Ryan had previously given. As a stop-gap measure, this entailed Ryan's stipend of £540 per annum being split equally between the two men: this worked out at £270 each.[77] In the spring of 1954, whilst this arrangement still obtained, it was clear that the Governing Body's Finance Committee had under serious review the state of staffing in the Law School.[78] In October the Governing Body acted by appointing three new Assistants for the Law School at a rate of £250 per annum each, soon raised to £300.[79] The three included two of the individuals who had been beaten by Henchy in the competition for Binchy's old chair: these were John (or Sean) Kenny and Gerard A. Lee. The third Assistant, and, as it happens, a future Dean of the Law School was William D. Finlay. Accompanying this development, it was announced that there were no plans for the moment to fill Ryan's chair.[80] This major initiative did not win universal approval. An element on the Governing Body protested that the Academic Council had not had the opportunity to express an opinion on the proposed appointments.[81] The President, Dr Tierney, arranged for such approval to be expressed (as it was before the next ensuing meeting of the Governing Body),[82] adding, however, that the manner in which he as President, together with Professors McGilligan and Henchy, in conclave, had chosen the three Assistants had been in accord with College convention and practice.

In advance of the session 1957–1958 Gerard Lee intimated that he would not be available for re-appointment as an Assistant.[83] Two new Assistants were appointed, bringing the total of such appointments (taking in John Kenny and William Finlay) up to four. The new appointees were the Revd J.G. Sheehy, BA, DD, who would be lecturing on Canon Law in the revised LLB programme (that we have earlier set down),[84] and John Kelly, MA, DPhil, another future Dean of the Law Faculty, who, in the short term, would be lecturing on Roman Law.[85] Sheehy was to be paid at the rate of 3 guineas per lecture; Kelly was put on a stipend of £400 per annum.[86] Before the session 1957–8 had got underway, the Law Faculty sought the recruitment of yet another Assistant as a specific replacement for Lee. The Faculty's choice was Kevin Kenny, and Tierney, in signalling his concurrence to the Governing Body, indicated that the approval of the Academic Council would also be sought.[87] There were thus five Assistants set down for renewal for the session 1958–9, viz. John Kenny, William Finlay, Kevin Kenny, John Kelly and Dr Sheehy. In the interim, Ehler had been promoted to the grade of Assistant Lecturer at a salary of £900 per annum,[88] which had risen to £1,050 by 1959.[89]

In the autumn of 1960 Dr Tierney announced that a Statute would soon be brought forward, to make provision for a number of part-time professorships in Law.[90] This long-awaited initiative finally occurred the following May.[91] Before then voices had been heard at the Governing Body critical of the delay in a proper re-moulding of the Law School. In June, 1959, for instance, Mrs Ó Dálaigh, wife of the future Chief Justice and a government nominee on the Governing Body, raised the possibility of having one or more full-time chairs in Law.[92] Tierney, in response, stated that it was advisable for the College to avail of the services of barristers, who would of necessity be part-time, 'for subjects such as Common Law, Law of Property or Criminal Law'. It scarcely added to the discussion when he went on to observe, as recorded in the minutes, 'that there already was a part-time Professor of Roman Law, Jurisprudence and Legal History' – a reference to Séamus Henchy.[93] Later in 1959, the Faculty of Law proposed a change to the description of one of the existing part-time professorships in a new draft Statute, Statute LII. They wanted it re-designated the Professorship of Common Law (Law of Contract and Tort) and Law of Evidence.[94] This provoked some further discussion at Governing Body level, Mr Justice Brian Walsh, a second government nominee, urging the adoption of a rule stipulating that the retirement age for Law Professors should be raised from 65 to 70.[95] Tierney again was not persuaded. The age 65 was the stated standard age for retirement throughout the College. Proper notice anyway would have to be given for any serious proposal to introduce such a change.[96] In this exchange Walsh, though he might have done so, elected not to allude to the fact that the retirement age for judges of the High Court and of the Supreme Court was set as long ago as 1924 at 72.[97] When Statute LII was being further considered in December, Professor Henchy raised a separate matter altogether – the legality of leaving statutory posts unfilled for an unconscionable length of time.[98] Henchy had taken the question up with the Registrar of the National University. Two pages listing unfilled vacancies appear in an appendix to the *Report of the Board of Visitors* in early 1960.[99]

In March 1961 Dr Tierney as President announced the broad outlines of Chapter IV – which would deal with chairs in the Law School – in a new College Statute, Statute LIV. It had proved impossible, Tierney revealed, to secure agreement for the establishment of any full- time chair in Law, though where the idea, if seriously canvassed by others besides Mrs Ó Dálaigh, had been shot down is not disclosed. In the circumstances, there would, in addition to Henchy's part-time chair in Roman Law and Jurisprudence, be three new part-time chairs. There would also be introduced at a nominal salary a new chair of International Law and International Relations.[100]

The detail in Chapter IV was revealed to the Governing Body in mid-May.[101] Ryan's old chair in Property, Common Law and Equity and McGilligan's in Constitutional Law, International Law and Criminal Law and Procedure were both to be abolished. They were to be replaced by

a) a part-time Professorship of Common Law (Law of Contract and Tort) and of the Law of Evidence at £600 per annum;
b) a part-time Professorship of the Law of Property and Equity at £600 per annum;
c) a part-time Professorship of Constitutional Law and of Criminal Law and Procedure, at £600 per annum; and
d) a part-time Professorship of International Law and International Relations at a nominal stipend of £100 per annum.

In a major departure from the previous dispensation, and which represented a return to the arrangements on tenure for Law Professors in both Statute A and Statute I in the very earliest days of the new UCD,[102] all these posts would be tenable for five years, though renewable for successive five-year periods up to the age of 65. In seeking to justify this reversion to the *status quo ante*, Tierney did not allude to the wish to satisfy the lecturing urges of successive cohorts of bright young barristers (affording them the bite at the proverbial cherry). He argued, rather, that with a five-year limit, rather than the seven years provided for in Statute A and Statute I, the Law Faculty would be facilitated in a more expeditious reallocation of subjects in the Faculty should that be found necessary.[103] The grouping for Evidence and for International Law, for some reason, was singled out by Tierney as worthy of consideration. The explanation for the nominal salary being attached to the new chair in International Law and International Relations bordered on the indiscreet. If Ehler was successful in his bid for the chair, the promised £100 would represent a satisfactory extra emolument to what he currently earned as an Assistant Lecturer in the Arts Faculty.[104]

Following adoption of Statute LII, the closing date for applications was set at 15 September.[105] Applications had been invited before the NUI in its own Statutes had finally authorised all the new chairs, which had the effect – much to the annoyance of Tierney, after unsuccessful representations on the matter to Seamus Wilmot, the NUI Registrar and, through him, to Eamon de Valera, the NUI Chancellor – of delaying the earliest date at which the winners in the four impending competitions could be announced.[106] The Governing Body was in a position to forward its recommendations in all four contests by 22 November with a view to the NUI Senate making the appointments at its scheduled meeting of 30 November. But, as a consequence of the kerfuffle between Tierney and Wilmot/de Valera over NUI procedures, the Governing Body's recommendations were only dealt with by the NUI Senate on 29 March 1962, when all the various appointments were finally made.[107] By then Henchy had resigned on his appointment as a judge of the High Court, leading to McGilligan being named an Acting Professor of Roman Law, Jurisprudence and Legal History.[108]

Four candidates had applied for the part-time chair in Contract, Tort and Evidence. The Faculty of Law adjudged all four suitable, but recommended William Finlay, one of the Law School Assistants for the post. The Academic Council agreed, and at the conventional Governing Body ballot Finlay came top with 21 votes at the first count and 20 at the second.[109] Finlay was appointed. Five candidates applied for the job to teach Property and Equity, three of whom had also been in contention for the chair in Contract, Tort and Evidence. Again the Law Faculty adjudged them all suitable for appointment but backed Kevin Kenny. The Academic Council did not disagree, and Kevin Kenny topped the voting at Governing Body level – 15 on the first round, 17 on the second.[110] Kevin Kenny was appointed. There were a very large number of contestants for the chair in Constitutional Law, and Criminal Law and Procedure. The three unsuccessful applicants for the first two chairs applied again, and once more their efforts were rebuffed, but on this occasion they were joined by six others, including among the four who likewise were unsuccessful – one other having withdrawn from the fray. The Faculty of Law adjudged all nine suitable, ranking R.J. O'Hanlon first, followed by the two individuals who would also later become judges, in what for the Faculty was the first of the votes it held. The Academic Council held a vote as well, where O'Hanlon was equally successful. At Governing Body level, O'Hanlon was again the top scorer – 13 at the first ballot, 12 at the second.[111] The Senate appointed O'Hanlon. There were three candidates for the new chair in International Law. All were considered suitable, but the recommendation went in favour of Ehler. The Academic Council accepted the recommendation, as did the Governing Body at its two customary votes.[112] Ehler was appointed by the NUI Senate.

With the exception of O'Hanlon, all the other victors had been in post in the College, either as Assistants (Finlay, Kevin Kenny) or as an Assistant Lecturer (Ehler), so the delay at NUI Senate level in making the appointments, however much it may have irritated Tierney, leading him to question the role and function of the National University,[113] is unlikely to have interfered very much with the smooth running of the Law Faculty itself.

In 1960, two years earlier, John Kenny who had been made an Assistant in 1954,[114] indicated his intention to resign. From October 1960, it was arranged that the remaining Assistants at that date would assume responsibility for the lecture courses for which Kenny had been responsible. Kenny's departure from the College was followed by his appointment to the High Court bench from which, in due course, in 1975, there was promotion to the Supreme Court. It is doubtful whether, so far as the College was concerned, this parting of the way was altogether amicable, for Kenny had been the prime mover in the agitation that led to the Visitation of 1959–1960 on the system of appointments in UCD. This extraordinary intervention in the affairs of the College was not of immediate consequence for the Law School any more than it was for other College Faculties and Departments, but since Kenny was at the heart of the opposition to Michael Tierney's modus operandi in the making of appointments and he was a member of the Law School staff at the time – though only on the lowest tier of all as an Assistant – it seems only right, briefly, to describe the controversy and pinpoint Kenny's role.

The bandwagon started rolling in May 1959 when Kenny wrote a key letter to Tierney challenging the College's system of appointments.[115] But this was no bolt from the blue. At a Governing Body meeting in June 1957 concern had been expressed at the legality of the College's appointment of what it termed 'College Lecturers', and 'Assistant Lecturers'.[116] Contributors to the discussion pointed out that several legal luminaries, T.K. Liston, SC, Andreas O'Keefe, SC (the Attorney General), together with the solicitor Arthur Cox, had intimated to members of the Governing Body that the controverted appointments were not legal. The Revd Professor Aubrey Gwynn, the distinguished medieval historian, backed Tierney's assertion that nothing was amiss, as did J.J. Hogan, the then Registrar and later President, and emphasised the advantages of the system so far as junior staff were concerned. Tierney was already in fighting mood, for he could not let the occasion pass without commenting that it was quite extraordinary for members of the Governing Body to, as it were, break ranks, and seek outside legal advice on the matter.[117]

John Kenny returned to the fray with his letter to Tierney of 18 May 1959. The Governing Body, he argued, could legally appoint Assistants on a year-by-year basis, but only the NUI Senate could legally make any other kind of appointments of staff. For UCD to bypass the Senate with its appointment of so-called College Lecturers and Assistant Lecturers was in contravention of both the Charter and statute law. What he termed such unauthorised appointments involved irregular payments out of College funds, and for obvious reasons ought to cease. The critical threat was then conveyed. Unless, Kenny wrote, the Governing Body was prepared to disclaim the power to appoint 'College Professors', 'College Lecturers' and 'Assistant Lecturers', he would be pressing the government for the appointment of Visitors.

Three days later, J.P. MacHale, the Secretary and Bursar, responded formally.[118] The question of 'the alleged illegality' of these staff titles had been before the Governing Body and the NUI Senate on several occasions. So far as the Governing Body was concerned, it was not prepared to alter its practice which it was satisfied was entirely proper and had been in operation as a benefit to the College for a considerable time. Nor was the Senate prepared to take any action. Then came an addendum inspired from on high that was scarcely calculated to win friends and influence people. 'The President has instructed me', MacHale concluded,[119]

> to inquire whether you think it altogether proper that you, as an Assistant in the College, should query the actions of the Governing Body in a matter which does not appear to him to be of any direct concern of you.

Kenny responded in detail on 23 May.[120]

(i) Whether this system of appointments was of benefit was a matter on which opinions differed. The key question, however, was whether such appointments were authorised.

(ii) In 1911 or 1912 University College Cork had sought to appoint a College Professor of Russian,[121] thus bypassing the Senate. The Senate appealed against the UCC Statute sanctioning such appointment to the Irish University Committee of the Irish Privy Council, and that appeal had been successful.

(iii) The assertion that the practice had been in existence for a considerable length of time was contradicted. He (Kenny) had been a student in UCD from 1936 to 1938, and, so far as he was aware, there then existed neither College Professor, nor College Lecturer, nor Assistant Lecturer.

(iv) He (Kenny) requested sight of any legal opinion the College had received which found legal this system of appointments.

(v) Kenny's objection to the practice – an allusion to the reference to this in the Tierney-inspired addendum to MacHale's letter– was not made as an Assistant but 'as a member and graduate of UCD'.

Kenny ended by assuring MacHale that, on the assumption that the Governing Body would still take no action, he would press for the projected Visitation.

Having received no further reply, Kenny proceeded to draft a petition for forwarding to the government seeking the appointment of Visitors. This petition is dated 29 May. On 24 June two members of the Governing Body at the meeting on that date sought to avoid the inevitable. This was when Mr Justice Walsh and Mrs Ó Dálaigh moved that the Governing Body should itself seek legal opinion on the question. The move was defeated on a show of hands, Tierney then going on to point out that with a Visitation now imminent, at least the entire matter would be thrashed out.[122] The meeting of 24 June continued by endorsing, on the recommendation of the Finance Committee, the appointment of a number of College Lecturers and Assistant Lecturers.[123] No rebuff could have been more theatrically expressed.

In the ensuing autumn the government announced the appointment of Visitors with the following terms of reference:

> To consider the petition dated the 29th of May 1959 of Mr John Kenny, SC, and to make such determinations and declarations in respect of the matters therein raised as may be appropriate and to report to the Government thereon.

Three judges were appointed: Mr Justice Kevin Dixon, Mr Justice Thomas Teevan and Judge Michael Binchy. Dixon died on 25 October, and was replaced by Mr Justice George Murnaghan. UCD chose Henry J. Molony, SC and Professor McGilligan to represent the College at oral hearings conducted by the Visitors at the Land Commission premises in Upper Merrion Street.[124] These were held between November 1959 and January 1960.

The Visitors in their short *Report* upheld the gravamen of the complaint in the Kenny petition, while recognising the unwieldy nature of NUI procedures for making appointments whether to existing or new posts.[125] Remedial legislation was introduced, and later enacted, that dealt with the controverted appointments made in the past which were retrospectively validated and with similar appointments that could in the short term be made in the future.[126]

An ill-natured debate in the Dáil on the measure that became the remedial Act offered Patrick McGilligan, a TD as well as one of the Law School's professors, who had, as we have seen, represented the College at the hearings before the Board of Visitors, the opportunity to pronounce his verdict on what the three judges on the Board had determined.[127] He was not impressed, castigating it as a bad report that had not done justice to the issues raised. In essence, he repeated the view that had been expressed at meetings of the Governing Body that this had been a storm in a teacup, an inconsequential dispute about titles for jobs. Turning to critics of Michael Tierney and of UCD's Governing Body who had preceded him in the Dáil's Second Stage debate, McGilligan left his audience and those who might chance to peruse the Dáil debate in no doubt that 'the lines of this debate have given great comfort to those who have been traditionally opposed to higher education for Catholics'.[128]

John Kenny, who had started the ball rolling, as we have already noted,[129] resigned his post as Assistant in the Law School not long after the report of the Visitors had been followed by adoption of the University College Dublin Act of 1960. He did not go quietly, committing his thoughts on the entire controversy in a short article he was fortunate enough to have published in the now-defunct journal, *Science and Freedom,* and which appeared in December 1960.[130] The choice of this journal merits a word of explanation. It was administered by a high-powered group of European intellectuals who were known as the Committee on Science and Freedom, a group established in 1954, under the auspices of the Congress for Cultural Freedom, to carry on the discussion of issues in the field of academic freedom started at the Conference on Science and Freedom held in Hamburg in 1953. The same issue of *Science and Freedom* in which Kenny's article appeared also featured a fine essay on scholarly activity in Poland's eight universities of the period, activity naturally overshadowed, if not quite overwhelmed, by the Communist regime that then ran the country.

Kenny's striking contribution to *Science and Freedom* began with a potted history of the Irish university question down to 1908.[131] The system of appointments in UCD that were properly made (i.e., by the NUI Senate), Kenny was to agree with the Board of Visitors was indeed 'costly, undignified and undesirable'.[132] This was a reference to 150 copies of applications having to be presented by any candidate seeking a statutory appointment. There then followed a brief history of the introduction of categories of appointment he, and the Visitors, had in turn termed illegal and objectionable: in 1949 there came 'Assistant Lecturers', of which in 1959 there were 30; in 1953 'College Lecturers', of which in 1959 there were 44; in 1955 one 'College Professor' (abortive).[133] The appointments under these headings that had been made since 1949, Kenny was satisfied, contravened the rule of law. They also, he contended, weakened academic freedom. The system, he went on,

> consisted in substituting numerous appointments on an annual basis, in place of the statutory appointments on long-period tenure which should (according to the Charter) have been made and which were, in fact, being left vacant.

Kenny attempted to understand the mindset of those in the College, from the President and Governing Body down, who supported this system of appointments bypassing the NUI Senate.[134] Most Statutory Lecturers had a seven-year tenure which was renewable. This was adjudged an inconvenience which did not work well. A speedy system of College appointments militated against the risk that brighter graduates would seek to be employed elsewhere. A third reason may have been influential – bypassing the NUI could well bring in its train the ultimate *desideratum*: the abolition of the NUI itself.

Kenny speculated, in addition, on why the Governing Body, despite repeated suggestions that it should, never took legal advice.[135] It was a matter of support for the President who was, seemingly, against this course of action, and thus involved the College's prestige. There was held, too, the conviction that any legal opinion condemning these appointments as unlawful was not 'honestly held'. And the belief, frequently articulated, that the system was for the good of the College, and that the boat accordingly should not be rocked. At this juncture, Kenny added this expression of belief. 'There were', he wrote,

> certainly some on the Governing Body who believed that a professor should be the head of his Department, with the power of the sword, and that lecturers who held office for seven years were a nuisance.

The attack on the three judges who made up the Board of Visitors and the defence of the College by one professor in the Dáil – a reference to McGilligan, one of Kenny's former senior colleagues – and of another professor in the Seanad, Kenny averred came as a considerable shock.[136] He continued, not wanting to leave matters there, with this expression of his heartfelt relief. 'It is', he opined,[137]

> a quiet tribute to our political maturity that these attacks on the Judges did UCD far more harm than did the findings of the Board of Visitors.

It is worth noting that, for his part, Henchy was inspired by the entire sequence of events to pen a magisterial essay on the powers possessed by a Board of Visitors such as the one appointed by the Irish Government in the autumn of 1959.[138]

The bitterness which the entire episode engendered is certainly conveyed by McCartney in his account of the Visitation and the background to it.[139] The report of the Visitors, McCartney was to write, 'deeply offended the president'.[140] Tierney's hands-on approach to all matters connected with the College – the acquisition of the suburban estates that would be the makings of the Belfield campus, the great expansion in the numbers of junior staff, 'especially the post-war influx of young scholars from British universities', even the 'sprinkling of refugees from the war-torn Continent', including the likes of Ehler from Prague – deserved, it might well have been imagined, far more generous recognition. 'Against such an achievement', McCartney concludes,[141]

> to be denigrated for a mere dispute over nomenclature (as the appointments argument appeared to the president and his closest confidants) was understandable cause for deeply felt anger.

McCartney, in his revisiting of the conflict, has room, even so, for certain of the critics of Tierney. 'The would-be reformers', he wrote,[142]

> resented what struck them as autocratic decision-making by a clique that had no exclusive right to determine the direction of development. In the president's benevolent despotism they increasingly perceived the despotism rather than the benevolence.

What had offended, of course, was an absence of transparency in the making of appointments – no advertising of posts and the impression whether rightly or wrongly conveyed – that UCD was content to employ its own favourite sons and, perhaps, a few daughters.

By the summer of 1962 there were in post in the Law School a number of part-time professors – Finlay (Contract, Tort and Evidence); Kevin Kenny (Property and Equity);[143] O'Hanlon (Constitutional Law and Criminal Law and Procedure); Ehler (International Law and International Relations); and two Assistants (Kelly and Sheehy).[144] Henchy had resigned his chair in Roman Law and Jurisprudence, with McGilligan, as we have seen, being brought back into service temporarily as his replacement, but plainly this was just a stop-gap measure.

The year 1963 saw Kelly confirmed yet again as an Assistant to teach Roman Law and Sheehy likewise as an Assistant to do justice to Canon Law.[145] For the forthcoming session, 1963–4, another Assistant was added – to teach Common Law. This was John Blayney, again, another future judge.[146] The Law Faculty also sought approval at the same time for the recruitment of four tutors – the first time such a move is recorded. They were to be paid £150 each per annum,[147] increased to £175 (for two tutorials a week) in 1965.[148]

A new Statute, Statute LIX, brought forward in 1964, marked a major new departure. It provided for a full-time chair in Roman Law and Jurisprudence and a statutory lectureship in Legal History[149] – a development that can be viewed as a partial fulfilment of the Law Faculty's plan from as long ago as 1946–7. There were three candidates for the chair, which was filled in March 1965.[150] Kelly, the long-serving Assistant, abandoning the prospect of continuing his career at Trinity College, Oxford, was appointed. Four candidates sought the Statutory Lectureship in Legal History, and here, a newcomer, Geoffrey Hand, was successful. Two of the candidates for the job the Law Faculty determined had no special studies in History under their belt, and they were therefore removed from consideration. Law's endorsement of Hand was backed by the Faculty of Arts.

The starting salaries for both Kelly and Hand were increased when the matter was revisited shortly after their formal appointment, in the early summer of 1965.[151] Following the death of Kevin Kenny in the spring of 1966, Hugh O'Flaherty, another future judge, was brought in as his replacement on a fee per lecture basis.[152]

Early in 1967, three of the part-time professorships filled in 1962 came up for renewal, the tenure of each having been restricted, as we noted, to five years. Jeremiah Hogan, President since 1964, explained to the Governing Body how it was planned to proceed.[153] If the existing holders – these were Finlay, O'Hanlon and Ehler – wished to reapply, they should so advise the Secretary, and the mandatory advertisement for each chair would state that the existing incumbent would be a candidate. He added – and this could be trumpeted as a clear financial saving – whatever else one might be tempted to say about it – in the circumstances it would not be necessary to advertise the posts widely. The end of February 1967 was set as the last date for the receipt of applications. The three professors – Finlay, O'Hanlon and Ehler – were the only candidates. The Law Faculty approved their reappointment, which had been passed through the Senate and reported back to the Governing Body by mid-March.[154]

Finlay, however, was a few months later to signify his intention to resign, and to concentrate on his practice at the Bar. The resignation took effect at the end of September 1967.[155] He had served as Dean for five years. There was now a sizeable gap in the Law Faculty's teaching strength, following, first, the death of Kevin Kenny and, second, the announced resignation of William Finlay. Steps were speedily taken to deal with this situation – scarcely without precedent in the history of the Law Faculty – but charting what these critical measures were must needs be postponed to the next chapter.

The year 1966 saw the appearance of a legal journal, which since that date has been linked with the Law School and forms therefore part of the latter's modern story. This was *The Irish Jurist*, edited for its first few years by John Kelly, the recently appointed Professor of Roman Law and Jurisprudence. The journal was to become a vehicle for the publishing of original legal research, the absence of which had increasingly become the focus of an amount of criticism.

Journals entitled *The Irish Jurist* had a long pedigree, going back to the middle years of the nineteenth century. The last in this sequence of titles came to an end with the volume for 1965, and the first of the new *Jurists* appeared under Kelly's editorship the following year. Its inauguration that year, as explained elsewhere, did not take place in the most auspicious of circumstances[156] – there were to be rival claimants to the acquisition of the title, following the death of the previous editor, Vincent Delany, the Regius Professor at Trinity College, and such other goodwill as attached. In the end, it was a UCD consortium that was to prevail and *The Irish Jurist* thus came to UCD. The consortium consisted, apart from Kelly himself, of R.J. O'Hanlon, Kevin Kenny, Geoffrey Hand and the Dean at the time, William Finlay. All became shareholders in the Jurist Publishing Company which the consortium had acquired. Finlay played a key role in extracting from the Governing Body an advance of £500 to help launch *The Jurist*.[157] The marketing plan had been to circulate the first number free to learned institutions and legal scholars across the globe 'as part of the effort to establish it as a legal journal of international standard'.

Kelly's approach as editor betokened a radical approach. The law report section, certainly a valued feature in the preceding *Jurist* series, was jettisoned. He envisaged a journal that aimed not only to satisfy the needs of professional lawyers (primarily, as was only to expected, ones based in Ireland), but also to provide a forum for the publication in Ireland of legal scholarship of both a less parochial and, arguably, a less ephemeral sort. The solution he hit upon – to divide each issue of *The Jurist* into modern and historical jurisprudence sections, a division inspired by his knowledge of arrangements in vogue in German academic literature – furnished the blueprint for the ensuing forty odd volumes of *The Jurist*. That division has only recently been abandoned.

SÉAMUS HENCHY (1917–2009)

Henchy, who hailed from Co. Clare, was educated locally and then at University College Galway, now known as the National University of Ireland Galway, UCD and King's Inns.[158] The same year that he was called to the Bar – 1943 – he earned a PhD from NUI for his thesis 'Fosterage in Early Irish Law'. This thesis, prepared under the supervision of Dr K. Mulchrone of UCG and incorporating, as Henchy admits in the preface, suggestions and corrections in the handling of the legal material from Binchy, the man to whose chair in UCD he was to succeed, firmly established Henchy's scholarly attainments. The thesis was in two parts. In Part I he collected and translated all the extant legal material, published and unpublished, dealing with the topic of Fosterage. For the unpublished material and for all surviving fragments of *Cáin Iarraith*, he was to consult the original manuscripts, though in a few instances forced to rely on the O'Curry and O'Donovan transcripts in the Royal Irish Academy. Part I is thus devoted to an attempt to reconstruct, so far as this is possible, the rules governing Fosterage in early Irish Law. In Part II Henchy aimed, as he himself phrased it,

> to trace the development, and assess the importance, of Fosterage from earliest times up the time of its collapse and disappearance.

The last sections of this Part thus touch on a relatively unexplored aspect to the death of the Gaelic social order.

Four years later – in 1947 – two years before he was appointed to the part-time chair of Roman Law and Jurisprudence – Henchy demonstrated once again his grasp of early Irish history. This was in the edition he published, with translation, of three Irish annals governing the years from 1114 to 1437.[159] Featured here was the longest of these, the so-called MacCarthaigh Book (pp 2–115 in Henchy's volume), which dealt with this entire period (1114–1437) and which is held by the National Library; but also two fragmentary annals, from the manuscript Rawlinson B 488 held by the Bodleian Library in Oxford, the first of which (pp 116–142 in the Henchy volume) straddles the years 1237–1314, and the second (pp 143–185) the years 1392–1407. As Henchy (or Ó hInnse – to employ the Irish form of the surname linked to this volume brought out under the aegis of the Dublin Institute for Advanced Studies) points out in his introduction, entries in these particular annals complement our knowledge of medieval Ireland in several respects. MacCarthaigh's Book revisits the arrival of the Normans (see pp 46–53), and adds a little to the accounts to be found in the *Expugnatio Hibernica* and *The Song of Dermot and the Earl*. In addition, it furnishes a good deal of information on events in the south of the country, notorious for their omission from other annalistic sources. The second fragment, taken from Rawlinson B 488 deals, *inter alia*, with Richard II's expedition to Ireland in 1394. The portrait of Richard is favourable. Among the marginalia preserved in this fragment one will find set down a cure for warts in which step no.1 – several others were to follow – is stated to have been 'put a hen's legs under embers'.

Lacunae in the coverage in the annals as such and challenges in deciphering individual words in the manuscripts presented unusual difficulties for any editor. Proposed editorial solutions and the accompanying editorial apparatus all testify to Henchy's scholarly credentials, and one cannot but surmise that when Henchy finally decided that his career interests lay elsewhere – in the practice and in the teaching of law – the study of early Ireland and even of early Irish law lost a veritable champion.

This impressive scholarly background could well have weighed the scales in Henchy's favour at the level of the NUI Senate, where, arguably, against the odds, he emerged the preferred candidate.[160] Nevertheless, it merits saying that the new professor in the Law School did not publish too extensively.

A piece on Communism and the law that appeared in 1957[161] portrayed the PhD scholar and the editor of *Miscellaneous Irish Annals* admittedly in a somewhat different light – that of the Jurisprudence professor. 'To the faithful Marxist', Henchy began the piece,

> law is a concept with a disreputable past and a limited future. While neither Marx nor Engels attempted to formulate a theory of law, they make it quite clear that they regarded law as an essential part of the apparatus of the bourgeois state which would perish with the bourgeois

> state. The view of law as part of the fortifications of capitalist society which were to be stormed and razed to the ground may have stiffened the anarchic zeal of the early revolutionaries, but it rendered the victors in the October Revolution singularly unqualified to produce a convincing basis for the continued existence of the Communist state which emerged from the revolution.

In later pages Henchy was to discuss the significance of the adoption of the New Economic Policy of 1921, the career and thinking of Pashukanis, and the implications of the trials late in the 1930s of Zinoviev, Kamenev, Bukharin and Radek with Vyshinsky as chief prosecutor.

At the Visitation into the system of staff appointments at UCD, the visitation provoked by John Kenny's petition of May 1959, Henchy gave evidence in support of the petition at the oral hearings held by the Visitors over December 1949 – January 1960. The experience of this and that gained the year before in connection with Henchy's own petition over changes in the composition of the several NUI Law Faculties, leading to the appointment of an earlier Board of Visitors, doubtless whetted Henchy's appetite to find out more about such Boards, their powers and procedures, particularly in a university context. The result was a learned legal essay with its focus on this very topic.[162] It appeared in the autumn of 1961, doubtless after the dust inspired by the reports of both Boards of Visitors had settled.

The next year – 1962 – the same year that he was appointed to the Bench, Henchy published another article perhaps more self-evidently within the range of interests of a Jurisprudence professor. This was his well-regarded essay 'Precedent in the Irish Supreme Court'.[163]

Henchy resigned in January 1962, following his appointment to the High Court, apologising for the short notice.[164] That appointment was followed ten years later to the Supreme Court, where he served with great distinction until his retirement in 1989. Henchy was bestowed with an honorary LLD by NUI Galway in 1999. He died in April 2009 at the age of 91.

As a professor at UCD, Henchy's principal extra-curricular activity was to act as treasurer to the students' Law Society. In 1956 he sought, unsuccessfully, to win one of the seats on the College's Governing Body under the co-option procedure.[165] In 1958, as we have already recalled,[166] he presented a petition objecting to changes in membership of the Faculty brought about by the inclusion of a cluster of non-Law subjects in the new BCL degree course sanctioned in 1954. A Board of Visitors was appointed, but, disagreeing with Henchy's interpretation of the Charter and Statutes, found nothing was legally amiss, and thus refused the petition.[167] When his colleague, John Kenny, moved another petition objecting to UCD's system of appointments that involved bypassing the role of the National University's Senate,[168] Henchy was supportive.

Extraordinarily, on the occasion of both Visitations, another colleague of Henchy's, Patrick McGilligan, represented the other side – the Senate of NUI in 1958 and Tierney and the Governing Body in 1959–60.

In 1961 Henchy was to join Dr Roger McHugh in opposing the President, Dr Tierney's insistence that, in the then quarrel with the L & H Society, the proper course of action to pursue was straightaway to suspend the society until further notice. In what sounds as if it could well have been an acrimonious Academic Council meeting where the matter was discussed, McHugh and Henchy, in their role as 'honest brokers', constituted the lone two votes against Tierney's call for instant draconian action.[169]

Once on the Bench, somewhat more prestigious calls on Henchy's services were the result.[170] In 1965, the International Commission of Jurists asked him to investigate allegations of racial discrimination in British Guiana. In 1972 he was made chairman of the International Committee on Mentally and Maladjusted Persons. A member of the Irish delegation appointed to the Anglo-Irish Commission on Law Enforcement established under the Sunningdale Agreement in 1974, he also sat on the tribunal of inquiry into allegations made in Dáil Eireann against the then Minister for Labour, Jim Tully, in 1975. He served as an observer for the International Commission of Jurists at the trial of Bishop Donal Lamont in Rhodesia in 1976. Henchy served two terms as Chairman of the Censorship of Publications Board and he was appointed Chairman of the Independent Radio and Television Commission in 1988.

As a judge, he is, perhaps, best remembered for presiding over the Arms Trial in 1970. But to his colleagues on the Bench, to members of the legal profession and to law students, he is probably recalled for the excellence of his judgments – getting it right and expressing himself in the most attractive of prose styles.

That dual accolade is nowhere better expressed than in the heartfelt appreciation penned by Mr Justice Hogan which appeared in *The Irish Jurist* in 2011.[171]

In the future, historians may well choose to point in particular to Henchy's strong dissenting voice in *Norris* v. *Attorney General* in 1983[172] or to the crescendo of disbelief that marked Henchy's supporting judgment in the case where a section in an Act of 1935[173] banning the sale or import for sale of contraceptives was struck down as unconstitutional. 'It is the informed and conscientious wish of the plaintiff and her husband', Henchy wrote in this case, *McGee* v. *Attorney General*,[174]

> to maintain full marital relations without incurring the risk of a pregnancy that may very well result in her death or in a crippling paralysis. Section 17 of the Act of 1935 frustrates that wish. It goes further; it brings the implementation of the wish within the range of the criminal law. Its effect, therefore, is to condemn the plaintiff and her husband to a way of life which, at best, will be fraught with worry, tension and

1 The study of Roman Law was long an ingredient of instruction in university law schools in Ireland no less than elsewhere. Shown here is the title page of a first volume in a set of Corpus Iuris Civilis, including the *Digest*, brought out in Lyons in 1584. A recent English translation of the Digest was published in four volumes in Philadelphia in 1985.

2 John Henry Newman, Rector of the Catholic University. Sketch in pastel by Lady Coleridge, née Seymour (see p. 244) '[Lady Coleridge's] genius as an artist will be perpetuated by a likeness of Newman, incomparably superior, not only to that by Millais, but to any other': Sir Mountstuart Grant Duff.

3 Chistopher Palles, Chief Baron of the Irish Exchequer, chairman of the Dublin Commissioners, 1909. Portrait by Sir Hubert von Herkomer. '[A]s one returns to [the portrait], one discerns in it a strange fascination and the dominating influence of a strong personality': V.T.H. Delany.

4 Henry Brougham Leech, Regius Professor of Laws, Trinity College, Dublin. Portrait by his son, William J. Leech. In evidence to the Fry Commission in 1906 Professor Leech welcomed the prospect of a second university law school being opened in Dublin (see pp 23–4).

5 William J. Walsh, Archbishop of Dublin, first Chancellor of the National University of Ireland, purchased and presented to UCD the library of Chief Baron Palles.

6 J.G. Swift MacNeill, Professor of Constitutional Law and Public and Private Wrongs. Cartoon by 'Spy' in *Vanity Fair.*

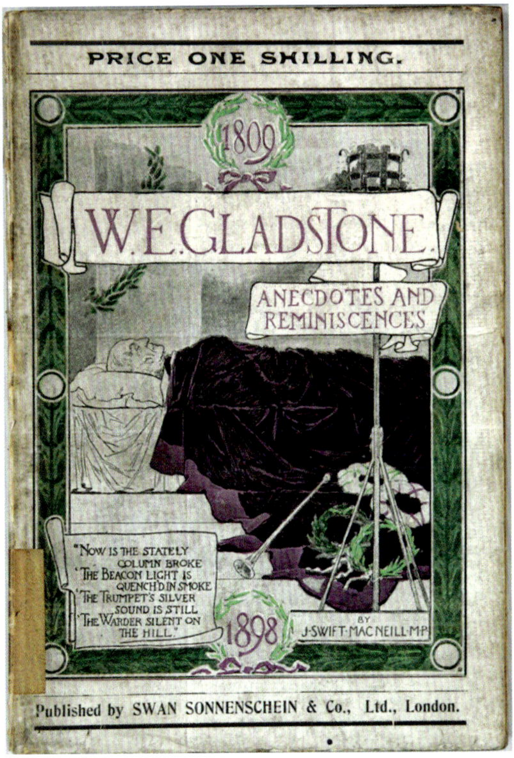

7 Cover of Swift MacNeill's tribute to Gladstone – *W.E. Gladstone, Anecdotes and Reminiscences* (1898), design by W.H. Margetson, reproduced by kind permission of the Board of Trinity College, Dublin.

8 Arthur Clery, Professor of Law of Property, Equity and Law of Contracts. Portrait by Leo Whelan.

"WHOSE CARRIAGE IS THIS?"—*p.* 60.

9 The would-be James III and his companion Cathleen interrupted on their journey north from Macroom – an incident recounted in Clery's *The Coming of the King: a Jacobite Romance* (1909), reproduced by kind permission of the Board of Trinity College Dublin.

10 Daniel A. Binchy, Professor of Roman Law, Jurisprudence and Legal History. Published *Corpus Iuris Hibernici* (1978). Dean, 1933–6.

11 Michael J. Ryan, Professor of Constitutional Law and the Law of Public and Private Wrongs, 1927–34; Professor of the Law of Property and Equity, 1934–52; Dean 1938–52.

12 Patrick McGilligan, Professor of Constitutional Law, International Law and Criminal Law. Dean, 1952–9.

13 A medieval allegory for the relationship of Church and State. Part of an eighth-century wall mosaic in remains of a dining-hall called Triclinium Leonianum Lateran. It shows St Peter bestowing a pallium on Pope Leo III and a standard on Charlemagne. Reproduced in Sidney Ehler's *Twenty centuries of Church and State* (1957).

14 Séamus Henchy, Professor of Roman Law, Jurisprudence and Legal History, 1949–62, prior to his elevation to the bench. Precipitated visitation into changes in the composition of NUI college law faculties.

15 John Kenny, Assistant Lecturer, 1954–60. Procured visitation into UCD's system of appointments, 1959–60. Elevated to the bench, 1960.

16

17

18

16 William D. Finlay, Professor of Law of Contract, Tort and Evidence. Dean, 1962–7.
17 John M. Kelly, Professor of Jurisprudence and Roman Law. Author of classic texts on Roman Law, legal philosophy and constitutional law. First editor of relaunched *Irish Jurist*. Dean 1967–70.
18 Presentation by Australian ambassador, Vincent Gair, to UCD president, Dr Thomas Murphy, of set of Commonwealth Law Reports, summer 1975.

19 Geoffrey J. Hand, Professor of Legal and Constitutional History. Dean, 1970–5.

20 Meeting of student law society, November 1970. Showing (*L to R*): Colm Allen, auditor, Dr Geoffrey Head, President of the Society and Dean of the Law Faculty, Desmond O'Malley TD, Minister for Justice; and Sean MacBride, Secretary-General, International Commission of Jurists.

21 Student activism in 1960s and 70s: 1 – March for prison reform.

22 Student activism in 1960s and 70s: 2 – Meeting pressing for introduction of free legal aid. Showing (*L to R*): Colm Kenny, Brendan Walsh, Paul McCartán and Mairin de Burca

23

24

25

23 James C. Brady, Professor of Law of Property and Equity. Dean, 1978–81; 1986–9.
24 James P. Casey, Professor of Law. Dean, 1981–6; 1989–92.
25 Paul A. O'Connor, Associate Professor of Law. Dean, 1992–2007.

26 Law staff bidding farewell to their base at Roebuck Castle, spring 2013.

27 Law students bidding farewell to Roebuck Castle, spring 2013.

> uncertainty that cannot but adversely affect their lives and, at worst, will result in an unwanted pregnancy causing death or serious illness with the obvious tragic consequences to the lives of her husband and young children. And this in the context of a Constitution which in its preamble proclaims as one of its aims the dignity and freedom of the individual; which in sub-s.2 of s.3 of Article 40 casts on the State a duty to protect as best it may from unjust attack and, in the case of injustice done, to vindicate the life and person of every citizen; which in Article 41, after recognising the family as the natural primary and fundamental unit group of society, and as a moral institution possessing inalienable and imprescriptible rights antecedent and superior to all positive law, guarantees to protect it in its constitution and authority as the necessary basis of social order and as indispensable to the welfare of the nation and the State; and which, also in Article 41, pledges the State to guard with special care the institution of marriage, on which the family is founded, and to protect it against attack.

Of this excerpt it may be remarked that, whilst Henchy's adoption of the strategy of anadiplosis might not have appealed to everyone, one generation of law students is likely to have been won over by such memorable forthrightness and so memorable a performance.

Henchy's assault denying the constitutionality of section 4 of the Vagrancy Act of 1824[175] evoked another sustained legal Philippic.[176] The ingredients of the offence [in section 4], he wrote,[177]

> and the mode by which its commission may be proved are so arbitrary, so vague, so difficult to rebut, so related to rumour or ill-repute or past conduct, so ambiguous in failing to distinguish between apparent and real behaviour of a criminal nature, so prone to make a man's lawful occasion become unlawful and criminal by the breadth and arbitrariness of the discretion that is vested in both the prosecutor and the judge, so indiscriminately contrived to mark as criminal conduct committed by one person in certain circumstances when the same conduct, when engaged in by another person in similar circumstances, would be free of the taint of criminality, so out of keeping with the basic concept inherent in our legal system that a man may walk abroad in the secure knowledge that he will not be singled out from his fellow-citizens and branded and punished as a criminal unless it has been established beyond doubt that he has deviated from a clearly prescribed standard of conduct, and generally so singularly at variance with both the explicit and implicit characteristics and limitations of the criminal law as to onus of proof and mode of proof, that it is not so much a question of ruling unconstitutional the type of offence we

> are now considering as identifying the particular constitutional provisions with which such an offence is at variance.

Two cases where the spotlight was focused on politicians as a group can usefully be added to this short inventory of the more memorable judgments of Mr Justice Henchy. In one case in 1981,[178] the Supreme Court was invited to rule on whether the plaintiff's election leaflet was 'grossly offensive' within the meaning of the Inland Post Warrant, 1939.[179] The leaflet in question had claimed that 'today's politicians are dishonest because they are being political and must please the largest number of people'. Henchy, for one, was not convinced that the criterion of gross offensiveness had been attained. 'Those who practice what is often dubbed the art of the possible', he wrote,

> would not feel grossly offended by such an expression which, denigratory and cynical though it might be thought by some, is no more than the small coinage of the currency of political controversy. Some of the most revered and successful politicians who have lived have failed at least in the eyes of reputable historians, to align great political acumen and success with moral or intellectual honesty. A charge of dishonesty is one that rarely penetrates the epidermis of any seasoned politician.

Also deserving of recall are observations which Henchy let fall in an otherwise unremarkable libel action in 1986: *Barrett* v. *Independent Newspapers Ltd.*[180]

Michael Barrett, the plaintiff, was a member of the Fianna Fáil party, and a TD for a Dublin constituency. The defendant published the *Evening Herald* newspaper. On 7 February 1983, a meeting of the Fianna Fáil parliamentary party was held at Leinster House to consider a motion that Mr Charles Haughey be removed from the leadership of the party. The meeting was a lengthy one, and ended with the defeat of the resolution. Members of the party leaving Leinster House had to negotiate the foyer where a number of journalists had gathered to await the outcome.

On 8 February, the *Evening Herald* reported that 'There were savage scenes as TDs left Leinster House early today. Michael Barrett, TD, a Dublin Haugheyite, leaned over and pulled at my beard, and said, "You thought you'd dance on his grave".' This was the basis for Barrett's libel action against the newspaper.

At the trial of the action, Mr Justice Egan ruled that the item was defamatory, thus trespassing on the function of the jury. The jury went on to hold that damages of £65,000 were appropriate. The Supreme Court was to hold that the trial judge had exceeded his jurisdiction. The members of the Court also held that the award of £65,000 was excessive. In Henchy's estimation, the jury had not been given any real help as to how to assess the damages in the case. He then personally sought to remedy the defect.[181] 'A helpful guide for a jury in a case such as this', he began,

> would have been to ask them to reduce to actuality the allegation complained of, namely, that in an excess of triumphalism at his leader's success the plaintiff attempted to tweak the beard of an unfriendly journalist. The jury might then have been asked to fit that allegation into its appropriate place in the scale of defamatory remarks to which the plaintiff might have been subjected.

'Had they approached the matter in this way', Henchy went on,

> I venture to think that having regard to the various kinds of allegations of criminal immoral and otherwise contemptible conduct that might have been made against a politician, the allegation actually complained of would have come fairly low in the scale of damaging accusations.

Overall, it is hard to disagree with Gerard Hogan's verdict on Séamus Henchy that 'his judicial thought and prose occupies a unique place in contemporary Irish legal history and jurisprudence'.[182]

ZDENĚK SYDNEY EHLER (d. 1972)

Prior to the recruitment on to the staff of the Law Faculty of qualified continental lawyers to teach courses in the Diploma in European Law which was set up in 1968, a cosmopolitan element on the staff was represented in the person of Zdeněk Sydney Ehler, a Czech émigré. Sydney Ehler, as he was known locally, began his association with UCD, when in 1950, two years after he had left Czechoslovakia, he was named an Assistant in the History Department (Assistant Lecturer 1956),[183] a job he retained throughout his years in the College. There his task was to teach Modern European History. In a little while it became clear that his talents would also be of use to the Law Faculty, where he was to teach International Law and International Relations, becoming the Professor in these subjects in 1962, as previously explained.[184]

Ehler studied law at Charles University in Prague where he graduated with a doctorate in civil and canon law. He was to continue his studies in Paris at the École Libre des Sciences Politiques, before entering the diplomatic service of the Czechoslovak Republic; for a while he worked in the Czechoslovak Embassy in London. He was later secretary to the Czech foreign minister Kamil Krofta. When in London he was to translate several English literary works into Czech.

Something of an expert in Church-State relations, Ehler after his arrival in

UCD, made his mark in this area with his publications. *Church and State through the Centuries* was, as its subtitle proclaimed, 'A collection of historic documents with commentaries'.[185] With his co-editor, John B. Morrall, also on the staff of UCD at the time, Ehler takes us on an extraordinary intellectual journey that commences, as Michael Tierney the UCD President explains in his preface, with the letter of the Emperor Trajan on the treatment of the early Christians and concludes with the Irish Constitution of 1937 and the Czechoslovak Communist Law on Church Affairs of October 1949.[186] *Church and State through the Centuries* was published in 1954.

Three years later Ehler alone covered much of the same ground in a volume consisting of a continuous narrative on the Church-State relationship. *Twenty Centuries of Church and State: a Survey of their Relations in Past and Present*, a more slender volume, was to be translated into German, Italian and Spanish.[187] The chronological span is again impressive. Ehler starts with the persecutions under Nero and Diocletian before reaching the Edict of Milan of AD 313; and he ends with a chapter on 'Church and State in the Cold War', that includes the tussle with Juan Perón of Argentina and the declaration of June 1955 of the Roman Congregation of the Consistory 'defining publicly the infractions of canon law committed by the Argentinian State authorities and stating the censures which they had incurred'.[188]

Twenty Centuries of Church and State is embellished by an illustration facing the title page depicting a medieval allegory for the relationship between Church and State – that of a wall mosaic of the eighth century showing St Peter bestowing a pallium on Pope Leo III and a standard on Charlemagne. The book carries a 'Nihil obstat' and an 'Imprimatur', the latter from the Archbishop of Baltimore.

In a series of essays published in the *Capuchin Annual*, Ehler continued the story of the Church and State relationship, giving particular attention to the fortunes of the Roman Catholic Church in the face of the Communist takeover in Eastern Europe after the Second World War. 'Decline of Communism', dealing with what he termed the 'Church of Silence', appeared in the *Annual* for 1965.[189] A longer piece with a global reach, 'Church and State in the present world' followed in 1966.[190] Here Ehler details the tribulations of certain of the princes of the Church, of Cardinal Beran from Czechoslovakia for instance, for whom Ehler was to act as interpreter during Beran's visit to Ireland following his release from captivity in 1965.[191] The conflict between the Catholic Church and the Communist government of Poland that boiled over into rival mass demonstrations in May 1966 is described and analysed in the *Capuchin Annual* for 1967.[192] Somewhat different in emphasis was 'The question of the Holy Places in Palestine' published again in the *Capuchin Annual,* in the issue for 1971.[193]

One feature of the first opus in this impressive sequence of publications, *Church and State through the Centuries,* that merits a special mention is that Ehler and Morrall's collection of documents put together in 1954 includes a large number of these appearing for the first time in an English translation. There are 30 of them in total, and among these are to be found the *Compacts of Prague made with the Hussites* at the Council of Basel (1433), the *Religious Peace of Augsburg* (1555), Pope Paul IV's Bull *Ex Apostolatus Officio* deposing heretical princes (1559), the *Edict of Nantes* (1598), and its *Revocation* (1685), the *Decree naming the Jesuit Order as Protector of the Indians of Paraguay* (1636), the *Law on the Appointment of Clergy* at the time of the German 'Kulturkampf' (1874), and the *French Law on the Separation of Church and State* (1905).

Ehler's comment on a corollary of *Ex Apostolatus Officio*, the Bull *Regnans in Excelsis* of 1570 declaring Elizabeth I excommunicate and deposed as Queen, is not without interest. It failed of its purpose, he wrote, and it had become 'obvious that hierocracy had run its course'.[194] Even within the twentieth-century Vatican it was to be adjudged a blunder, so much so in fact that, as Owen Chadwick was to tell Diarmaid MacCulloch and as recorded by the latter, the episode was employed by discreet voices in the Vatican to dissuade Pope Pius XI from mounting a frontal attack on Nazism: this would backfire.[195] Pius' Encyclical, *Mit Brennender Sorge* (1937), bristled with indignation, but was limited in scope.

Ehler would regularly attend summer and autumn meetings of the Academy of International Law at The Hague. He also attended the get-together of Hague attendees and alumni in Dubrovnik in May 1962.[196] A Hague Academy meeting in Istanbul the next year again saw Ehler in attendance.[197] In 1959 he lectured at The Hague on 'The international organisation of the feudal Middle Ages',[198] a theme to which he returned in his contribution to the Festschrift for Aubrey Gwynn, SJ, published in 1961.[199] For his 1961 lecture at The Hague, he turned his attention again to Church and State with an offering on 'The recent concordats' – a talk also given at Maynooth a year or so later.[200] In 1962, back in Dublin, he had, at the request of the Law Faculty, delivered a special lecture on the then European Communities.[201] He was at Rennes in 1965, lecturing on 'Legal aspects of World War II',[202] and in Paris in 1970, on the invitation of the University of Paris, lecturing on 'New trends in the International Law of Neutrality'.[203] In May 1965 Ehler edited a special supplement in the French newspaper *Le Monde* devoted to Ireland: *L'Essor de l'Irlande*.[204] Ehler had become the newspaper's Dublin correspondent. Ehler was a faithful contributor to the Czech journal, *Nový Život*, under the pseudonym, Zdeněk Petr.[205]

Ehler's wife, Astrid Baecklund, was also appointed to the UCD staff, when, in 1961, she was made Director of Studies for Slavonic Languages.[206] She was to resign four years later on obtaining the Professorship of Slavonic Philology at the University of Lund in Sweden.[207] It was in Lund where Sydney Ehler died early in 1972 towards the end of his second five-year term as holder of the chair of International Law and International Relations.

WILLIAM D. FINLAY (1921–2010)

William D. Finlay was called to the Irish Bar in 1942,[208] and his association with the Law Faculty commenced in 1954 when he was named one of the three new Assistants. In 1956 he was made a Senior Counsel, and following his appointment in 1962 to one of the four new part-time chairs – Finlay's was that of Common Law (Contract and Tort) and Evidence – he became Dean. During his Deanship, as we have recorded, Finlay successfully negotiated an advance from the Governing Body to help launch as a Law Faculty publication the revamped *Irish Jurist*.[209]

Finlay inherited as Dean the task of acting as treasurer for the student Law Society. He was also occasionally asked to tender legal advice to the President – this occurred for instance in connection with the plans for a church on the Belfield Campus – but the days when this had been a frequent occurrence were now decidedly at an end, and the President and Governing Body conspicuously went outside the Law School to secure comprehensive and, hopefully, rock-solid advice on that same vexed issue, which T.K. Liston, SC, in two very long and detailed opinions was good enough to furnish.

Finlay's part-time chair of Contract, Tort and Evidence came up for renewal in 1967, as it was only originally tenable for the five years since the initial appointment in March 1962. The renewal was confirmed in March 1967,[210] but three months later Finlay announced he was resigning. In a letter to the President, Jeremiah Hogan, Finlay recalled a conversation he had had, in which he had expressed to Hogan the concern he had felt over the conflict between the demands of his academic work and his Bar practice. 'When', he continued,[211]

> the term of my chair ended earlier in the year I hoped to be able to continue my work in the College in which I am deeply interested, but I am now reluctantly convinced that it is impossible.

'If it would be helpful', he added, 'I would continue to act until the start of October to deal with the exams.' Pressure was applied to get Finlay to stay on until Christmas, but it was unavailing, and Finlay finally resigned on 30 September 1967.[212]

Finlay's presence at the lecturing podium was recalled by Charles Lysaght, a student at the law school in the early 1960s. Finlay was viewed as 'a stylish figure in an institution that seemed to spurn style'. Lysaght's recollections continued. Finlay, he wrote,[213]

> arrived for lectures carrying a bowler hat, a dapper, breezy figure with wavy hair combed back, always attired in a well-cut suit, and even a flower in his button hole. He delivered lectures off the cuff, entertaining

> his students with anecdotes from his practice and occasional references to shooting and fishing which were his main relaxations.

Finlay maintained a close association with his *alma mater*. Until ill-health supervened, he could be encountered walking his dog in the grounds of Belfield. On the establishment of the UCD Association in 1984, Finlay became its first chairman and would preside at the functions the Association organised. In October 1986 he led the Association on the excursion they paid to the College's experimental farm at the Lyons Estate, which furnished at the time the teaching centre of the Faculty of Agriculture.[214]

JOHN GERARD SHEEHY (1924–2003)

To teach and examine in the subject Canon Law, introduced into the LLB in 1955, the Revd J.G. Sheehy was recruited as an Assistant, commencing with the session 1957–8. Sheehy qualified as a barrister in 1958, and was later to preside as a judge of the Marriage Tribunal in the Roman Catholic Archdiocese of Dublin. Sheehy would regularly attend the annual London January meetings of the Canon Law Society of Great Britain.[215] The focus of his published writings covered certain topics of practical use to him as a judge of the Marriage Tribunal. These included 'Male psychical impotence in judicial proceedings',[216] and, together with John Marshal, MD, 'The problem of female impotence with specific reference to the artificial vagina'.[217]

In 1968, an issue of the journal *Studies* was devoted to the laws on marriage, and the issue of the introduction of provision for civil divorce that had been recommended by a committee reviewing the Constitution (which at the time contained a complete ban on divorce). Sheehy was among the contributors who responded to the leading article penned by Cahir Davitt, who had recently retired as President of the High Court.[218] In common with a number of the other contributors, Sheehy evinced a degree of astonishment at the proposal that had emanated from the committee. 'No responsible body of opinion' he wrote,[219]

> even of minority opinion, has emerged to support the Committee's suggestion that civil divorce is a need in this country.

The depth of his feelings on the entire question is captured in another extract from his essay. 'The ban on divorce', he continued,[220]

> is an obvious and an integral part of our legal heritage. If we were to change it now, we should be reversing the process of centuries. Antiquity itself is not perhaps an absolute value, but in the interest of a nation's

> legal inheritance and in a matter of such fundamental importance to society, what lawyers would sweep aside such a tradition for something to which it has always been diametrically opposed?

Canon Law did not survive on the Law Faculty's curriculum following the replacement of the new LLB in 1970 by the taught LLM. Sheehy's association with the Law Faculty thus came to an end. Latterly, Sheehy had experienced difficulty in maintaining his teaching schedule – a circumstance that on one occasion provoked a number of his student charges to contemplate litigation.

Sheehy died in March 2003.[221]

JOHN MAURICE KELLY (1931–91)

John Kelly, a native of Dublin, was educated at Glenstal Abbey, Co. Limerick, from where he won an open scholarship to UCD. Graduating in Classics, he secured a travelling scholarship which took him as a postgraduate student to Heidelberg where he earned the first of his doctorates. Oxford was to bestow a second. Following his call to the Irish Bar and a period of practice on the Leinster Circuit, Kelly was elected a fellow of Trinity College, Oxford in 1961. He stayed there for four years, serving concurrently (from 1962), at the conclusion of the short Oxford terms, as an Assistant in the UCD Law School, teaching Roman Law.[222]

In 1965 Kelly, as we have already noted,[223] was appointed to the chair in Roman Law and Jurisprudence which again became full-time. The gap that had existed since Henchy was translated to the High Court Bench was thus finally filled. Kelly held the chair until his death at the age of 59 in January 1991. In honour of Kelly a lecture series named after him was inaugurated by the Law Faculty in 1994. This involves an annual lecture delivered by a distinguished judge or jurist.

Kelly succeeded Finlay as dean in 1967 and was responsible for key developments undertaken in the Law School at this time.[224] These included the inauguration of a taught Master's degree (the LLM), the inauguration of a Diploma in European Law, the expansion of holdings of European legal material in the Law section of the Library and a programme for the recruitment of more full-time staff. Not to be omitted from the reckoning either was the acquisition at this time by the UCD staff consortium of *The Irish Jurist*, which Kelly edited from 1966 until 1973. Kelly set his stamp on the new series of *The Irish Jurist* in impressive fashion – the deliberate division of the subject-matter of each issue into 'Modern Jurisprudence' and 'Historical Jurisprudence'. There was the risk, as Kelly saw it – and others would agree – that legal writing and legal research would degenerate to the point where undue emphasis was accorded the insular and the ephemeral. In the plans for *The Jurist* any such trend would almost certainly not be encouraged; rather the reverse. So a place from the outset was set aside for those who discerned the immensity of the legal heritage, outside Ireland no less than within, and across the centuries besides, and wished to write about, and discuss that – a tactic successfully designed to guarantee the international appeal of the journal.[225]

Kelly was a prolific author, publishing three works of his own on Roman Law between 1957 and 1976 and one translation of a German classic in the area, in 1966. His first major foray into Irish constitutional law appeared in 1961 as well. And there was the writing of novels besides – all of which will be dealt with in more detail below.[226]

Kelly entered politics in 1969, serving first as a Senator, and then, whilst a member of Dáil Éireann (from 1973), holding ministerial office. He served as Parliamentary Secretary to the Taoiseach, 1973–7, to the Minister for Defence, 1973–5, to the Minister for Foreign Affairs, 1975–7. He had a brief stint as Attorney-General in 1977 and enjoyed a rather longer period in office, 1981–1982, as Minister for Trade, Commerce and Tourism. Granted leave of office for certain of the periods Kelly held these ministerial appointments, Kelly yet retained a keen interest in the Law School and its activities, while unable, naturally enough, to assist with the increasing burden shouldered by his colleagues who, not having been bitten by any political bug, were left to man the fort – and undertake the manifold administrative tasks that this involved – 'ploughing the sands', as Kelly was wont dismissively to label a fair few of them, especially attendance at committees. Occasionally, in his political role, Kelly was nevertheless to act as champion for interests that the country's academic lawyers had taken to heart as well: the problem of the delay in the appearance of Irish law reports for instance, and the need to do something about it.[227]

Politically, Kelly proved no friend of the Labour Party with which Fine Gael necessarily was allied in the short sequence of Coalition administrations. His preference was for a coming together ultimately of Fine Gael and Fianna Fáil, once the latter had learned fiscal rectitude and ditched much of its Republican posturing.[228] As Downey put it in his obituary, Kelly was himself 'a Republican in the antique, austere mould', despising pretension and ostentation.[229] Returning to the back benches in 1982, he continued, as another obituarist phrased it,[230] 'to make stimulating contributions to political debate often laced with uproarious humour, invective and irreverence'. There was a down side though, it was claimed by the same writer:[231]

> But there was an idiosyncratic and unpredictable quality about his pronouncements which devalued his standing as a contender for political office.

John Kelly, as we have already acknowledged, was to prove a prolific author: from his pen were to come three books on Roman law, two on Irish constitutional law, one on legal philosophy, three novels and one translated work. In addition, there were a number of shorter offerings that were of importance in their own right. It may be an idiosyncratic selection, but among these offerings, I would highlight 'The inner nature of the tort action';[232] 'Equality before the law in three European jurisdictions' [Germany, Italy, Ireland];[233] and 'Hidden treasure and the Constitution'.[234] Such productivity on the part of any academic linked to the Law Faculty was not only unheralded; it was unprecedented. There can be little doubt that this personal achievement contributed hugely to the growing reputation of the Faculty itself.

Kelly's first book, one of the three on facets of the history of Roman law and written in German, was published in Weimar in 1957. *Princeps Iudex*, as its full title – *Princeps Iudex: eine Untersuchung zur Entwicklung und zu den Grundlagen der Kaiserlichen Gerichtsbarkeit*[235] – explains, wrestles with the problem of the changes wrought in the Roman legal system by the establishment of the Augustan principate. It is split into two parts, dealing separately with criminal law and with private law. The text itself was the key portion of work presented in fulfilment of the requirements for the award of the doctorate which Kelly received from the University of Heidelberg in 1956.[236] How Raphael Houlihan, another Irish postgraduate student (in fiction) earned his doctorate from the same university – a matter dealt with in a novel published by Kelly under a pseudonym[237] – can usefully be compared.

Roman Litigation,[238] Kelly's second book in the area of Roman law, came out nearly a decade later, and had benefited from a sojourn the author had spent at the Leopold – Wenger – Institut attached to the University of Munich. Its publication occurred in 1966, just after Kelly had left Trinity College, Oxford on being appointed Professor of Roman Law and Jurisprudence at UCD. (The first of Kelly's volumes on Irish constitutional law and the novel written under the pseudonym had also emerged in the interval between *Princeps Iudex* and *Roman Litigation*.) *Roman Litigation* comprised a series of studies on the realities of Roman judicial practice and, in particular, of its shortcomings. The latter were listed as the handicaps faced by the socially weaker party; corruption on the part of praetors and judges; and the general ineffectiveness of the judicial system. There was a certain nobility about the mission statement we find at the start of Justinian's *Institutes: Justitia est constans et perpetua voluntas jus suum cuique tribuens.* Kelly, however, finds himself coerced into pronouncing a gloomy verdict. 'A powerful and intractable defendant', he concluded,[239]

> who was not sensitive about his public reputation, could and very often did frustrate the just claim of a plaintiff by resisting summons or execution.

'This situation', he went on,[240]

> must have continued so long as the State took no hand in physically assisting the wronged plaintiff.

Only when Antoninus Pius became emperor – in AD 138 – was that situation to alter. To drive home the points Kelly felt compelled to reach, he was to make considerable use of the detail of which only a person with a good knowledge of the classics was in a position to avail. We thus read[241] that

> the violence of which Roman litigants were capable is evidenced by what is no doubt the extreme case of A. Sempronius Asellio, praetor in 89 BC, who was actually murdered by a crowd of capitalist creditors because he was favouring the debtor defendants by applying old laws against usury.

On the theme of corruption, Kelly makes a predictable acknowledgement of Cicero's express opposition, but adds, tellingly, of the frequency in Cicero's private correspondence of recommendations to magistrates on behalf of his litigant friends, invariably accompanied by the anodyne (?) qualification, *quod tua fides dignitasque patietur*.[242] Inevitably, Kelly finds room to mention the case of the judge L. Tubulus, who in 142 BC was condemned by a special *quaestio* for taking bribes during a murder trial.[243]

Reviewers of *Roman Litigation* were broadly enthusiastic. This book, wrote Yale,[244]

> refreshingly requires the student of Roman law to consider many questions about the facts of Roman litigation, questions which the writings of the Jurists do not generally ask, let alone answer.

Kelly's work, wrote Duff,[245]

> may be more valuable for the questions it asks than for the answers it propounds. But for his choice of target, for the attempt to place the abstract rules of Roman law in a realistic setting of Roman social and political life, there can be nothing but praise.

Binchy, the erstwhile occupant of the chair to which Kelly had so recently been appointed, joined in the refrain. 'Works on Roman law', he wrote in his review,[246]

> which can claim the interest of the specialist and the general reader alike are extremely rare. This is undoubtedly one of them. Dr Kelly is just as

> much at home with the poets, the dramatists, the philosophers and the historians as with the jurisconsults. The testimony of Cicero or Plautus is invoked as frequently as that of Gaius or Ulpian. The result is that his book never loses contact with the realities of Roman life even when the author is discussing highly technical points of legal procedure.

The highest of praise then ensues. 'It is', Binchy concludes,[247]

> surely a matter for rejoicing that this country, for the first time in its history, has a scholar of international reputation in the field of Roman law.[248]

There was to be brought out in 1966 the 1st English edition of Wolfgang Kunkel's *Römische Rechtsgeschichte* in the latter's fourth edition. Kelly was the translator, as he was for the 2nd English edition of 1973 based on Kunkel's sixth edition.[249] A succinct and up-to-date history of Roman law and its constitutional background was in this fashion introduced to the English-speaking world. In these two English editions, Kelly's handiwork is to the fore, not just in the translation itself but in the admirable, detailed and lengthy Bibliographical Appendix (pp 192–228) in the 2nd English edition.

Kelly himself returned as an author in his own right, with his *Studies in the Civil Judicature of the Roman Republic*, published in 1976,[250] and preceded by a study sojourn at the Institut für geschichtliche Rechtswissenschaft in Heidelberg. Here Kelly sought to establish the respective functions of the three forms of court that occupied the space of civil judicature under the Republic: the *centumviri,* the *recuperatores* and, last but not least, the *unus judex*. An attempt is made to estimate statistically the relative frequency with which the various departments of the civil law were litigated – the *unus judex* scoring 50 per cent, the *recuperatores* under 10 per cent. The origins of the role of the *recuperatores*, which has been controversial, are revisited, Kelly concluding that they seem to have acquired jurisdiction in cases concerning free/unfree status, manumission on succession, and a few linked to certain quasi-criminal delicts. The *centumviri* throughout retained their jurisdiction, which was of ancient pedigree, in the sphere of inheritance; and here it was important to note that they continued to judge by *legis actio* even after the procedure by *formula* applied in the other jurisdictions: this older procedure, unlike the new, did not constrain the court to pronounce a judgment in purely money terms.

More even than in the case of *Roman Litigation* Kelly makes substantial use of non-legal sources, to which, indeed, a separate index is furnished. In between Cato/Catullus and Varro/ Vitruvius, the reader will find sundry references for Cicero, Gellius, Livy, Plautus and Suetonius and so forth. Kelly sought to guard against criticism of his endeavours in this volume with the averment[251] that his 'statement of the conception of the Republic's judicial complex [was] offered not as the last word, but as the first in a long overdue discussion'.

Stein, in his review, is gently critical.[252] Kelly, he was to write, 'by smooth, flowing, modest suggestions', had lulled himself, 'into accepting quite revolutionary ideas'. Watson, in his observations, is a good deal more robust. 'When reading Kelly', he began,[253]

> you should keep alert or he will slip a quick Irish one past you. Concentrate on the evidence and on what other scholars say, as well as on what he says is the evidence or the claims of others. Otherwise you will lose a few tricks.

There is no let-up. 'Much of what is said is suspect'. 'So many of the conclusions are hypothetical'. The book should be approached 'with extreme caution'. It is 'brilliant in its conception but less satisfactory in its execution'.

Fundamental Rights in the Irish Law and Constitution, Kelly's first major foray into Irish Constitutional Law, was published in 1961.[254] A second edition followed in 1967.[255] It was to be welcomed as the first book on the practical workings of the Irish Constitution, an exercise executed extremely well. The initial chapter, charting the essence of the political and constitutional history of the South from the time of the Easter Rising down to the adoption of the 1937 Constitution and beyond is a masterly synopsis. We are reminded of the slim majority that greeted the backing of the new constitution – 685,105 votes in favour, and 526,945 against – and the extent to which certain provisions of the new dispensation, but not of course all, revisited what was to be found in the document of 1922. That there had even been organic growth extending over a longer period is recalled in the reviewing of cases such as *Humphries* v. *Connor*,[256] *O'Kelly* v. *Harvey*,[257] and *Coyne* v. *Tweedy*[258] for what they tell us about the rights linked to freedom of assembly.[259]

Kelly addresses a question that has since been examined in even greater detail: the extent to which fundamental rights provisions were intended merely to serve as guiding headlines for the Oireachtas rather than to serve as an inspiration for activist judicial review in the courts. Declan Costello, in an early assessment,[260] welcomed what he termed 'a balanced and unemotional account of human rights in our legal system and how they are derived and protected'. But he does not let Kelly off the hook when Kelly chooses to term 'natural law' as affording 'hardly anything more than the precept of loving justice and hating iniquity'. There was much more to 'natural law' than that.

In the foreward to the second edition of *Fundamental Rights in the Irish Law and Constitution,* Kelly comments as follows on the radical changes already influencing the evolution of the indigenous legal system. 'Both Bench and Bar', Kelly was to write,

> are increasingly tending to fertilise Irish jurisprudence by implanting in it concrete propositions evolved from fundamental principles, and the rate of development over the next few years is likely to be rapid.

And so, indeed, it turned out, which led Kelly to plan a different stratagem to keep abreast of developments in Irish constitutionalism – a different kind of book. Thus was *The Irish Constitution* conceived. It was to appear in its first edition in 1980.[261] It is now in its fourth edition, being edited after Kelly's death in 1991, by the team of Gerard Hogan, now a judge of the High Court and Gerry Whyte, now a professor at Trinity College.[262]

The book is arranged round the text of the 1937 Constitution itself which is supplied in bold type in the two official languages, Irish and English. We thus start with the Preamble or Brollach and end with Article 52 and the other transitional Articles, the force of which is long since spent.

Carolan has considered at some length the impact of this seminal work in its several editions on Irish Constitutional Law and its scholarship.[263] They have had, he writes,[264] 'a profound influence on the development of constitutional law'. 'There can be few, if any, persons', he continues,[265]

> with a professional or pedagogical interest in Irish constitutional law who have not had cause to refer to and rely upon this text in the last 30 years.

The principal difference between the new text and that of the earlier volume of 1961 with its second edition of 1967, is that, whereas *Fundamental Rights* dealt, as its title indicated, with all the assorted fundamental rights, *The Irish Constitution* dealt with the Constitution as a whole. Carolan's praise is certainly heartfelt, and, if he is correct, this entails that Kelly's *The Irish Constitution* bodes fair to being the volume by which he will best be remembered. '*The Irish Constitution*', Carolan writes,[266] 'stands as a tribute to the possibilities of academic leadership in a small jurisdiction like ours – and is a challenge to those who continue to work in its wake'.

Kelly aimed to blaze a trail in a very different area of legal studies with his *A Short History of Western Legal Theory*.[267] Like the second of the two published novels which we will be dealing with shortly, *A Short History* was to be published posthumously – in 1992, a year after his death. The message about the subject Jurisprudence which Kelly was intent to put across is brilliantly realised in the two opening paragraphs of his Preface 'The book', Kelly writes,

> is an attempt to offer students of law and politics a guide of manageable size to the history of the leading themes in the legal theory of Western civilisation.
>
> The idea of writing it came from my own teaching experience at Dublin. Under the rubric Jurisprudence, or Legal Theory, lecturers are

> notably freer to choose their own material and method than when dealing with the practical parts of the law. The lack of a fixed conventional content in the subject can be seen in the very different plans adopted by those who have written textbooks in the field, as a quick glance at Dias, Friedmann, Lloyd, Paton, Salmond, and Wortley will demonstrate. My own preference is to try and take my class through the history of the main themes of legal theory, starting with the Greeks and going up to the present day. But the approach of most of my colleagues in the common-law world is different. They prefer to concentrate on contemporary legal theory, on the doctrines of legal philosophers still alive, or not long dead.

Or to express it more succinctly, in a note to Tony Honoré, who undertook the chore of reading and checking the typescript, following Kelly's death: *Vixere fortes ante Hart et Dworkin multi*. Indeed, they did.

Inevitably, given the structure around which the book is arranged – a succession of accounts of historical periods in which different kinds of legal theory evolved – there was to be an amount of repetition which does, alas, grate. But the achievement nonetheless is very considerable, and helps to reposition the study of law centrally within the humanities where it belongs.

Of the reviews that accompanied the publication of *A Short History*, that by Quinn in the *Irish Jurist* can be counted among the more acute.[268] Kelly, he writes, 'makes a valiant and largely successful attempt to portray the history of Western legal theory on an integrated continuum stretching from the ancient past to the present'. Much can be forgiven for the shortcomings linked to Kelly's dismissal of certain of the more recent writers on jurisprudence, for these 'pale in comparison with the erudition and clarity of the book as a whole'.

Ibbetson's assessment, for a variety of reasons, is more critical.[269] But he has this to say, which is worth repeating 'The recognition', he writes,

> that the ideas of contemporary writers have a history in the ideas of earlier generations, and that these earlier writers existed in a context of their own, inevitably leads to the recognition that the writers of our own time are as much a part of the historical process as were their forebears. This might be an uncomfortable (and salutary) realisation for those seduced into the belief that the present generation has a monopoly of truth.

The late Mr Justice Niall McCarthy, for his part, found the volume 'fascinating, entertaining and humbling'.[270] It is easy enough to see why.

John Kelly was a man of many parts, and this was reflected above all in the circumstances that he wrote three novels. Two of the latter were to be published, the first during his life-time under a pseudonym, and the second, two years after his death, under his own name.

Matters of Honour, authored by 'John Boyle' and published in Hutchinson's New Authors series in 1964,[271] is in the tradition of the *Bildungsroman* which places it in the same genre as Flaubert's *L'Éducation Sentimentale* and Thomas Mann's *Der Zauberberg*. Raphael Houlihan has won a postgraduate scholarship enabling him to travel to Heidelberg to complete a doctorate on 'Land values in the Roman republic' under the supervision of a Professor Theodor Gottlieb, a professor of ancient history. The novel charts the fortunes of Raphael during his year in Heidelberg.

At one level, the novel furnishes an explanation of how Gottlieb's imaginary classic tome, *Wirtschaftstheorie und – Praxis der Römischen Republic* was finally accepted for publication by his publishers, Schloss-Verlag. At another, it is a tale of the two passionate love affairs in which Raphael becomes embroiled. The first affair which would, we are led to think, possibly endure, was with Ingelore Chmiet, 'a gentle fair-haired girl', whom Raphael encounters by chance by the waters of a public fountain.[272] This last boasted rioting stone cherubs and bore, along with armorial devices of one kind or another, an apt Latin tag: 'calidis refrigeror lymphis'. Raphael doubtless will have been aware that, according to legend, Numa Pompilius and Egeria made their acquaintance at just such a place. Raphael's second affair involved Marta Lukas, Professor Gottlieb's unhappily married daughter.

There is much else besides. The fairy-tale atmosphere of Heidelberg itself is splendidly evoked: the narrow cobbled streets, the onion towers, the steeply pitched snow-covered roofs. If the neighbourhood also hid many delights, Raphael's eviction from his student quarters at the behest of an unforgiving Frau Globke, the landlady – taking a bath in a bathroom the use of which was restricted exclusively to the Globke family – demonstrated that life in Heidelberg could not be relied on to proceed on an harmonious or even keel.[273] Raphael is also to be found at a duel fought under the auspices of the Saxo-Thuringian Corps in a low-ceilinged stone-floored room under the gaze of Kaiser Wilhelm I.[274] For an assault on Szegety, one of Inge's other lovers, Raphael is convicted and fined.[275] And he is admitted to hospital suffering from a bout of pneumonia contracted when caught in a thunderstorm at the conclusion of a fireworks display.[276]

The affair with Marta Lukas eventually turns a little sour. But well before that Raphael and Marta had enjoyed an especially sensual spring break in Rome.[277] They would sit naked on their bedroom's balcony, splashing each other with wine. They would go swimming in the Mediterranean at Ostia, 'embracing wildly as the sea closed over our heads'.

Raphael never completes his thesis on 'Land values in the Roman republic', but he nevertheless obtains a DPhil for his work on revising for publication Professor Gottlieb's classic tome.[278] The achievement puts Raphael in line for a prestigious academic appointment back in Dublin, a city to which by the conclusion of the novel we sense he is determined to introduce Inge and where he will marry her. Nevertheless, throughout the book, a tone of self-deprecation is evident, even emphatic. It is his Mullingar confrère Kastenbummel, Szegety's adversary in the duel, who expresses the sentiment at one point:[279] 'What woman of spirit wants to live with a bloody old ancient historian?' But it is no flight of fancy to imagine Raphael identifying with the same school of thought, for elsewhere our principal protagonist in this yarn expresses clear doubts about what he was at. 'Vivid pictures of little Italian farms in the age of Horace', Raphael tells us,[280]

> flashed cross my mind; little fields of olives and maize, slim brown-skinned girls with shining black hair walking across them in bare feet, carrying pitchers of wine to men lying beneath plane-trees and waiting for them. How Lalage and Phryne would laugh from their dust to think of someone like me spending the best time of his life buried in a library trying to discover how much their fields of olives were worth, buried in a library while other girls passed beneath his window, passed on their way and disregarded him.[281]

There are contradictions even so, for Raphael, on hearing of the bestowal of the DPhil and the prospect that this has opened up of the academic post in Dublin starts to sing a different tune. 'I sat already', Raphael hypothesises,[282]

> in the cosy library with its deep alcoves and its windows looking across the dignified square, already I was being lionised at the inaugural meetings of student societies, I was planning another book.

Inimitable Kelly touches abound. American tourists flocking to Heidelberg are admonished for their greasy, spotty complexions, which were attributed to their eating 'fried eggs and chocolate cake for breakfast'.[283] A German who confides in Raphael his considered opinion that Ireland was to be congratulated for remaining neutral during the Second World War, would have been taken aback by Raphael's response, only thought, not uttered:[284] it was 'small honour to us not to have played our part in beating down an inhuman tyranny'. Believing erroneously that he would never in fact earn his postgraduate degree, Raphael is found ruminating once again:[285]

> I'd be lucky to end up as a junior executive officer in the Civil Service or as the public relations officer of a baby-powder factory.

Matters of Honour ends with Raphael returning to the railway station at Aachen to rendezvous with Inge, only a few pages after it looked as if he was intent on standing her up.[286] Kelly has earlier taken steps to dissuade any reader or critic from proceeding to pronounce some solemn judgment on this opus by printing at the outset six well-known lines of Latin, intended, perhaps, as a kind of health warning:

> Gaudeamus igitur
> Juvenes dum sumus:
> Post jucundam juventutem
> Post molestam senectutem
> Nos habebit humus
> Nos habebit humus.

The Polling of the Dead, Kelly's second novel and published posthumously,[287] is very different. This is a political thriller set in the Ireland of the 1960s which features one contemporary homicide, a petrol bomb attack on the Leeson Street flat of the principal protagonist, the young barrister and Opposition activist, Redmond Byrne (conceivably Kelly's second *alter ego*), skulduggery at the Aliens Office in Dublin Castle and a cover-up for a murder on the Dublin–Liverpool boat in the mid-1940s. The unravelling of a sequence of mysterious events, the appearance of a war-time Belgian passport and two travel tickets and much else besides, enables the political Opposition to put pressure on Bradley, no. 2 in the Government party, who is found to have known exactly what had been going on, to prevent him announcing a financial bonanza likely to turn the political tide in the Government's favour at the critical juncture, for the events in *The Polling of the Dead*, with side shows outside Dublin, in Naas, Newbridge, The Curragh and Athy, all take place on the eve of a General Election. As a result of that, at the end of the day, we are told, the Opposition are returned to power, with the capture of 14 new seats in the Dáil.[288]

As the mystery starts to unfold, our barrister hero – soon to travel down a garbage chute in a multi-storey apartment block, and to be savagely beaten up – argues a wrongful dismissal case in the High Court before Mr Justice Ganly. A sketch of the judge follows, one of the few passages in the novel of legal import. Ganly, we are informed,[289] was

> fair and polite; but when you had said that much about him, you had said nearly everything. He was not exactly stupid, but had an absolute flair for getting hold of the wrong end of the stick; and opening a case to him involved hard work, if you didn't want to waste half a day later on trying to disentangle some basic misapprehensions formed at the outset.

An important early scene takes place in the penthouse flat in the apartment block that contains the garbage chute. The flat belonged to a Government senator, one

Shane Boyne, who had made a success as a businessmen with a chain of large garages and motor showrooms. The sociologist in Redmond Byrne (Kelly?) takes over at this point apropos Boyne. The empire Boyne had built up, we are told,[290] was

> not a bad business in a country where the car starts as a status symbol very far down the income-bracket scale, and where farmers leave thirty acres starved of lime and phosphate so that their sons will be able to drive forty miles to a marquee dance and back, three nights a week.

That the country was facing a general election is indicated by Kelly right at the start, when Redmond Byrne describes the streetscape at dawn as he looks out of the window in his Leeson Street flat:[291]

> The street was squalid with election posters. Sodden cardboard, poorly printed, they sagged on slack twine from the green lamp-posts, those of them that had not fallen to the ground and been mashed by the weather and the traffic.

Byrne spots a Government poster. It read:[292]

> 'Forward into the future' – then photographs of Grealish and Bradley smirking – 'With the Men You Have Trusted in the Past'. 'The claptrap', Byrne continues,
>
>> which our party put up was just as bad, though our posters were not as numerous, since we weren't getting four-figure subscriptions from industrialists and building speculators.

Content for the plot, as it is made to unfold, for the key events occurring in the 1940s (which Bradley, it becomes clear, very well knew about) happens to be furnished by two cases in the *Irish Reports*: *The State (Goertz)* v. *Minister for Justice*[293] (deportation of an undesirable alien); and *The People (A.G.)* v. *Thomas*[294] (disappearance at sea). The *Goertz* case, as it happens, is alluded to twice in *The Polling of the Dead*, once by name.[295]

The identification of Bradley as the villain at the Aliens Office is made possible through spotting his signature in the Irish version of his surname on a key document. This was 'Ó Brolcháin'. Using your name in Irish, we are informed,[296] 'is common in the Civil Service as a token that one's heart is in the right place'.

Quincke, alias Claes, the holder of the mysterious Belgian passport, disappears, and though he is later espied at the Venice Film Festival, 'opulent behind dark glasses and in opulent company',[297] he does not return to Belgium. We had earlier learnt why such an outcome would have been unlikely.[298] As Claes, he had served in a Flemish police unit which had collaborated with the Germans in rounding up the Jews of Antwerp for forward despatch in cattle-trucks to Poland. This was, indeed, a horrific business. 'Belgian Jews', writes Matthew Cobb, in revisiting these events,[299]

> were herded into a concentration camp in Mechelen near Antwerp and housed in an old barracks. By the end of the war, over 26,000 Mechelen inmates had been deported to Auschwitz, all of them Jews, apart from 365 Gypsies. Nearly 16,000 of them, including virtually all the children, were gassed as soon as they arrived in Auschwitz.

There is a not unimportant disclaimer that greets the reader of *The Polling of the Dead* at the outset. 'This is a work of fiction', we are told, and any similarity between characters in the novel and individuals, whether living or dead, 'is purely coincidental'. As to the calibre of the book itself, there is not perhaps to be found the depth of portrayal of character such as we encounter in *Matters of Honour.* Still it is a sprightly enough venture, and it is, arguably, a trifle harsh to dismiss this thriller, as Ronan Keane has done,[300] as 'more laboured and less successful'.

A third volume appeared posthumously. *Belling the Cat* was a collection of Kelly's political speeches and articles, testimony to his reputation as a fine parliamentary orator.[301] Brought together in this compact volume are thus Kelly's thoughts 'on subjects as diverse as the day-to-day life of a TD, the humbug of Irish neutrality, the scourge of socialism and the need to aim hefty kicks at our sacred cows and sleeping dogs'.

5

Merger Talk and Further Growth: the Law School, 1967–2000

The publication of the *Report of the Commission on Higher Education* in 1967 furnishes us with a glimpse of the pattern of education in law at university level – not least at UCD – as well as in science, the humanities generally, and training for other professions. The views on the new BCL of Tierney and Hogan, the former's successor as President, have already been set down. 'Very few of the submissions received [by the Commission]', we are told, 'dealt with legal education'.[1] But, as we shall see, submissions and evidence from UCD sources even so were conspicuous by their presence and need to be recorded.

Despite this apparent lack of interest, the commission report is remarkable for the vigour with which it makes the case for the study of law in the university, and how this should be approached. 'There can be no doubt', the *Report* reads,[2]

> that law should be studied in the university. Law is founded on the philosophical and ethical principles that inform society, and it is influenced by, and in turn influences, the history of that society.

It goes on:[3]

> The study of law, no less than the study of languages or science must be established in the university, to be pursued in depth and to the highest level of scholarship, not merely for purposes of the professional practice of law, but also because of the broad cultural value of the subject and of its value to persons who are to engage in politics, administration, business, industry and other callings.

And it continues, adopting a refrain oft-repeated elsewhere, not least in submissions to the commission itself:[4]

> If law is to be studied in the university, the university must support its study properly. The evidence, however, is that law studies in our university colleges have been inadequately supported. The law schools of the NUI colleges and of Trinity College have, until quite recently, been conducted entirely by part-time staff, with the result that research in law has been neglected. We consider … that university law schools should

> have an adequate complement of full-time professors and other teachers to provide not only for teaching requirements but also for the active pursuit of legal research.

A blueprint is then attached, which, regrettably, it has to be conceded, has not in every particular been embraced in the interval between then – 1967 – and today. 'Such subjects as Roman law, jurisprudence, constitutional law and international law', the commission's *Report* continues,[5]

> should be firmly established in the Irish university system. In particular, the Irish Constitution requires to be studied and expounded as a document containing philosophical, political and social concepts, which in great measure are beyond the traditional intellectual range encountered in the study of common and statute law.[6] Nor is the value of comparative law studies to be overlooked.

Aside altogether from the evidence presented by two Presidents of UCD, there were submissions too from two erstwhile members of the staff, Séamus Henchy and John Kenny. Kenny's radical proposals we will turn to in a moment. There is an intriguing footnote at one point in the commission's summary of evidence which merits immediate attention. 'In a summary of a proposed submission (the full submission was not received)', we are told,[7]

> Mr Dermot Bouchier-Hayes, solicitor and graduate in civil law from University College, Dublin, also adverted to a number of the matters mentioned by Mr Justice Henchy and referred, too, to the absence of an adequate programme of lectures, to the lack of tutorial classes for students, and to the failure to provide proper guidance for students on their selection of courses of studies.

The commission rightly dubbed Mr Justice Kenny's proposals for legal education 'the most comprehensive'.[8] Too many institutions involved, the relatively small number of students, and the comparative absence of full-time teachers, persuaded him that the existing institutions should be shut down and a single 'Institute of Law', based at King's Inns, should be responsible for all instruction. It has to be said that these ideas got short shrift. If ever there was a non-starter, this was it. But at the same time, it has to be acknowledged that talk of mergers at least was in the air. The great political conundrum, stretching from 1967 to 1974 – and, possibly, even beyond – was whether a merger should take place in Dublin between Trinity and UCD to create a single new University of Dublin.[9] The Commission of Higher Education considered such a plan but ultimately set its face against it.[10] Though this, as we are about to discover, did not dissuade the government of the day. The merger debate, therefore, is not one that can be omitted in this account of the history of UCD Law School.

Before we turn to the 'lift-off' in staffing terms for the UCD Law School – the dramatic upturn in its fortunes which dates from the late 1960s and early 1970s, it is incumbent upon us to revisit this remarkable episode in the history of higher education in Dublin.

It was in April 1967 that Donogh O'Malley, the then Minister for Education in a Fianna Fáil administration, announced that it had become government policy to bring about the merger of TCD and UCD.[11] The authorities of the two institutions held meetings as a result, but in the autumn of 1967 announced that they had not been able to agree on a possible merger plan. In July 1968 it was signalled that there would be a single University in Dublin. The Higher Education Authority, whose immediate first remit was to oversee this planned merger, was set up in August 1968, and under pressure from it detailed arrangements for the prospective merger saw the light of day in the NUI/TCD agreement of April 1970. It was under this agreement that UCD's Law School was to be moved to the Trinity campus and merged with the TCD Law School there.

From the outset UCD's Law Faculty had been involved in plotting a way forward in the light of the apparent determination on the part of the government of the day that a merger of some kind should materialise. But, in a sign of the times, at a meeting of the Faculty in October 1967 there was to be a pronounced difference of opinion on the route that should be taken.[12] On this occasion the President, J.J. Hogan, and Monsignor Horgan proposed the adoption of a motion under which the Faculty would agree to exploring the possibility of unifying certain departments in the two Colleges. This was shot down, on a vote of six–four against. Instead, on a vote of six–four in favour, the Faculty agreed to adopt as its views on the question a document presumably prepared in advance by certain members of the Faculty and designated the 'Report of the Faculty of Law'.[13] This is a long document, but needs to be set down *in extenso*:[14]

1. The Faculty of Law welcomes the Government proposal to create a formal association between this College and Trinity College, and assures its practical cooperation in this development.
2. The Faculty believes that considerations of justice and of national and educational policy require this association to be effected in such a way as to enable each College to retain its identity and character.
3. The Faculty does not believe this end can be achieved if the association involves the geographical consolidation of every pair of faculties in one College or the other.
4. The Faculty considers, however, that it should be possible to associate, under the superstructure of University Faculties, existing

pairs of College Faculties, and to consolidate their systems of administration, appointments, teaching and degrees; and believes that, with proper planning, such University Faculties could function efficiently even through geographically divided College Faculties.

5. The Faculty realises, however, that the optimum situation, whereby each College would retain all its existing faculties, is likely to be economic and effective only where the total numbers concerned are large enough to justify, on educational grounds, a certain number of parallel lectures and classes, and recognises that in some smaller Faculties – or where the alternative would be duplication of expensive equipment – an adherence to the existing division would be unduly costly and inefficient.
6. The Faculty notes an extreme divergence between its structure, staffing, student numbers, teaching system, curriculum and degrees and those of the Law Faculty at Trinity, and suspects that this divergence is greater than that existing between any other pair of Faculties.
7. The Faculty considers that the task of associating the two Law Faculties will be complicated and slow, and will involve, among other problems, planning an academic curriculum in law from first principles. The Faculty already has this matter under consideration.

Twice in the succeeding year – 1968 – the question was to be revisited. Separate proposals vis-à-vis the projected merger – one originating in UCD, one in TCD – were brought before the Faculty at a special meeting in March, when it was asked to convey its views on them to the Academic Council. The Faculty reported as follows:[15]

1. In the opinion of the Faculty of Law the proposals submitted to it for consideration at this meeting do not provide a wholly satisfactory solution of the university question in Dublin. The Faculty of Law, therefore, suggests that other means should be considered for carrying the proposed merger into effect. [This resolution was carried on a four – three vote.]
2. On the question of the best geographical site for the Faculty of Law, the Faculty considered that reasons of convenience were strongly in favour of a central rather than an outer site. Subject to this, the Faculty considered that it would be an advantage to maintain geographical proximity to the Faculty of Arts.
3. The Faculty was asked, notwithstanding its resolution set out above [no. 1], to indicate a conditional preference between the UCD and the TCD merger proposals. On this question four members of the

Faculty favoured the UCD proposal, two members favoured the TCD proposal and one member abstained.

The Government's tentative final decision (it turned out to be anything but) was promulgated in July. The Faculty's response is clear in this resolution adopted by the Faculty on the 23rd of the month:[16]

> Within the context of the University solution proposed by the Minister for Education on 6th July 1968, whereby both Colleges are to retain Faculties of Arts and Science, and are thus intended to preserve their identities as separate Colleges, the Faculty of Law considers that the distribution of Faculties proposed, in particular the location of both the Faculties of Law and Medicine in TCD, is highly detrimental to this College.

The authorities of NUI and of Trinity College were subsequently mandated to agree a merger scheme – something that UCD and TCD originally had been unable to do. In April 1970 a document, R 70–95, the fruit of these talks, was then circulated for consideration. By now, the UCD Faculty of Law appears to have been prepared to bow to the inevitable and agree to the merger with the Trinity Law School. Their thoughts on document R 70–95 are entered up thus in the Law Faculty minutes:[17]

> The Faculty of Law approves in principle the Faculty arrangements contained in the document agreed between the negotiators of the NUI and TCD and numbered R 70–95; but believes that if the Faculty's main teaching staff is transferred to TCD, the provision at UCD of professional law training under current professional regulations will not be possible.

Matters dragged on, but late in 1972, invited again to discuss the lineaments of another 'final' solution, the Faculty repeated its grudging acceptance of the plan, which augured the extinction of its separate existence.[18] In reporting on the matter to the Academic Council and to the Governing Body, the Faculty coupled this expression of assent with a number of qualifications. It protested, first, that there had been no consultation either with their Trinity counterparts or themselves in the bringing forward of the plan. It warned, second, that if the plan was to be progressed, there would have to be a radical improvement in the staff-student ratio in the merged law school. It stipulated, third, that it would not consent to a merger with a structurally unaltered TCD law school. Fourth, the Faculty asserted there would have to be a new degree structure for the merged entity. The fifth *caveat* concerned deficiencies in the law library collection and the future of the UCD Library's collection of law books in the Palles holdings.[19]

Under pressure from the UCD Arts Faculty, the Governing Body was to make a strong case for the retention of elements of law teaching in UCD and thus, though unaware of it at the time, in effect to produce a life line of sorts for UCD's Law School.[20] 'Arts at UCD', the Governing Body would resolve, 'still needs Roman Law, Constitutional Law, Jurisprudence, and Constitutional and Legal History.' Instruction here, the Governing Body went on to declare,

> cannot be done by means of service teaching which would be appropriate at a quite different level (e.g., the provision of teaching in the Law of Contract in the Faculty of Engineering and Architecture). Failure to make such provision [of appropriate teachers at the appropriate level] could seriously damage the present work and future development of the Arts Faculty. We would hold on to law books as would be appropriate for the law teaching retained.

By the autumn of 1973 the stance of the Governing Body had sensibly hardened. They were not now prepared to hand over the law school to Trinity. Five considerations informed this key resolution:[21]

(i) A University without a Faculty of Law would be at a considerable disadvantage.

(ii) The retention of full-time academic staff for non-professional Law subjects will be necessary in order to make provision for the teaching of academic law in Arts, Commerce and other Faculties.

(iii) In the years during which university reorganisation has been under consideration, the number of students taking Law increased considerably in both Colleges. University College has now reached the stage of having to restrict the number of students entering the Faculty.[22]

(iv) There would be little financial advantage in unification of the two Faculties of Law. The staff: student ratio will not be greatly dissimilar whether there is one or two faculties.

(v) University College would have no objection to participating in changes in professional law training leading to rationalisation and sharing of facilities such as libraries.

A new Minister for Education, Richard Burke, announced government decisions on a range of issues that the merger proposal had thrown up, in December 1974.[23] What is significant here is that the plan to close UCD's Law School merging it with Trinity's was simply abandoned. What *was* achieved as a consequence of the protracted merger talks was that Veterinary Medicine would be concentrated in UCD, and Pharmacy and Dentistry in Trinity – a dénouement that was to prompt McCartney in his summary of the events over these extraordinary seven years to term it something of a damp squid:[24]

> … [T]he great merger plan that Donogh O'Malley had announced in April 1967 was now, after seven years of hectic negotiations and vast quantities of memoranda, allowed to fizzle out and disappear off the Government's agenda.

The announcement of April 1967, and the frenzied talk that ensued, did not dissuade the powers-that-be from attending to the staffing needs of the Law School, on which, as we have seen, the Commission on Higher Education had cast a critical eye. For the autumn of 1967, as we have previously set down, a sizeable gap in the Law School's teaching strength had manifested itself – a gap occasioned by the death of Kevin Kenny and the retirement of William Finlay. In November 1967, as a stop-gap measure, sanction was sought and given for the recruitment of two part-time Assistants to cover for the pertinent lecture courses. These were Hugh O'Flaherty, whom we have already encountered, who was to go on to enjoy a judicial career, and Ronan Keane, a future Chief Justice.

An altogether new course in the Law School, leading to the award of a Diploma in European Law, was scheduled for inauguration in the autumn of 1968. This presaged the need for another new appointment. The plan for the course envisaged the study and analysis of European Law *stricto sensu,* i.e., that emerging from European Community institutions, such as the Court of Justice of the Community. But, significantly, in addition, room was to be found for the study of Civil Law systems, and especially the legal systems of France and Germany. A private law focus was thus being helpfully retained – which satisfied the Commission on Higher Education's enthusiasm for comparative law studies.

A sequence of appointments to service this new departure for the Faculty, in the years that followed, saw the recruitment of a succession of staff from the Continent – Edward Lissone from the Netherlands, Paris Niflis from Thessaloniki in Greece, and Arnaud Cras from France. Lissone inaugurated the Diploma. It was an interesting pick. Lissone was a graduate of the University of Amsterdam who had done postgraduate work, like the present author, at Tulane University in New Orleans. He had also been a research assistant at the Institute of Comparative Law in Paris. Lissone had an extraordinary personal background besides, having been raised in a Japanese prisoner-of-war camp in the former Dutch East Indies, and who endured fragile health from the side effects: he suffered badly from the cold, insisting to the present writer that the temperature in his apartment in Dublin's Appian Way should be an invariable 80° Fahrenheit.

With the death of Kevin Kenny and the retirement of William Finlay – now that the gaps there had been plugged – the Governing Body decided to collapse both chairs, and chart a new way forward. Statute LXIV was brought forward to achieve this outcome, the President, J.J. Hogan, explaining at the time that the College was discounting the option of instituting full-time chairs, the prospects of securing the talents of suitable candidates for full-time posts at that level being adjudged slight. The plan now was to create two full-time posts – one at College Lecturer level and the other at Assistant Lecturer level. Leaving no time for the grass to grow under anyone's feet, Hogan employed the opportunity afforded by the same meeting to announce that Nial Osborough, the present writer, would now be appointed to the College Lecturer post, having passed earlier hurdles at both the Faculty of Law and the Academic Council.[25] At the ensuing March meeting, it was revealed that Osborough would start as from 1 October 1968 on a salary of £2,020 per annum as recommended by the Finance Committee.[26] The post at Assistant level was filled by the appointment of Peter Shanley, another future High Court judge, to teach Contract and Equity at a salary of £1,040 per annum.

When the session 1968–1969 commenced, there were thus in post:

one full professor (Kelly)
two part-time professors (O'Hanlon, Ehler)
one statutory lecturer (Hand)
one College lecturer (Osborough)
one 'special lecturer' (Lissone)
one Assistant Lecturer (Shanley)
four Assistants (Sheehy, Blayney, O'Flaherty, Keane).

Further changes to the staff in the Law School were foreshadowed by President Hogan, in an announcement to the Governing Body in November 1968.[27] There were to be two new full-time posts that would be advertised – one at College Lecturer level and one at Assistant Lecturer level. Mr Justice Walsh was not exactly enamoured at the news, repeating his refrain that more full-time professors were required who could only be attracted if special salaries were offered.[28] There was to be no follow-up to this intervention.

The two new posts were advertised in mid-January 1969,[29] and in March it was announced that the College Lectureship had been filled by the appointment of Jim Brady as from October 1969.[30] The following October retrospective sanction was given to the appointment of Niflis the successor to Lissone as 'special lecturer' for the Diploma in European Law.[31] Late in 1970 the Assistant Lectureship, not previously filled, saw the appointment of James O'Reilly: he would be placed on the pay roll as from 1 January 1971. At the same time a new Statute (Statute LXX) was going through the process of adoption. This provided for a chair in Legal and

Constitutional History, to which in time the then holder of the statutory post in the area, Geoffrey Hand, would be appointed.

What represented a fresh recruitment policy owed a great deal to the reservations that the Law Faculty itself had come to express over practices followed in the past. At a meeting of the Faculty on the last day of August 1967 where Finlay, the then dean, signalled his retirement, he employed the occasion to warn his colleagues, and indeed, the College, of the need for a new approach. 'It was no longer possible', Finlay is recorded as having declared,[32]

> to cope with the students and the day-to-day running of the Faculty on a part-time basis. Teaching could be carried out by members of the Bar and suitably qualified Solicitors, but they would not have the time to look after the needs of the students.

'There existed', Finlay concluded, 'a serious conflict between the need to cater for the normal problems of a Faculty and outside work'. Professor O'Hanlon heartily agreed, as did John Kelly. The President, J.J. Hogan, for his part, as has already been indicated, proposed the collapse of the new part-time chairs (of Kenny and Finlay). At this point Hogan contemplated their replacement, ideally, with one full-time chair, and a statutory lectureship or a College lectureship.[33] By the time of the Governing Body meeting later in the session Hogan had shifted his opinion: full-time chairs for the moment at least were to be ruled out.[34] In the end of the day, what the Faculty was to achieve was the two College lectureships spread over two years – 1968 and 1969 – and which has been rehearsed above – the move that saw added to the full-time staff Osborough and Brady, together with the more junior appointments.

The appointment of the likes of Osborough and Brady was unusual in one respect: neither individual possessed a professional qualification, though both had postgraduate academic backgrounds. But their addition to the team of instructors in the Law School focused attention yet again on the technical composition of the Law Faculty as such.

The Visitation procured at the instigation of Séamus Henchy in 1958 into membership of the Law Faculty highlighted the acceptability or otherwise of a non-Law majority of statutory personnel on the Faculty.[35] This new predicament in which the Law Faculty found itself concentrated attention rather on the non-representative character of the governing organ for the law school, where non-statutory full-time teachers of legal subjects were deprived of a voice. When a principal grievance regarding tenure for such fresh appointees was removed – College Lecturers and Assistant Lecturers had, first of all, merely been made annually renewable, even if advisedly 'full-time'[36] – it seemed all the more indefensible that the exclusion of full-time law teachers from any voice in the conduct of affairs was maintained.

The Academic Staff Association which had been established in 1960, along with the report of the committee of inquiry set up by the Governing Body in the wake of the student unrest and occupation of 1968–1969, known as the 'Gentle Revolution', insisted, together, that the College should go this extra mile, and rectify a situation that was so glaringly unacceptable. And so it did, from 1971 onwards, with, first, College Lecturers (Assistants I in UCD's post-Visitation terminology) earning faculty entitlement, and somewhat later Assistant Lecturers (Assistants II), in both instances after a three-year probationary period, by virtue of UCD Statute LXVII, Chap. III.[37] The final instalment in what had been a long drawn-out saga came in 1982 with the adoption and coming into force of Statute CXX.[38] Statute CXX provided as follows:

> Table 'A' to Chapter II of Statute LV of UCD is hereby amended by the addition to the appropriate College Faculty, as determined by the Governing Body, of full-time Assistants II deemed by the Governing Body to be Assistant Lecturers and appointed to the age of 65 years (subject to six months notice on either side). Such Assistants II (Assistant Lecturers) shall not be entitled to vote on a statutory appointment and shall not be eligible for election as Dean of the Faculty.

Before the inevitable came to pass, a series of incidents occurred that merit mention here. As protests first began to be voiced – non-statutory law staff[39] actually gate-crashing one meeting of the Law Faculty held in the Board Room in Earlsfort Terrace[40] – the President, Jeremiah Hogan, reiterated the position that membership of faculties, including that of the Law Faculty, was restricted to statutory appointees. It was at the same time conceded that individual full-time non-statutory staff might be invited to attend meetings of the Faculty where items on the agenda could be reckoned to be of particular interest to them.[41] As a further sop to 'the disenfranchised', provision was subsequently made for a report based on the minutes of each Law Faculty meeting to be circulated to all non-statutory staff lecturing in legal subjects in the Faculty.[42] Difficulties persisted.[43] Thus when a sub-committee of all staff was set up in 1971 to study workloads, the President was to observe that since membership of the committee included non-statutory staff, the committee itself would be precluded from considering matters of staffing.[44] In due course a legal opinion was sought on the entire question of the attendance of non-statutory staff at faculty meetings. The opinion was sought from Professor O'Hanlon, who was to argue that while the presence of non-statutory staff could be conceded, active participation was ruled out: to be silent observers, in short.[45] There can be no denying that this represented something of a volte-face. And as late as 1975 the proof was there for all to see when, for the election of a new dean in the Law Faculty, non-statutory staff not technically members of the Faculty were asked to withdraw.[46]

The edited version of minutes of Faculty meetings, to which reference has just been made, it deserves to be noted, was also to be circulated to members of the Faculty's staff-student committee.[47] This constituted another development that might be thought to have gone some way to reducing 'the democratic deficit'. The creation of such committees had been urged by the Commission on Higher Education in its *Report* of 1967. They had been introduced generally in the College in 1968.[48] In the Law School, the committee comprised three staff members and eight student members. The committee as such was mandated to meet twice a term.[49]

To return to more straightforward faculty business: in April 1972, two of the Faculty's five-year chairs, originally established in 1962 – those occupied by O'Hanlon and Ehler – came up for renewal. Early in the year, O'Hanlon, as Professor of Constitutional Law and Criminal Law, signified that he would not be applying to be reappointed. Also falling due for renewal was Sidney Ehler's chair in International Law and International Relations. Here the chair was re-advertised together with an accompanying note to the effect that the incumbent (Ehler) would be a candidate. The unexpected now occurred, with Ehler's sudden death. (This posed one major question on which O'Hanlon was asked to advise:[50] could the question of the filling of Ehler's chair be dropped entirely, although one other person had signified their wish to be regarded as a candidate?)

The Law Faculty was asked to advise the President and Governing Body on whether they wished to continue to fill these two chairs or to collapse them altogether. Seizing the bit between their teeth, and possibly mindful of the views both Hogan himself and Séamus Henchy had expressed to the Commission on Higher Education in the 1960s, the Faculty decided to adopt the latter course. They were to announce at the same time a marked change of emphasis. In February 1972, the Faculty resolved

> that the proportion of full-time teachers in the Faculty should be increased and believe that part-time service from practitioners should be arranged on a different basis from that of professorships and statutory lectureships.[51]

Legally trained specialists from the Continent – Lissone, Niflis, Cras – in succession continued to shoulder responsibility for the Comparative Law elements both in the Diploma in European Law and in the BCL. A succession of full-time Assistants were appointed, not all of whom remained on the staff. Mention has already been made of Peter Shanley and James O'Reilly. Appointed as well were to be the likes of A.V. Gill, Finbar McAuley, Mary Matthews, Finbar Murphy, E.P. Fanning, Robert Clark, Paul Brand, John Caldwell, William O'Dea, Tony Kerr, Tom Cooney, Mark Cooney and Paul O'Connor –

to take us down to no further than 1978. Two appointees, not named here, declined to take up their appointments, and, among those listed above, only Gill, McAuley, Clark, Tom Cooney and O'Connor eked out their careers in UCD as, too, did Brady and Osborough (though the latter interrupted it with a stint as a Professor in Trinity College).

If practitioners were increasingly to be numbered among the Faculty's tutors, a significant number continued to render service as teachers, albeit on a part-time basis. These included John Blayney, later a judge of the Supreme Court, Ronan Keane (later Chief Justice); Hugh O'Flaherty (later a judge of the Supreme Court); Donal Barrington (later a judge of the Supreme Court); Eoghan FitzSimons, SC (later Attorney-General); and Ralph Sutton, SC.

A tutorial system appears to have been inaugurated in the early 1960s. The plan was that students would be divided into groups of ten who would meet as a group once a fortnight during term time. In the early days tutorials were arranged only for certain subjects, viz. Contract, Tort, Real Property and Equity. Constitutional Law was instantly recognised as a serious omission, and the situation here was quickly rectified. Tutors were expected to set and correct essays and were remunerated accordingly. A list of tutors for 1965–6 is extant: Ronan Keane, Hugh O'Flaherty, Hugh Geoghegan, Maurice Curran, Enda O'Carroll. In due course, full-time staff members were also to become involved in the organisation and participation in tutorials.[52]

The deanship itself had passed from Finlay to Kelly (1967), then on to Hand in 1970, Osborough in 1975 and Brady in 1978. A complaint conveyed by Osborough as dean in the spring of 1977 to the then President, Dr Thomas Murphy, and passed on for the consideration of the Governing Body by the latter, drew attention to one ironical element in this slow and overdue growth in the full-time teaching strength of the Faculty.[53] Osborough, as dean, wrote that the staff had noted 'with concern that no member of the then teaching staff enjoyed professorial status', felt that the views and interests of the Faculty were 'not being properly represented in the decision-making bodies of the University', and argued that 'the length of leave of absence accorded to the current holders of professorial posts in the Faculty' was 'a disincentive to the staff' and 'constituted an unjustifiable restriction of promotional possibilities at all levels'.

The Osborough letter drew attention to what, on any view, was an extraordinary situation. Hand who had become the Professor of Legal and Constitutional History in 1972 had been honoured with the appointment as one of the first professors at the new European University Institute in Florence. This was a three-year appointment, later extended for a further year. The Governing Body granted Hand leave of absence for the duration – on a part-time basis from 1 September 1975 to 31 May 1976, later extended to 30 June 1976 – this involving a 20 per cent cut in salary – and on a full-time basis (without pay) from that last date until 31 August 1979, later extended by one more year, i.e., to the end of August 1980.[54] Authorisation was given for this final extension in June 1978. Hand was not, however, to return to UCD, signalling his resignation from his chair there in 1980.[55]

The other professor that the Osborough letter had in its sights was John Kelly, Professor, since 1965, of Roman Law and Jurisprudence. On the election of a Coalition government in 1973 Kelly, who was to hold ministerial office, had been granted leave of absence for the duration of his membership of that government. As Parliamentary Secretary to the Taoiseach, Kelly represented to the College that he would still be in a position to teach Roman Law on the basis of two lectures a week. This was found agreeable, as a consequence of which the Governing Body sanctioned a special payment for those lectures and for examining in the subject of £750 per annum. There was to be a readjustment in the autumn of 1975 when Kelly indicated that his teaching load in Roman Law would be decreasing. In June 1977, with the fall of the government, Kelly indicated that he would be ending his leave of absence and returning to full-time duties.[56] At the election that month Kelly had, however, been returned as a TD. Was there, therefore, still a problem? It would seem so, if the history of the matter was turned to.

In 1969, the Finance Committee of the Governing Body and the Governing Body itself addressed the issue of what to do about members of staff who sought to combine active politics with their academic careers.[57] In the past, McGilligan and Ryan and even for a short while, long before then, Clery and before him, Swift MacNeill, sought to do just that, but they had all held their posts on a part-time basis, and no serious issue of principle was thought to have been raised. With the establishment of full-time statutory and non-statutory posts in the Law School, a process that gets under way in the 1960s, the issue could scarcely avoid being tackled, even if some of the more high profile individual cases brought to the attention of the Governing Body, at least in the early days, had not arisen within the membership of the Law Faculty.

The issue itself raised two separate questions: the legitimacy of letting staff members continue to draw two distinct salaries and the impact of a less than wholehearted commitment on the part of the individual 'full-time' staff member to the work of the department (inevitably involving the thrusting of an extra burden on the other members of the department – in lecturing, in supervision of postgraduates and in administration).

In June 1969, the Finance Committee, possibly for the first time, wrestled with a problem in a manner that served to distance the College from the days when the assistance via politics in building the new State was no ground for complaint at all – indeed quite the reverse: earning a panoply of brownie points. They concluded that election to Seánad Éireann was compatible with full-time employment in the College,[58] but that election as a TD to Dáil Éireann was not.

Here they recommended that the individual staff member elected a TD should be permitted to proceed on leave of absence without pay.[59]

The Governing Body duly noted these conclusions and the attached recommendation,[60] but when, in the ensuing December, the issue was squarely presented before them, in the case of two staff members who had just been made TDs – Professor John O'Donovan and Dr Garrett FitzGerald – they adopted a far more generous attitude than that which had apparently prevailed in June.[61] A staff member elected to the Dáil might be expected to devote 20 per cent of his time and energies to the Oireachtas: they therefore proposed a deduction of 20 per cent in the individual staff member's salary, which could be made at source or the member could be asked to refund the College by that amount. The new rules would apply from 1 January 1970, and were expressly restricted to the two cases that had come before them – those of O'Donovan and FitzGerald. The Governing Body voted unanimously for the planned 20 per cent reduction in salary to be deducted at source.

To return to the Osborough letter to the President discussed by the Governing Body in May 1977, it is of importance to note the outcome. Dr Murphy indicated that he would be approaching the Higher Education Authority to secure sanction for two additional Chairs in Law in basic law subjects. On the heels of the hunt, only one of these was immediately forthcoming. Statute CIII of 1978, by chapter I, provided for a Chair of the Law of Property and Equity,[62] to which the then holder of the lectureship in these subjects, Jim Brady, was appointed. As for Osborough, he had applied for and obtained a Professorship in Trinity College in the interim, and it was at that other Dublin College from 1978 that he was to pursue his career before returning to UCD in 1993 to occupy the chair left vacant by the death of Kelly in February 1991. The second new chair in Law, when finally sanctioned, was obtained in 1980 by James Casey, a graduate of Queen's, Belfast, who had spent several years as a Lecturer in Trinity College. Casey was to serve two stints as Dean, and it was during the latter of these – 1989–92 – that the move of the Law School to Roebuck Castle came about.

The consequences flowing from the resignation of Hand in 1980 and the death of Kelly in 1991 now need to be briefly set down. Hand's chair in Legal and Constitutional History, effectively a promotional appointment – he had previously been the Statutory Lecturer in these two subjects – was to be abolished at the request of the Law Faculty.[63] It was, however, replaced by a new Lectureship in Law, which it was hoped, could enable coverage of such historical topics to be maintained.[64] That hope was realised when in 1983, following the customary competition, Paul Brand secured the appointment. Brand, however, had determined in his own mind to return to England and pursue his research interests there, and his tenure of the new Statutory Lectureship was short-lived, a matter of a few months in fact. In view of Brand's staggering productivity as measured by his later publications, his departure represented a considerable loss for UCD. On the other hand, given the nature of those publications, it is difficult to see how he could have juggled, if still based in Dublin, a teaching commitment here and research work in London, Oxford and Cambridge. Brand in the years after leaving UCD was to publish an important monograph on the origins of the legal profession in England,[65] a collection of his legal history articles – many of them dealing with Ireland[66] – and no less than four major volumes of Early English Law Reports for the Selden Society. A fifth volume in the Selden Society series – no. 125 – was also produced by another UCD Law staff member, now retired. This was the volume brought out by Dr Andrew Lyall: *Irish Exchequer Reports: Reports of Cases in the Courts of Exchequer and Chancery in Ireland, 1716–1734* (London, 2009).[67]

Brand's vacant Lectureship produced another contest, from which Robert Clark, a modern Contract Law expert, was to emerge victorious. The aftermath following John Kelly's unexpected death in 1991 was somewhat different. His chair had been designated a chair of Roman Law and Jurisprudence. Following his death in January 1991 the Faculty, as was the custom, were invited to pronounce on the question whether they wished any change to be made in the governing statute. At a meeting of the Faculty in May a clear majority indicated a preference for the chair to be a non-designated chair in Law – a stratagem designed to attract a somewhat broader field of applicants.[68] Dr Lyall registered his opposition to make any change, and Mr Cooney followed suit in October when the matter again came before the Faculty. The two subjects – Jurisprudence and Roman Law – Cooney averred were unique in the contribution they made to the intellectual and educational elements of law courses.[69] Lyall was to point out at another Faculty meeting in November that many of those who had previously voted for the change in the statute had not technically been members of the Faculty and that their votes therefore had been invalid. The upshot here was an alteration in the minutes to record the fact that by a substantial majority of academic members appointed to, and teaching in, the Faculty of Law had agreed to changing the statute to provide for a non-designated chair in Law.[70] In a possible sop to the opponents of the change, the Faculty had previously decided at its October meeting that the new statute should include a clause to the effect that the Governing Body should have the power, on the recommendation of the Faculty and of the Academic Council, to attach to the chair a specific designation reflecting the interests of the current holder of the chair when appointed.[71] When all is said and done, however, the die had been cast. A chair with its long pedigree, and held by a distinguished group of individuals, from John Kelly back through Séamus Henchy and Daniel Binchy to James Murnaghan, was to exist no more. Well might it have been said, 'Veneration is dead among us; the present age has buried it, without a stone to mark the place'.[72]

A certain irony attaches to the circumstance that the individual who was appointed to this new non-designated chair in law and who entered into office in 1993 – the present writer, as it turned out – was to embark on an enterprise, ultimately proving abortive, to secure the services of a lecturer in Roman Law for the law school.[73] A small committee was established, which recommended that efforts should be made to obtain the services of such a person. Romanists, Osborough was to argue, were universally scholars of outstanding ability, who would certainly be able to contribute to teaching in areas other than Roman Law itself. The direction in which the Law Faculty appeared to be travelling left little room for this argument. Should a vacancy arise in the lecturing of a core subject, there could be no dispute concerning the manner in which the resultant gap would have to be filled. Osborough's allied plea that staff members should be prepared to learn to teach subjects other than those that were their own specialisation plainly fell on deaf ears as well.

The years from 1967 onwards witnessed a number of changes to the curriculum for the BCL degree. The number of Arts-style subjects in 1BCL was reduced when History and Philosophy were replaced by a single option of History or Philosophy or Political Economy. The language options – English, French, German, Greek, Irish, Italian and Latin – had Spanish added as a further choice. These changes took effect in 1969 and 1970. In 1970 a change was made to the curriculum for the 3rd and final year of the BCL: Comparative Law was listed as an alternative to Politics, a development made possible, of course, by the recruitment of the succession of special lecturers linked to the Diploma in European Law.

Throughout these years an allied matter regularly canvassed concerned the question of what should be the annual intake of students into 1BCL. In 1979, possibly with something of a heavy heart, the Faculty resolved for the first time to restrict numbers.[74] There would seem to have been three factors that weighed with members of the Faculty at the time: the *numerus clausus* being operated by the Incorporated Law Society on admissions to the solicitors' profession; the continuing unacceptability of the poor staff-student ratio; and, finally, the pressure on library resources. A few years down the road there was to be another break with the past. As from the session 1982–3 the course laid on for non-Law graduate King's Inns students would be discontinued.[75]

Around this time, as it chanced, the *President's Report* (for 1981–2) furnished a vignette devoted to the account of the Law School. As regards curriculum changes in the BCL this vignette, of uncertain authorship, celebrated the transfer of Roman Law and Legal History, erstwhile mandatory 1BCL subjects, to the list of optional subjects taken in later years. It celebrated, too, the availability to students in the later years of the BCL of 'more popular' subjects such as Family Law, Criminology, Human Rights and Labour Law. EEC Law, as it was then called, had also been made an obligatory subject in 2BCL. There had been a major change besides in the teaching of Constitutional Law and Administrative Law. These had been replaced by two new courses designated Public Law – 1 and Public Law – 2: testimony of course to the exponential growth both of Irish constitutional law and of resort to judicial review.

More major surgery of the BCL degree programme began to be implemented as from the session 1991–2. The changes then introduced increased the range of optional subjects, making a number of those even available in 2nd year. Under the new regulations 1st BCL was to consist of Legal System, Criminal Law, Constitutional Law, Tort and Contract. In 2BCL there were to be but two obligatory subjects, viz. EEC Law and Land Law. The student was also obliged to sit and pass examinations in three subjects from a long list of options (which is given below). In 3BCL, the final year, a single mandatory subject was retained, viz. Jurisprudence. In addition, the student was required to take four options from the same long list prescribed for 2BCL students as added to by a shorter list of six options reserved exclusively for 3BCL students. The long list comprised the following subjects:

Administrative Law	Advanced Public Law
Company Law	Comparative Law
Criminal Procedure	Evidence
Family Law	Intellectual Property Law
International Protection of Human Rights	Labour Law
	Legal History
Private International Law	Public International Law
Revenue Law	Roman Law
Social Welfare Law	

The shorter list available exclusively to 3BCL students embraced:

African Law	Criminology
Environmental Law	Equity
Law and Economics	Planning and Development Law

All this was much more than tinkering, since it made available to the undergraduate law students a range of options unthinkable a generation earlier. In addition, in the decade leading up to the millennium note requires to be taken of two significant 'structural' additions to the work of the Law School. The first was the inauguration of an entirely new undergraduate degree: the Bachelor of Business and Legal Studies (BBLS). Run jointly with the Faculty of Commerce, it became available for qualified students as from the session 1991–2. (The second, we will come to in a moment.)

Needless to say, planning for its inauguration went back a number of years.

The Faculty's Development Plan of early 1987 might be reckoned to have paved the way.[76] Without formally committing itself to the new degree which came on stream in the autumn of 1991, this document supported the idea of option clusters in the final year of the BCL, one of which foresaw the grouping of a number of topics in the Law and Business area – Commercial Law, Company Law, Business Administration and International Commercial Transactions. There were more general considerations that would equally appear to have been operative. 'The Faculty of Law', the document recites,

> would … wish to avoid any suggestion that it has traditionally perceived its role as one of educating students exclusively for the practice of law in the orthodox sense.

The Development Plan continued:

> While we would be prepared to concede that in the past we have tended to acquiesce complacently in an almost exclusive orientation of students towards practice of law in the traditional sense, we feel now that the structure of the undergraduate programme should be such as will heighten student awareness that there exists a greater variety of law-jobs, both in Ireland and abroad, to which our graduates should aspire.

This well-argued document had started with a complaint, regularly aired by deans of this epoch, which might have created the impression that the Law School would have been loath to engage with the future: the old sore that the university law school was uncommonly cheap to run. 'The unit cost per law student', the Development Plan pontificates,[77]

> is the lowest of any Faculty in the College, and it does not detract from our cost argument that there may be a Department within another Faculty which might have a marginally lower unit cost per student. Law we believe is one of the oldest and most prestigious Faculties and merits a better share of albeit dwindling resources.

The higher echelons may or may not have agreed: it is impossible to say. What is clear, though, is that a perception existed at the highest level in the College that, whatever the reason, the Law School had chosen not to play as full a part in the life of the College as it might have done. This helps to explain, I think, another factor in the motivation to launch the BBLS: pressure from above. Dr Patrick Masterson, who served as President from 1986 to 1993, seems to have been of this school of thought. At a Faculty meeting in May 1987, he went on record to bewail the Law School's policy 'to make itself a professional hermetically sealed

Faculty'.[78] The criticism was to be repeated in a lengthy statement to the Faculty from Masterson welcoming progress in talks between Law and Commerce foreshadowing the launch of the BBLS degree.[79] 'There was', Masterson is reported to have declared in 1989,

> a demand for more interfaculty degrees. There was a perception that the Faculty of Law was too professionally orientated. He had been advised that the Government was most anxious to increase student numbers, and one of the areas suggested was Law and Business.

Now the carrot. 'Should', Dr Masterson is recorded as having told the Law Faculty,

> the College agree to take on more students and put on more interfaculty degrees, it would be in a strong bargaining position to say that it needed more funding for teachers and library resources before this could be done.

Masterson concluded this unusual intervention by encouraging the Law School to look at areas in other Faculties which could be combined with Law. In the resultant general discussion, alternative degree models included Law/Humanities, Law/Philosophy and Law with a European language. (A new BCL with French law was to be introduced in 1999;[80] other products of this discussion of 1989, Law with Philosophy, for example, were destined to be launched after the turn of the century.)

The BBLS, as we have seen, was started in 1991. There were a number of teething problems that needed to be tackled. The innovation coincided with a movement involving the abandonment of the old term structure of Michaelmas, Hilary and Trinity and its replacement by semesters which required examinations twice a year. The Commerce Faculty moved swiftly to accept semesterisation; the Law Faculty did not. The embarrassing scenario now manifested itself. Students would be preparing for exams in Commerce components of the BBLS while simultaneously supposed to be attending lectures in the Law components of the degree. Another difficulty presented itself: securing recognition of the new degree from the two professional legal bodies – the Law Society and King's Inns. As was perhaps to be expected, this required the Law School to show that the mandatory core subjects of a recognised degree would remain within reach of the BBLS students.

No less significant than the creation of the new BBLS degree was the establishment in the year 2000, in alliance with the Law School, of the Irish State's first and – so far only – Institute of Criminology. The intention to establish this Institute was announced by the then dean, Paul O'Connor, in June 1989 in *Law*

Alumni UCD, the first alumni journal of the UCD Law Faculty. The Institute would, O'Connor declared on the occasion, enable studies to be undertaken in the State on crime 'in all its manifestations'. The Institute was formally launched a few months later – in February 2000 – appropriately enough perhaps, in Mountjoy Prison in Dublin, by the Minister for Justice, Equality and Law Reform, Mr John O'Donoghue, TD.

Initial funding for the venture – which now boasts a Director and a number of Research Associates – was furnished by a US charity, Atlantic Philanthropies. Physically located in the same building as the law school at the time – Roebuck Castle – the Institute planned at the outset to conduct a survey to measure the true extent of crime in Ireland. 'Trends and patterns of crime', 'The relationship between crime and opportunity' and 'The nature and operation of penal sanctions' were identified at an early date as among the Institute's research priorities. The team at the Institute, aside from their research interests, would be responsible for instruction in Criminology at both undergraduate and postgraduate levels. The Institute's first Director, Dr Peter Young, took up his position in the autumn of 2000. A year later the first Annual Public Lecture under the aegis of the Institute was given by Professor Roger Hood of the Centre of Criminological Research in Oxford. His topic was 'Capital punishment: what progress towards worldwide abolition?' An earlier act of munificence, of which it is proper to take note, was the inauguration in 1977 by the Bank of Ireland of the annual award of prizes acknowledging academic excellence spread over successive years in the BCL undergraduate course. For other prizes awardable in the Law School, see the most recent *Calendar* (only available online).

Student exchanges with continental Europe, made possible by the Erasmus and later the Socrates schemes, and with universities in the United States and in Australia under a series of bilateral agreements, led to the BCL degree in many instances becoming a four-year degree, with the third year spent abroad. Hence the BCL (European Legal Studies) and BCL (International). BBLS students in due course became entitled to avail of the identical extended programmes. Students from continental Europe spending a year in UCD became entitled, if academic progress was satisfactory, to earn a Diploma of Common Law. The success of these exchange programmes demonstrated that the students at whom they were aimed plainly rejected the philosophy reflected in the Latin tag, '*Domi manere convenit felicibus*'. They had been persuaded rather by Petronius' well-known injunction, '*Linque tuas sedes, alienaque litora quaere/ o juvenis*', with its encouragement of much better things to come: '*maior tibi nascitur ordo*'.

College policy dictated that fully-fledged postgraduate diploma courses were to be re-labelled Higher Diplomas. Thus it came about that the Law School's first diploma, the Diploma in European Law became the Higher Diploma in European Law. This redesignated diploma was not destined to establish itself over a number of years, for in time it was to be totally replaced by the LLM in

European Law. Another new departure was the launch in 1990 of the LLM in Commercial Law – another taught Master's programme. The Irish Centre for Commercial Law was set up in tandem with this innovation.[81]

Despite these changes it remained possible to secure an LLM by thesis, and in the dying decades of the twentieth century, much interest in the Law Faculty minutes at least attaches to the listing of LLM thesis topics for which Faculty approval was obligatory. Under the original replacement for the old LLB the Faculty had introduced a taught Masters which had no specific focus. This was quietly abandoned as first the LLM by thesis and the two specific LLM taught courses – European Law and Commercial Law – proved more popular. Fashion was to change things once more. An unsatisfactory completion rate for LLM theses was later to provoke concern;[82] in subsequent years the realisation that research of enduring value was more likely to result from work at PhD level witnessed a marked shift towards applications to do PhDs. The Faculty's own scholarships programme came to the assistance of a small number of PhD applicants. Of greater immediate benefit of a financial kind was the establishment in 1998 of the Irish Research Council for the Humanities and the Social Sciences, with the scholarship funds at its disposal. The Law Faculty was not to be slow to encourage applicants to apply for these IRCHSS grants.

There was to be a creditable amount of soul-searching on the part of the Law School staff on two separate issues, at one of its last meetings in 1999 and at one of its first in 2000. A paper presented to the staff on the function and purpose of tutorials provoked a lively discussion.[83] Support was expressed for the involvement of all full-time staff and care was to be taken over the recruitment of part-time tutors. The best way, it was agreed, to secure the desideratum of students using the tutorial to maximise the development by them of their powers of legal reasoning was for tutors to employ a strategy of encouraging a good deal of advance preparation: setting problems and suggesting helpful preparatory reading. It would remain important even so to ensure that students fully grasped what they were being invited to comprehend in the standard lectures. Good liaison between lecturers and tutors was taken as a *sine qua non*.

Early in 2000 an attempt was made – which might have proved abortive – to secure a consensus on an entirely different matter, but one, again, of key importance to the professional academic: should the Law School permit staff on a full-time contract to continue in practice either as a barrister or as solicitor?.[84] There was a certain irony attaching to the raising of the issue at the time and in the manner of its raising. For well over half of its existence the Law Faculty had been served, and served faithfully, by a coterie of part-timers who remained active in the professions. There had been occasions, too, when it was sought to defer the filling of vacancies on the grounds that no qualified barrister was there to throw his hat in the ring. By the late twentieth century things had changed a lot: not all those embarking on a teaching career in the law school had professional qualifications, and the pronounced preference of university administrators to appoint holders of PhDs and to stimulate the publication of research now had to be reckoned with. The staff would seem to have acknowledged that the Law Faculty was indeed fortunate 'to have on board' practitioners who had made a substantial contribution to the Law School and who had indeed added lustre to it. At the same time, however, the view was expressed, as recorded in the minutes, that care was to be extended 'not to give succour to the fallacy that the academic approach to law remained inchoate unless and until fructified by input from the practitioner'. Another contributor expressed unease over one critical matter. 'The dismal fact remained', it was suggested, 'that colleagues who practised at the Bar were apt to dishonour their teaching commitments when exigencies of practice required them to be elsewhere'. Promotion blockages, others suggested, could have provoked this drift into practice. But even so, others again protested, the new universities legislation highlighted the importance of research (which active practitioners were likely to eschew) and made administrations accountable to the Oireachtas for how their money was spent. The point here is that if *X*, on a full-timer's academic salary, was spending part of his time, however meagre, down at the courts, the State was not receiving full value at the university from his paid services. Adjustments to contractual arrangements for staff members wishing to continue in practice (or even to commence it) appeared to some of the contributors to represent the way forward on this vexed but scarcely negligible issue.

It is worth recalling at this juncture that within the College there had been a short history of controversy over what might be termed 'double jobbing'. One case concerned the History Department.[85] More immediately germane (arguably) was a case raised by President Masterson at a meeting of the Governing Body in the autumn of 1986.[86] Masterson had learnt that a full-time member of staff was in active practice at the Bar. (In the formal record of the matter neither the name of the individual concerned nor the College Department is furnished.) Masterson's first letter to *X*, stated what he believed was the case, and that no permission for such practice had been given. *X*, in reply, intimated an intention to continue to practise at the Bar, whereupon Masterson, in a second letter, stated that this was unacceptable, and that under *X's* contract any outside work had to be approved by the President on the recommendation of the Head of Department.[87] The Governing Body set up a sub-committee under the then Registrar to pursue the matter and report. Within two months what looked like irreconcilable differences of opinion had been resolved. The matter was adjudged settled; and no report was called for. No details are revealed.[88]

It is useful to recall the words of J.B. Ames, a distinguished dean of the Harvard Law School over a century ago. Speaking at the dedication of a new law building for the Law School at the University of Pennsylvania in February 1901, he leaves us in doubt where he stood on the issue that these exchanges in the Dublin of 1986 brought into focus. 'The faculty', Ames insisted,[89]

> should be made up almost wholly of men [*sic*] who devote the whole of their time to the university. The work of a law professor is strenuous enough to tax the energy of the most vigorous and demands an undivided allegiance.

In short, as he went on to express it,[90] 'a law professorship should be regarded as a vocation not as an avocation'. But even Ames added a caveat. 'There are, of course', he was to suggest in other remarks,[91]

> occasional instances of men of exceptional ability, facility and capacity for work, and of such abundant loyalty ... from whom it is better to accept the half loaf that they are ready to give, than the whole loaf of the next best obtainable person.

An entirely different matter touching on staffing merits an airing here as well. A decision taken by the Governing Body in November 1987 inaugurated a regime of mandatory retirement for academic staff at the age of 65. Under Statute I of 11 April 1911 the possibility of continued employment in the case of statutory staff for five more years, at the discretion of the Governing Body with the approval of the President (subject to annual NUI Senate sanction)[92] had been preserved, but by a vote recorded on 24 November 1987 this arrangement seemingly was ended.[93] It was not an unanimous choice, concern having been expressed 'that with the loss through retirement of its most senior staff, the College would be without a source of wisdom and experience at a particularly difficult period in its history'.[94] At the same time it was perhaps something of an exaggeration to claim that that loss 'would affect the whole fabric of the College'. Masterson, the President at the time, had supported an end to the discretion he had undoubtedly inherited when elected to the post. It was important, he argued, to improve the age profile of staff, weighted at the time too heavily in favour of older personnel.[95] That a tactic accelerating change could contribute to the removal of blockages on promotions was not overplayed, but was certainly involved.[96]

Two professors, thwarted in their endeavours to be continued in post after attaining the age of 65, were to go to law over the question. Revd Professor F.X. Martin, the Professor of Medieval History, insisted that the Governing Body's vote or resolution of November 1987 was ultra vires, citing paragraph 18 of Chapter IV of Statute I. Paragraph 18 provided as follows:

> At least three months before he [i.e., the President] attains the age of seventy years, and also at least three months before any Professor,

> Lecturer or Officer who is liable to retire at the age of sixty-five years, attains that age, he shall report to the Senate and to the Governing Body the fact of himself or of such Professor, Lecturer, or Officer approaching the respective ages mentioned; and in the case of any Professor, Lecturer, or Officer shall state at the same time his opinion as to the fitness of such Professor, Lecturer, or Officer for continuance in office; and he shall furnish to the Professor, Lecturer or Officer concerned a copy of such Report.

This provision can rightly be viewed as part of the procedure laid down in paragraph 10 of Chapter XV of the same Statute – Statute I – for continuing statutory personnel in office for the five years after age 65. Nowhere does it appear in any record whether, in the case of the Revd Professor Martin, a report in respect of his fitness for continuance in office had been furnished (as paragraph 18 stipulated) to both the NUI Senate and the UCD Governing Body. In the event, the Revd Professor Martin's action was settled out of court, with none of the details being disclosed.[97]

The Labour Court was to be invited to pronounce on the entire question of the earlier retirement age, and how this had been introduced – clear evidence of the ripples that the Governing Body's resolution of November 1987 were continuing to make. Its recommendation – no. LCR 12847 – deserves to be recorded.[98] The Court refused to pronounce on the legality of what the Governing Body had done, but there was to be criticism nonetheless. A potted history of the background was first supplied. Until November 1987, the Labour Court explained, continuance in office until the age of 70 was 'a reasonable expectation'. But there had been changes in staffing and financial circumstances and that had created a situation in which management was obliged to seek reasonable cost reductions in all areas including staffing. However, the College's decision to introduce the lower retirement age without adequate consultation and negotiation with the Unions concerned on behalf of their members was 'contrary to good industrial relations practice'. There should ensue discussions to ameliorate the effect of the reduction with the two Unions concerned – the Irish Federation of University Teachers and SIPTU.

One consequence of F.X. Martin's lawsuit was the appearance in the Governing Body's minute book of reports from the President on the fitness to continuance in office of personnel approaching the age of 65 – invariably accompanied by notes of a Governing Body decision, endorsed by the President, to end the appointment at age 65 even so. In one breath the President was saying 'You are fit to go on'; in the next, 'No, not at all'. Franz Kafka would not have been perturbed by this, whatever about other observers.

The saga was to throw up another disappointed UCD Professor, George Eogan, the distinguished Professor of Celtic Archaeology, to which post he had been appointed in 1979. Eogan pressed his case as far as the High Court, but, in a ruling handed down in May 1996, Mr Justice Shanley, who had been on the staff of the Law School in the late 1960s and early 1970s, held against him on the key question: the legality of the Governing Body's resolution of November 1987. This was in a decision, let it be said, that is not entirely satisfactory.[99]

An excuse for this protracted excursus – recalling episodes that do not directly impinge on the Law School or its history – is furnished by the circumstance that the excursus itself can be reckoned to serve as a coda of sorts to the discussion in previous chapters of arrangements on tenure for an earlier law professoriate. There is, as it happens, a further explanation or justification, in a curious personal encounter: on a summer's afternoon in 1996 the present writer was waylaid on a corridor in the Newman building and commiserated with at some length over the loss of 'my' High Court action: I had been mistaken for George Eogan, as it eventually dawned on me.

One other consequence of the Governing Body's discussion of the retirement age in November 1987 could be viewed as a sop by some: this was the adoption of a strategy to foster participation by retired staff in the cultural, academic and social life of the College.[100] A survey was planned on what might need to be done; in the end a work room for retired staff was reserved adjacent to the Common Room in the Newman building, a room named after Maurice Kennedy, a former Registrar.[101] This is Room B102.

It will be recalled that there was a marked reticence in the records regarding the identification of the full-time staff member to whom the President, Dr Masterson, had in 1986 written concerning that staff member's continued full-time practice at the Bar. Anonymity, it is worth noting, was also maintained in the cases of two law students brought before the Committee of Discipline in the period that this chapter covers – neither is named. The first case, dealt with in 1982, concerned a 2 BCL student who applied for a replacement student card. He (she) had reported it as lost. This was not the case.[102] The 'offence' was found proved, and a fine of £50 imposed. The second case – in 1987 – was that of another 2 BCL student reported for breach of the examination regulations on the occasion of the summer examinations. The breach was found established, and the student was prohibited from re-presenting at the autumn re-sits. He – or she – would have to wait until the summer of 1988. In the meantime, attendance at lectures during the session 1987–8 would be allowed.[103] A first year BBLS student, likewise unnamed, was brought before the Committee of Discipline in the autumn of 1992 for a further breach of examination regulations. The judgment in this case declared that the student was to be adjudged to have failed the Business subjects sat in the June examinations that year.[104]

Retracing our steps a number of years – to the late 1960s in fact – brings into focus a very different aspect to student life on campus. This was the period when there was ushered in an era of law student activism, marked in particular by groups of young men and women venturing into pastures new for a cohort customarily viewed as conservative and indifferent to calls for social or legal reform.

Justice, an Irish Student Law Review, made its first appearance in Trinity term 1968. Edited by Barry McAuley, a UCD law graduate, who would go on some years later to become editor of the *Irish Jurist*, prevailed on a coterie of authors from the Inns and the solicitors' profession to communicate the thoughts of a younger generation of lawyers on a range of topics. The very first issue covered topics as diverse as petty sessions; criminology ('science or nonsense'?); academic and professional legal education; and judicial activism. McAuley in his editorial pleaded for research to be carried out into the effectiveness of the disparate penal sanctions available to the courts. 'The lay of the law student to his lass', a five-stanza poem, accompanied by an editorial apparatus of bewitching obscurity, was not perhaps in quite so serious a vein.

UCD law students were also to the fore in programmes of what one should term 'political action'. Colum Kenny, a barrister and Professor of Communications at Dublin City University, recalled, in a one-day conference at UCD in 2011, the ambience of the late 1960s and early 1970s.[105] From the signing of a petition for the release of Martin Dolphin it was no long journey to the establishment of the Phoenix Society, named in memory of O'Donovan Rossa, the mission statement for which, according to one newspaper,[106] was the examination of the court system and of the laws in force; the encouragement of proper behaviour in the Gardaí; the campaign for free and adequate legal aid; the consolidation of the legal educational system; and much else. Kenny was to recall that 'the Phoenix Society … went the way of many small student organisations', but out of the ashes there arose the Law Students Union for Action, who soon made headlines with a picket on Mountjoy Gaol in connection with their demand for an inquiry into the prison system. The LSUA was described at the time as an 'organising committee of law students at UCD, Kings Inns and the Incorporated Law Society'.

Reform in the educational arrangements for solicitors' apprentices, which were ushered in by the Incorporated Law Society in the 1970s, precipitated litigation in the outcome of which law students in the College as well as elsewhere in the Republic had much more than a passing interest. Under the previous dispensation, the Law Society had required apprentices to take courses of lectures in the university law schools, and those who did so, without wishing to obtain a degree – as indeed was the majority situation until a very late hour – were admitted to UCD's Law School and the other university law schools as non-matriculated students, a far from ideal strategy. The Law Society became increasingly concerned by the small number of would-be solicitors taking degrees, and planned a number of changes accordingly, which would divide preliminary education and training into academic and practical components.

A strategy adopted by the Society of Young Solicitors in 1967 charted the way forward.[107] A newly fashioned preliminary examination was raised to that of university degree level, and exemption from this was to be given to university graduates. There was also to be established the Society's own law school, which would handle the rest of pre-qualification education and training, and entry to this would be by competitive examination.

In the end, further concessions were planned to be extended to certain categories of law graduates. This was an exemption from what was termed the Final Examination First Part – one of the preliminaries to entering the Law Society's own law school. Under regulations adopted in 1991, this examination required the student to sit and pass examinations in the following subjects, viz., Company Law, Constitutional Law, Law of Contract, Criminal Law, Law of Property and Law of Torts (Equity and the Law of the European Union were to be added to the original list of six obligatory subjects in 1997).

What proved to be the fly in the ointment was the wording of article 15 in the regulations of 1991 itemising the university law degrees, the holders of which would be exempted from the Final Examination First Part. The law degrees sanctioned in this manner were those of Trinity College, the NUI through its constituent colleges in Cork, Dublin (UCD) and Galway, the University of Limerick and Dublin City University.

In 1994 Alison Bloomer and a number of the other law students studying for the LLB degree at Queen's University, Belfast launched proceedings to object to the exclusion of degrees of QUB from the list set out in article 15. In essence, what they sought to achieve was to have the position of Queen's law graduates assimilated to that of law graduates of universities in the Republic with regard to admission to apprenticeships and the Law Society's vocational training course.

Ms Justice Laffoy, in her decision of 22 September 1995, found in favour of the plaintiffs to this limited extent, pronouncing article 15 *ultra vires* the powers of the Law Society and accordingly invalid.[108] In the judge's estimation there were indeed grounds for distinguishing between law graduates from universities in the Republic and those from Queen's, Belfast, but article 15 was disproportionate even so. The article indirectly contravened the prohibition on discrimination on nationality grounds in Article 6 of the Treaty of Rome of 1957; it was thus null and void.

The Law Society sought to mend its hand so far as Queen's, Belfast law graduates were concerned by employing its authority in the pertinent regulations to modify their provisions 'in exceptional circumstances', and this was done on 31 October 1995, the resultant benefit – exemptions from the Final Examination First Part – being extended, after the declaration on article 15's invalidity, to all the other relevant law graduates as well.[109]

But this was not the end of the story. The nullification of article 15 meant that, prospectively, no exemptions at all were there to be availed of by law graduates whether in the South or in the North. This then became the bone of contention on the part of a group of law students, including a number from UCD, who had entered on their course of studies at a time when article 15 was in force, and enjoyed the reasonable anticipation that, at the conclusion of their law degree course (assuming they obtained their degree), they would still be able to secure an exemption from the Law Society's Final Examination Part One. These were the issues to be explored in *Abrahamson* v. *Law Society of Ireland*.[110] The resultant judgment, delivered by Mr Justice McCracken on 15 July 1996, held that the respective plaintiffs had indeed a legitimate expectation that the particular regulation condemned in *Bloomer's* case would remain in force, the advantage it contained continuing to inure for their benefit.

Exemptions from the Final Examination First Part – the examination which, when passed, conferred an entitlement to enter the Law Society's vocational training law school – came to an end when new regulations were introduced in 1997.[111] The imbroglio, occasioned by the results of the twin cases of *Bloomer* and *Abrahamson*, precipitated this verdict pronounced by John Buckley:[112]

> The effect of this decision [in *Abrahamson's* case] was to entitle a large number of law graduates, all emerging from the universities within a very short space of time, to entry to the [Society's] law school. This 'free ticket' became increasingly attractive as the employment prospects for newly qualified solicitors improved dramatically during the late 1990s. This put significant pressure on the Society's resources, both human and physical, and the Society's response was later adjudged by the Education Policy Review Group to have been inadequate.

The enactment of the Universities Act of 1997[113] promised major changes in the manner in which the several constituent colleges – now, more correctly, described as constituent universities – went about their business. This impacted on the Law School as well as on all the other academic disciplines on the campus. The General Board of Studies died a death straightaway. The straitjacket linked to NUI Senate's overarching control was set to disappear as well. Few probably would mourn the abandonment of the cumbersome appointments system – from the enactment or modification of internal Statutes for chairs and senior lecturers to the retention of the Senate's power to confirm or repudiate the Governing Body's verdict on each senior academic competition.

There were other changes foreshadowed by this major piece of legislation. But in the case of UCD these were not to be implemented until we were well into the new century. They will be briefly highlighted in the Epilogue.

GEOFFREY J. HAND (b. 1931)

Geoffrey Hand was educated at Blackrock College and at UCD. He obtained 1st class honours in his BA in History, and won various prizes in Law, capping this with the award to him of the Swift MacNeill prize for King's Inns students and the NUI Travelling Studentship in History. He obtained a DPhil from Oxford for his thesis on English law in Ireland, 1290–1324, with special reference to the Court of the Justiciar. This was in 1960, the same year that he qualified at the Irish Bar. He began his lecturing career in Edinburgh, moving on to Southampton, before returning to UCD in 1965, where he became, successively, Statutory Lecturer in Legal and Constitutional History and then, from 1972, Professor in the same subjects. He served as Dean of the Law School from 1970 to 1975, at which period he also acted for a while as chairman of the Arts Council (1973–5). He was named one of the first Professors of the new European University Institute in Florence in 1976, returning in 1980 to Britain as Barber Professor of Jurisprudence at the University of Birmingham. With colleagues in Florence he co-edited the *European Electoral Systems Handbook*, brought out in the late 1970s.[114]

It is his publications in areas of Irish history and Irish law, however, that merit special emphasis here.[115] His seminal volume on the arrival of the Common Law in Ireland was, as might have been expected, the outcome in part of time spent in Oxford doing research for his DPhil. *English Law in Ireland, 1290–1324*, published in 1967 in the Cambridge Studies in English Legal History series, broke fresh ground in the array of problems Hand explored, and the care taken to ensure the sources consulted yielded up their secrets. This was a major event in the rebirth of research into Irish legal history, the bibliography alone setting a standard for all to follow. The same year – 1967 – saw the publication in an Irish periodical journal of an article touching on litigation and how it was conducted under what may be termed 'the feudal legal order'.[116] The portion of it dealing with the controverted Comyn inheritance revealed Hand's mastery of the legal aspects to medieval history as much for England as for Ireland. This could well explain the invitation to him to collaborate with Lord Cross of Chelsea to revise the first part of the edition of Radcliffe and Cross' classic text on the legal system of England that came out in 1971.[117] A major preoccupation of Hand throughout his career was ecclesiastical history, as a listing of his published work reveals. The fortunes of medieval Irish cathedrals and cathedral chapters were of special interest, and these furnished the focus for the first Aubrey Gwynn lecture delivered by Hand in Dublin in October 1981: 'The dual secularity of the cathedrals of medieval Anglo-Ireland'.[118]

Turning to a more modern period, Hand was to produce in 1970 an edition of the *Report of the Irish Boundary Commission* completed in 1925, but, in controversial circumstances, suppressed at the time.[119] An important companion piece, focusing on Eoin MacNeill's membership of that commission, was published contemporaneously.[120] Here Hand, among other things, made telling use of the reminiscences of a predecessor on the UCD law school professoriate, Patrick McGilligan, who had known MacNeill well.

Hand was also to edit two important original-source legal texts from seventeenth-century Ireland, the first of these in collaboration with Victor Treadwell: James I's directions for the Irish Courts of 1622,[121] and the Irish Chancery Court rules of 1659.[122]

Hand was elected a Member of the Royal Irish Academy as well as a Fellow of the Royal Historical Society. He has also been awarded the Gold Medal of the Irish Legal History Society.

When he resigned from UCD in 1980, following his appointment to Birmingham, his chair in Legal and Constitutional History, at the urging of the then Law Faculty, was to be abolished.[123]

JAMES C. BRADY (1940–98)

Jim Brady was a graduate of UCD, holding both the BCL and the LLB. He also earned a PhD from Queen's University, Belfast. Before joining the staff of the Law School in UCD he served a stint lecturing in law at the University of Hull. His forte was teaching in the areas of Real Property and Equity, where he became the Statutory Lecturer in these subjects in 1974, moving on to the appropriate Chair in 1979. He held his post until his death in June 1998. He published *Religion and the Law of Charities in Ireland* in 1975 and *Succession Law in Ireland* in 1989. With Anthony Kerr he wrote *Limitation of Actions in the Republic of Ireland* which came out in 1984. This last and the *Succession* book made it to second editions, in 1994 and 1996 respectively. Brady succeeded Osborough as Dean in 1978, serving for a further period in that capacity from 1986 to 1989. He also served on a sub-committee of the Governing Body to consider the future of International Studies in the College; this was in 1987.[124]

Jim, in his last years, suffered from multiple sclerosis. If, as the *President's Report for 1997–1998* conceded, this untoward development restricted Jim's movements, it by no means affected his enthusiasm for Property and Equity, or his capacity to communicate that enthusiasm.

On his death a memorial prize named after him was established in the Faculty; it is awarded to the top student in Equity each year.

JAMES P. CASEY

James Casey, like Jim Brady, a native of Newry, gained his primary law degree, an LLB, at Queen's University, Belfast. In 1972 he obtained a Lectureship in

Trinity College, Dublin, and it was there too that he was awarded his doctorate. An LLD on published work from NUI was eventually to follow.

In 1980, Casey was appointed to a chair in Law at UCD, and in due course was to serve twice as Dean (1981–6; 1989–92). A scholar of rare talent, his early published work betrayed a breadth of interests that was increasingly uncommon among potential candidates for elevation to the rank of professor. There were to be two pioneering studies of the Dáil Courts,[125] a review of electoral law in the State,[126] and an intriguing foray into British, and essentially Scottish, political history over Ramsay McDonald's difficulties in securing the services of a Lord Advocate for Scotland in 1924.[127] McDonald seems to have been keen on appointing a Glasgow solicitor, one Rosslyn Mitchell, only to backtrack over such a break with precedent, which led to the choice of a Tory advocate instead, the future Lord Macmillan. As Casey was to recall, the move did not commend itself to James Maxton, the fiery Labour Clydeside MP. Casey wrote:

> He [Maxton] would not have allowed the Faculty of Advocates to say who should not or should be Lord Advocate. If he continued to have health and strength (he did), he would smash the Scottish Faculty of Advocates (he did not).

This is all very nicely expressed.

It is possible that Casey's revisiting of this political affair in the sister island in early 1924 inspired the choice of one of his later books, *The Office of the Attorney-general in Ireland* (1980), which was destined to be expanded and given an appropriately lengthened fresh title, *The Irish Law Officers: Rules and Responsibilities of the Attorney-general and the Director of Public Prosecutions* (1996).

Mr Justice Hogan, in his review of the 1996 volume,[128] welcomed the mélange of parliamentary debate, newspaper reports, and archival material in the Public Record Office that Casey had mined to produce an 'enormously impressive' piece of work, which represented 'a major addition to Irish legal literature'.

In the interval between the two books on the law officers, Casey had found time to produce another major piece of work, his *Constitutional Law in Ireland* (1987). When this key text reached its third edition in 2000,[129] it had expanded from 570 pages in the first edition to 719 in the third – eloquent testimony, naturally, to the exponential growth of Irish constitutional law in so short a period. A year's leave of absence spent at the University of Granada enabled Casey to bring out his survey of the Spanish Constitutional Court,[130] one of a number of related public law studies that flowed from Casey's pen. These include a study of constitutional law developments under Chief Justice T.F. O'Higgins,[131] as well as a personal favourite of the present writer, a piece where the constitutional mandate of trial by jury received different interpretations – in Australia and in the Republic – as to whether this mandate necessarily implied jury unanimity. Australia said 'yes': *Cheatle* v. *The Queen* (1993) 177 CLR 571; Ireland said 'no': *O'Callaghan* v. *A.G.* [1993] 2 IR 17. Casey, a straight talker here as in much else, makes it crystal-clear that the High Court of Australia put in a much more impressive intellectual performance.[132] Casey has also discussed in some detail the constitutional dimension to the Church/State relationship.[133]

Casey was Dean when the opportunity to move the Law School from the Library Annexe to Roebuck Castle arose; it was immediately seized and the move took effect in 1991. Less successful was Casey's raising of his objection to the customary practice, associated with the award of honorary degrees, to bestow honorary doctorates in Law, LLDs, when the powers that be or the beneficiaries of their largesse could not think of some more apt acknowledgment of the beneficiaries' personal accomplishments. When, in 2006, the Ryder Cup was held in Ireland and six LLDs were awarded to Ian Woosnam, the Captain of Europe, Tom Lehmen, the Captain of America, and four other figures in golf administration,[134] it is not difficult to see that Casey had a point.

Casey was elected a Member of the Royal Irish Academy in 1998. He served for several years as Book Review Editor for *The Irish Jurist*. He retired in 2006.

6

The Law Collection in the College Library

The sources are generally silent on the adequacy of the facilities for the study of law in the years before the opening of the new UCD and indeed for several years subsequently. The predominant role of Bar students on the early editorial team that produced *St. Stephen's* could well mean that a complaint directed at the National Library in Kildare Street came from a UCD student group that were accustomed, *faute de mieux,* to patronise the Library's august reading-room. 'When', a piece in *St. Stephen's* in 1902 asked,[1]

> will the Library authorities [of the National Library] think of installing efficient electric light? The present installation is interesting but unsuccessful. We are treated nightly to admirable imitations of a kettle boiling, interspersed with lovely violet and heliotrope effects. It is also a pleasant interruption of the dull routine of work, when a red hot chip of carbon falls on the table with brilliant scintillations. Such things are pretty, but not conducive to study.

The premises of the Royal University at Earlsfort Terrace contained a library as might have been expected, but neither then, nor in the decade and more after the new UCD opened its doors in 1909 and the new Law School was born, is there much evidence to hand of the utility of whatever collection of law books was available to whet the appetite of the early generations of law students. As the academic lawyers of more recent vintage have been want to proclaim, for them and for their students a decent law library with its assemblage of statutes, law reports and textbooks was as essential as the laboratory for the scientist. Some progress even so is on record. In 1911 authority was sought and obtained for the expenditure of £150 on English law reports.[2] A further £102 15*s.* for purchases in the same area was sanctioned in 1929.[3] Irish law reports were bought both in 1912, when £130 was spent, and in 1914, another £50.[4] In addition, it merits mention that in 1918, 17 volumes of transcripts of the Brehon laws were acquired from the Royal Irish Academy.[5] There is no hard information regarding legal textbooks.

But in truth it was only with the arrival in 1921 of the substantial law library of the recently deceased Chief Baron of the Irish Exchequer, Christopher Palles, that it could be argued that the in-house library collection was finally adequate to the needs of a law student population that was slowly destined to grow.

Palles, aside from his career as a distinguished judge, had long played a role in the reform and modernisation of the Irish education system – at all levels.[6] It will be recalled that under the Irish Universities Act of 1908 he was named chairman of the Dublin Commissioners. He had earlier served on the Senate of the old Royal University, so his involvement with the third level tier of education represented a continuum. Remarkably, in addition to serving as head of the Commissioners who regulated the affairs of the new UCD until their powers were brought to an end in July 1911, Palles was also appointed a member of the College's first Governing Body. It is impossible – even if proof for this is lacking – that Palles' handiwork, inspired by his knowledge of how things were managed at King's Inns, could have lain behind the new College's early preference for the first three law professors, in contradistinction to all the other professors, just to be given seven-year contracts with no immediate entitlement to be continued until age 65.[7]

Palles died on 14 February 1920.[8]

Archbishop Walsh, the Roman Catholic archbishop of Dublin and a long-time friend of Palles, purchased the Chief Baron's library after his death for £1,000 with a view to presenting it to the new UCD.[9] Dr Coffey and UCD's Governing Body first became aware of the impending donation when the archbishop's solicitor contacted the College late in 1920 with details of the proposed gift and the terms and conditions that it was proposed should attach. In 1959–60, as we will see, allegations that these terms and conditions had been breached lay at the heart of prospective litigation.[10] The Palles deed of trust, as we can call it, was also specifically singled out as the template Senator Alice Stopford Green indicated she wished followed – with one significant variation – when a few years after Walsh's gift she donated the library of her husband, J.R. Green, to the College.[11] Thus, some familiarity with the terms and conditions of the deed of trust seems unavoidable.

On 18 December 1920, Richard Ryan of the firm of Arthur O'Hagan & Sons, Walsh's solicitors, advised the College that he was submitting to its Governing Body a deed by which Walsh would be declaring certain trusts covering the projected donation of books. The preamble was lengthy, but merits reproduction:[12]

> Whereas the Founder has acquired the Law Library of the right Honourable Christopher Palles, Lord Chief Baron of the Exchequer, lately deceased;
>
> And whereas the Founder is desirous of establishing a Law Library in University College, Dublin, to bear the Name of the Chief Baron Palles Library, in grateful recollection of many acts of personal kindness, of his appreciation of the enduring work done by the Chief Baron as member

and chairman of the Dublin Commissioners appointed by the Irish Universities Act 1908;

And whereas the Founder has transferred to University College Dublin the said Law Library consisting of 2,169 volumes, as is testified by the catalogue or inventory thereof hereto attached and signed by the Founder and Denis J. Coffey, President of the said College;

And whereas the Founder is desirous of declaring the trusts upon which the said Law Library shall be held ...

The draft deed of trust went on to prescribe conditions for the housing, control and care of the collection. These insisted on all the books being kept together, and being stamped with the legend 'the Chief Baron Palles Library'. The draft deed also required that a report on the Library should be made to the Roman Catholic archbishop of Dublin every three years.

On 21 December 1920 UCD's Governing Body accepted the proposed gift, and the terms and conditions attaching. On the occasion Mr John Dillon proposed, and Dr Sigerson seconded, the following resolution, which was unanimously agreed:[13]

That the Governing Body of University College Dublin hereby declares its acceptance of the donation of the Chief Baron Palles Library made to the College by His Grace the Most Revd William J. Walsh, D.D., Archbishop of Dublin and Chancellor of the National University of Dublin, under the conditions of Trust set forth in the Deed by which his Grace as founder of the Chief Baron Palles Library declares the conditions of Trust. That the Governing Body of University College Dublin begs to tender to his Grace the Most Revd Wm. J. Walsh, D.D., archbishop of Dublin and Chancellor of the National University of Ireland, an expression of the most respectful appreciation and grateful thanks for the noble gift now made by his Grace to the College, by the foundation in the College of the most valuable Law Library accumulated by the late Lord Chief Baron Palles, by which the higher study of the Faculty of Law of this College will be encouraged and promoted in all the future work of the College and by which at the same time there will be forever associated with the College the memory of a great Irish judge, whose enduring work in relation to the university and to this College, as chairman of the Dublin Commissioners under the Irish Universities Act is specially named by His Grace.

By the middle of February in 1921 it was reported to the Governing Body that the books had arrived and proper arrangements for their housing had been made. This was in one of the Council Chambers on the ground floor of Earlsfort Terrace where the books would stay until an alternative location was found in the late 1950s.[14] Formal meetings of College authorities were to take place on occasion in the so-called Chief Baron Palles Library which, one presumes, while meetings were in progress, could not have facilitated access by law students. In February 1921, plans were laid for a formal opening of the Library with Archbishop Walsh in attendance.[15] This, however, does not appear to have taken place, for Walsh himself was to die on 9 April. Noting the death of the National University's first Chancellor, its Senate at its meeting on 19 April unanimously adopted the following resolution:[16]

> Profoundly interested in Irish education, and intimately acquainted with its ideals and problems and with the conditions interfering with its extension and development, His Grace devoted his great abilities throughout his life to its advancement.

The resolution went on to pay tribute to Walsh's 'wise guidance' and the role he had played in assuring for the National University the success it had enjoyed 'in surmounting the great difficulties of its early years'. The UCD Governing Body was to pay its respects at its meeting two days later. 'We recall', the resolution adopted on the occasion ran,[17]

> with special gratitude the constant interest which his Grace has shown in the work and progress of our College, and in the well-being of our students; his yearly visits to the College on the opening of each session and, during last term, the final act by which he manifested his love for the College in making his generous gift of the Chief Baron Palles Library. In the death of His Grace, the Chancellor, we mourn the loss of a kind friend, a wish counsellor and a great Irishman.

At the end of 1924 Coffey dealt with one facet of unfinished business.[18] Walsh's deed of trust envisaged three-yearly reports on the Palles Library. Two visitors were appointed by the Governing Body on Coffey's recommendation. The reports were to be made to successive archbishops of Dublin; in 1924 the incumbent was the Most Revd Edward Byrne. The Governing Body picked the Rt. Revd Monsignor Hickey and the Very Revd Canon Cronin. It is not clear whether Hickey joined in producing his first report, for not long after his appointment Hickey died. It is not clear either when the last of these three-yearly reports was carried out; they have certainly ceased – if indeed, they ever began. Nor is it clear, alas, in view of the seeming disappearance of the original deed of trust, what consequences were intended should proof emerge that the planned regular reports had not been carried out. Reference at this point may not altogether inappropriately be made to the conditions attached by Archbishop Matthew Parker (1504–75) to the bequest by him of his collection of medieval manuscripts and early printed books to Corpus Christi College in Cambridge.[19] An annual audit to be conducted by two other colleges – Gonville and Caius, and Trinity Hall – was prescribed. Stray books, identifiable as such from lists drawn up by Parker and furnished to each college, were to be replaced; fines were laid down for missing items; but, most seriously, if serious losses, interpreted as 6 large or 12 small books, were found to have been lost, through idle neglect (*per … supinam negligentiam*), the entire collection was to be transferred in the first instance to Gonville and Caius. Likewise, if the latter failed in its superintendence of the collection, the whole was to go to Trinity Hall. And if Trinity Hall failed to pass the key test at the annual audit, everything would come back to Corpus Christi. And so on *ad infinitum.*

Early in 1925 Senator Alice Stopford Green announced the gift of the library of her late husband, John Richard Green.[20] A variation in the terms of the trust, by comparison with that laid down for the Palles collection, showed that Mrs Stopford Green was anxious to avoid the imposition of a straitjacket on the College's library administration as to the housing of the collection, seeing the need to be flexible and anticipating the need for rearrangement in the light of possible College library development in the future – a contingency conspicuously omitted in Archbishop Walsh's vision for the Palles collection in the future.

Down until the 1950s, that collection – or at least the major part of it – was housed in one of the Council Chamber rooms on the ground floor of Earlsfort Terrace. The books were installed in handsome book cases that we happen to know, from a record left by the Governing Body, were polished in 1947 for the sum of £15 10*s.* 6*d.*.[21] This arrangement, however, was not to last – to the clear dismay of the late 1950s generation of law students.

In 1959 three students of the Law School, M.J. Hogan, Dermot Bouchier-Hayes and Aidan F. Browne, set in train a sequence of events that threatened at one point to be as damaging as John Kenny's protest over the appointments system which contemporaneously had brought about the Visitation. Their target was the state of the law collection in the library in Earlsfort Terrace and, in particular, the fate of the Palles Library, the collection of the law volumes that Archbishop Walsh had donated back in 1920. Aware of the broad outlines of the terms of the trust under which UCD held the books, the three students wrote to the Commissioners of Charitable Donations and Bequests, complaining that the terms of that trust were not being observed. The Commissioners in turn then wrote to the President of the day, Dr Michael Tierney, advising him of this complaint. Thus the matter came before the College's Governing Body.[22]

Tierney explained what had happened at a meeting of the Governing Body in June 1960. The reconstruction of the main Library had led to books previously housed in the History Library and the Law, or Palles, Library, formerly in the Council Chambers being moved to new quarters in the O'Curry Hall and the Coffey Hall. This had freed up the Council Chamber for use as extra classrooms. Resulting from discussions occurring there and then, Tierney instructed J.P. MacHale, the Secretary and Bursar, to write to the College Solicitors to apply to the Commissioners for a variation in the terms of the trust. What had particularly rankled was the splitting up of the Palles Collection in violation of what was understood to be one of the main conditions of the donation that the books be kept together. MacHale, in his letter of 17 August to the solicitors, pondered the question whether the present Catholic archbishop of Dublin might seize the bull by the horns as it were, and vary the terms of the original trust himself. Equally remarkably, a final instruction Tierney gave MacHale was for the latter to tell the solicitors that, if it proved impossible to vary the terms of the trust, the College would be prepared to abandon the trust and return the books to the legal representatives of the late archbishop.[23]

Much earlier, the Commissioners, anxious, it would undoubtedly appear, to avoid under any shape or form court proceedings, had sought advice from Andreas O'Keeffe, the then Attorney-general. The latter came in person to the Terrace early in 1960, to be shown where the books were then installed. Subsequently, the identity of the complainants to the Commissioners had become known; and they continued to press for the books to be brought together, labelling the dispersal 'a disgrace' and accusing the authorities of hypocrisy, having proclaimed back in 1920 the Governing Body's 'respectful appreciation and grateful thanks' for Walsh's gift.[24] At the end of May they had threatened to go to court if the College – in effect, Tierney and the Governing Body – refused to budge. At this stage, though a search was doubtless carried out, the original document setting out the terms of the deed of trust could not be found. The mystery of its disappearance fuelled a number of conspiracy theories.

When MacHale took O'Keeffe on a tour of the Terrace after the Commissioners had sought guidance from the latter, O'Keeffe will doubtless have been told that even as early as the time of the original receipt of Palles' books, the collection had been split up – many of them being stored in a corridor adjacent to the Great Hall. The position at the time of his visit in February 1960 was that books frequently required were housed in stacks at the back of the Great Hall, the main Library facility. Books less frequently required were housed in a stack room under the O'Curry Hall. Certain law reports and other volumes rarely required were kept in bookcases stationed along the walls in the Great Hall. MacHale, doubtless prompted by the new Librarian, Ellen Power,[25] pointed out one perhaps insurmountable difficulty. All law volumes, whether part of the original Walsh donation or subsequently acquired, bore the stamp 'Chief Baron Palles Library'. O'Keeffe, at the end of his visit, intimated that he would wish a plaque to be erected at some convenient location on the wall of the Great Hall commemorating Walsh's donation; he also wanted to have presented to him before a prescribed date a list of all the books in the Palles Library. MacHale indicated that there would be no difficulty in complying with both requirements, adding, for good measure, that the College would accompany the plaque with a portrait of Walsh. He also told O'Keeffe that there was no desire on the part of the College to have the power either to dispose of, or to exchange, books in the Palles collection. On this agreed basis O'Keeffe then advised MacHale that he would be asking the Commissioners of Charitable Donations and Bequests to vary the terms of the trust.[26] How this was to be accomplished, given that the original deed of trust was still apparently missing, was not to be explained. It never was.

When all this was reported to the Governing Body, two of its members urged MacHale to see to it that the Attorney-general expedited what he had promised to secure.[27] In such fashion, it was calculated, the law student protagonists, with their threat of legal action, might be kept at bay.

Doubts continued regarding the identification of the exact volumes to be considered part of the donation made by Archbishop Walsh in view of the abandon with which all law books even those acquired after the donation were stamped 'Chief Baron Palles Library'. Whether any splitting up of the entire collection at all would be allowed was another key issue. Both were raised in a letter sent by MacHale to the College solicitors on 28 July 1960 where at the same time it was indicated that the plan now was to house the books in a raised balcony at the end of the O'Curry Hall.[28] When Ellen Power heard of this last scheme, she protested at once. The balcony was needed, she argued, for office space, and the balcony itself could not support the weight of the books. Though, as MacHale wrote to the College solicitors on 2 August, the Professor of Architecture was of opinion that the balcony could support the books if properly placed, the College was now proposing an alternative plan: the housing of all the Palles books in glass-fronted cases to be erected along the sides of the O'Curry Hall.[29] Later, as reported by MacHale to the Governing Body in December,[30] the solicitors had advised that the College would be deemed to be in compliance with the terms of the trust if, as had been proposed, the books were now to be kept in the projected glass book-cases for the O'Curry Hall. Books previously stored in an adjacent corridor were adjudged part of the collection and were to be dealt with similarly. The College was then urged to end the practice of stamping all law books with the stamp 'Chief Baron Palles Library'. As the very last stage in the saga, the Governing Body intimated that the three original student complainants should be informed of the legal opinion on the whole question that the College had received and the practical steps it was now planned to take in compliance with that opinion.[31]

McCartney, in his account of the affair, makes the obvious point that the makeshift arrangements that had been introduced in the case of the Palles books had in a sense been forced on the College as a result of 'the immense pressure on space in the years before the move to Belfield'.[32] Whether Tierney's exasperation at the way the 'crisis' was handled by his student adversaries – they had another agenda, as McCartney points out[33] – in any way justified the threat to abandon the trust and jettison the books, the threat MacHale at one stage was asked to convey, is a question which it is not too easy to determine. University CEOs – presidents, provosts, rectors and vice-chancellors – usually avoid seeming to take a sledgehammer to crack a nut. It might not be altogether out of place at this precise juncture to note that a recent assessment of Tierney has drawn attention to his apparent capacity 'to court unpopularity with intemperate language'.[34]

At an early stage in the affair one of the prime movers among the students raised a point that MacHale, for one, considered perfectly valid, and which it was only right for the Librarian to deal with. This was the Library's practice of requiring the law student to fill out a separate docket each time he or she wished to consult a law report. This was destined to remain the case even after the final solution, involving the installation of an array of glass-fronted bookcases in the O'Curry Hall, had been achieved. The era preceding that of 'open access' was, indeed, nothing to be proud of. Timothy Forbes, one suspects, would not have been the only one to express concurrence with that view.[35]

Despite the reference to a catalogue of the Palles collection in Archbishop Walsh's deed of gift as communicated by Walsh's solicitors to the College in December 1920, and Andreas O'Keeffe's insistence in 1960 that another listing should be prepared, no such catalogue or listing would seem to be extant today. This is unfortunate. Establishing what exactly was comprised in the original gift is, of course, made difficult – as Ellen Power was aware, and as MacHale explained to O'Keeffe – by the practice that grew up for all additions to the College's law collection to be stamped 'Chief Baron Palles Library'. Whether this is the reason that the task does not seem ever to have been undertaken it is impossible to say. As regards the topic itself, one addendum is worth producing. On the removal of the collection from Earlsfort Terrace, its first resting place, to the new UCD Main Library on the Belfield campus, the then Assistant Librarian in charge of the law books, Esther Semple, attempted an up-to-date catalogue partly on index cards, that, hopefully, would assist in building up the best picture available to us of the entire collection. Sadly, however, the work was not completed.[36]

Something in excess of 2,000 volumes, as we have seen, made up the original gift. The Chief Baron's Library was indeed a working lawyer's library, and the majority of the volumes are text books, and treatises of assistance to any practitioner working in Ireland at the end of the nineteenth century and the start of the twentieth. The imprints are variously English or Irish and consist of predictable enough fodder. In addition, there are 'runs' of English and Irish reports from the start in the 1860s of the respective 'official' series down to 1916, the year of Palles' retirement from the Bench. There are also some so-called

English nominate reports from before the 1860s. Among the miscellaneous additional material – and perhaps the main interest of the entire collection – is an assemblage of volumes dealing with the succession of nineteenth-century Irish special commissions, a few printed yearbooks, a couple of original single copies of acts of James II's Irish parliament of 1689 and two curious folio volumes. The latter consist in the main of judgments composed by Palles himself, not all of which, however, we can say, were actually delivered. The judgments survive in various forms: some are printed, others typed and others again handwritten. No study of these judgments has to date been carried out. One of them – a typewritten exemplar – which I happened to peruse some years ago was Palles' undelivered judgment for the Court of Appeal in the pre-natal injury lawsuit that arose out of the Armagh rail disaster of June 1889: *Walker* v. *Great Northern Railway Co.*.[37] In another case arising out of the same accident, *Bell* v. *Great Northern Railway Co.*,[38] the Irish judiciary, at the instigation partly of Palles, pioneered an innovative approach that inspired the development of liability for nervous shock. In the *Walker* case, was the appellate court, reviewing the decision of the court below which, on a demurrer, had disallowed the action, about to strike out in a new direction as well? In a comment on the proceedings on the appeal, brought to an abrupt end by the death of the young plaintiff, Mabel Walker, an anonymous author in the pages of the *Irish Law Times & Solicitors' Journal* did not preclude the possibility. 'Nor was it at all certain, at the conclusion of the arguments', this commentator wrote,[39]

> that the Court of Appeal had determined unanimously to uphold the decision arrived at by the Court below [allowing the demurrer]. The arguments were learned and interesting, the interlocutory *dicta* suggestive, and were important by reason of the fatality that has precluded the delivery of the long-deferred judgments.

Palles' undelivered judgment in the case, which is accompanied by a note in his handwriting, 'not finished – having before completing it received notice that p'tf had died', and which is included in the collection of the Chief Baron's judgments alluded to above and held by Special Collections in the UCD Library,[40] makes it quite clear, however, that the doctrinal breakthrough, the focus of speculation in the *Irish Law Times*, was not, on this occasion at least, about to take place. Most certainly not if these represented the views of the majority on the Court of Appeal. The first paragraph of this undelivered and uncompleted 11-page judgment makes it plain where Palles stood. 'The question upon this appeal', the Chief Baron began,[41]

> is, whether a child who was born crippled, in consequence of injuries sustained before its birth by the negligent management of a train upon a railway, can maintain an action to recover damages for its injuries. It is

> admitted that there is no trace of such an action having been heretofore sustained, or even instituted; but it is said that there are principles of our law the inevitable result of which is that the action is maintainable. Having carefully considered all the cases which have been referred to, and some which were not mentioned, I have arrived at the clear conclusion that this proposition cannot be maintained, and that, consistently with the settled and established doctrine of our law, the action is not maintainable.

In truth, no coup de grâce could have been more forcefully expressed.[42]

Controversy continued to dog the Palles collection even after the move of the College and the entirety of the Library's holdings to the new Belfield campus. Under the abortive plan to merge UCD and Trinity College that came to be examined in the early 1970s, there was to be a single Law School situated in Trinity College. The fate of the Palles collection under such a dispensation necessarily called for a decision: could the College rightly claim entitlement to retain possession boasting neither law school nor law students? Early in 1973 the Law Faculty reported on the implications of the proposed merger so far as the holdings of law books, including those in the Palles collection, in the UCD Library were concerned. They recommended that the law collection *in toto* should be transferred to Trinity, and that application should be made to effect an alteration in the terms of the deed of trust regarding the Palles collection. By the time these suggestions reached the Governing Body, opposition had materialised however.[43] Responding to pressure from the Arts Faculty, the Governing Body noted that it continued to be the desire of Arts to continue teaching in the areas of Roman Law, Constitutional Law, Jurisprudence and Constitutional and Legal History. Failure to continue to make such provision, the Governing Body determined, 'could seriously damage the present work and future development of the Arts Faculty'. As a corollary, it was additionally resolved that the College should hold on to such law books as would be appropriate for the limited law teaching that was to be retained.

The agitation engendered by this particular controversy was soon enough to be shown to be a waste of emotional energy when the grandiose merger plan itself was finally abandoned, and UCD was set to retain its own Law School. In the new library building at Belfield, however, the Palles collection itself continued to be split up, most of the volumes at the time of writing being housed in a 'closed access' section adjacent to the Law issue desk with the remainder being placed in Special Collections. For many months until the new library building was completed, the general law collection was also fated to be split up – between Earlsfort Terrace and new cramped conditions in Stage One of the Library – a state of affairs, naturally, that attracted the ire and concern of members of the Law Faculty.[44]

Conflict over the housing of Archbishop Walsh's munificent donation represents one facet to the immense problems that the College's Library as such faced prior to the move to Belfield. In Earlsfort Terrace the cramped conditions in which the Library was obliged to operate left a very great deal to be desired. Late in 1927, a major report was drawn up on the needs of the Library;[45] perhaps significantly, it makes no reference at all to the Palles collection housed at the time in one of the Council Chambers. This report bluntly announced that a properly equipped Library building was 'one of the most pressing needs of the College at the moment'. Space was at a considerable premium, so much so at the time that on account of the congestion the Librarian had on occasion to refuse admission to would-be student readers. The conditions in which the lion's share of the general collection was housed, the report happily concluded, were satisfactory; where the residue was held in a room in the north wing of the Terrace, however, conditions were anything but. The roof was in a shocking state; the windows broken; and there was inadequate shelving. Moreover, pigeons and other birds often secured access, so poor was the facility. In such circumstances – and here there is gross understatement in the report – the task of preserving the books from injury, it was declared, was 'rendered very difficult'. There was no heating, so the books were prone to deteriorate on account of the dampness, and there was no artificial light: this meant that after nightfall there was no access to relevant books and periodicals.

The Academic Council considered this gloomy report in January 1928.[46] While it was agreed that something had to be done – any other reaction would have been laughable – progress, because of the financial constraints, was necessarily slow. And, of course, the principal thrust of the report – the case that is made for an independent library building – would only finally come to be realised after the move of the College to the Belfield site.

Meanwhile, law students, in common with the rest of the student body, had to cope as best they could. Slips were filled out for any volume – textbook or report – that the student wished to consult, and although books could be borrowed, a number of them – those most in demand – formed part of the 'reserved collection' which could in no circumstances be borrowed at all – the regulation which, as we have seen, in 1928 the student Timothy Forbes sought dramatically to challenge.[47]

The expansion of the Law School from the mid-1960s on – reflected in the increases in student numbers, in the recruitment of extra staff and, not least, in the launching of new courses and the teaching of new subjects – presented, as in other law schools, a particular challenge for the law library and for those whose business it was to administer it.

Ireland became a member of the European Economic Community, and the European Union, on 1 January 1973. But well in advance of that, with the inauguration, in 1968, of the Faculty's Diploma in European Law (of which

EEC Law was a constituent part), steps had been taken to enter subscriptions to a small number of French and German language law reports and legal periodicals. Monographs and text books dealing with the law in the constituent member countries were also to be acquired, a process that was to continue. A straw in the wind, too, was the acquisition for £110, almost certainly at the suggestion of John Kelly, of a set of the *Zeitschrift für geschichtliche Rechtswissenschaft* for the years 1815–48.[48]

Of equal significance, the Library in UCD had in 1967 been recognised as a European Documentation Centre, a status that was confirmed in 1972 and to be renewed in 1996. One development regarding European Law legal material, presaged at the time to confer considerable benefit on UCD and its Law Library, did not in the end materialise. This was the plan for a single major European Law Centre in Dublin, proposed in 1973 by the then President of the Incorporated Law Society, Mr James O'Donovan. Meetings of law librarians, academic lawyers and representatives of the two branches of the profession were held over a three-year period, and although much ground was covered at these meetings – especially in agreeing on the lists of books, reports, periodicals and official publications that needed to be furnished for such a central library – in the end nothing was done, partly because government funding, at first thought a possibility, was refused, and partly, I surmise, because every law library of any standing in the State wished to go its own way. One decision arrived at by the representatives who met over this three-year period was that the central library, should the project go ahead, would most appropriately be based in UCD. Space elsewhere simply could not be found. The King's Inns offer at these meetings to make their Library basement available could not, at this remove in time, be viewed as especially appetising. If the original scheme had come within an ace of being implemented, in the months that lay ahead a very considerable obstacle to the library ever opening under UCD auspices came to pass: the proposal in the high-powered report on the tentative merger between Trinity College and UCD that the merged Law Schools should be located at Trinity.[49]

The strength of the Republic's tradition in constitutional law, aided and abetted by an increasingly activist judicial bench, made it imperative that steps should early be taken to ensure access in the Library at least to judgments of the United States Supreme Court. Early in the 1980s, the relevant development was achieved when the UCD Library agreed with the National Library to become the national depository for United States Government Publications. The National Library, notoriously underfunded, and hampered space-wise, cannot have been proud to admit that a great deal of material it received from Washington had over many years lain in unopened parcels in some garage – described elsewhere as a dilapidated former warehouse with a leaking roof and walls and exposed, as it was coyly put, 'to other environmental hazards'. Damp, mould and insect infestation had wrought so much havoc that a proportion of the pre-1985 documentation eventually transferred to UCD that year had simply to be disposed of, the remainder requiring treatment in the storage facility at the Blackrock campus. Subsequent to 1985 a good deal of the relevant material was to be made available on microfiche. Included in the eventual transfer was a pristine set of the United States Supreme Court Reports (mercifully uninfested).

Until 1971 and 1972 when the Law Faculty moved out to Belfield, the Law Library formed part of the general collection housed in the main library in Earlsfort Terrace. There was but one complete set of *Irish Reports* and one complete set of English law reports available. Reports in the Palles collection were housed there too, but 'runs' finished circa 1916, and like the principal collection of both the Irish and English law reports were not on 'open access', and a docket had to be filled out for any individual volume the student might wish to consult. Given the number of students, the situation, of course, was indefensible. Following the move to Belfield, two fresh sets of the *Irish Reports* were acquired – the collection of the late Thomas McCann, Dun Laoghaire, and the entire Professional Books reprint of 1976. Additional subscriptions to the English Reports, i.e., the volumes produced by the Council of Law Reporting for England and Wales, were also entered up.[50] One other development from the 1970s should be noted. Prior to the launching of the new Irish report series, *Irish Law Reports Monthly*, a not-inconsiderable delay would occur before key judgments of the Supreme Court, the High Court and the Court of Criminal Appeal ever appeared in print. Representations on the matter were made to the Department of Justice and in due course it was agreed that copies of each so-called 'unreported judgment' could be made available to all of the law schools in the State as well as to the law school of Queen's University, Belfast.[51] Similar representations were made in Northern Ireland, the judgments of its superior courts being made available, doubtless on a similar basis. (Eventually, the so-called *Northern Ireland Judgment Bulletins* superseded this development.)

Gifts of law books from various donors have assisted in the building up of today's UCD law collection. In the late 1950s Fergus Clarke presented the College with 300 law reports.[52] An earlier gift of books from Professor J. McGrath contained many legal volumes.[53] In 1975 the Australian government presented a set of the *Commonwealth Law Reports*.[54] The following year an anonymous benefactor gifted a set of the *Revised Reports*, a set not perhaps often opened, but containing reports of some cases not to be found in the better-known 178-volume *English Reports*. (I discovered *Gorham* v. *Bishop of Exeter* at Privy Council level in RR,[55] even though, surprisingly, it is not in Eng. Rep.). In 1983 there came a gift of the *World Law of Competition*, and two years later the first of two donations from the St Louis University Law School in Missouri. In 2009 there came the gift of a 'run' of UK parliamentary statutes from the mid-nineteenth century (the Sweetman donation).

Further gaps in the holdings were plugged by the Library agreeing to take out subscriptions. A run of *Session Cases* (the Scots law reports), the *Lloyd List Law Reports*, *Restrictive Practices Cases*, the *Dominion Law Reports* (Canada), and the *New Zealand Law Reports*[56] – all to be found in the Society of Public Teachers of Law minimum holdings listing – were to be acquired in this fashion. Successive deans, law staff members, law librarians and College librarians have all played a part in overseeing the expansion. The late Henry Heaney, College Librarian at the time, in the spring of 1975, made a general case for increasing the law library holdings, in an important letter to J.P. MacHale, the then Secretary and Bursar. Heaney made four principal points. In the first place, he wrote,[57]

> For lawyers, periodicals and, in particular, law reports are the raw material of education. Expenditure on books is the major expense for a law faculty's continued existence.

Second, he argued,

> Emphasis in recent years in the Faculty has moved from teaching out of text-books to use of primary materials, particularly reports, by students. To meet the changed demand long runs of such reports are necessary for undergraduate use.

Third (an oblique reference to the abortive merger plan for the law schools of TCD and UCD):

> The Faculty and my predecessor have deliberately underspent on Law, other than textbooks, in recent years because of uncertainty as to the future of the Faculty. These deficiencies should now be made good.

And fourth, and last:

> Because of their nature, law reports are not easily available on inter-library loan, and a high level of self-sufficiency is necessary.

None of the deans who were to press for action over the law library both earlier, then and in later years – as all did – could have improved on Heaney's statement of the case.

A number of these other representations on the library problem are worth revisiting. A report on the Faculty of Law, prepared in 1973 with the help of its staff by the then dean, Geoffrey Hand, was the first in a sequence of more recent surveys undertaken by the Faculty itself, which highlighted the importance to the Faculty and its operations of an adequately stocked and properly funded Law Library.[58] The resources of that library, Hand averred, were 'still quite inadequate for a law school the size of UCD's'. Those resources, he stressed, of what was 'after all the premier law school in the State' were 'well below par'. Anticipating the College Librarian's forceful letter to the College's Secretary and Bursar of May 1975, Hand[59] sensed it was

> crucial to emphasise the peculiar importance of the library in legal education, almost certainly surpassing, in a common law system like ours, its importance in any other field of undergraduate study.

Hand's report of 1973 went on to applaud one of the major benefits accruing from the move to Belfield – the operation from the outset at the new library building of an 'open access' system. 'The advantages', he argued,[60]

> of a system of access under which the law student is at liberty to serve himself to the large number of statutes, law reports and … legal periodicals he requires to consult in any one visit to the library are self-evident.

Another dean, Jim Casey, wrote directly to the College Secretary and Bursar, reiterating the case for extra investment in the law library, previously forcefully expressed by Heaney and Hand.[61] Casey drew attention to the Faculty's low demands on the College so far as plant and equipment were concerned, the relatively poor staff/student ratio in the Faculty at the time and (restating one of Heaney's contentions) the actual research and teaching needs of the Faculty. For good measure, he added a fourth consideration, something that the powers that be had constantly to be reminded of: the imperative need for the academic lawyer to be up-to-date in national and international legal developments. This last important coda puts one in mind of a law lord in the late nineteenth century who scornfully rejected the suggestion, aired in a decision appealed from Scotland, that the self-respecting university professor or lecturer could get by, offering a series of lectures that never altered from one year to the next.[62] The sheriff-substitute of Lanarkshire had sensed that it strengthened the claim of a Professor Caird, a professor in Glasgow University, to copyright in his lectures that his lectures would be unlikely to change from year to year. At the hearing in the House of Lords, Lord Fitzgerald attacked the logic, basing his argument on what he perceived to be the proper responsibility of any university lecturer worth his salt. The sheriff-substitute's contention, Lord Fitzgerald began,[63]

> would seem to assimilate the professor's duty to the cuckoo cry of repetition. I rather think that this eminent professor would repudiate such a suggestion, and tell us that the lecturer should remember that

> 'Beneath this starry arch,
> Naught resteth or is still',[64]

> And that his duty is to watch over and criticise new modes of thought, new works, the march of intellect, and those discoveries which

> 'Make old knowledge
> Pale before the new.'

> 'Even in pure mathematics', Lord FitzGerald concluded,[65] 'there may be alterations and additions, and ethical science [Professors Caird's area of expertise] is not free from the inexorable law of mutability.'

A submission on library needs was drawn up also in 1986 by Paul O'Connor, acting as chairman of the Faculty's Library committee and shortly to become dean.[66] In the introduction to this seven-page document, O'Connor placed on record the Faculty's appreciation of 'the co-operation, understanding and sheer devotion to the task of bettering the Law section shown by the staff of the Law Library'. At the same time, he left the authorities in no doubt that the library fell far short of meeting 'the routine research needs of members of staff'. In an appendix, the submission itemised the more serious lacunae. In the submission itself emphasis was placed on gaps in the holdings of reports from common law jurisdictions. 'Unless', O'Connor's report observed,[67]

> the Faculty obtains a constant flow of information on legally significant developments in the common law world our legal vision will be narrowed and we will be perceived, from an international perspective, to be insular in outlook and, as jurisdictions go, something of a backwater.

Many of the representations to the College Librarian and to the College authorities bolstered the case for extra investment by rehearsing, sometimes in considerable detail, the extent to which UCD's law library fell short of the minimum standards for university law libraries drawn up in England by the Society of Public Teachers of Law. The O'Connor submission, in the introduction, did so too, adding a reference to the matter of library holdings in the approach of the American Bar Association towards the recognition of prospective new law schools in the United States. 'The U.C.D. Law Library', the submission contended,[68]

> certainly falls short of the *minimum* holdings recommended by the Society of Public Teachers of Law … and would certainly fall short of the standards required for approval by the American Bar Association.

Note at this juncture might be taken of the decision of the United State's Supreme Court in the case of *Sweatt* v. *Painter* in 1949.[69] There the Supreme Court held that the legal education being offered to Negroes at a planned new Texas law school for Negroes was not substantially equal to that being offered at the long-established University of Texas Law School, comparing unfavourably, inter alia, the 16,500 volumes at the new school's library with the 65,000 volumes held at the older law school.[70]

Even with the passage of time, this Faculty of Law document on what were perceived as the Faculty's library needs at mid-point in the 1980s makes interesting reading.

A multiple copy collection of textbooks for law undergraduates was finally put together in the late 1970s. It came not a moment too soon, for the story of the law library is not invariably one of progress over the years. It is possible to write this, given the thrust of the document headed 'Rules for Good Library Conduct', which was introduced around the late 1970s. These asked students to observe silence in the law library, never to consult more than three volumes of law reports at any one time, and always to re-shelve law reports. But there was more. There should occur no mutilation of law books: that could be taken for granted. But there was also this:

> The wilful concealment of reports, journals and official publications in non-law sections of the Main Library is a reprehensible and anti-social practice which must be eliminated. Law students especially should not indulge in underhand strategies of this kind.

Cut-backs and reductions in Library funding have equally affected the Law School. Not all the details have been meticulously recorded, but it is on file that, as a result of financial pressure in 1984, the Law Faculty acquiesced in the cancellation of the subscription to the *Anuario de historia del derecho español*. And in 1995 a request to the College Librarian for an explanation for the reduction in Law's allocation in the general Library budget from 5.3 per cent to 5.1 per cent prompted Sean Phillips to respond that four factors entered into the equation: the average of book prices, the average of periodical subscriptions, the number of research users and the number of other users.[71] Other cancellations have occurred in later years.

A variety of problems continued to manifest itself. In 1988 students attending the Diploma in European Law sought access to the European Documentation Centre in the evenings and on Saturdays. The same year, the then dean, Jim Brady, wrote at the behest of Andrew Lyall, asking for copies of the pre-1860 statutes and a number of Irish nominate reports to be transferred from Special Collections and placed on open access. 'We should', Brady wrote,[72]

> keep on open access in the law library in a readily accessible form the text of all the laws currently in force ... Since the affected materials have this formal status as law we feel that they should be treated on a different basis to materials that are of purely historical interest or only of interest to scholars.

The Librarian, Sean Phillips, was unmoved. Replying, he considered that the open shelves were not the most appropriate location; the materials in question would, he accepted, be readily accessible, but they would also be vulnerable. In Special Collections they would be 'very much more secure':[73]

> Special Collections represents the best balance between the need for accessibility to readers and the security and environmental requirements for older and rarer materials.

A turning-point in the development of the law library was reached in 1986 when the then dean, Jim Brady, argued for the taking out of a subscription to Lexis, one of the first electronic legal data bases to make appearance. Today the availability on-line of a range of reports and periodicals has transformed the very look of the law library itself. All this seems a far cry from the 1970s and even the early 1980s when the then Law Librarian, Esther Semple, would make application to remedy deficiencies in essential furniture for the Law Librarian's office. A filing cabinet, tables and stands for the display of catalogues were all requested in 1977.[74] Seven years later Miss Semple found herself still bereft of essentials, 'I would like to ask', she wrote to the Deputy Librarian in 1984,[75]

> for three desks with drawers for our office. The tables used by the library assistants are no longer satisfactory, as they very quickly get overcrowded and they also leave the staff with nowhere to lock away their possessions.

And there was more:[76]

> Could we also please have four anglepoise lamps? The present arrangement of lighting is satisfactory as long as the daylight lasts, but in the evening those sitting near the windows are in shade.

7

Housing the Law School

It was to be early in 1910 when the Governing Body effectively resolved that the main base for the new UCD for the first half century and more of its existence should be in a remodelled and extended building at Earlsfort Terrace close to St Stephen's Green and in the city centre. This was by no means the foreseeable conclusion when the Governing Body's Sites Committee was asked to ponder the options. A report delivered to the Governing Body in January 1910 argued that there was no suitable site on the north side, but on the south side there were a number of possibilities: the Royal Hospital at Kilmainham, Elm Park (near where St Vincent's University Hospital is located today), Nolan-Whelan's property at Harold's Cross and Rathfarnham Castle.[1] Matters had been put in hand to secure the availability for the new College through leasing of the premises of the old UCD, heirs to the Catholic University, on St Stephen's Green, and of its medical school on Cecilia Street in Temple Bar.

The attractions of a city centre site close to the houses, including numbers 85 and 86, on St Stephen's Green proved overwhelming, and thus it came about that, despite the inquiries made by the Sites Committee, the lion's share of the parliamentary grant of £150,000 designed to secure headquarters for the new institution was to be spent on the Earlsfort Terrace site. The Governing Body successfully argued for £110,000 of that block grant to be earmarked for UCD. The National University, the new supervisory body for the three constituent colleges, UCC (the old Queen's College, Cork), UCG (the old Queen's College, Galway) and the new UCD, would be evicted from the old Royal University premises at Earlsfort Terrace, and with the £40,000 remaining out of the £150,000 were to set up shop in new premises some distance away at Merrion Square.[2] By March 1910 the die was finally cast when the Governing Body made formal application to the Dublin Commissioners appointed under the 1908 Act for the appropriation to UCD and the National University of the Earlsfort Terrace site.[3]

In due course there began the taxing business of organising a competition for the design of the new Earlsfort Terrace building, choosing an architect, a contractor and a quantity surveyor, and keeping a watchful eye on cost. The Treasury were regularly in touch to ensure no money was wasted but, perhaps inevitably, expenditure quickly consumed the £110,000 which had been allocated to UCD.[4] In the summer of 1918, the Governing Body successfully negotiated an overdraft of some £12,000 or £15,000 (sources differ as to the amount) from the National Bank, the President, Dr Denis Coffey, in his letter stressing the fact that when the original allocation had been made there were some 530 students on the books, a figure that had since risen to 1,100.[5]

The lack of a permanent home for the new institution was expressly alluded to in the address of welcome presented to King George V and Queen Mary at Dublin Castle by Dr Coffey and the Registrar, Dr Conway, in July 1911 during the visit to Dublin by their majesties that month.[6] And so it remained until the first stage of demolition and construction was completed in 1919 and it became possible for students and staff to move in. Work itself appears to have commenced in 1914 but, as McCartney explains in his history of the College, it was not to be a case of smooth sailing; far from it. 'The work began', he writes,[7]

> and so, almost immediately, did a formidable array of problems. Flooding delayed the supply of limestone from Stradbally quarry; costs mounted when unforeseen work arose because an underground passage was discovered, which had to be filled in and buttressed; a strike by Crampton labourers in 1916 hampered construction more effectively than the Rising, with which it coincided; and, above all, prices rocketed as a consequence of the Great War, then in progress.

From the outset a base of sorts had been found for the Law School at no. 86 St Stephen's Green. Neither there nor in the Terrace (when construction was completed) will its demands have been onerous, for the new law school was a very small operation.

A base nevertheless was made available in the Terrace which was called, appropriately enough, the Law Room. The small – not to say exiguous – Law professoriate would not appear to have had exclusive possession, to judge from a tantalisingly obscure entry in the records of both the Academic Council and of the Governing Body from December 1945.[8] This reads, in the case of the Governing Body:

> Law Room to be suitably decorated, and placed at the disposal of College staff as a reading and writing room, and that a selection of reference books and current periodicals be placed there.

This sounds very much like the origins of a Common Room for staff, involving as it undoubtedly does the part-eviction of the lawyers.

When the present writer joined the staff in the late 1960s, whatever had been done to accommodate the Law Faculty's staff in the intervening years, the Faculty then occupied two large rooms on the first floor of the North Wing of the Terrace, one of which had earlier in 1964 or 1965 been earmarked for Law.[9] Four full-timers and sundry part-timers shared these facilities, and a single, doubtless overworked secretary, Irene Geraghty, saw to the Faculty's official business a couple of afternoons in the week. She shared duties there with two History departments – Medieval History and Early Irish History.[10]

The Law Faculty remained there until in 1972 it moved out to the new Belfield campus, and into what was then denominated the Arts – Commerce – Law Building – today's Newman Building. The Law Faculty delayed its move to Belfield in the absence of any concurrent move of the College's Law collection. And only when steps had been taken to provide a modest law library service in the new Library building was the time adjudged opportune for the Faculty to move to space that had been reserved for it at Belfield. The Faculty opted to occupy a suite of rooms on the fourth floor of D block. For the first time, each staff member had an individual office and there was a single office too for the Faculty's secretarial staff, now about to be raised to two permanent positions. The Faculty shared the lecture theatres in the building with the Faculties of Arts and of Commerce.

The fourth floor of D block in the Arts Building, however, was soon found to be less-than-adequate in terms of office space for the burgeoning Faculty. In the summer of 1980, Professor Brady, the then dean, bewailed the shortage of satisfactory staff accommodation, pointing out that two members of staff were situated in rooms without telephones three floors away from the Faculty's principal base.[11] The President, Dr Murphy, promised to raise the question with the Buildings Officer, while pointing out there could be no early solution: 'the current cash crisis inhibited the university's plans to resolve the accommodation crisis'.

Four years later, with the prospect of the completion in the near future of phase II of the Library building, the Law Faculty was apprised of one possible solution to its accommodation problem.[12] This was to move en bloc to one floor in the new building. Professor Casey, now Dean, had been made *au fait* with the thinking of the Rooms Committee, who had advanced this proposal. Casey insisted that the Law School would require 27 rooms in the new building, adding that even if the Law Faculty were allocated all of the fourth floor in Block D of the Arts Building, 'we would get nothing like this amount of space'. The Law Faculty's assent to the proposed move was conditional 'on the understanding that the Law Faculty's accommodation would be an identifiable block of rooms in the new building'.

That in the autumn of 1985 the promised move had not as yet taken place found the Law Faculty grumbling again.[13] In the end, the move finally took place late in 1987.[14]

The Library Annexe, to which the Law School had been moved, was adjacent to the Library itself – a considerable advantage – but all the offices were small and the corridor linking them narrow. But once again, it was the problem of expanding staff members that continued to concentrate peoples' minds. And so, late in 1991 the Law Faculty moved its headquarters yet again from the upper floor in the Library Annexe to one of the old buildings on the expanded Belfield campus.

This was Roebuck Castle, whose immediately preceding occupants had been the College's Graduate School of Business. Following the purchase by the College of the former Carysfort Teaching Training College in Blackrock, the Graduate School of Business had transferred to these sumptuous new premises, and Roebuck became vacant. The Law Faculty was in desperate need of expanded facilities at this juncture in its fortunes and, although Roebuck was situated on the periphery of the campus, alongside Roebuck Road which formed the connecting route between Foster's Avenue and the Clonskeagh Road, and thus was several minutes walking-time away from the centre of the campus, it very obviously was in a position to cater for that need. It was no surprise then when the decision was made to allocate the vacant building, with its generous supply of space – 3,000 square metres on one calculation[15] – to the Law Faculty. The Faculty would have the exclusive use of its own lecture theatres and seminar rooms.

The move, when it took place in the autumn of 1991, was not without its teething problems.[16] Students complained of the lack of facilities – an omission regarded as legally indictable in the view of one sympathetic staff member. The Buildings Office moved quickly to set up a reading room, and a recreation area. This was followed by the installation of food and drinks vending machines, both superseded sometime later by a small cafe. Acoustics in the theatres were poor in the estimation of the lecturing staff; even with the installation of a microphone system, adjustments had to be carried out. Heating and ventilation presented problems as well, together with insufficient lighting along the road or path to the Castle from the centre of the campus. Early plans to convert the church into a library were dropped; instead, the space was converted into two separate large lecture theatres, which, as the years passed and funds became available, were modernised, wired and tiered. Lack of consultation with staff over the planned move – a further bone of contention – was dismissed as unrealistic in terms of the manner in which decisions such as this one were reached. Students who wanted Jurisprudence lectures at least given in the Arts Building received equally short shrift.

The building that the Law Faculty came to occupy in 1991 had a number of interesting legal historical associations, though none of these involved actual residence by a superior court judge, unlike at Merville, also now part of the expanded Belfield campus, where in the early nineteenth century the chief justice of the Irish King's Bench, Chief Justice Downes had had his residence;[17] or at Roebuck House (now demolished, which for several years operated the UCD crèche), which had been the residence of Abraham Brewster, lord chancellor in 1867; or at Newstead House (now also demolished), the residence for a while of Hugh Kennedy, first chief justice of the Irish Free State.[18]

Two families were to be closely connected with the Roebuck site and merit a mention here. These were the Barnewalls in possession down to 1810, and the Westbys, who in the 1870s built today's Roebuck Castle.

The Barnewalls played a conspicuous role in Irish legal and political history across the centuries. In the fifteenth century two Barnewalls, father and son, served as Chief Justices of the King's Bench; in the sixteenth, another member of the family served as lord chancellor. The senior branch had been elevated to the peerage as the Barons Trimleston by Edward IV in 1462.

Nicholas, the 14th Baron Trimleston, died at the age of 86 in 1813. There then ensued a major dispute on the validity of his will, a dispute in which his son John Thomas, the 15th Baron, was ranged against Alicia, Nicholas' widow and actually his second wife. Nicholas had spent his earlier years in France, and through his first marriage, to the daughter of Joseph D'Auguin, the president of the Parlement of Toulouse, he had acquired substantial property in France, which was expropriated by revolutionary decree in 1793. The legal battle between John Thomas and Alicia over Nicholas' will was, as it turned out, also a struggle over who was entitled to claim compensation under the regime established by the Commissioners for Claims on France set up by statute in 1819.[19] It was a battle which John Thomas was ultimately to lose, following litigation extending over two decades.[20]

Prior to Nicholas' death, and in the face of considerable pressure on his income, he resolved in 1810 to sell Roebuck Castle, and thus it came about that the property fell into the hands of the Crofton family where it remained until it was acquired in 1856 by the trustees of one Edward Perceval Westby. It was this Westby who demolished the old ruined castle and remodelled the site to create the impressive building that remains today.

It was to be in the 1930s, after the death of Francis Vandeleur Westby, Edward Perceval's son, that the Westbys were in turn to leave their imprint on Irish law. Of Francis Vandeleur's three sons, two predecessed him – Perceval who was killed in action in September 1917 and Horace who died in August 1926. John, from the earlier death of Horace, his father, stood to inherit a substantial inheritance on the death of his grandfather, Francis Vandeleur Westby, which took place in September 1930. In the circumstances, it was a prudent move to arrange for both John and his brother David to be made wards of court, and this was duly done.

The previous generation of Westby boys – including Francis Vandeleur's third son – and father of Lois Valletta – Granville – had been educated at Harrow in England. It was hoped to make similar arrangements in the cases of both John and David; in fact, in the end, they were despatched to Cranleigh instead. However, the question arose: was any such course of action available in the case of an infant ward of the Irish court? In celebrated proceedings, *In re Westby Minors (No. 2)*,[21] the Irish chief justice, Chief Justice Hugh Kennedy, thought not. But that decision was overturned by a majority in the Supreme Court (Mr Justice FitzGibbon and Mr Justice Murnaghan; Mr Justice Sullivan, the President of the High Court, dissenting).

John in later life was to return to Ireland to take up residence in the glebe house in Timoleague, Co. Cork. He died in September 1995, but arranged for a number of Westby family portraits to be returned to Roebuck Castle. None of these portraits, it seems safe to assume, will have been *in situ* when one more critical episode in the history of Roebuck was fated to occur. This was the accompaniment to the sale of Roebuck to the Little Sisters of the Poor – the auction in September 1943 of the entire contents of the former Westby family home. The auction catalogue is extant.[22] As Pearson explains,[23] the auction itself constituted a major clearing-out, where

> everything, from an important collection of jewellery and silver down to a Ford van and an Austin Landaulette car, was sold. There was a large library of books, many carpets and quantities of antique furniture.

The Little Sisters of the Poor made changes to Roebuck when they acquired the Castle in 1944. UCD were to make changes as well – the nuns' chapel was divided in two to make two large lecture theatres. After the Law School came into possession, a one-storey building separate from the main edifice was erected on land that must have formed part of a former orchard, to judge from the fruit – small, hard pears – produced by a group of what I recall as sad, neglected fruit trees felled during the salient clearance work – not far, either, from the stables brought into service to house the horses during the filming in 1944 of Olivier's *Henry V*.[24] This building was to be dubbed the Legal Education Centre, which became the College's Confucius Institute in 2011, a bare two years before the Law School was set to move its base yet again.

The various associations of Roebuck Castle, which I have contrived to summarize here, prompt the conclusion that the UCD Law School, staff and students alike, was indeed fortunate to have been housed for over twenty years in a building so obviously redolent of its historic past. Nick Guest, the London postgraduate of one of Alan Hollinghurst's novels, confesses his dismay at the discovery that University College London's English Department had once been a mattress factory.[25] A generation of denizens of Roebuck Castle can surely, I would have thought, afford to commiserate.

8

Epilogue: Changes All Round – the Law School since 2000

President Masterson's taunt that the Law Faculty was perceived by the College at large of being 'hermetically sealed' had provoked well before the millennium was reached two initiatives designed to repudiate any such notion – the inauguration in the year 1991 of the new degree course, the BBLS – and just ahead of the millennium itself – the establishment of the Institute of Criminology.

There were, and there remain, valid educational arguments in favour of all the courses taken by the undergraduate over his or her three or four years in a law school having a distinct legal flavour – and there is no need to apologise for this. Comprehending and mastering the doctrines of core legal topics are not things to be undertaken in the expectation of quick or easy success: the rule in *Shelley's Case*, springing and shifting uses, even *volenti non fit iniuria* and *mens rea* in murder are none of them simple to fully understand. There persists, against the odds perhaps, a swathe of opinion to the effect that in the formation of the lawyer, the study of the law itself faces other rivals at least equally valuable. The point has recently been adopted by Lord Sumption, a recent appointment to the United Kingdom Supreme Court. 'The study of something involving the analysis of evidence, like history or classics', he is recently reported to have declared,[1] 'or the study of a subject close to pure logic, like maths, is at least as valuable preparation for legal practice as the study of law'.

If this is the true state of affairs, one can hardly object to a development scheduled to 'take off' in UCD after the year 2000: joint degrees in which the undergraduate was at liberty to acquire an amount of knowledge of law at the same time as an amount of knowledge of some other discipline. A start was made in 1989, as we have seen, with Law with French Law. By the year 2012 it was possible at UCD to study Law at undergraduate level together with History, with Economics, with Philosophy (all introduced in 2007).

There had been other innovations as well. In 1999 there had come the Diploma in Arbitration, followed the ensuing year by the Diploma in Employment Law. The year 2009 was to see the introduction of the BCL /Maitrise as well as an MSc in Criminology and Criminal Justice. Two new LLM programmes saw the light of day the following year – one in Human Rights Law and another in European Public Law and Governance.

Two major lecture series founded by the Law Faculty in the 1990s were continued in the new century and, as before, were recognised as important events in the Law School's annual calendar. These were the J.M. Kelly memorial series established in 1994 and the Joint UCD/RTÉ 'Broadcasting Society and the Law' series, which was started in 1997.

President Masterson's criticism to the effect that the Law School was 'hermetically sealed' could have been understood by certain observers to imply that the Law School was both inward-looking and closed to the outside world, both professionally and globally. This would be a fatal misunderstanding of what the Law Faculty – or, to adopt the post-2005 vocabulary, the Law School – had achieved as it celebrated not just its ninetieth year but its centenary as well. The Commercial Law Centre, the Irish European Law Forum, with their attendant programmes, and the various Diploma courses testify to an unheralded commitment to links with the profession and, indeed, to 'continuing education'. Of significance in this context must be counted the Judge in Residence programme established in 1991. As regards the student body, the development of a substantial international dimension represents a critical departure – and a lot of hard work for those who oversee its success. By 2004 some 40 per cent of UCD students were going abroad at the end of their second year of legal study to study for one year. There were exchange programmes with universities in the United States, Canada and Australia. In addition, under the Erasmus / Socrates exchange scheme, links were to be established with some twenty law schools in continental Europe. Post-2000, internationalisation of the Law School has seen student exchanges take in Asia as well (National University of Singapore and new agreements with Chinese and Indian partners). Major conferences held under the aegis of the Law School enter into the reckoning as well. These have brought delegates to UCD and the Belfield campus literally from all over the world. One such conference was the 16th British Legal History Conference in 2003. Contributors to the publication based on the proceedings of the conference hailed from England, Scotland, Wales, Australia, New Zealand, Belgium, Germany and the United States as well as from Ireland, both North and South.[2] Accommodation for the delegates was provided in the campus' blocks of student residences during vacation periods. In 1972 the annual conference of the Société Internationale Fernand de Visscher pour l'Histoire des Droits de l'Antiquité, had also been held in UCD. The Société's previous hosts had been in Bordeaux, Vienna and Perugia. The list of countries represented at the 1972 conference was again extremely varied. This was to be the case also when the 5th Irish Criminology conference was hosted by UCD's Institute of Criminology in 2009.

The Law School, arguably, continues to punch above its weight in the matter of publications. For the middle of 2014, it can be recorded that UCD now houses both *The Irish Jurist* under its fourth post-1965 editor, Paul O'Connor, and, as a result of competitive tendering, *Legal Studies*, the successor to the *Journal of the Society of Public Teachers of Law*. The flyer produced by the new editorial team at *Legal Studies* conveys very well the nature of the constituency they reckoned the periodical was designed to serve. They were keen to encourage the submission of articles which analysed 'the history, development and contemporary status of law', placed 'current legal developments in historical and theoretical perspectives', or analysed 'contributions to the study of law in the fields of jurisprudence, legal history, and international and comparative law'.

An initiative taken by the Irish Association of Law Teachers led to the appearance in 2011 of a volume celebrating three decades of legal research and writing in Ireland.[3] No less than five of the 28 contributors to this key volume were to be counted UCD staff (though one has since fled the coop to Trinity College). Aside from this, a visit to the landing outside the principal secretaries' office in Roebuck Castle, where two display cases were installed, would have introduced the passer-by to the range of published work produced by staff members in the last few years. Also on display were some of the leading periodicals in which articles written by staff members were on show – *Law Quarterly Review*, *Public Law*, *Journal of Legal History*, *British Journal of Criminology*, *Journal of Law and Society*, *Law and Policy*, *European Business Organization Law Review*, *Yearbook of European Law*. Absent at the time of composing this short survey had been any textbook in a particular branch of Irish Law on display outside the secretaries' office, but if we travel back a few years, we may be forgiven (at least I hope so) for asserting that staff members then were not so taciturn – as important texts on constitutional law, company law and contract law authored by them, and still of utility, bore witness. At the end of the nineteenth century the redoubtable Lord Bowen found an excuse for this limitation on the sphere of activity of the legal author (though whether it would apply to the author in the early twenty-first century UCD Law School can be doubted). To write a legal textbook, Bowen was to pronounce, was a task too ephemeral to be worth the effect. From the same oracle there was to emerge another deflationary remark: 'Professional life is not worth the sacrifice it entails'.[4]

At first, talk of joint programmes such as Law with History or Politics led to such being termed 'interfaculty degrees', but the nomenclature had to change after 2005, following the adoption of a major change in the internal government of the College, which saw the abolition of faculties and the consequential metamorphosis of the Law Faculty into a Law School. The Universities Act of 1997 had given an organ such as UCD's Governing Body (now the Governing Authority) the power to amend or even abolish its existing statutes.[5] Faculties were itemised in Statute I of 1910, and were therefore at risk of being set aside should any post-1997 Governing Body determine on such a course of action. This was done by a new post-1997 Statute in June 2005,[6] which, in the name of greater efficiency, abolished all existing faculties, substituting for them seven multi-school Colleges: Human Sciences; Arts and Celtic Studies; Science; Engineering and Architecture; Health Sciences; Business and Law; and

Agriculture, Food Science and Veterinary Medicine. There was some uncertainty as regards the College that Law, a small Faculty in College terms, would be obliged to enter under the new dispensation. One or other of the two Humanities-sounding Colleges was a possible choice. In the end, however, the fall of the dice suggested that Commerce, i.e., Business, should be Law's bedfellow in the new combined School of Business and Law, not, note, School of Law and Business. The Dean at the time these changes were first mooted, Paul O'Connor, assessed the desirability of proceeding down the path that Statute 6 was to prescribe.[7] While acknowledging what he terms 'uncomfortable political realities', O'Connor by no means conceded the case that the then Faculty of Law should be abolished and replaced by a School within some broader administrative reconfiguration, the reconfiguration which in the end did result. O'Connor found six reasons to support the status quo. 'This' he argued,

> provides a stable environment for achieving academic goals; permits fast responses in decision-making; facilitates the development of academic and institutional partnerships; facilitates co-operation with other academic units within the University; provides a strong sense of identity for alumni and prospective students; and facilitates contact and development of relationships with the professional legal bodies.

The same Statute which introduced the changes of June 2005 also dispensed with the clause in Statute I of 1910 which provided for the election of Deans. Deans, as Heads of School, would henceforth be appointed by the President, albeit after a procedure providing for consultation. The matter was regulated by clause 7 of Chapter 17 in Statute 6:

> Upon the recommendation of the Head of College, the President, having consulted the Academic Council, shall appoint the Head of School, by whatever name known. The Head of College shall consult with the members of the School and take all reasonable steps to determine their views and where possible achieve consensus on the appointment of the Head of School before making a recommendation to the President. Where the Head of College, having consulted with the members of the School, determines that the post of Head of School should be advertised inside and/or outside the University, the School shall be represented on any search, selection or interview panel.

Despite the checks and balances to be found in clause 7, in a longer historical perspective, the clear overthrow of the provision in Statute I for decanal elections brings to mind one achievement notched up by the emperor Tiberius in the first year of his reign (AD 14–15): the abandonment of the system of the election of magistrates by popular vote. 'In the first year of Tiberius' reign', we are told by a historian of Ancient Rome,[8]

> one of the sheet-authors of the republican constitution was slipped, when the election of magistrates by the Popular Assemblies was discontinued, so the Comitia henceforth were merely called upon to ratify, *pro forma*, lists of candidates approved by the emperor and the Senate.

This particular change, introduced in 2005, is all the more remarkable, given the circumstance that when in 1992 the Governing Body had discussed this very issue, they came out strongly in favour of retaining provision for the formal electing of deans.[9] Even so, it can scarcely be claimed that the implementation of this change or the allied alteration in nomenclature from law faculty to law school constituted any sort of shirt of Nessus.

A good question to ask, however, is whether one should be rather more uneasy over the possible introduction, by way of a borrowing from Britain, of formal rankings by government, with all their financial sequelae, especially on staffing levels. Such sponsored league tables, now a feature in third-level administration in the United Kingdom, have not as yet 'muddied the plot' so far as the Republic is concerned. It is right to record that critics in the UK would obviously wish us to be on our guard. In a trenchant criticism, carried in *The Times* of London in July 2012,[10] David Colquhoun, Professor of Pharmacology at University College London, assailed a memorandum produced by another constituent College of the University of London (Queen Mary College) that announced the publications profile to be demanded of professors and lecturers at QMC. Professors were expected to have produced 11 papers in the period 2008 to 2011, of which two were to be 'high-quality'; lecturers, 5 papers in the same period, 'one of which was to be high-quality'. In addition, it would be incumbent that one student under one's charge had successfully completed their PhD during that four-year period. 'Like so much managerialism', Colquhoun warned, 'the rules are an encouragement to dishonesty'. One can only agree.

There are many obvious differences between the small-scale operation that was the Faculty in St Stephen's Green in 1909 and the major business that is the Law School of 2013 or 2014. Some statistics will help to emphasise the extent of the change.[11] In the session 1909–10 a mere five students (all male) registered for the course in Law. For the years when the LLB was the key academic qualification in law that the Law Faculty bestowed, a period going from 1909 to the mid-1950s, in no single year did the number of LLB degrees awarded reach double figures. The first of the new BCL degrees were awarded in 1957–8; by 1970–1 the number of such degrees awarded reached 100, a figure which remained reasonably stable thereafter. Another change worth recording has been an alteration in the gender balance within each year's undergraduate intake. Six of the 43 students enrolled for Law in 1939–40 were female. In 2000–1, of the total enrolment of 338 for the BCL, 223 of that number were female.

Also, very obviously, courses of study have diversified, in none more so than in the case of the LLM. In addition to a general LLM, there are today Masters programmes in Intellectual Property and Information Technology; Criminology and Criminal Justice; and Human Rights, alongside the longer established LLMs in Commercial Law and European Law. The new MCL (Master of Common Law) is a two-year programme aimed at students who have not previously studied Law at undergraduate level.

Courses themselves are denominated modules, and the academic year is divided into semesters: no mention any more of Michaelmas, Hilary and Trinity. There exist staff-student committees, and a mentor system for the benefit of each student. Appeals on examination results are allowable.

Scholarships and prizes remain there to be won. And if the Dunbar Barton Prize founded in the early years is no more – the money soon ran out – a number of other forms of subvention or awards of distinction have been introduced, not least, of course, the scholarships made available by the Irish Research Council for the Humanities and Social Sciences. And the Swift MacNeill Prize, established shortly after MacNeill's death, is still going strong, albeit that it is confined to King's Inns students.

In the law section of the College library, books and periodicals are shelved on open access. Dockets have only to be filled out if the student or staff member wishes to borrow. In a sign of the times (which some may regret and protest about), certain periodicals may only now be accessible on-line, hard copy subscriptions having been abandoned, albeit, surely, with but marginal savings – whatever about freeing up shelf space.

Staff numbers have been massively expanded. And where in 1909 lecturing was monopolised by full professors in Roman Law and Jurisprudence, Constitutional Law and Criminal Law, Property and Contract (all part-time), in today's Law School the student is as likely to be harangued by non-professorial staff (admittedly all full-time or supposed to be). And in the modern School the full professors boast titles or an expertise very different from that insisted on in 1909 – European Law, EU Regulation and Governance, Criminology and Commercial Law. The autumn 2012 and spring 2013 advertisements for a new President of UCD[12] – Dr Hugh Brady having been scheduled to retire at the end of 2013 – impressed upon potential applicants that they should 'understand and value the diversity of academic disciplines within UCD and have the ability to advance and cultivate each unique discipline'. Strengths of a similar kind are rightly expected of those who aspire to guide the fortunes of any self-respecting Law School. It is trite to stress it, but it is plain that within such a school research and teaching embrace a vast empire and each constituent element merits close attention and support. This is what is occurring.

The last of the changes to be noted in this Epilogue is of major proportions – a case no less of a planned physical upheaval. Over the summer and autumn of 2013 the Law School was scheduled to move into a new purpose-built Law School Building – the UCD Sutherland School of Law. The vision and much of the funding for it was furnished by the family trust of Peter Sutherland, a former Irish attorney-general and EU Commissioner (Sutherland had previously funded the Sutherland Professorship of European Law currently held since 2006, by Imelda Maher, the first woman full professor in the history of the Law School). The Sutherland Trust benefaction was generously supported by a number of major Dublin solicitors' firms, and the realisation of the enterprise owed a great deal to the efforts of one of the School's longest serving deans, Professor Paul O'Connor, who finally yielded up the reins of office after a 15-year stint in 2007. (He was to be succeeded by Joseph McMahon (2007–8) and John Jackson (2008–11) before the present incumbent, Colin Scott, came into office in 2011.)

The UCD Sutherland School of Law is situated at the heart of the UCD campus, and will accommodate staff, administration and all law teaching within the one building. The Law collection, however, remains in the College Library. Otherwise this state of the art facility was certain to be very broadly welcomed, once it was up and running. One consequence of this upheaval merits a short note. The Law School was to be obliged to surrender its purpose-built Legal Education Centre, which now houses the College's Confucius Institute.

One constant in the midst of all these changes, both actual and forthcoming, must be counted the presence of the law student – working hard (hopefully) and relaxing too. His or her well-being is catered for in a number of different fashions. On the one hand, we have the record of learned extra-curricular talks being given by Professor James Murnaghan in the early years of the Legal and Economic Society.[13] The serious side to things was emphasised again at a meeting of the newfangled Law Society in December 1970, when Austin Currie addressed his student audience on 'the spirit of Nationality' in the North – an episode recalled in a recent essay on the creation of the SDLP in Northern Ireland.[14] And, of course, there have been debates and debating competitions – lots of them.

Contrast with this the rather different sort of occasion when the honorary vice-presidency of the students' Law Society is conferred on some celebrity, from the world of sport or of entertainment. Contrast, too, the detailed programme of events laid on for the law student on a typical contemporary Law Day (when all lectures and tutorials are cancelled) and sporting challenges are addressed to law staff and charity collection boxes are rattled. Contrast, again, the attractions with which some executive committee of students might seek to beguile their compatriots into attending a Law Ball:[15]

four course meal	law ball king and queen
champagne reception	magician
wine on the table	professional photographer
return transport	fire performers
DJ	caricature artist
late bar	old school sweet shop
goodie bags	professional make-up artist

Plainly, in some persons' eyes, there was more to the world than the Man on the Clapham Omnibus or, indeed, *Fearne on Contingent Reminders*.[16]

APPENDIX I

Deans of the Faculty of Law, 1909–2000

1909–10	Charles F. Doyle
1911–24	James A. Murnaghan
1928–32	Arthur E. Clery
1933–6	Daniel A. Binchy
1938–52	Michael J. Ryan
1952–9	Patrick McGilligan
1962–7	William D. Finlay
1967–70	John M. Kelly
1970–5	Geoffrey J. Hand
1975–8	W. Nial Osborough
1978–81	James C. Brady
1981–6	James P. Casey
1986–9	James C. Brady
1989–92	James P. Casey
1992–2007	Paul A. O'Connor

NOTE

The information above is taken from data furnished in the respective College *Calendars*. The *President's Report for 1981–1982* at p. 17 would appear to explain the many gaps (1924–8; 1937; 1959–62) by saying that 'Acting Deans' were not shown. In evidence to the Commission on Higher Education, Mr Justice Henchy targeted rather some 'breach' of College statutes or straightforward 'illegality' (*II Report*, Vol. I, p. 304).

APPENDIX II

Newman and the Law

The role of the law and its practitioners in the protection of civil rights was emphasised in an early seventeenth-century Irish will. Sir Richard Shee of Kilkenny in his will of 23 December 1603 left a collection of law books to his son Marcus.[1] The precise injunction laid on Shee's executors in regard to young Marcus' education is illuminating. They were charged to keep Marcus

> to the studdye of the Kinges Lawe, at his own personal chardges, yf he be desirous thereof, and not wantonlye given, in hope he maye be the better member of the commonwealthe, and to be better able in this unfortunate countrie to defend himself, his brethren, and friends from wronges.

Whether the young Newman was prompted by considerations of this sort when faced with his choice of career (or over the establishment of a Law Faculty at the Catholic University)[2] it is impossible to say, but it is certainly worthy of note that he did apparently quite seriously at one stage contemplate a career in the law. Newman entered Lincoln's Inn in the autumn of 1819 and kept three terms there. After he took his fellowship at Oriel College, Oxford in 1822, a colleague was to project two possible vocations for him:

> [I]n Holy Orders, taking pupils in College, and having a Curacy within a short distance, then Public Tutor, Vicar of –, Provost, Regius Professor of Divinity, Bishop of – , Archbishop of Canterbury. Or shall we say thus –, student-at-law, Barrister, Lord Chancellor, or at least Lord Chief Justice of the King's Bench.

Newman's regard for the law, even though he was never to become a lawyer (nor, for that matter, archbishop of Canterbury), is evident from his correspondence. During his trial for criminal libel in the 1850s (of which more anon), Newman remarked to one of his lawyers who had urged Cardinal Wiseman to provide further help to Newman: '[W]hat a wonderful gift it is to be a Lawyer'. That was in November 1851. The following April when his trial was impending, Newman we know from another letter refused to 'make any appeal to the Public against the Law'. 'If the Law brings me into trouble', he wrote, as indeed, assuredly it was to do, 'the Law must bring me out'. A Socratic touch, if there ever was one.

In the 1851 publication that was to cause Newman so much trouble, anguish and even alarm, his *Lectures on the Present Position of Catholics in England,* aside altogether from the question of the style constituting that 'cloistral silver-veined prose' that Joyce attributes to Newman,[3] there is ample evidence from the content of the *Lectures* that its author knew a great deal about the law in the England of Queen Victoria. In the first lecture Newman writes of the British constitution that it was 'rightfully the object of our wonder and veneration'. There were flaws in it even so: acceptance of the doctrine that the King can do no wrong and the principle of the omnipotence of parliament. Turning to his particular preoccupation – the position and treatment of Catholics – Newman then asserts that

> no conceivable absurdities can surpass the absurdities which are firmly believed of Catholics by sensible, kind-hearted, well-intentioned Protestants.

But if, Newman argues, we are making any kind of intelligent inventory of absurdities, we must not exclude those linked to the law and constitution. There were

> the sophisms *De minimis non curat lex* … Possession is nine points of the law … The greater the truth the greater the libel – principles which sap the very foundation of morals.

In addition, there were the 'blighting superstitions of primogeniture, gavelkind, mortmain and contingent remainders'. Could one do other than to 'detest, abhor and abjure the tortuous maxims and perfidious provisions of [the law's] *habeas corpus, quare expedit* and *qui tam*'? And 'scorn the mummeries of its wigs, and bands, and coifs …'? And 'trample and spit upon its accursed fee simple and fee tail, villanage [*sic*], and free soccage [*sic*], and fiefs, heriots, seizins [*sic*], feuds'?

In Newman's third lecture, the author unwittingly gave a hostage to fortune when he averred that 'It is a principle of English law, that no one should bring a charge against another without being under the obligation of supporting it'. The principle thus evoked enabled Newman to repudiate a tale visiting churchmen had brought back from Belgium that at the entrance to the cathedral of St Gudule there was displayed a board listing sins and the prices at which such sins could be remitted. On a charitable view, it was the difficulty in comprehending a foreign language that had misled the visiting churchmen. The board in fact merely listed charges for seats in the cathedral (like charges for sun beds on some beach in Lanzarote we might say today):

> A chair without cushion one cent (about a farthing);
> a chair with cushion 2 cents,

> On great festival days, a chair without cushion 2 cents;
> a chair with cushion 4 cents.

Newman then adds a public declaration on the entire matter issued from Brussels on 2 April 1851 under the names of the dean of Brussels, four clergymen, churchwardens and members of the local judiciary. They were to declare upon their honour

> that such a notice as the one spoken of by the said clergymen has never disgraced the entrance, either of the church of St Gudule, or of any church of Brussels or of the whole country. They further declare that they have never even suspected for one instant that permission to sin could, for any possible motive, be granted, nor that any one could ever obtain remission of his sins for money. Such a doctrine they repudiate with indignation, as it is, and always has been repudiated by the whole of the Catholic Church.

All this represented a hostage to fortune, for, as we are about to discover, Newman was not to be in a position to substantiate all the charges he was to level against Achilli and which had resulted in his trial for criminal libel.

For all his regard and respect for the law (despite the well-informed if slightly mischievous attacks he could also level at it), Newman very likely held to a different point of view before, during and after his prosecution for criminal libel. The case which, as we shall see, Newman was led wrongly to believe would never get off the ground provided a sore trial for him from the summer of 1851, when it became certain it would in fact take place, until early in 1853 when the final instalment was reached and sentence handed down. That it constituted a distraction while Newman wrestled with problems at the Birmingham Oratory, accepted appointment as rector of the Catholic University in Dublin, and planned and delivered his lectures on university education can scarcely admit of any doubt. The trial and all that pertained to it Newman was to find totally unreal. 'If the devil', he confided,[4]

> raised a physical whirlwind, rolled me up in sand, whirled me round, and then transported me some thousands of miles, it would not be more strange, though it would be more imposing a visitation.

Newman's prosecution stemmed from language he had employed in respect of the Catholic convert Giovanni Giacinto Achilli in the fifth of his *Lectures on the Present Position of Catholics in England,* published in London in 1851. Following his conversion, Achilli, a former Dominican priest had, in the 1840s, been embraced within the Protestant fold in England, gaining the support of the

Evangelical Alliance and its formidable standard-bearer, Sir Culeen Eardley Eardley. Welcomed on to the lecturing circuit, Achilli won over audiences in places such as Birmingham, Leamington, Brighton, Bath, Cambridge, Huntingdon and Winchester. His diatribes against the Church of Rome were also heard in Ireland, in Belfast where he had been 'fed with muffins', but also in Dublin where he had delivered his thoughts on chapter 12 of the Acts of the Apostles – the chapter telling of the persecution of the church by King Herod – at a meeting held in the Rotunda under the benign auspices of Sir William Betham.

Among Catholics, particularly in England, Achilli was viewed with both distaste and suspicion. Inquests launched primarily in Italy confirmed the rumours regarding his background and character. What would now be termed 'a hatchet job' on Achilli found its way into print in June 1850. This was in an article, ostensibly a review of two books treating of Achilli[5], that appeared in the pages of the *Dublin Review*, the periodical founded by the triumvirate of Daniel O'Connell, Michael Joseph Quinn and Nicholas Patrick Wiseman.[6] The *Review* was designed to address issues of concern to Catholics and to respond to non-Catholic critics. This article, so critical of Achilli – quoting chapter and verse for his career pre-eminently of serial seducer – was unsigned, but it was soon known that the author was none other than one of the founders of the *Review*, Nicholas Wiseman.[7] A few months after publication, the Roman Catholic hierarchy was to be re-established in England and Wiseman himself returned to London as Cardinal Archbishop of Westminster. Wiseman sought to justify his approach to the task in hand by recalling that St Jerome had 'felt himself compelled to unmask the licentiousness of a Vigilantius or a Helvidius'.[8] 'We must examine', he had earlier explained, 'Achilli's pretensions as to the character, we will not say of a martyr, but of a decent member of civilised or moral society'.[9] The need to tackle Achilli, Wiseman had asserted, derived largely from the falsehoods he had been so adept at peddling. The man's lecturing technique had to be exposed. 'You would find him', Wiseman wrote,[10]

> telling the people, as they listen to him with gaping mouths and rolling eyes, that those Christians, whom he has left, worship secretly an ass's head, and indulge in Thyestian banquets, murdering every day a suckling babe to feast on him, and that they riot in other abominations too gross for a modest convert to paganism to detail.

Nearly twenty pages in the *Dublin Review* article then follow in which Achilli's career is rehearsed and, in effect, his entitlement to be deemed, as the *Oxford DNB* expresses it, not only, 'an anti-Catholic polemicist' but also 'a seducer' – and a serial seducer at that.[11] The essence of this was to be repeated by Newman, and again brought into broad daylight during the hearing of the criminal libel prosecution.

Achilli's sexual exploits, it was to be maintained, had extended from the year 1831 when he was reputed to have seduced an 18-year-old girl, Elena Valente, in the diocese of Viterbo in Italy, down to the years 1847–51 (one year after the *Dublin Review* article had appeared), when it was claimed he had attempted to seduce five women in London – Harriet Harris, Jane Legg, Sarah Wood, Catherine Gorman and a Mademoiselle Fortay. Also charged against Achilli, was his dismissal from office in 1848 as a professor of theology at the Protestant St Julian's College in Malta for hindering an inquiry at the college into allegations of fornication against Fortunato Saccares and Pietro Leonini. Arguably, an even more damning piece of evidence was the condemnation in 1841 by the Holy Office or the Inquisition in Rome, as a consequence of which Achilli, a Dominican priest, had been suspended from saying Mass, and banned from preaching, hearing confession and generally exercising his sacerdotal office.

The author of the 'review' in the *Dublin Review*, having covered all this ground (which Newman was to do as well, but in far less detail), then addressed his audience which he trusted was composed of a majority of level-headed, right-thinking individuals – almost certainly an approach which Newman in the *Lectures* sought to emulate:[12]

> We trust, therefore, that this contradiction of the calumnies spread over the whole empire by this man, will have due weight. We have so much confidence in the uprightness and sense of justice of our fellow-countrymen, so much reliance too on the matronly dignity and modesty of our countrywomen, that we cannot for a moment fear that they will continue to countenance a man so little worthy to treat the same boards with either, still less to allow him to be exalted any longer on platforms, to bear witness against us, instead of hiding his head in penance in some obscure retreat.

There was just a chance, our author conceded, that this would not occur – a prophetic utterance, in view of what we now know the special jury was to decide in Newman's criminal libel case. Against such a scenario, a little mischievously perhaps, Wiseman offered a suggestion that might bring consolation to a few. If Achilli, he wrote,[13] is still accepted as hero,

> we shall propose to have it written over the hall door of the evangelical alliance, wherever that might be: 'Aude aliquid brevibus Gyaris aut carcere dignum, si vis aliquid'.

The Latin is from Juvenal's first satire,[14] and reads: 'If you want to be anybody nowadays, you must dare some crime that merits narrow Gyara or a gaol'. Gyara was a small island in the Aegean Sea on which criminals were confined. For some unfathomable reason, the next four words in Juvenal Wiseman omitted which is a shame. These were:

probitas laudatur et alget,

which may be rendered:

honesty is praised and is left to shiver.

A change in the law at the time persuaded Newman that he had nothing to fear from repeating the thrust of Wiseman's attack in his own *Lectures on the Position of Catholics*. Legislative reform, ironically by Lord Campbell, who as lord chief justice would preside at Newman's trial, made truth a complete defence in a libel action, if the revelation of it could be said to be in the public interest.[15] Wiseman had gathered documentary proof of Achilli's assorted delinquencies, and Newman harboured no doubts that he would himself be able to avail of this information, should the worst come to the worst, and a libel action be instituted. Such documents could be adduced in evidence to demonstrate the proof of the allegations, and given the current state of the debate within the churches in England, it could scarcely be accepted that such revelations would not be regarded as being within the public interest. By late 1851, however, the decision of the Evangelical Alliance to support Achilli having been taken, and a second decision to pursue Newman rather than the anonymous author of the piece in the *Dublin Review*, having been reached, an affidavit sworn by Achilli and accepted in the Queen's Bench enabled an indictment to be drawn up, which served as a precursor for the trial itself. This was in November. The previous month Newman who now knew he was to be proceeded against arranged for two brothers from the Birmingham Oratory to travel to Italy to gather the proofs he would need to substantiate the allegations against Achilli. Wiseman, before he composed his *Dublin Review* article, had had access to just this key material, but over a year later this was no longer to hand, having been inadvertently destroyed. The mission undertaken by the Oratory brothers was designed to remedy the deficiency. Unfortunately, in another blow that Newman was to suffer, the letters of introduction the brothers carried with them were not expressed in sufficiently forceful or authoritative terms to secure the critical data from the archives where such data reposed.[16]

The trial of Newman on the charge of criminal libel opened before the lord chief justice of the Queen's Bench, Lord Campbell, and a special jury on 21 June 1852. The trial lasted four days.[17] The two law officers, Frederick Thesiger, the attorney-general, and Fitzroy Kelly, the solicitor-general, together with the barrister T.F. Ellis, represented the crown. Newman's legal team comprised Sir Alexander Cockburn (who was to ascend to the Bench in 1856), Serjeant

Wilkins, and three barristers – Addison, Badeley and Bramwell. Through his counsel, Newman contended that the allegations against Achilli contained in the controversial lecture 5 of his *Lectures on the Position of Catholics* were true in substance and in fact. They also amounted to fair and reasonable comment. Publication additionally was for the public benefit; in terms of the controversy between the Church of England and the Roman Catholic Church which had spawned discussion in which Achilli was prominent, it was necessary to demonstrate, as Newman contended, that Achilli was not deserving of credit.[18]

The court made two rulings on evidence in a manner adverse to Newman's defence. Documentary proof of the proceedings against Achilli by the Inquisition in 1841 was admitted, not as evidence of the acts of seduction to which the final sentence alluded, but solely as evidence of such proceedings having taken place. For Newman, Cockburn also sought to put in evidence a copy of the *Dublin Review* for 1850 (which contained the same details on Achilli's sexual exploits as Newman had reproduced) 'with a view of showing that these charges against Achilli could not have been got up for the purpose of making out the justification of Newman in the case'. Lord Campbell, however, refused to admit the evidence.

Defence witnesses called by Newman included a number of the women who were alleged to have engaged in sexual relations with Achilli. Certain of Campbell's comments on the evidence thus given were decidedly against Newman.[19] Achilli himself gave evidence for the prosecution. Here he insisted that the judgment against him in the court of the Inquisition had been for heresy. Equally, that no charge of immorality had been brought against him and that, contrary to an assertion contained in a document that had been obtained from Rome, he had never made any confession in the court.

The Queen's Bench special jury very largely accepted the crown's case and Achilli's point of view for, with the exception of two not insignificant findings, they adjudged Newman guilty, the generality of his claims against Achilli not being established to their satisfaction.[20] In their ruling, they made it plain that they accepted Achilli had been suspended from the priestly office and also that he had been dismissed from his post in Malta. But the overall result of course was adverse to Newman.

Newman and his legal team did not as yet admit defeat. On 22 November 1852 application was made to the full Queen's Bench court – Mr Justice Coleridge, Mr Justice Wightman and Mr Justice Erle in addition to Lord Campbell himself – to grant a new trial.[21] Three grounds were advanced: the wrongful exclusion of corroborative evidence (the treatment accorded the document emanating from the Inquisition in Rome) and the ruling that the *Dublin Review* article from March/June 1850 was inadmissible; misdirection by the court; and the verdict of the jury being against the weight of the evidence. The crown's law officers, who had presented arguments on Achilli's behalf, argued that Newman's lawyers had moved the application for a new trial too late. Contemporary procedural rules apparently required such an application to be presented within the first four days of the next ensuing law term, but this had not been done. For the first and only time Newman scored a minor victory: Lord Campbell, while admitting that the rules had been breached, was not prepared to shut Newman out. The court, however, went on to refuse to grant an order for a new trial on the first two grounds advanced. At the conclusion of the hearing on 22 November 1852, they thus granted a rule nisi for a rule to show cause only on the ground that the jury's verdict on 21 June was against the weight of the evidence.

It was this single matter that preoccupied that same court when it proceeded to hear the rule nisi on 20, 21 and 23 January 1853. (In the interim Newman had been holidaying in Scotland at Abbotsford, the house Walter Scott had built in the Borders (where a friend had married Scott's granddaughter)).[22] On 26 January the court pronounced itself satisfied with the jury's verdict and refused to grant a new trial.[23] The matter of Newman's sentence which had, in effect, been adjourned, was thus finally disposed of. It was now announced by one of the puisnes, Mr Justice Coleridge, on 31 January. Newman was sentenced to a £100 fine with the prospect of a spell in prison until such fine was paid. In advance of the promulgation of this sentence, evidence, over the objections of the crown's lawyers, had been adduced, in accordance with the section in Lord Campbell's Act,[24] that allowed, where the defence of truth was unsuccessful, the sentencing authority 'to consider whether the guilt of the defendant is aggravated or mitigated by the said plea, and by the evidence given to prove or disprove the same'. This, in effect, permitted Newman's lawyers to repeat much of the evidence that in the trial proper had placed such a critical interpretation on Achilli's character.[25] In passing sentence, Mr Justice Coleridge is recorded to have said the following in addressing the future cardinal, already appointed the rector of the Catholic University in Dublin.[26]

> The great controversy between the Churches will go on, we know not, through God's pleasure, how long. Whether, henceforward, you will take part in it or not, it will be for you to determine; but I think the pages before me should give you this warning, upon calm consideration, that if you again engage in this controversy, you should engage in it neither personally nor bitterly … If you, for the future, sustain, as you may think you are bound to do, by your publications, the Church of Rome, I intreat you to do it in a spirit of charity and of humility – in a spirit worthy of your great abilities, of your ardent piety, of your holy life, and of our common Christianity.

In view of the circumstance that the special jury's conclusions indicated that part of what Newman had alleged was true, the issue of costs proved a final tricky conundrum. The judges of the Queen's Bench court prudently left this conundrum to the court's own taxing authority to resolve.[27]

A collection to enable Newman to fight his case had been raised from subscribers in England, France, Ireland, Germany and from North and South America. Not all of the £12,000 raised was needed, and the surplus was later utilised to part-defray the costs incurred by Newman as rector of the Catholic University in connection with the new University Church on St Stephen's Green in Dublin.[28]

The fine imposed on Newman was of course ludicrously low even if, as Minow points out, it seemed to be in line with other contemporary fines for criminal libels by newspapers.[29] Writing shortly after the event to Archbishop Cullen, Newman was overjoyed. 'Thus have the judges', he declared, 'virtually revised and reversed the verdict of the jury, and I am grateful to all four for this act of justice'.[30]

Commentators on what had transpired were far from sharing anything approaching Newman's generosity of interpretation. Finlason, who has left us the most comprehensive available account of the trial itself, was far less sanguine. The verdict of the special jury, he declared, had been 'in defiance of evidence, justice, common sense and law, and ... revolted most reputable persons in court'.[31] Contemporary critics were no less severe in pronouncing their views on Lord Campbell, the judge at the trial. When, in the course of that trial, Campbell admitted as evidence, albeit, as we have seen, on a limited basis, the decree of the Inquisition in Rome in the case involving Achilli, Campbell was reported to have made the quite gratuitous additional remark, 'Thank God, we have not in this country a tribunal of Inquisition'. The *Morning Chronicle* took umbrage at the aside: 'Of course, the expected cheers of an ultra-Protestant audience greeted this irrelevant appeal to their prejudices'.[32] Finlason leaves us in no doubt that he believed Campbell had pandered to the anti-Catholic prejudices of the special jury.[33] In his meticulous commentary on Campbell's charge to the jury, Finlason finds fault with nearly every analysis of the evidence of each of Newman's defence witnesses – primarily the women who had been the objects of Achilli's attentions.[34] Seeming to adopt Thesiger, the attorney-general's thesis that Achilli had been the victim of perjury and forgery, besides stretching the uncommitted observer's credulity to breaking-point, once more reflected badly on Campbell. At the outset of his charge, Campbell proffered a view of the entire case which, alongside certain of the procedural or evidential rulings which did not advance Newman's cause, might be thought by some to display bias. 'Newman', he is reported to have declared,[35]

> in attacking Dr Achilli, as he has done, has acted rashly and recklessly, even though he might well believe in the truth of what he said.

Remarkably, a little later, he was to reply to one of the criticisms Newman in his *Lectures on the Present Position of Catholics* had levelled at the common law. The change in the law of libel, so recently introduced, that enabled truth to be pleaded as a defence, 'takes away the reproach embedded in the saying "The greater the truth, the greater the libel"'.[36] A modern writer is as blunt as could be imagined. Campbell, Gilley writes, was 'a militant Protestant' who 'was hostile to Newman from the first'.[37]

As against all of this, it bears recalling, as Finlason to his credit does not omit to do, that in his charge to the jury Campbell clearly expressed the view that certain of the charges preferred against Achilli by Newman were indeed true,[38] and that, as a prelude to sentence, he sanctioned an interpolation of the new law that enabled fresh evidence to be tendered after Newman's trial so as to mitigate the latter's sentence.[39] Foss' assessment of the man argues for a more rounded view too, even if the generality of the language employed does not altogether inspire confidence in the author's critical armoury. 'During the nine years that [Campbell] filled [the office of chief justice of Queen's Bench]', Foss declares,[40]

> he is acknowledged to have performed its important duties in a most exemplary manner, preserving the dignity of the place, and administering the law with apparent ease and strict impartiality.

It is not easy to choose between these two nineteenth-century legal writers. History – or at least the pages of the *Oxford DNB* – has been kinder to Edward Foss (1787–1870) than to W. F. Finlason (1818–95). Foss' work of reference on the English judges is still regarded as 'the standard authority in its field'.[41] Foss became a solicitor and actually served a two-year term as president of the English Law Society. Finlason became a barrister in 1851, two years after he had converted to Catholicism. In 1869, many years after he had supplied us with his account of Newman's criminal libel trial, he published a revised edition of Reeves' *History of English Law*. In his entry for Finlason in the *Oxford DNB* Michael Lobban writes that it was 'not a job well done'. He continues:[42]

> contradicting many of Reeves' arguments, Finlason sought to argue that all of the important institutions of the common law were derived from the period of the Roman occupation of Britain, but in doing so he revealed both a lack of historical sense and an approach to the sources which had little intellectual vigour.[43]

This matter of possible bias on the bench merits being taken just a little further. Whatever about his being correctly denigrated as 'a militant Protestant', Campbell was, by accident of birth, a son of the manse from Fife. A second Scot, William Wightman, from Dumfriesshire, also sat in the Queen's Bench court that dealt with the sequel to the original trial conducted by Campbell.

Data on John Taylor Coleridge, the puisne who actually announced the sentence on Newman in January 1853 is, if anything, somewhat more revealing.[44] First appointed to the bench in 1858, he and Newman later became acquaintances and correspondents. Even more remarkable was Newman's relationship with Coleridge's son, another judge, and ultimately as Lord Coleridge, lord chief justice, and with the latter's first wife, Jane Fortescue Seymour.[45] Lord Coleridge and Newman were more than acquaintances, the former claiming to be a close friend of the Tractarians. As for Jane Fortescue Seymour: Newman sat for her. Seymour's portrait in pastel of Newman survives in the Park Place Pastoral Centre, Wickham in Hampshire.

The case itself still leaves a sour taste. Achilli vanished into obscurity – little is known of his later life.[46] Newman went on to achieve higher things. *R. (at the prosecution of Achilli)* v. *Newman* survives as a squalid business, best relegated to obliquity, if such could be arranged. Unfortunately, this truly cannot be done. The verdict of *The Times* summed matters up very well. Making no bones about it,[47] the Thunderer lambasted

> proceedings so indecorous in their nature, so unsatisfactory in their result, so little calculated to increase the respect of people for the administration of justice, in the estimation by foreign nations of the English name and character.

The barbs continued:[48]

> A great blow has been given to the administration of justice in this country, and … Roman Catholics will have henceforth only too good reason for asserting that there is no justice for them in cases tending to arouse the Protestant feelings of judges and juries.

Minow's focusing on the significance for Newman of this extraordinary episode in his career merits repetition as well. 'The case', he writes,[49]

> also provides further insight into Newman's life. As Newman scholarship continues on its present and generally more objective course, it must take into account the importance of the vocation not chosen in Newman's life, the law. Even before this trial, Newman's thought appears to have been significantly influenced by his interest in English common law. This trial made him even more aware of the power and importance of law in society.

This being so, the fact that the law faculty planned by Newman for his Catholic University on the latter's opening in Dublin in 1854 never got off the ground has to be accounted a grave disappointment.

APPENDIX III

Chief Baron Palles' Judgment in the *Mabel Walker* Case

Printed below is the previously unpublished but incomplete and undelivered judgment of Chief Baron Palles for the Irish Court of Appeal in the case of *Walker* v. *Great Northern Railway Co.*[1] Mabel Walker, a child, suffered pre-natal injuries on the occasion of the Armagh rail disaster of June 1889. Through her mother she sued, alleging negligence, but in the Queen's Bench Division the defendant railway company successfully raised the demurrer that the action was not maintainable. Mabel died after the hearing in the Court of Appeal but before judgment was pronounced. It is clear from this draft but incomplete judgment of the Chief Baron that he, for one, was not about to disagree with the Queen's Bench Division, overrule the allowance of the demurrer, and thus permit an action for pre-natal injuries to succeed. Palles' incomplete draft survives in the second of two folio volumes of his judgments held by Special Collections in the UCD Library.[2] It is probable that these arrived in the College when the Roman Catholic archbishop of Dublin and Chancellor of the new National University of Ireland, Dr William Walsh, purchased Palles' library and presented it to UCD. It is apposite that Palles' judgment, incomplete as it is, as he, or an amanuensis explains, is extant,[3] for contemporary speculation proceeded along the lines that the demurrer might have been disallowed in the Court of Appeal, enabling *Walker's* case to join *Bell's* case (*Bell* v. *Great Northern Railway Co.*), arising out of the same railway accident, where liability for nervous shock had been conceded,[4] as a second revolutionary tort decision of the 1890s. A contemporary commentator had this to say at the conclusion of the hearing of the appeal in *Walker's* case in the Court of Appeal. 'Nor was it at all certain, at the conclusion of the arguments', we are told,[5]

> that the Court of Appeal had determined unanimously to uphold the decision arrived at by the Court below [allowing the demurrer]. The arguments were learned and interesting, the interlocutory *dicta* suggestive, and were important by reason of the fatality that has precluded the delivery of the long-deferred judgments.

This transcript of Chief Baron Palles' judgment has been kindly supplied by Dr Andrew Lyall.

UCD, Special Collections, MS 14
Palles CB, Judgments and Charges
-54-
COURT OF APPEAL

WALKER v. GREAT NORTHERN RAILWAY COMPANY <1>[6]

Judgment of the Lord Chief Baron [Palles].
(Undelivered and incomplete: see note at end)

The question upon this appeal is, whether a child who was born crippled, in consequence of injuries sustained before its birth by the negligent management of a train upon a railway, can maintain an action to recover damages for its injuries. It is admitted that there is no trace of such an action having been heretofore sustained, or even instituted; but it is said that there are principles of our law the inevitable result of which is that the action is maintainable. Having carefully considered all the cases which have been referred to, and some which were not mentioned, I have arrived at the clear conclusion that this proposition cannot be maintained, and that, consistently with the settled and established doctrines of our law, the action is not sustainable.

From the mode in which the argument was presented to us, it will be convenient that I should, in the first place, eliminate from the case such of the authorities cited as, in my opinion, have no true bearing upon the question in controversy; and thus reduce the subject-matter for consideration to that really bearing upon the question.

It is said that there are dicta of three judges, viz. Lord Hardwicke, Chief Justice Eyre, and Mr Justice Buller, that a child *en ventre sa mère*[7] is as much a person as if born.

<2>

In *Wallis* v. *Hodson*[8] the question arose as to the share which Towers Walker took in his father's personal estate, that father having died intestate. Towers Walker, who also died intestate, left him surviving his mother, who was then *enceinte* with the plaintiff, who was born after the death of Towers. The mother claimed the entire. The posthumous sister claimed a moiety, under 1st James 2nd, chapter 17, s.7.[9]

'Lord Hardwicke said,

> "To be sure if the plaintiff, the sister, had been born before the death of the brother, out of controversy she would have been thus entitled. But the doubt is, whether she is so entitled, as she was a posthumous child; and I am of opinion it will make no material difference. It has been admitted that the debt of nature which the father owes to provide for his children will extend to posthumous ones; for as it is an event which must happen

within nine months, no inconvenience can arise from it. But then it is objected that there is no such debt of nature as to collaterals, viz. brothers and sisters … With regard to the difference that has been taken between the collateral and lineal succession, to be sure the principal and primary object of this statute of James the 2nd was to preserve the estate of the father to his own children in a reasonable degree, and not to let the mother run away with too much to her children by a second husband. Though it is in general settled that the shares vest immediately upon the death of the intestate, and holds equally in lineal and collateral succession, yet notwithstanding it has been determined that there is an exception to this rule in the case of a posthumous child; for in *Edwards* v. *Freeman*[10] it is said a distributive share does not in all events vest in the issue on the intestate's death, because if there be a posthumous child, such child shall be let in for its share, though not in *esse* at the intestate's death <3>.

The principal reason I go upon in the question is that the plaintiff was *en ventre sa mère* at the time of her brother's death, and consequently a person in *rerum natura*,[11] so that both by the rules of the common and civil law she was, to all intents and purposes, a child, as much as born in her father's lifetime. First as to the common law, there is the trite case of an infant *en ventre sa mère* being vouched in a common recovery; the mother may also justify the detaining of charters on behalf of it; a devise to him is good, by the opinion of Treby and Powell in *Scattergood* and *Edge*;[12] a bill may be brought in his behalf; and this court will grant an injunction in his favour to stay waste.[13] I now take it to be fully settled that this Act (Statute of Distributions, Charles the 2nd) is to be construed by the rules of civil law; and the statute of 1st James the 2nd I think ought to be construed in the same manner, which is an Act of continuance of the statute of Charles the 2nd, with three additional clauses, and is to be construed as if the statute of Charles the 2nd had been re-enacted and repeated with these clauses. Secondly, as to the civil law, nothing is more clear than that this law considered a child in the mother's womb absolutely born to all intents and purposes, for the child's benefit … It may possibly be said that these rules are only laid down with regard to lineals, but you will find it they are equally with regard to collaterals… The last passage in the Digest is more explicit than any other, but then it makes a difference between a child *en ventre sa mère in esse* at the father's death, and only conceived. The latter is not considered as having any relation to the intestate, being (according to the term made use of there) not animax."'

In *Doe* v. *Clarke*[14] there was a devise to the testator's brother Henry for life, and after his decease to <4> all and every such child or children of him as should be living at the time of his decease, other than and except one Bridget, in fee, as tenants in common, and not as joint tenants; and the decision was that a posthumous child should share equally with those who were born in his lifetime. Eyre, C.J., says,

> 'It is plain on the words of the will that the testator meant that all the children whom his brother should leave behind him should be benefitted; but independent of this intention I hold that an infant *en ventre sa mère*, who by the course and order of nature is then living, comes fairly within the description of "children living at the time of his decease".'

Buller, J., says,

> In equity there are two classes of cases on this subject: the first, where the bequest is in the nature of a portion or provision for children, and there an after born child takes his share with the rest; ... the second, where the bequest arises from some motives of personal affection, and there it is confined to children actually in existence. It seems indeed now settled that an infant *en ventre sa mère* shall be considered, generally speaking, as born for all purposes for his own benefit,[15] *Lancashire* v *Lancashire* [5 Term. Rep. B. R. 49];[16] and in a sensible treatise, lately published (Watkins, *Law of Descents*, page 142), after a discussion of the interest of posthumous issue, the whole is well summed upon by saying 'It is now laid down as a fixed principle that, wherever such consideration would be for his benefit, a child *en ventre mère* shall be considered as absolutely borne'.

Heath and Rooke, JJ., were of the same opinion; and Chief Justice Eyre added, 'The two classes of cases in equity proceed on a distinction which has always appeared to me extremely unsatisfactory, and unfit to be the ground of any decision whatever'.

The decision in *Lancashire* v *Lancashire*,[17] re-<5>ferred to by Buller, J., was that marriage and birth of a posthumous child amounted to an implied revocation of a will of lands made before marriage. All the court there treated it as fully established that marriage and the birth of a child were such circumstances as amounted to a revocation of a will of lands. Buller, J., said,[18]

> Then the only question which remains to be discussed is whether a child *en ventre sa mère* be or be not in the same situation as a child actually born ... Then the great question is, whether a posthumous child is considered in the same situation as one born during the parent's life? On this head

many cases have been cited to shew that there is no distinction. Without going through them again, I will only add one to them, in 1 Ves. 85,[19] where on a bond given on marriage to raise £2,000 for such child or children of the marriage *as should be living* at the death of the father or mother, a posthumous child was held entitled to take as coming within the description. And indeed all the cases cited, as well as that of *White* v. *Barber*,[20] establish this point, that there is no distinction between a child *en ventre sa mère* and one actually born.

Grose, J., says[21]

It is now too late to doubt whether in the case of marriage and the birth of a child during the father's life, the law presumes a will of lands made before that marriage to be revoked... The only question here is whether in point of law, justice, and good sense, there be any difference between that case and the present. I know of no argument founded on law and natural justice in favour of the child who is born during his father's life, that does not equally extend to a posthumous child. And I think that, when once the law has interfered and presumed in favour of one child, it would stop far short of justice if it did not 'raise the same presumption in favour of the other'. The presumption in favour of the child who is actually born is <6> that at the time of the father's death he could not intend that the will should take effect, or rather that at the time he made the will, he did not intend that it should stand in the event of his afterwards marrying and having children. Then the law which makes that presumption in favour of a child born in the parent's life, must make the same presumption in favour of one born afterwards. The objection which has been made against this is that the will speaks from the devisor's death, and that it must be decided whether or not at that moment it be a valid will. I agree that it does speak from that time; but the instant the child is born, he is considered, by retrospect, as born during the parent's life. For this opinion I refer to the civil law, as was done in *Christopher* v. *Christopher*,[22] and the other cases which were founded on that law. Vinnius says "*Si modo postea nascatur, tunc enim fictione juris nativitas retrotrahitur*". And in another learned writer on this subject, Domat, I find this passage, 'The children who are not as yet born when their fathers die, whom we call posthumous children ... are reckoned in the number of children who succeed. And although they are not as yet born when the successions which they are to inherit fall to them by the death of their father, mother, or others their relations, yet they belong to them upon condition that they shall be born alive, and they are considered as heirs already before their birth'.

In *Thellusson* v. *Woodford*[23] the question was whether a remainder, limited to take effect upon the expiration of an estate previously granted, during the lives of certain persons, including "such sons as A, B and C, may have, and such issue as such sons may have as should be living at the time of testator's decease, or born in due time afterwards", was or was not void for remoteness, as contravening the rule against perpetuities. Buller, J., <7> there says,[24]

> 'The next objection is that supposing he meant a child *en ventre sa mère*, and had expressly said so, yet the limitation is bad; such a child has been considered a nonentity. Let us see what this nonentity can do. He may be vouched in a recovery, though it is for the purpose of making him answer over in value; he may be an executor; he may take under the statute of distributions; he may take by devise; he may be entitled under a charge for raising portions; he may have an injunction, and he may have a guardian. Some other cases put this beyond all doubt'.

And after citing Lord Hardwicke's judgment in *Wallis* v. *Hodson*,[25] he proceeds, 'In the same case Lord Hardwicke takes notice that the civil law confines the rule to cases where it is for the benefit of the child to be considered as born; but, notwithstanding, he states the rule to be that such child is to be considered living to all intents and purposes;' and after referring to a settlement of the Duke of Norfolk's drawn by Mr Booth, in which the property was settled 'with remainder to the use of the first child, if a male, where of Juliana —— is *enceinte* …' with remainders over, he proceeds,

> *Lancashire* v. *Lancashire*[26] and *Doe* v. *Clarke*[27] go upon the same principle. In both a child *en ventre sa mère* was held to be a child living at the death of the testator… In *Doe* v. *Clarke* the words 'that wherever such consideration would be for his benefit, a child *en ventre sa mère* shall be considered as absolutely born' were used by me because I found them in the book from whence the passage was taken; but there is no reason for so confining the rule. Why should not children *en ventre sa mère* be considered generally as in existence? They are entitled to all the privileges of other persons. In this case it is enough to say such a child is capable of having an estate given to him and consequently to another person, for his life. The <8> infant is not hurt, nor is the law transgressed, by giving the interest to a third person, any more than by giving it to the infant himself.

I need not say that none of the above cases are in point here as authority. They can be relied upon only for the *dicta* of the eminent judges by whom they are decided. I admit the authority of each of those cases as to the point decided in it; but I entertain a strong opinion that none of them was intended to lay down a rule otherwise than in reference to the matters then before the courts that is, as to the succession to property, the limits of the rule against perpetuities, and the intention, in certain cases, to be gathered from wills and statutes.

In 3rd Institute[28] it is said

> 'If a woman, be quick with child, and by a potion or otherwise killeth it in her womb, or if a man beat her whereby the child dieth in her body, and she is delivered of a dead child; this is a great misprision, and no murder. But if the child be born alive, and dieth of the potion, battery, or other cause, this is murder; for in law it is accounted a reasonable creature *in rerum natura* when it is born alive.'

This passage makes a distinction of the gravest materiality between a child *en ventre sa mère* and a child actually born; and this very passage, which is now settled law, is cited with approval and acted upon, both by Harcourt, L.C., in 1713 and Parker, L.C., in 1718.

In the first of these cases – *Beale* v. *Beale*,[29] Harcourt L.C., says,

> 'As to the other objection, it would be very hard in a court of equity that a child, because it happened not to be born at such a time, must therefore be unprovided for. But as the law in many respects regards an infant *en ventre sa mère*, so as to allow such child to be (a) vouched; also as the mother may be guilty of the murder (b) of a child *en ventre sa mère* if she <9> takes poison with intent to poison it, *and the child is born alive and afterwards dies of that poison,* there is more reason that equity should consider such child, in order to its being *provided for*; and therefore this posthumous child may be well looked upon in equity to be living at her father's death *en ventre sa mère*.'

Burdett v. *Hopegood*[30] was the case of a devise to A, in case the testator left no son at the time of his death. At the time of his death the testator's wife was *enceinte* with a son, and the decision was that A was not entitled.

The report says,

> 'Lord Chancellor Parker referred it to the judges of the King's Bench, who were unanimously of opinion that the plaintiff, Sir Robert, though not born, had yet an existence in the eye of the law, as *en ventre sa mère*, which in many respects was regarded as if a woman takes poison to kill her child when in her womb, and the child is born alive, and afterwards dies of that poison, the woman is guilty of murder. Also a child *en ventre sa mère* may be vouched, and may be a devisee and it would be hard to

disinherit such an only child, nor could it be imagined the testator ever intended to do so.

Having regard to the decisions in *Rex* v. *Senior*, *Rex* v. *Enoch*, and the *Queen* v. *West*, it would be mere pedantry to enter into an elaborate argument to show that the passage I have cited from Coke is now settled law, also though, no doubt, it is contrary to the passages from Bracton and Fleta which have been cited during the argument.

In result, then, it appears to me that we must take it that, for some purposes, a child *en ventre sa mère* is to be treated as living; and for certain other purposes it is not treated as living; and the question is whether it is to be treated as living for the purpose of bringing an action for injuries sustained before birth.

<10>
I desire to point out that in none of the cases (except those of indictments for murder or manslaughter), [in] which the child *en ventre sa mère* was treated as a living child, did the case relate to injuries to the body of the child.

The general rule of law is that the body of the child until birth is *pars viscerum matris*;[31] and it appears to me that it is one thing to say that the living soul of the child, existent in that which in law is deemed part of the body of the mother, is recognised by law as having, for certain purposes, a separate individuality, which relates back to the earliest period at which the law recognises that soul as being in existence; and that it is a wholly different thing to say that the body in which the soul exists is, at one and the same moment of time to be deemed for one purpose, the body of the mother, and for another separate and distinct purpose the body of the child; and unless the cases decided upon the criminal law make or involve such a doctrine as to the body of the child, I can find no trace of it in our law.

The main argument for the plaintiff was, that every criminal offence involves a private wrong; that the only person, against whom the private wrong included in injuries before birth which may be the subject of murder or manslaughter can be committed, must be the unborn child; and therefore it is argued that the fact of an indictment lying involves that an action will also lie. In support of this, the following passage from Sir William Blackstone is cited:[32] 'In all cases a crime includes an injury. Every public offence is also a private wrong, and somewhat more. It affects the individual and it likewise affects the community.' I should be unwilling to express an opinion upon this passage, were it not absolutely necessary, for the purposes of this case, to do so; but as it does become necessary, I feel bound to say that, in my opinion, in this passage Sir William Blackstone is not as <11> accurate as he usually is. No doubt the vast majority of offences involve private injuries; but, in my opinion, every offence does not necessarily do so. In my view the law is more accurately stated in the judgment of Barry, L. J. in the

Queen v. *Parnell*. 'All offences, it need hardly be observed, are *either* in their nature offences against the community, or are primarily offences against individuals.' Suicide and bestiality are felonies: what private injury do they involve, unless in the sense that one may commit a wrong against himself? But I need not say that in this sense, 'wrong' does not mean an actionable wrong.

[MS Note: Not finished – having before completing it received notice that p'tf [plaintiff] had died]

Notes

1 LEGAL EDUCATION AND THE UNIVERSITY: THE HISTORICAL CONTEXT

1 Hastings Rashdall, *The Universities of Europe in the Middle Ages*, new ed. by F.M. Powicke and A.B. Emden, 3 vols (Oxford, 1936), i, 97.
2 Ibid., p. 98.
3 Ibid., p. 120.
4 Quoted, J.B. Ames, *Lectures in Legal History and Miscellaneous Legal Essays* (Cambridge, MA and London, 1913), p. 355.
5 [1965] AC 75.
6 33 Hen. VIII, sess 2, c. 3. This, to an extent, replicated previous practice: see Paul Brand, 'Irish law students and lawyers in later medieval England', *IHS*, 32 (2000), 161.
7 T.C. Barnard, 'Lawyers and the law in later seventeenth-century Ireland', *IHS*, 28 (1993), 256 at 259.
8 Colum Kenny, *King's Inns and the Kingdom of Ireland: the Irish 'Inn of Court' 1541–1800* (Dublin, 1992), p. 21.
9 PROI, Ferguson MS 1a. 49. 136, f.52.
10 Kenny, *King's Inns*, p. 21.
11 Ibid.
12 See F.W. Eheling, *Archivalische Beiträge zur Geschichte Frankreichs unter Carl ix* (Leipzig, 1872), p. 129.
13 H.M. Baird, *History of the Rise of the Huguenots*, 2 vols (New York, 1879), ii, 570.
14 Quoted, Baird, *Rise of the Huguenots*, ii, 570.
15 Ibid.
16 And see *Cal. S.P. Ire., 1666–1669*, p. 654.
17 Quoted, H.L. Murphy, *A History of Trinity College Dublin from its Foundation to 1702* (Dublin, 1951), p. 77.
18 R.B. McDowell and D.A. Webb, *Trinity College Dublin 1592–1952: an Academic History* (Cambridge, 1982), p. 193.
19 Ibid.
20 Ibid.
21 Ibid.
22 Ibid., p. 65, and see the modern edition of *An Historical Treatise* by S.P. Donlan under the title *Lectures on the Constitution and Laws of England with a commentary on Magna Carta* (Clark, NJ, 2003).
23 McDowell & Webb, *Trinity College Dublin: an Academic History*, p. 81, and see the appreciation by Paul O'Higgins in *NILQ*, 20 (1969), at 255 as well as J.M.G. Sweeney's account of Browne's work on admiralty law in *Journal of Maritime Law and Commerce*, 26 (1993), 58.
24 The Queen's Colleges (Ireland) Act 1845: 8 & 9 Vict., c.66. The long title deserves to be better known: An Act to enable Her Majesty to endow new Colleges for the Advancement of Learning in Ireland.
25 T.W. Moody and J.C. Beckett, *Queen's Belfast 1845–1949: the History of a University*, 2 vols (London, 1959), i, 77.
26 Colum Kenny, *Tristram Kennedy and the Revival of Irish Legal Training, 1835–1885* (Dublin, 1996).
27 Colum Kenny, 'Adventures in training: the Irish genesis of the "remarkable and far-sighted" select committee on legal education, 1846' in Paul Brand, Kevin Costello and W.N. Osborough (eds), *Adventures of the Law: Proceedings of the Sixteenth British Legal History Conference, Dublin 2003* (Dublin, 2005), p. 289.
28 Newman to Disraeli, 19 July 1858: *Letters and Diaries of J.H. Newman*, ed. C.S. Dessain et al., 31 vols (Oxford and London, 1965–77), xviii, 415.
29 It is possible that the admission may have been intended by Newman to have referred to the Faculty of Theology.
30 *Weekly Reporter*, 30 Jan. 1858, reproduced in *Letters and Diaries of J.H. Newman*, xviii, App. I, p. 567 at p. 568.
31 Murray to Newman 16 May 1854: Birmingham Oratory Archives, Newman Dublin Papers, Folder Number 5, File 5.1.

32 Newman to Ambrose St. John, 16 Jan. 1857: *Letters and Diaries of J.H. Newman*, xvii, 499.
33 *Letters and Diaries of J.H. Newman*, xviii, App. 2, p. 584.
34 *DIB*, viii, 119 (Georgina Clinton and Sinead Sturgeon).
35 Denis Gwynn, 'John E. Pigot and Thomas Davis', *Studies*, 38 (1949), 145.
36 *Letters and Diaries of J.H. Newman*, xvi, 138, 145.
37 *Letters and Diaries of J.H. Newman*, xvi, 360 (a view of Newman's recorded by Dessaint after Pigot's death).
38 Moriarty, quoted, ibid., 456.
39 Ibid., 360.
40 Pigot to Newman, 3 Mar. 1855: *Letters and Diaries of J.H. Newman*, xvi, 403.
41 Newman to Pigot, 5 Mar. 1855: ibid., xvi, 403.
42 Pigot to Newman, 7 Mar. 1858: *Letters and Diaries of J.H. Newman*, xvi, 404.
43 Newman to Moriarty, 29 Apr. 1855: *Letters and Diaries of J.H. Newman*, xvi, 456.
44 *King's Inns Admission Papers, 1607–1867*, ed. Edward Keane, P.B. Phair and T.U. Sadleir (Dublin, 1982), p. 402.
45 *Letters and Diaries of J.H. Newman*, xvi, 623 (biographical note).
46 Colin Barr, *Paul Cullen, John Henry Newman, and the Catholic University, 1845–1865* (Leominster, 2003), pp 135, 139.
47 Ibid., p. 138.
48 *Letters and Diaries of J.H. Newman*, xviii, App. 2, p. 584; Gwynn, 'Pigot and Davis', *Studies*, 38 (1949), at 157.
49 Barr, *Cullen, Newman and the Catholic University*, p. 135.
50 Ibid., p. 251, n.8.
51 Professors and Lecturers of the Catholic University, before 6 Nov. 1858: *Letters and Diaries of J.H. Newman*, xviii, 503.
52 Newman to Professors at the Catholic University, 6 Nov. 1858: ibid., 504.
53 Newman to Hayden, Dean of Faculty of Medicine of the Catholic University, 25 Sept. 1859: *Letters and Diaries of J.H. Newman*, xix, 216.
54 Sheridan Gilley, in *The Cambridge Companion to John Henry Newman*, ed. Ian Ker and Terrence Merrigan (Cambridge, 2009), p. 19.
55 Ibid.
56 Reproduced in *Letters and Diaries of J.H. Newman*, xviii, App. 1, p. 567.
57 Moody & Beckett, *Queen's Belfast*, i, 279.
58 Ibid.
59 Ibid., p. 280.
60 Ibid., p. 281.
61 Ibid.
62 *Hansard 3*, clxxxvii, 1431.
63 See *McCormack* v. *The Queen's University* (1867) 1 Ir Eq Rep 160.
64 Better known, perhaps, as the author of *Ireland Sixty Years Ago*, brought out in 1847.
65 1 Ir Eq Rep at 172.
66 *Hansard, 3*, clxxxvii, 3–4 (6 May 1867), 1431–1456 (31 May 1867); cxcii, 956 (28 May 1868); cxciii, 313 (29 June 1868).
67 Moody & Beckett, *Queen's Belfast*, i, 281.
68 42 & 43 Vict., c.65, s.9.
69 44 & 45 Vict., c.52.
70 32 & 33 Vict., c.42.
71 Robertson Commission, *First Report, Appendix*, p. 360.
72 Moody & Beckett, *Queen's Belfast*, i, 289.
73 In evidence to the Robertson Commission, *First Report, Appendix*, p. 19.
74 M. Mc D. Bodkin, *Recollections of an Irish Judge, Press, Bar and Parliament* (London, 1914), p. 25.
75 *DIB*, vi, 898 (Colin Barr).
76 Ibid., at 900.
77 *Hansard, 3*, clxxxvii, 1452.
78 Ibid., 1454.
79 *The University Education Question in Ireland: its Difficulties and their Solution* (Belfast, 1899). The pamphlet is reproduced in the Robertson Commission's *First Report, Appendix*, p. 367.
80 Ibid., at 369.
81 *Hansard, 3*, clxxxvii, 1445.
82 Robertson Commission, *First Report, Appendix*, p. 18.
83 See chapter 6.
84 William Walsh, *The Irish University Question* (Dublin, 1890).
85 Ibid., p. 23. The passage is quoted by Whitla in his very different piece: Robertson Commission, *First Report, Appendix*, p. 369.
86 For Walsh's involvement in the Irish university question, see P.J. Walsh, *William J. Walsh, Archbishop of Dublin* (Dublin, 1928), ch. 20.
87 Moody & Beckett, *Queen's Belfast*, i, 289.

88 Royal Archives, Windsor, entry for 29 April 1900, quoted Elizabeth Longford, *Victoria R.I.* (London, 1966), p. 698.
89 33 Hen. VIII, sess. 2, c. 3.
90 'The Catholic University and legal education', *Dublin Review*, 41 (1856), 226.
91 At 234.
92 Ibid.
93 Royal Commission on University Education in Ireland (Robertson Commission), *Appendix to First Report*, 1901 (Cd. 826).
94 See Robertson Commission, *Appendix to First Report*, p. 301.
95 Mr Justice Madden, the Irish judge, was one of the twelve.
96 Royal Commission on University Education in Ireland, *First Report*, 1901, Cd. 825; *Appendix to First Report*, 1901, Cd.826; *Second Report*, 1901, Cd.899; *Appendix to Second Report*, 1902, Cd. 900; *Third Report*, 1902, Cd.1228; *Appendix to Third Report*, 1902, Cd. 1229; *Final Report*, 1903, Cd. 1483; *Appendix to Final Report*, 1903, Cd. 1484.
97 Printed, Robertson Commission, *Second Report*, *Appendix*, p. 328.
98 Robertson Commission, *Final Report*, p. 29.
99 Ibid.
100 Ibid.
101 Ibid.
102 Ibid.
103 See, for example, *St. Stephen's*, i, no. 1 (June 1901), no. 2 (Nov. 1901), ii, no. 1 (Dec. 1903), no. 5 (Nov. 1904).
104 *St. Stephen's*, ii, no. 1.
105 Ibid.
106 See p. 26.
107 *St. Stephen's*, ii, no. 1.
108 36 Vict., c. 21. See McDowell & Webb, *Trinity College Dublin: an Academic History*, ch. 9.
109 *The Queen* v. *Visitors of Trinity College Dublin* (1845) 9 ILR 41.
110 *Heron* v. *Trinity College* (1845) 9 ILR 56n; McDowell & Webb, *Trinity College Dublin; an Academic History*, pp 213–14.
111 D.C. Heron, *An Introduction to the History of Jurisprudence* (London, 1860).
112 McDowell & Webb, *Trinity College Dublin: an Academic History*, p. 214.
113 Royal Commission on Trinity College and the University of Dublin (Fry Commission), *First Report*, 1906, Cd. 3174; *Appendix to First Report*, 1906, Cd. 3176; *Final Report*, 1907, Cd. 3311; *Appendix to Final Report*, 1907, Cd. 3312.
114 Fry Commission, *Appendix to Final Report*, p. 282.
115 Ibid.
116 Ibid.
117 *St. Stephen's*, ii, no. 3 (Mar. 1904).
118 Fry Commission, *Final Report*, p. 22.
119 Ibid.
120 Ibid.
121 *Who Was Who, 1916–1928*, 4th ed. (London, 1967), p. 866.
122 Fry Commission, *Appendix to Final Report*, p. 282.
123 Ibid.
124 *St. Stephen's*, i, no. 7 (Jan. 1902).
125 *St. Stephen's*, i, no. 1 (June 1901).
126 Fry Commission, *Appendix to Final Report*, pp 196–207.
127 McDowell & Webb, *Trinity College Dublin: an Academic History*, p. 413.
128 Ibid., p. 414.
129 Fry Commission, *Appendix to Final Report*, p. 20 (evidence of the Provost, Dr Anthony Traill), p. 160 (evidence of Mr Justice Madden).
130 Ibid., p. 206.
131 Ibid.
132 Ibid.
133 Ibid.
134 Ibid.

2 FRESH BEGINNINGS: THE UCD LAW SCHOOL, 1909–25

1 8 Edw. VII, c. 38.
2 S.1 (1), (3).
3 Ss. 2(1), 2; 1 (i). UCD's Charter is conveniently reproduced in the early UCD *Calendars*.
4 S.1 (3).
5 Statute A of 15 May 1909, Chap X, replaced by Statute I of 15 Apr. 1911, Chap XI.
6 Irish Universities Act 1908, s.12.
7 For the LLB under the Royal University dispensation (1881), see the Robertson Commission, *Appendix to First Report 1901*, pp 239, 255.
8 See Robertson Commission, *Appendix to First Report 1901*, p. 255.
9 Denis J. Coffey to R. Armstrong, Under Treasurer, 15 Apr. 1911: Governing Body minutes, 29 June 1911.

10 Armstrong to Coffey, 14 June 1911: Governing Body minutes, 29 June 1911.
11 Governing Body minutes, 29 June 1911.
12 *Final Report of the Commission on University Education Ireland*, 1903 HC xxxii, pp 43, 58.
13 *Report of the President of Queen's College, Cork, for 1908–09*, 1909 HC xx, 803, pp 9, 14 (821, 826).
14 *Report of the President of Queen's College, Galway, for 1908–09*, 1909 HC xx, 831, pp 3, 9 (833, 839).
15 *ILT & SJ*, 74 (1940), 49.
16 *ILT & SJ*, 73 (1939), 229.
17 *Report of the President of Queen's College, Belfast, for 1908–09*, 1909 HC xx, 715, pp 3, 25 (717, 739).
18 See further T.W. Moody and J.C. Beckett, *Queen's Belfast, 1845–1949: the History of a University*, 2 vols (London, 1959), ii, 588 and 589.
19 *Appendix to First Report of the Royal Commission on Trinity College Dublin, and the University of Dublin*, 1906 HC lvi, 607, at p. 20 (627).
20 Ibid., at pp 16–17 (623–24).
21 In 1905–6 he is listed as 'Reid Honour Lecturer' which gave him a stipend of £71 8*s*. His total earnings of over £124 included sums for 'exam fees' and for the 'Army Class lecture fee'.
22 R.B. McDowell and D.A. Webb, *Trinity College Dublin: an Academic History* (Cambridge, 1982), p. 414.
23 *Twenty-seventh Report of the Royal University of Ireland, for 1908*, 1909 HC xx, 869, pp 5, 6 and 10 (873, 874, 878).
24 *Report of the President of Queen's College, Galway, for 1908–09*, at p. 6 (836).
25 *Report of the President of Queen's College, Belfast, for 1908–09*, at p. 19 (734).
26 8 Edw VII, c. 38.
27 S. 6.
28 S.15. Re-engagement of professors, etc. at the two erstwhile Queen's Colleges of Cork and Galway was also left to the Dublin Commissioners to handle: see ss. 15 and 16.
29 E.g., *ILT & SJ*, 43 (1909), 139.
30 The salary for one professorship in law at Queen's University, Belfast, concurrently advertised by the Belfast Commissioners was only £200 per annum: *ILT & SJ*, 43 (1909) 109.
31 1908 Act, s. 15(2), (4).
32 As was done in the case of the three individuals concerned: UCD, Governing Body minute book 1915–1917, 23 May 1916. There was a repetition of the process in 1923; for the NUI Senate's then endorsement, see the NUI Senate minutes, ix (1922–1925), 117 (6 July 1923).
33 Benchers' minute books for the second half of the nineteenth century make it plain that sometimes King's Inns professors were not eligible for reappointment at all; or, if they were, not in the subjects of their first appointment: King's Inns, Benchers' minute book, 1856–1869, p. 400: entry for 22 May 1868.
34 Quoted, J.B. Ames, 'The vocation of the law professor' in his *Lectures in Legal History and Miscellaneous Essays* (Cambridge, MA, and London, 1913), p. 356.
35 Ibid., p. 357.
36 Governing Body minute book, 1925–1927, 22 Dec. 1925.
37 Governing Body minute book, 1931–1933, 31 Jan. 1933.
38 Irish Universities Act, s. 6 (10).
39 Order of 23 Jan. 1911: *Dublin Gazette, Jan.–June 1911*, p. 195.
40 *King's Inns Barristers, 1868–2004*, ed. Kenneth Ferguson (Dublin, 2005), p. 444.
41 Royal Commission on Trinity College, Dublin and the University of Dublin (Fry Commission), *Appendix to Final Report, 1907*, Cd.3312, p. 309.
42 NUI Senate minutes, i (1909–1911), 16 (19 April 1909).
43 *ILT & SJ*, 47 (1913), 29.
44 NUI Senate minutes, i, 24 (11 Nov. 1909).
45 UCD Governing Body minute book, Dec. 1908–June 1911, 4 Jan. 1910.
46 *The Old Munster Circuit* (London, 1948), p. 158.
47 *King's Inns Barristers, 1868–2004*, p. 145.
48 UCD Governing Body minute book, 1908–1911, 7 Oct. 1909.
49 UCD Governing Body minute book, Dec. 1908 – June 1911, 7 Oct. 1909, 4 Jan. 1910.
50 *King's Inns Barristers, 1868–2004*, p. 251.
51 McDowell and Webb, *Trinity College Dublin, 1592–1952*, p. 414.
52 Royal Commission on University Education in Ireland, *Appendix to First Report, 1901*, Cd. 826, p. 279.

53 NUI Senate minutes, i (1909–1911), 193 (20 Dec. 1910), 199 (7 Jan. 1911).
54 T.J. Morrissey, *Towards a National University: William Delany SJ (1835–1924)* (Dublin, 1983), p. 256.
55 Ibid., pp 256–7.
56 NUI Senate minutes, xi (1927–9), 212 (7 Dec. 1928).
57 *King's Inns Barristers, 1868–2004*, p. 178; obituary, *ILT & SJ*, 62 (1928), 241.
58 Governing Body minute book, 1908–1911, 14 Feb. 1911.
59 The *DIB* is wrong to say that appointment was to the chair of Jurisprudence etc. (vi, 160).
60 Edward MacLysaght, *More Irish Families* (Galway and Dublin, 1960), p. 190. See, too, M.C.P. MacNeill, *A Blessed Life, being a Biographical Sketch of the Rev. John Gordon Swift MacNeill, MA* (Dublin, 1891), p. 5.
61 J.G. Swift MacNeill, *What I Have Seen and Heard* (London, 1925), p. 18.
62 The failed incursion during the Napoleonic Wars.
63 D.L. Macnie and Moray McLaren (eds), *New Shell Guide to Scotland* (London, 1977), p. 424.
64 Other texts followed: *Contracts, Instruments for Social Cooperation – East Africa: Text, Cases, Materials* (South Hackensack, NJ, 1968); *Cases and Materials on Contracts: Exchange Transactions and Relationships* (Mineola, NY, 1971).
65 See *Students and Decision-making: a Report by Robert S. Morison, Chairman of Cornell's Commission on Student Involvement in Decision-Making, and Comments by Iain MacNeil* (Washington, DC, 1970).
66 MacNeill, *What I Have Seen and Heard*, p. 21.
67 Ibid., p. 32.
68 Ibid., p. 39.
69 Ibid., p. 47.
70 Ibid., p. 62.
71 Ibid., p. 64.
72 Ibid.
73 *What I Have Seen and Heard*, p. 71.
74 F.H. Lawson, *The Oxford Law School, 1850–1965* (Oxford, 1968), p. 25.
75 *What I Have Seen and Heard*, p. 76.
76 Lawson, *The Oxford Law School*, p. 45.
77 *What I Have Seen and Heard*, p .97.
78 Ibid., p. 107.
79 *King's Inns Barristers, 1968–2004*, p. 444; *What I Have Seen and Heard*, p. 112.
80 Ibid., p. 164.
81 Ibid., p. 196.
82 Ibid., p. 197; King's Inns, Benchers' minute book, 1885–1901, pp 6, 100.
83 *What I Have Seen and Heard*, pp 189, 201. Confirmation of MacNeill's academic talents is to be found in the published *Report of the Education Committee* [of King's Inns] (Dublin, 1876), at p. 8: 'J.G. Swift MacNeill passed a very brilliant examination and obtained the First exhibition'.
84 *What I Have Seen and Heard*, p. 201.
85 *What I Have Seen and Heard*, pp 259, 267.
86 In James Meenan (ed.), *Centenary History of the Literary and Historical Society of University College Dublin, 1855–1955* (Dublin, 2005), p. 109.
87 *DIB*, vi, 160 (entry by Patrick Maume).
88 Meenan (ed.), *History of the L & H*, pp 129–47.
89 Ibid., pp 131–2.
90 Ibid. O'Higgins' extraordinary academic journey through UCD and the NUI is discussed on p. 81.
91 *What I Have Seen and Heard*, p. 210.
92 King's Inns, Benchers' minute book, 1856–1869, p. 401; GEC, *Complete Peerage*, x, 743. Plunket represented Dublin University from 1870 to 1895.
93 *What I Have Seen and Heard*, p. 210.
94 King's Inns, Benchers' minute book, 1885–1901, p. 83 (entry for 1 June 1888), *ILT & SJ*, 22 (1888), 285 (9 June 1888), MacNeill, *What I Have Seen and Heard*, p. 211.
95 London, Paris, New York and Melbourne, 1885.
96 J.G. Swift MacNeill, *The Irish Parliament: What it Was and What it Did*, p. xi.
97 Ibid., pp 18–19.
98 Quoted, MacNeill, *What I Have Seen and Heard*, p. 203.
99 J.G. Swift MacNeill, *English Interference with Irish Industries*, 2nd ed. (London, Paris, New York, Melbourne, 1886).
100 Ibid., at pp vii–viii.
101 Ibid., p. ix.
102 See J.A. Froude, *The English in Ireland in the Eighteenth Century*, 3 vols (London, 1872–4), ii, 230.

103 Quoted, *English Interference*, p. 45n.
104 Ibid., p. 40.
105 Ibid., p. 59.
106 Ibid., p. 73n.
107 J.G. Swift MacNeill, *Titled Corruption: the Sordid Origin of Some Irish Peerages* (London, 1894).
108 Juvenal, *Sat.* viii. 20.
109 Sadly, the printer has '*nobilitus*'.
110 The whole of Juvenal's eighth satire, as it happens, is germane to MacNeill's purpose.
111 See p. 38.
112 W.E.H. Lecky, *History of England in the Eighteenth Century*, 8 vols (London, 1878–90), iv, 518.
113 *Titled Corruption*, p.v.
114 Ibid., pp vi–vii.
115 J.G. Swift MacNeill, *W.E. Gladstone: Anecdotes and Reminiscences* (London, 1898).
116 Ibid., pp 34–5.
117 *Scott: Poetical Works*, ed. J. Logie Robertson (London, 1904), p. 90.
118 J.G. Swift MacNeill, *Home Rule and Religious Intolerance: a Refutation of Unionist Charges in a Forgotten Speech of Mr Gladstone Recalled* (London, 1912).
119 Ibid., p. 6.
120 Ibid., pp 10–11.
121 Ibid., pp 15–17.
122 Ibid., p. 3. MacNeill acknowledged that other Protestants had been elected in NUI to positions of trust for the teaching of students.
123 The NUI Senate balloted its members on the three candidates who had offered themselves for the post. MacNeill received seven votes, Arthur Clery six, J.J. Macken five. The Dublin Commissioners appointed MacNeill: NUI Senate minutes, i, 199 (20 Dec. 1910), 227 (7 Jan. 1911).
124 *Home Rule and Religious Intolerance*, p. 4.
125 UCD Governing Body minute book, 1913–1915, 9 Feb. 1915.
126 NUI Senate minutes, ix, 247 (23 May 1924), 268 (9 July 1924).
127 MacNeill, *What I Have Seen and Heard*, p. 197.
128 Ibid., pp 201, 237.
129 Ibid., p. 239.
130 *DIB*, vi, 160.
131 *What I Have Seen and Heard*, p. 240.
132 Accession Declaration Act 1910: 10 Edw. VII & 1 Geo. V, c. 29.
133 30 Chas. II, stat. 2, c.1 (1678).
134 1 Will. & Mary, sess.2, c.2 (by s.1).
135 12 & 13 Will. III, c.2 (by s.2).
136 The declaration is required 'to be made, subscribed, and audibly repeated' by the Sovereign, s.1.
137 *Hansard, 5*, xix, cols. 2129–41.
138 Ibid., cols. 2213–16.
139 Ibid., col. 2215.
140 Ibid., 3 & 4 Vict., c. 52; speech of duke of Sussex: *Hansard, 3*, lv, col. 850 f. (21 July 1840).
141 *Hansard, 5*, xix, col. 2383.
142 Ibid., col. 2391. MacNeill did not ignore the Bill of Right's alternative date – at the Coronation of the monarch. And the further provision that the earlier of the two dates (at the first parliament or at the Coronation) was requisite: *Hansard, 5*, xix, col. 2379.
143 *Hansard, 5*, xix, col. 2216.
144 Ibid.
145 *Hansard, 5*, xxviii, col. 875 (18 July 1911).
146 7 & 8 Geo. V, c. 47.
147 *What I Have Seen and Heard*, p. 285.
148 'The Irish Parliament and the mandate for Union', *Contemporary Review*, 105 (1914), 331.
149 'The breakdown of the Dublin Castle regime', *Contemporary Review*, 110 (1916), 22.
150 Ibid., at 29.
151 Ibid.
152 12 Geo. III, c. 11 (G.B.).
153 'The Prince's Marriage and the Royal Marriage Act, 1772: A Plea for Repeal': *LQR*, 38 (1922), 74.
154 Ibid., at 74.
155 Ibid., at 79.
156 Ibid., at 75.
157 *Irish Times*, 22 April 2011.
158 Dublin, 1925.
159 *Journal of Comparative Legislation and International Law*, 3rd series, 5 (1923), 52.
160 *Studies in IFS Constitution*, p. 36 ff.
161 Quoted, *Studies in IFS Constitution*, p. 49.
162 *Studies in IFS Constitution*, p. 27.
163 Ibid., p. x.
164 Ibid., p. xxiii.
165 Thus one reviewer wrote (*ILT & SJ*, 59 (1925), 105): 'If any criticism of Mr MacNeill's method may be made, it is that

he fixes his attention too much upon Dicey and historical parallels and too little upon the very far-reaching efforts that this Constitution and the circumstances under which it originated are likely to have upon empire policy in the future'.

166 Leo Kohn, *The Constitution of the Irish Free State* (London, 1932).

167 *DNB, 1922–1930*, ed. J.R.H. Weaver (London, 1937), 549–50.

168 This passage is omitted from the *Oxford DNB* entry (xxxv, 960).

169 *DIB*, vi, 160.

170 *What I Have Seen and Heard*, p. 293.

171 See, too, Nehemiah 3:15; John 9:7, 11.

172 NUI Senate minutes, x (1925–1927), 201 (16 July 1926).

173 NUI Senate minutes, x, 221 (17 Sept. 1926), 232 (29 Oct. 1926). The need for a Statute to authorise retrospectively the award of this gratuity was discussed by the Senate early in 1928: NUI Senate minutes, xi (1927–1929), 97 (9 Mar. 1928).

174 James Meenan (ed.), *Centenary History of the Literary and Historical Society of University College Dublin, 1855–1955* (Dublin, 2005), p. 264.

175 Ibid., p. 39.

176 Ibid., p. 58 (Thomas F. Bacon).

177 *St Stephen's*, vol. 2, no. 1 (Dec. 1903), p. 22. In May 1899, Murnaghan had signed the student protest against Yeats' *The Countess Cathleen*: Meenan (ed.), *History of the L & H*, p. 48n.

178 *St Stephen's*, vol. 1, no. 2 (Nov. 1901), p. 34.

179 *St Stephen's*, vol. 1, no. 3 (Dec. 1901), p. 44.

180 Ibid.

181 Meenan (ed.), *History of the L & H*, p. 109.

182 *Studies*, 1 (1912), 130.

183 *Studies*, 2 (1913), 846.

184 'The Parliament of the Pale', *LQR*, 34 (1918), 291; 'The first adventure of the Common Law', *LQR*, 36 (1920), 9; 'Ireland in the medieval law courts', *Studies*, 12 (1923), 553; 'The English legislature and Irish courts', *LQR*, 40 (1924), 91.

185 [1929] IR 191.

186 [1934] IR 44.

187 At 55.

188 *Governors of Erasmus Smith Schools* v. *AG* (1932) 66 ILTR 57.

189 Erasmus Smith Schools Act 1938: no. 1 (private) of 1938.

190 Swift MacNeill naturally can also lay claim to this tradition. In this case, however, it needs to be said that his focus was obdurately on constitutional history.

191 Meenan (ed.), *History of the L & H*, p. 104.

192 Murnaghan to Coffey, 11 June 1924: Governing Body minute book, 1923–1925, 12 June 1924.

193 Ibid.

194 NUI Senate minutes, iii, 3 (27 Feb. 1913).

195 *King's Inns Barristers, 1868–2004*, p. 261.

196 Governing Body minute book, 1913–1915, 19 Dec. 1913 (£30); 1915–1917, 11 May 1915 (£20), 23 May 1916 (£20); 1917–1919, 3 July 1917 (£20); 1919–1921, 22 July 1919 (£20), 1921–1923, 26 July 1921 (£20); 1923–1925, 30 June 1924 (£20).

197 See p. 34.

198 NUI Senate minutes, i, 85 (6 May 1910).

199 NUI Senate minutes, i, 35 (22 Dec. 1909), 40 (23 Feb. 1910).

200 Ibid., 124 (24 June 1910).

201 Ibid., 177 (29 Oct. 1910).

202 Ibid., 249 (12 May 1911).

203 Ibid., 67 (24 Feb. 1910).

204 NUI Senate minutes, iii, 136 (4 July 1913). The Senate ruled earlier in 1913 that no special courses for such RUI matriculated students were to be maintained after 1914: ibid., 2 (27 Feb. 1913).

205 NUI Senate minutes, ii, 527 (30 Oct. 1912).

206 NUI Senate minutes, iii, 372 (27 May 1914); iv, 249 (21 May 1915).

207 NUI Senate minutes, v, 194 (27 Oct. 1916).

208 A.D. McDonnell, *The Life of Sir Denis Henry, Catholic Unionist* (Belfast, 2000).

209 NUI Senate minutes, vi, 341 (28 Feb. 1919).

210 See p. 52.

211 NUI Senate minutes, vii, 156 (16 Dec. 1919).

212 NUI Senate minutes, vii, 224 (14 May 1920).

213 NUI Senate minutes, vii, 237 (16 May 1920).

214 NUI Senate minutes, vii, 192, 349 (5 Mar., 22 Oct. 1920).

215 NUI Senate minutes, vii, 393 (17 Dec. 1920).
216 NUI Senate minutes, viii, 47 (13 May 1921).
217 NUI Senate minutes, ix, 42, 91, 172 (27 Mar., 18 May, 7 Dec. 1923). Queen's was duly to pay its share.
218 NUI Senate minutes, viii, 142 (28 Oct. 1921).
219 NUI Senate minutes, iii, 130 (4 July 1913).
220 NUI Senate minutes, iv, 224 (21 May 1915).
221 NUI Senate minutes, v, 292 (2 Mar. 1917).
222 NUI Senate minutes, vi, 121 (1 Mar. 1918).
223 NUI Senate minutes, vi, 358 (28 Feb. 1919).
224 NUI Senate minutes, vii, 205 (15 Mar. 1920).
225 NUI Senate minutes, viii, 25 (11 Mar. 1921).
226 NUI Senate minutes, viii, 223 (10 Mar. 1922).
227 NUI Senate minutes, ix, 44 (27 Mar. 1923).
228 NUI Senate minutes, ix, 216 (16 Mar. 1924).
229 Governing Body minute book, 1911–1913, 29 Dec. 1911, 29 June 1912.
230 Governing Body minute book, 1915–1917, 30 Jan. 1917.
231 Governing Body minute book, 1923–1925, 30 June 1924.
232 [1930] IR 649.
233 [1930] IR at 700.
234 [1935] IR 170.
235 Constitution (Amendment No. 16) Act, 1929, No. 10 of 1929.
236 No. 37 of 1931.
237 [1935] IR at 237–8.
238 Meenan (ed.), *History of the L & H*, p. 109.
239 Brian Farrell, 'The drafting of the Irish Free State Constitution – I', *Ir Jur*, 5 (1970), 115; – II, *Ir Jur*, 5 (1970), 343; – III, *Ir Jur*; 6 (1971), 111; – IV, *Ir Jur*, 6 (1971), 345.
240 *Ir Jur*, 5, at 118.
241 *Ir Jur*, 5, at 345.
242 *Ir Jur*, 6, at 112.
243 Draft C is reproduced by Farrell in *Ir Jur*, 6, at pp 125–35.
244 E.G. Hall, *The Superior Courts of Law: 'Official' Law Reporting in Ireland, 1866–2006* (Dublin, 2007), p. 128.
245 Ibid., p. 143.
246 *DIB*, vi, 788.
247 See p. 34.
248 UCD, Governing Body minute book, 1908–1911, 10 Dec 1910.
249 NUI Senate minutes, i (1909–1911), 227 (7 Jan. 1911).
250 *King's Inns Barristers, 1868–2004*, p. 241; obituary, *ILT & SJ*, 77 (1943), 190.
251 Healy, *The Old Munster Circuit*, p. 248.
252 *A Portrait of the Artist as a Young Man* (London, 1960), p. 53 (ch. 1).
253 See p. 62.
254 Healy, *The Old Munster Circuit*, pp 98–102, 155–7.
255 Ibid., p. 155.
256 *DIB*, ii, 584 (Patrick Maume).
257 Edward MacLysaght, *Irish Families, their Names, Arms and Origins* (Dublin, 1957), p. 80.
258 Arthur Ua Clerigh, *The History of Ireland to the Coming of Henry II* (London, 1908).
259 In the King's Inns admission papers for Arthur Clery, junior, his father's address is given as Albert Street in London.
260 Ua Clerigh, *History of Ireland*, p. 412.
261 Ibid., preface.
262 Ibid.
263 Clery senior's *History* is probably regarded today with disfavour: it does not feature in the bibliography for vol. 1 of the *New History of Ireland*. Trinity College's copy of the volume which I consulted had not had its pages cut.
264 *The Franchises and the Registration of Parliamentary Voters in Ireland*, 3rd ed. (Dublin, 1886).
265 *Some Thoughts on Reform in the Irish and County Courts in Ireland*, printed for the author (Dublin, 1885). An early pamphlet, *The Queen's Colleges in Ireland* (Dublin, 1868) was also composed by Clery senior.
266 James Joyce, *Stephen Hero* (London, Paladin ed., 1991), p. 95.
267 *DIB*, ii, 584.
268 'Chanel', *The Idea of a Nation* (Dublin, 1907), p. 50.
269 Ibid., p. 49.
270 T.J. Morrissey, *Towards a National University: William Delany SJ (1835–1924) – an Era of Initiative in Irish Education* (Dublin, 1983), p. 163.
271 Joyce, *Stephen Hero*, p. 94.
272 Ibid., p. 95.

273 See further James Meenan (ed.), *Centenary History of the Literary and Historical Society of University College Dublin, 1855–1955* (Dublin, 2005), p. 50 (recollections of Felix Hackett).
274 Joyce, *Stephen Hero*, p. 105.
275 Ibid., p. 106.
276 Ibid.
277 Joyce, *Stephen Hero*, p. 176.
278 Meenan (ed.), *History of the L & H*, p. 264.
279 Morrissey, *William Delany SJ*, p. 160.
280 Meenan (ed.), *History of the L & H*, p. 47.
281 Ibid., pp 265–6.
282 Morrissey, *William Delany, SJ*, pp 273–4.
283 William Dawson, 'Arthur Clery', *Studies*, 22 (1933), 77 at 78, 81.
284 Ibid., p. 78.
285 Arthur E. Clery and J. McWalter, *The Public Health Acts Amendment Act 1907, with Explanation, Full Commentary upon the Sections and Summary of Recent Public Health Decisions* (Dublin, 1908).
286 Ibid., p. 17.
287 Ibid., p. 56.
288 *Tussaud* v. *LCC* (1893) 57 JP 194.
289 Clery & McWalter, *The Public Health Acts Amendment Act 1907*, pp 61–2.
290 It consisted of the name 'Madame Tussaud's': 'The letters forming the name are three feet in height, and two feet six inches in width. They are made of wood, five and a half inches wide by one and a quarter inches thick. They are fastened to a galvanised iron trellis which is about 35 feet long: the trellis is also braced or tied back to the dome by five galvanised iron bracings.' 57 JP at 184. The advertisement had been erected prior to the enactment of the London Sky Signs Act, 1891.
291 The reference was to *LCC* v. *Carwardine* (1893) 57 JP 181.
292 Clery & McWalter, *The Public Health Acts Amendment Act 1907*, p. 62.
293 *The Town Tenants (Ireland) Act 1906* (Dublin, 1907), reviewed, *ILT & SJ*, 41 (1907), 133.
294 Dublin, 1913.
295 Patrick Maume, 'Nationalism and Partition: the political thought of Arthur Clery', *IHS*, 31 (1998), 222 at 231; idem, *DIB*, ii, 584.
296 In Meenan (ed.), *History of the L & H*, p. 109.
297 Ibid., p. 110.
298 Dawson, 'Arthur Clery', *Studies*, 22 (1933), 77 at 82; C.P. Curran, *Under the Receding Wave* (Dublin, 1970) p. 127.
299 Above, p. 64.
300 Entry on Moran in new *Oxford DNB*, xxxviii, 1024 and in *DIB*, vi, 666 (both by Maume).
301 *DIB*, ii, 584 at 585.
302 'Chanel' (Arthur E. Clery), *The Idea of a Nation* (Dublin, 1907).
303 Maume, 'Political thought of Arthur Clery', *IHS*, 31 (1998), 222.
304 Morrissey, *William Delany SJ*, p. 144.
305 Maume, 'Political thought of Clery', 222 n. 2.
306 *Idea of a Nation*, p. 11.
307 Ibid., p. 7.
308 Ibid., p. 16.
309 Ibid.
310 *The Idea of a Nation*, p. 20.
311 Ibid., p. 22.
312 Ibid.
313 *The Idea of a Nation*, p. 46.
314 Ibid., p. 47.
315 Ibid., p. 29 ff.
316 Ibid., p. 17 ff.
317 See p. 75.
318 See p. 62.
319 In Meenan (ed.), *History of the L & H*, p. 48.
320 Ibid.
321 *The Idea of a Nation*, p. 70ff.
322 Ibid., p. 55.
323 *King's Inns Admission papers, 1607–1867*, ed. Edward Keane, P.B. Phair and T.U. Sadlier (Dublin, 1982), p. 88.
324 Dublin, 1909.
325 *The Coming of the King*, p. 83.
326 Ibid., p. 134.
327 At pp 142–3.
328 At p. 1.
329 Dawson, 'Arthur Clery', p. 85.
330 Dublin and London, 1919.
331 *Dublin Essays*, p. vii.
332 Dawson, 'Arthur Clery', p. 79.
333 *Dublin Essays*, p. vii.
334 Ibid., p. 2.
335 Ibid.
336 'The snobbery of Quintus Horatius Flaccus', *Dublin Essays*, pp 106–13; 'The pseudo-science of classics', ibid., pp 100–5.
337 'A Gaelic university', ibid., p. 15 at pp 24–5.

338 'Thomas Kettle', ibid., pp 1–14.
339 'Rugby Football and the "condumnium"', ibid., pp 66–70.
340 *Dublin Essays*, pp 15–16.
341 'The theatre: its educational value', ibid., pp 114–21; above, p. 62.
342 *Dublin Essays*, pp 93–9.
343 At pp 97–8.
344 At p. 99.
345 *Studies*, 10 (1921), 19.
346 *Studies*, 10 (1921), 299.
347 *Studies*, 10 (1921), 545.
348 *Studies*, 11 (1922), 571.
349 Hall, *The Superior Courts of Law*, pp 138–42.
350 Dawson, 'Arthur Clery', at 78, 80.
351 Curran, *Under the Receding Wave*, p. 129.
352 Maume, 'Political thought of Clery', at 233.
353 Healy, *The Old Munster Circuit*, p. 231.
354 NUI Senate minutes, ix (1922–1925), 309 (24 Oct. 1924). See too, ibid., 263 (9 July 1924). For drafting NUI Statute XXIX (minutes, x (1925–1928), 232 (29 Oct. 1926)) Clery earned £10.
355 *DIB*, ii, 584.
356 See Mary Kotsonouris, *Retreat from Revolution: the Dáil Courts, 1920–24* (Dublin, 2004).
357 Ibid., pp 28–9.
358 Conceivably in the accidental fashion described by Curran, *Under the Receding Wave*, pp 131–2.
359 See Dáil Eireann Courts (Winding-up) Act 1923, No. 36 of 1923.
360 Dáil Supreme Court (Pensions) Act 1925, No. 13 of 1925; Kotsonouris, *Retreat from Revolution*, p. 122.
361 *O'Crowley* v. *Minister for Justice and Minister for Finance* [1935] IR 536.
362 Kotsonouris, *Retreat from Revolution*, p. 85.
363 Ibid., p. 73.
364 Mary Kotsonouris, *The Winding up of the Dáil Courts, 1922–1925: an Obvious Duty* (Dublin, 2004).
365 Ibid., pp 142–3.
366 Maume, 'Political thought of Arthur Clery', 235.
367 Ibid., 237.
368 Dawson, 'Arthur Clery', 79.
369 Ibid., 87.
370 C.S. Andrews, *Man of No Property* (Dublin and Cork, 1982), p. 43; Christopher Murray, *Sean O'Casey: Writer at Work* (Dublin, 2004); Maume, 'Political thought of Arthur Clery', 238.
371 Dawson, 'Arthur Clery', 80; NUI Senate minutes, xiii (1931–1933), 231 (8 Dec. 1932).
372 Dawson, 'Arthur Clery', 88.
373 Ibid., 80.
374 Ibid., 81.
375 Governing Body minute book, 1931–1933, 31 Jan. 1933.
376 Pp 3–4.
377 See, for example, the *President's Report for 1935–36*, at pp 35 and 36.
378 In *The Leader*, in 1909, an essay reprinted in *A Page of Irish History: the Story of UCD, 1883–1909* (Dublin and Cork, 1930), p. 583 at p. 586.
379 Governing Body minute book, 1929–1931, 25 Feb., 19 Dec. 1930, 26 Feb. 1931.
380 Governing Body minute book, 1931–1933, 26 Jan. 1932.
381 Ibid., 14 June 1932, 11 Apr. 1933.
382 Governing Body minute book, 1931–1933, 11 April 1933; Governing Body minute book, 25 May 1971–22 Apr. 1972, 29 June 1971 (£1,000); Governing Body minute book, 13 May 1975–22 June 1976, 13 May 1975 (£1,800 for purchase of Eimpacher fine Four).
383 *DIB*, ii, 584.
384 Maume, 'Political thought of Arthur Clery', 239.
385 Curran, *Under the Receding Wave*, p. 125.
386 Ibid., p. 130.
387 Donal McCartney, *UCD, A National Idea: the History of University College Dublin* (Dublin, 1999), p. 64.
388 Governing Body minute book, 29 Oct. 1940 – 25 May 1943, 26 Nov. 1940.
389 See *ILT & SJ*, 46 (1912), 33: meeting of 31 Jan. 1912, chaired by Mr Justice Barton.
390 See *ILT & SJ*, 47 (1913), 62: meeting of 19 Feb. 1913, chaired by Lord Justice Cherry.
391 NUI Senate minutes, iii, 11 Dec. 1913. Other testimonials are reproduced in the early minutes, but the practice is soon abandoned. This entry, devoted to the testimonials received for all candidates in contention for a particular post, is probably unique.
392 T. Arkins, 'The commercial aspect of the Irish Penal Code', *Studies*, 1 (1912), 257;

idem, 'The Penal Laws and Irish land', *Studies*, 1 (1912), 514.
393 V.T.H. Delany, *Christopher Palles* (Dublin, 1960), p. 154.
394 Healy, *The Old Munster Circuit*, pp 248–9. See too, A.P. Quinn, *Wigs and Guns: Irish Barristers in the Great War* (Dublin, 2006), p. 32.
395 NUI Senate minutes, x (1926–1927), 355 (15 July 1927).
396 But not in 1923, as wrongly stated in the entry in the *Dictionary of Irish Biography*: vii, 562.
397 NUI Senate minutes, iv, 351 (28 Oct. 1915).
398 NUI Senate minutes, v, 190 (27 Oct. 1916).
399 NUI Senate minutes, v, 284 (2 Mar. 1917).
400 NUI Senate minutes, vi, 44 (26 Oct. 1917).
401 NUI Senate minutes, vi, 84 (7 Dec. 1917).
402 NUI Senate minutes, vii, 99 (24 Oct. 1919).
403 He earned a Pass LLB: NUI Senate minutes, vii, 76 (24 Oct. 1919).
404 Terence de Vere White, *Kevin O'Higgins* (Tralee, 1966), p. 47.
405 NUI Senate minutes, vii, 158.
406 de Vere White, *Kevin O'Higgins*, p. 28.
407 NUI Senate minutes, vii, 158.
408 *Municipal Government in Ireland, Medieval and Modern* (Dublin and London, 1918).
409 NUI Senate minutes, vi, 298, 346, 384 (12 Dec. 1918, 28 Feb., 28 Apr. 1919).
410 *Irish Times*, 24 Oct. 1924.
411 *The Guilds of Dublin* (Dublin and London, 1929). Webb's winning Coyne Memorial Scholarship Essay, *Industrial Dublin since 1698 and the Silk Industry in Dublin: Two Essays*, had been published by Maunsel in Dublin in 1913.
412 *King's Inns Barristers, 1868–2004*, p. 315.
413 Sir Brian MacKenna, 'Discretion', *Irish Jurist*, 9 (1974), 1.

3 NEW BROOMS: THE LAW SCHOOL, 1925–45

1 Governing Body minute book, 1913–1915, 20 Oct. 1914.
2 Governing Body minute book, 1925–1927, 30 Nov. 1926, 25 Jan. 1927.
3 Governing Body minute book, 1931–1933, 31 Jan. 1933.
4 See p. 86.
5 NUI Senate minutes, x (1926–1927), 275 (10 Dec. 1926).
6 NUI Senate minutes, x, 317 (11 Mar. 1927).
7 NUI Senate minutes, xi (1927–1929), 27 (4 Nov. 1927).
8 NUI Senate minutes, xi, 64 (9 Dec. 1927).
9 Governing Body minute book, 1927–1929, 3 Jan. 1928.
10 NUI Senate minutes, xi (1927–1929), 64 (9 Dec. 1927), 105 (11 May 1928).
11 An excellent piece of place name research informs Binchy's, 'The old name of Charleville, Co. Cork', *Eigse*, 10, pt. 3 (1962–3), 211.
12 District Justice John Farrell, in James Meenan (ed.), *Centenary History of the Literary and Historical Society of University College Dublin, 1855–1955* (Dublin, 2005), p. 136.
13 *King's Inns barristers, 1868–2004*, ed. Kenneth Ferguson (Dublin, 2005), p. 139.
14 See Binchy's 'The Irish Benedictine congregation in medieval Germany', *Studies*, 18 (1929), 194.
15 D.A. Binchy 'Irish history and Irish law: I', *Studia Hibernica*, 15 (1975), 7 at 23n.
16 *Studies*, 10 (1920), 353, 573; *Studies*, 11 (1921), 199; *Studies*, 12 (1922), 83, 461; *Studies*, 13 (1923), 115.
17 See entry in *DIB*, i, 531 by Michael Kennedy and Thomas Charles-Edwards.
18 Diarmaid MacCulloch, *Thomas Cranmer* (New Haven and London, 1996), p. 84.
19 V.T.H. Delany, *Christopher Palles: His Life and Times* (Dublin 1960), p. 84. Delany, in scotching the story, pointed out that Gladstone did indeed travel to Windsor on 17 Feb. 1874 to resign, but travelled from Waterloo.
20 Donal Cregan, 'Daniel Binchy – obituary: the road to Emmaus', *Irish University Review*, 19 (1989), 310.
21 Governing Body minute book, 1923–1925, 17 Oct. 1924.
22 The other candidates were Joseph Geraghty, James G. O'Connor and John J. Webb. Geraghty was a recent Brooke Scholar.
23 The Senate confirmed the choice on 24 Oct. 1924: NUI Senate minutes, ix, 298.
24 Ibid., 24 Feb. 1925.
25 Binchy himself would soon be engaged in standing in for others; in 1926 he substi-

tuted for the Professor of History, J.M. O'Sullivan: NUI Senate minutes, x (1925 – 1927), 205 (16 July 1926).

26 Binchy, 'Irish history and Irish law – I', 7.

27 'Our men in Berlin: some thoughts on Irish diplomats in Germany, 1929–39', *Irish Studies in International Affairs*, 10 (1999), 53 at 69.

28 Binchy to Joseph Walshe, 27 May 1930: *Documents on Irish Foreign Policy: vol. 3 – 1926–1932*, ed. Ronan Fanning, Michael Kennedy, Dermot Keogh, Eunan O'Halpin (Dublin, 2002), pp 542–3.

29 Binchy to Walshe, 2 Mar. 1931: *Documents on Irish Foreign Policy, vol. 3*, p. 754.

30 Binchy to Walshe, 5 Aug. 1931: *Documents on Irish Foreign Policy, vol. 3*, pp 809–14.

31 Binchy to Walshe, 1 Mar. 1932: *Documents on Irish Foreign Policy, vol. 3*, pp 915–16. See, too, D.A. Binchy, 'Adolf Hitler', *Studies*, 22 (1933), 29, at 46 n1.

32 Binchy to Walshe, 29 Oct. 1929: *Documents on Irish Foreign Policy, vol. 3*, pp 457–8; Binchy to Walshe, 14 Mar. 1932: *Documents on Irish Foreign Policy, vol. 4 – 1932–36*, ed. Catriona Crowe, Ronan Fanning, Michael Kennedy, Dermot Keogh and Eunan O'Halpin (Dublin, 2004), pp 15–16.

33 Binchy to Tierney, 4 Apr. 1930: *Documents on Irish Foreign Policy, vol. 3*, p. 521.

34 'What with lunches with Daniel Binchy, our Irish minister, and wanderings in the Tiergarten … and parties with stage and film people …. the time passed pleasantly': Micheál MacLiammóir, *All for Hecuba*, 2nd revised ed. (Dublin, 1961), p. 119.

35 Binchy to Tierney, 4 Apr. 1930: *Documents on Irish Foreign Policy, vol. 3*, pp 521–2.

36 Ibid.

37 Irish minister in Paris, 1929–1935.

38 Charles Plummer (1851–1927). Fellow of Corpus Christi College, Oxford, noted medieval historian with an expertise in Icelandic and Old Irish, author of *Vitae Sanctorum Hiberniae* (1910), awarded honorary doctorates by both Dublin University and NUI in 1925, a year in which he was also made an honorary MRIA.

39 Laurence Durrell, *Justine* (London, 1963), p. 18.

40 MacLiammóir, *All for Hecuba*, p. 118.

41 D.A. Binchy, 'Heinrich Brüning', *Studies*, 21 (1932), 385.

42 Ibid., at 403.

43 D.A. Binchy, 'Paul von Hindenburg', *Studies*, 26 (1937), 223.

44 J.W. Wheeler-Bennett, *Hindenburg: the Wooden Titan* (London, 1936).

45 Binchy, 'Hindenburg', at 246.

46 Ibid., at 236.

47 Ibid., at 237.

48 Ibid., at 242.

49 D.A. Binchy, 'Adolf Hitler', *Studies*, 22 (1933), 29.

50 Charles Bewley, *Hermann Göring and the Third Reich: a Biography based on Family and Official Records* (New York, 1962).

51 Kennedy, 'Our men in Berlin', p. 55.

52 Binchy, 'Hitler', p. 29.

53 Ibid.

54 Binchy, 'Hitler', p. 37.

55 Ibid., p. 31.

56 Ibid., p. 39.

57 Ibid., p. 47.

58 D.A. Binchy, *Church and State in Fascist Italy* (Oxford, 1941).

59 *President's Report for 1940–41*, pt. 2.

60 *Church and State in Fascist Italy*, pp 16–17.

61 P. viii.

62 The poetic excerpt at the end of this passage comes from an 1811 poem of William Wordsworth, 'Here pause: the poet claims at least this praise': *The poetical works of William Wordsworth*, ed. E. De Selincourt and Helen Darbishire, 2nd ed. (Oxford, 1954), p. 140.

63 *Church and State in Fascist Italy*, p. viii.

64 P. 120.

65 D.A. Binchy, 'Background of the Italian general election', *Studies*, 37 (1948), 257.

66 The quotation is from Schiller's *Wallensteins Tod*, act, 1, scene 7, lines 659 and 660. Wallenstein's warning over the vagaries of fortune is his rueful reaction to a show of triumph on the part of his sister-in-law, Countess Terzky, that he (Wallenstein) would commit treason, lead rebellion and ally himself with Sweden against Emperor Ferdinand. In view of the fate that later overwhelms the principal protagonists, the warning was not misplaced.

67 D.A. Binchy, *Church and State in Fascist Italy* (Oxford, 1970), pp v–vi. See, too, Binchy's, 'The diplomacy of the Vatican', *The Bell*, 12 (1946), 99.

68 Ibid., pp 722–5.
69 'Proposals for a new Senate', *Studies*, 25 (1936), 20.
70 'Partition and a policy of national unity', *Studies*, 24 (1935), 20.
71 Tomás Ó Criomhthain, *An t-Oileánach* (Dublin, 1929), Tomás Ó Crohan, *The Islandman*, trans. Robin Flower (Dublin, 1934); Muiris Ó Suileabhain, *Fiche Blian ag Fás* (Dublin, 1933), Maurice O'Sullivan, *Twenty Years A-growing*, rendered from Irish by Moya Llewellyn Davies and George Thomson (London, 1933).
72 D.A. Binchy, 'Two Blasket autobiographies', *Studies*, 23 (1934), 545.
73 Binchy, 'Two Blasket autobiographies', at 545.
74 Ibid., at 547.
75 Walshe to Coffey, 5 Mar. 1932, in Governing Body minute-book, 1931–1933, 8 Mar. 1932.
76 Governing Body minute book, 1931–1933, 11 Apr. 1933.
77 Ibid.
78 Academic Council minute book, 1915–1931, 15 and 22 Mar. 1929.
79 Statute I of the National University of Ireland, 15 Apr. 1911, conveniently reproduced in *ILT & SJ*, 45 (1911), Administration and Judicial Orders and Rules, 1911, at p. 41.
80 Governing Body minute book, 1931–1933, 11 Apr. 1933. See, too, Academic Council minute book, 12 Jan. 1932–26 June 1941, 30 May 1933.
81 The reference here is to just Jurisprudence and Roman Law.
82 It is not without interest that ten months earlier the Finance Committee and the Governing Body had approved the grant to Binchy of £75 to cover expenses linked to his collaboration with Rudolf Thurneysen in Bonn on work on the Brehon laws: Governing Body minute book, 1931–1933, 14 June 1932.
83 See the *1935–36 Calendar*.
84 Ibid.
85 In his review of J.M. Kelly's *Roman Litigation* (Oxford, 1966) in *Studies*, 55 (1966), 448.
86 'Irish history and Irish law: I', *Studia Hibernica*, 15 (1975), 7.
87 Ibid., at 8.
88 *Corpus Iuris Hibernici*, 6 vols (Dublin, 1978), i, p. vii.
89 Felix Liebermann, *Die Gesetze der Angelsachsen*, 4 vols (Halle, 1898–1916).
90 D.A. Binchy, 'The linguistic and historical value of the Irish law tracts', *Proceedings of the British Academy*, 29 (1943), 175.
91 Ibid., at 203.
92 F.W.H. Wasserschleben (ed.), *Die Irische Kanonensammlung*, 2nd ed. (Leipzig, 1885).
93 Quoted, *Corpus Iuris Hibernici*, i, at p. vii.
94 Eoin MacNeill, *Celtic Ireland* (Dublin, 1921), p. xiv.
95 'Irish history and Irish law: I', *Studia Hibernica*, 15 (1975), 7, at 11–12.
96 'Two Blasket autobiographies', *Studies*, 23 (1934), 545.
97 'Irish history and Irish law: I', *Studia Hibernica*, 15 (1975), at 12.
98 Daniel Binchy, reply to M. Tierney, 'Daniel O'Connell and the Gaelic past', *Studies*, 27 (1938), 369.
99 See the *President's Reports for 1941–42*, and *for 1945–46*.
100 Thomas Finlay, 'The class of "43"' in *UCD: Law Alumni Journal*, 1:1 (May 1999), 17.
101 Ibid.
102 Gearóid Ó Tuathaigh, 'The position of the Irish language' in Tom Dunne (ed.), *The National University of Ireland: 1908–2008 Centenary Essays* (Dublin, 2008), p. 33.
103 Academic Council minutes, 3 Oct. 1941–10 Oct. 1946: see the record of meetings between 1 April 1943 and 8 Feb. 1944. Binchy's refusal to continue to serve is recorded in the minutes of the meeting held on 22 June 1943.
104 Governing Body minute book, June 1943–Mar. 1947, 5 May 1946.
105 Ibid., 21 May 1946.
106 *President's Report for 1945–46*, pt. 2, p. 14.
107 Institute for Advanced Studies Act 1940 (No. 13 of 1940); *Dáil Eireann deb.*, lxxix, col. 1105, 10 Apr. 1940 (Mr de Valera).
108 Institute for Advanced Studies Act 1940, s.4. In *Matters of honour*, a novel published under the pseudonym John Boyle by John Kelly (London, 1965) – see above, p. 164 – the novel's principal character, Raphael Houlihan, after his year in Heidelberg, looks forward to an appointment as

lecturer in the School of Ancient History at the DIAS. For the functions prescribed for the School of Celtic Studies (which, unlike Boyle's School of Ancient History, actually exists) see s.5 of the Institute for Advanced Studies Act.

109 D.A. Binchy, 'The legal capacity of women, in regard to contracts', in Myles Dillon and D.A. Binchy (eds), *Studies in Early Irish Law* (Dublin, 1936), p. 207.

110 D.A. Binchy, 'Bretha Crólige', *Eriu*, 12 (1938), 1; 'Sick-maintenance in Irish law', *Eriu*, 12 (1938), 78.

111 Vv. 18 and 19.

112 D.A. Binchy, 'The linguistic and historical value of the Irish law tracts', *Proceedings of the British Academy*, 29 (1943), 195.

113 Ibid.

114 D. Coghlan, *The Ancient Land Tenures of Ireland* (Dublin, 1933).

115 At p. 194.

116 'Secular institutions' in Myles Dillon (ed.), *Early Irish Society* (Dublin, 1954), p. 52.

117 *The Science of History* (Cambridge, 1903).

118 'Secular institutions', pp 52–3.

119 'Irish history and Irish law: I', *Studia Hibernica*, 15 (1975), 7; 'Irish history and Irish law: II', *Studia Hibernica*, 16 (1976), 7.

120 Dafydd Jenkins (ed.), *Celtic Law Papers* (Brussels, 1973).

121 D.A. Binchy, 'Patrick and his biographers – ancient and modern', *Studia Hibernica*, 2 (1962), 7; Francis Shaw, 'Post-mortem on the Second Patrick', *Studies*, 51 (1962), 237.

122 Oxford, 1970.

123 Entry by Michael Kennedy and Thomas Charles-Edwards: *DIB*, i, 531.

124 The UCD *President's Report for 1942–43* also records that Binchy had been made Professor of Roman Law in the Faculty of Canon Law at St Patrick's College, Maynooth: pt. 2, p. 7.

125 Liam Breatnach, *A Companion to the Corpus Iuris Hibernici* (Dublin, 2005).

126 *Corpus Iuris Hibernici*, i, p. xxi.

127 *Collected Papers* (Cambridge, 1911), iii, 506.

128 *Dictionary of National Biography, 1941–1950*, ed. L.G. Wickham Legg and E.T. Williams (Oxford, 1959), p. 564.

129 'MacNeill's study of the ancient Irish laws' in F.X. Martin and F.J. Byrne (eds), *The Scholar Revolutionary: Eoin MacNeill, 1867–1945, and the Making of the New Ireland* (Shannon, 1973), p. 37.

130 Breatnach, *A Companion to the Corpus Iuris Hibernici*, p. 2.

131 'The passing of the old order', in Brian Ó Cuiv (ed.), *The Impact of the Scandinavian Invasion on the Celtic-speaking Peoples, c.800–1100 A.D.* (Dublin, 1975), 119; on this see Dáibhí Ó Cróinín, *Early Medieval Ireland, 400–1200* (London and New York, 1995), pp 260 ff.

132 'Ancient Irish Law', *Ir Jur*, 1 (1966), 84; intro. to Eoin MacNeill, 'Prolegomena to a study of the ancient laws of Ireland', *Ir Jur*, 2 (1967), 106; 'Celtic suretyship, a fossilised Indo-European institution?', *Ir Jur*, 7 (1972), 360.

133 See above, p. 95.

134 D.A. Binchy, 'The law and the universities', *Studies*, 38 (1949), 257.

135 Michael Tierney, Mr Justice Gavan Duffy, Very Revd Denis Canon O'Keeffe, Richard O'Sullivan, KC.

136 See p. 122.

137 William Binchy, 'Values and policies in tort law: the emerging Irish debate' in Thomas Mohr and Jennifer Schweppe (eds), *Thirty Years of Legal Scholarship* (Dublin, 2011), p. 162 n1.

138 'The law and the universities', at 260.

139 *Corpus Iuris Hibernici*, i, introduction, p. vii.

140 Ibid.

141 D.A. Binchy, 'Lawyers and chroniclers' in Brian Ó Cuív (ed.), *Seven Centuries of Irish Learning, 1000–1700* (Cork, 1971), 50 at 59.

142 For the Irish original, see *Annals of Ulster, vol. 3: 1379–1541*, ed. and trans. D. MacCarthy (Dublin, 1895), p. 428. MacCarthy's translation into English differs in a few respects from Binchy's, the one set out here.

143 *Studia Celtica*, 24–5 (1989–90), 153.

144 Governing Body minute book, 1925–1927, 30 Nov. 1926.

145 Ibid., 25 Jan. 1927: Governing Body minute book, 1927–1929, 28 June 1927.

146 Governing Body minute book, 1925–1927, 8 Mar. 1927.

147 NUI Senate minutes, x (1926–1927), 344 (13 May 1927).

148 Above, p. 95.
149 Above, pp 95–6.
150 Statute XIX, Chapter I, ss. 3 and 1.
151 Public Services (Temporary Economies) Act 1933 (No. 37 of 1933), s. 13; Governing Body minute book, 1933–1935, 4 May 1934.
152 Memorandum on the Public Services (Temporary Economies) Bill 1933, presented by Representatives of the Staff of three University Colleges (copy pasted in to UCD, Governing Body minute book, 1931–1933, 27 June 1933); Governing Body minute book, 1931–1933, 27 June 1933, recording the meeting with the Minister on 19 May.
153 The new section 13 thus prescribed: Where a grant is made annually, under statute or otherwise, out of public moneys to a University or University College, there shall be deducted from the amount of such grant which falls to be made in the current financial year such sum not exceeding five per cent of the amount of such grant, as the Minister shall determine.
154 Memorandum on the Temporary Economies Bill (n. 152 above), p. 7.
155 Eamon de Valera.
156 Memorandum on the Temporary Economies Bill, p. 9.
157 Ibid., p. 11.
158 A.D. Codling to Dr Coffey, 14 Mar. 1934: Governing Body minute book, 1933–1935, 22 Mar. 1934.
159 A.D. Codling to Dr Coffey, 13 Jan. 1934: Governing Body minute book, 1933–1935, 30 Jan. 1934.
160 Opinion of M.J. Ryan, KC: Governing Body minute book, 1933–1935, 30 Jan. 1934.
161 No. 27 of 1934.
162 Governing Body minute book, 1933–1935, 4 May 1934.
163 Governing Body minute book, 1933–1935, 28 June 1934.
164 Ibid.
165 Governing Body minute book, 1933–1935, 19 July 1934.
166 No. 35 of 1929.
167 NUI Senate minutes, xiv (1933–1935), 63 (7 Dec. 1933).
168 NUI Senate minutes, xiv, 307 (7 Feb. 1935); xv, 3 (23 May 1935).
169 NUI Senate minutes, xv, 300 (22 Oct. 1936).
170 NUI Senate minutes, xvi, 47 (14 Jan. 1937).
171 NUI Senate minutes, xvi, 49 (14 Jan. 1937), 91 (8 Apr. 1937).
172 NUI Senate minutes, xvii (1938–1939), 69 (27 Oct. 1938).
173 NUI Senate minutes, xxii, 200–01 (12 Jan. 1939).
174 NUI Senate minutes, xviii (1939–1941), 130 (18 Apr. 1940).
175 Above, p. 107.
176 Donal McCartney, *UCD: A National Idea – the History of University College Dublin* (Dublin, 1999), pp 127–33.
177 McCartney, *UCD: A National Idea*, pp 128–9.
178 Governing Body minute book, 1937–1939, 26 Jan. 1938.
179 Ibid., 21 June 1938; see, too, Governing Body minute book, 1935–1937, 23 Feb., 27 Apr. 1937.
180 Ryan to Coffey, 28 Dec. 1938: Governing Body minute book, 1937–1939, 30 Dec. 1938; Governing Body minute book, 1939–1940, 10 Nov. 1939, 25 June 1940.
181 Ryan to Coffey, 20 Mar. 1940: Governing Body minute book, 1939–1940, 28 Mar. 1940.
182 Above, p. 109.
183 Governing Body minute book, 1939–1940, 28 Mar. 1940.
184 Ibid., 9 Apr. 1940.
185 Ibid.
186 Ibid.
187 Governing Body minute book, 1939–1940, 30 Apr. 1940.
188 NUI Senate minutes, xiv (1941–1942), 332 (16 July 1942).
189 Governing Body minute book, 1937–1939, 14 July 1939; Governing Body minute book, 1939–1940, 31 Oct. 1939.
190 Governing Body minute book, 1943–1947, 14 Dec. 1944.
191 Ibid., 1 May 1945.
192 Governing Body minute book, 1943–1947; Governing Body minute book, 25 Mar. 1947–20 Nov. 1950, 24 June 1947.
193 Ibid., 5 Apr. 1949.
194 *Kirkwood Hackett* v. *Tierney* [1952] IR 185.
195 Governing Body minute book, 1947–1950, 12 Dec. 1949.
196 Ibid.

197 As were Cecil Lavery SC, the Attorney-general, J. Healy SC, and T.F. Bacon, BL.
198 Governing Body minute book, 19 Dec. 1950–20 Oct. 1953, 26 June 1951.
199 'The Irish university question', *Studies*, 51 (1962), 208 at 233.
200 Ibid., at 233–4.
201 Governing Body minute book, 1929–1931, 15 Oct. 1929 (£125 per annum to both Ryan and Clery).
202 Governing Body minute book, 1931–1933, 11 Apr. 1933 (£225 each to Binchy and Ryan for Nov. 1932–Sept. 1933).
203 Governing Body minute book, 29 June 1943–13 Mar. 1947, 15 Oct. 1946.
204 UCD Statute XXXVII; Governing Body minute book, 25 Mar. 1947–21 Nov. 1950, 25 Mar. 1947.
205 At pp 55–7.
206 Finlay, 'The class of "43"', pp 17–18.
207 NUI Senate minutes, vii (1919–1920), 92 (24 Oct. 1919).
208 NUI Senate minutes, vii, 388 (17 Dec. 1920); viii (1921–1922), 19 (11 Mar. 1921).
209 Edward MacLysaght, 'The railway problem: facts to be faced', *Studies*, 21 (1932), 353; Patrick McGilligan, ibid., 360.
210 *DIB*, v, 1038. What might be termed 'bluster' on McGilligan's part in his contributions to the fraught debates on ending the appeal to the Privy Council could lead to him being viewed in a somewhat different light: see Thomas Mohr, 'The Privy Council appeal as a minority safeguard for the Protestant community of the Irish Free State, 1922–1935', *NILQ*, 63 (2012), 365.
211 Academic Council minute book, 12 Jan. 1932–24 June 1941, 4 Oct. 1934.
212 Ibid.
213 Finlay, 'The class of "43"', p. 18.
214 Ibid.
215 Governing Body minute book, 1943–1947, 15 Oct. 1946; UCD Statute XXXVII; Governing Body minute book, 25 Mar. 1947–21 Nov. 1950, 25 Mar. 1947.
216 Governing Body minute book, 1956–1959, 17 Dec. 1957.
217 Ibid., 15 Apr. 1958.
218 Governing Body minute book, 1959–1961, 24 June 1959.
219 Ibid., 22 Oct. 1959; *Report of the Board of Visitors – National University of Ireland, August 1959* (see, above, p. 130), passim.
220 Governing Body minute book, 1947–1950, 18 Nov. 1947; *Irish Times*, 28 Jan. 1948.
221 *Irish Times*, 23 Feb. 1948.
222 Donal Barrington, 'The Constitution in the courts', *Administration*, 35 (1987), 110. See, too, *Irish Independent*, 3 Mar. 1988.
223 Macaulay to Randall, 23 May 1857, reproduced in the *Southern Literary Messenger*, 24 Mar. 1860.
224 *Administration*, 35 (1987), at 110.
225 *In re Art. 26 of the Constitution and Offences against the State (Amendment) Bill, 1940* [1940] IR 471.
226 It is worth noting that the Supreme Court's decision was a majority one: see [1940] IR at 475, per Sullivan C.J.
227 See the item under the heading 'Cula aris' [Backing off again] in the *Irish Press*, 24 Feb. 1948.
228 McGilligan also sat on the committee that drew up the course structure for the College's Diploma in Public Administration, introduced in 1942; see Academic Council minutes, 1941–1946, 11 Dec. 1941.
229 This passage is repeated in the 2nd ed. of *The Irish Constitution* (Dublin, 1984), pp xxviii–xxix.
230 *O'Donovan* v. *Attorney General* [1961] IR 114.
231 No. 33 of 1959.
232 Kelly, *The Irish Constitution*, 2nd ed., p. 107. And see *O'Donovan* v. *AG* [1961] IR at 116–117.
233 [1961] IR at 134.
234 [1961] IR at 149.
235 Many years after his resignation from UCD and his eventual retirement, Binchy was also to receive an honorary degree from NUI.
236 Above, p. 51.
237 NUI Senate minutes, xviii (1939–1941), 65 (11 Jan. 1940).
238 NUI Senate minutes, xviii, 94 (7 Mar. 1940).
239 NUI Senate minutes, xviii, 123 (11 Apr. 1940).
240 NUI Senate minutes, xviii (11 July 1940).
241 Governing Body minute book, 1950–1953, 27 Jan. 1953.
242 E.g., in connection with a Governing Body election – 5 guineas: Governing

Body minute book, 1953–1956, 31 Jan. 1956.

243 Governing Body minute book, 1950–1953, 26 June 1951.

244 Governing Body minute book, 1943–1947, 14, 28 Mar. 1944.

245 G.J. Hand, 'MacNeill and the Boundary Commission' in F.X. Martin and F.J. Byrne (ed.), *The Scholar Revolutionary: Eoin MacNeill and the Making of the New Ireland* (Shannon, 1970), p. 199.

246 *Ir Jur*, 1 (1966), iii.

247 Tadhg F. MacFirbheoigh to James O'Neill, 3 Nov. 1928: Academic Council minute book, 1915–1931, 5 Nov. 1928.

248 James O'Neill to Registrar, 5 Nov. 1928: Academic Council minute book, 1915–1931, 5 Nov. 1928.

249 Ibid.

250 Academic Council minute book, 1915–1931, 12 Dec. 1929, 6 Feb. 1930.

251 T.F. O'Higgins, *A Double Life* (Dublin, 1996), pp 48–9, an excerpt reprinted here by kind permission of the family.

252 NUI Senate minutes, xvi (1936–1938), 301, 13 Jan. 1938.

253 NUI Senate minutes, xix (1941–1942), 257, 5 Mar. 1942.

254 Academic Council minutes, 3 Oct. 1941–10 Oct. 1946, 11 Dec. 1941.

255 *Irish Times*, 3 Dec. 1943.

256 8 (no. 8) (1925), 466.

257 7 (no. 4) (1928), 1453.

258 *Irish Times*, 29 Apr. 1946, 19 Apr. 1947. In the same year 1946, Justice published an article entitled 'Droit anglais' in the *Journal des Tribunaux* in Brussels. At earlier stages in his career Justice had served in Cairo, Hamburg, Danzig and Berlin: *Irish Press*, 10 Apr. 1946.

259 *The Independent*, 7 July 1990; *The Guardian*, 10 July 1990.

260 *The Guardian*, 31 May 1999.

261 Academic Council minutes, 1941–1946, 12 Mar. 1941.

262 Thomas Finlay, 'The class of "43"' in *UCD Law Alumni Journal*, 1 no. 1 (May 1999), 18.

263 Ibid.

4 CHALLENGES AND A MAJOR REFORM: THE LAW SCHOOL, 1945–67

1 'The law and the universities', *Studies*, 38 (1949), 257–74.

2 Ibid., 257–65.

3 Above, p. 86.

4 *Studies*, 38 (1949), 257.

5 Ibid., 260.

6 Ibid.

7 Ibid.

8 Ibid.

9 Ibid., at 258.

10 Ibid., at 259.

11 Ibid.

12 Ibid.

13 At p. 258.

14 Ibid.

15 Ibid.

16 At p. 260.

17 At p. 261.

18 At p. 252.

19 Ibid.

20 Ibid.

21 Ibid.

22 P. 263, n.2.

23 P. 264.

24 P. 263.

25 P. 264.

26 P. 265.

27 Quoted, p. 265. Binchy omits any reference. The quotation is taken from Newman's *The Idea of a University* – see the 1976 edition by I.T. Ker (Oxford), at p. 145. Here the list of professions after 'physician' embraces 'a good landlord, a man of business, a soldier, an engineer, a chemist, a geologist, an antiquarian'.

28 *Studies*, 38 (1949), at 265.

29 Menander, *Monostichoi* 2: Siegfried Jaekel (ed.), *Menandri Sententiae* (Leipzig, 1964), p. 33.

30 P. 272.

31 See at p. 271.

32 At p. 268.

33 At p. 267.

34 At p. 268.

35 At p. 268.

36 At p. 269.

37 Ibid.

38 At pp 269–70.

39 At p. 270.

40 V.T.H. Delany, 'Legal studies in Trinity College, Dublin, since the Foundation', *Hermathena*, 89 (1957), 3, at 13.

41 *JSPTL*, 1 (1949), 258; see, too, L.C.B. Gower, 'English legal training', *Modern L. Rev.*, 13 (1960), 137.

42 Academic Council minute book, 14 Dec. 1951–9 Dec. 1958, 5 Nov. 1953.

43 Faculty of Law minute book, quoted in *Report of the Board of Visitors: National University of Ireland, August 1959*, p. 5.

44 The above synopsis follows that furnished in the *Report of the Board of Visitors: National University of Ireland, August 1959*, at pp 5–6.
45 Commission on Higher Education, 1960–1967, *II Report, Volume I*, ch. 11: 'Legal Education'.
46 Ibid., p. 305.
47 Ibid.
48 Ibid., p. 306.
49 Ibid., p. 303.
50 Academic Council minute book, 1951–1958, 5 Nov. 1953.
51 See p. 155.
52 See the *Calendars for 1954–1955, 1955–1956, 1956–1957*.
53 There is a brief allusion to this Visitation in a footnote to Mr Justice Henchy's summarised evidence to the Commission on Higher Education, 1960–1967, *Report, II, vol. I*, at p. 304.
54 Mr Justice Ó Dálaigh of the Supreme Court, Mr Justice Dixon of the High Court, and Judge Michael Binchy of the Circuit Court.
55 E.g., Professor P.J. Gallagher, Law, UCG and Professor M.M. Shea, German, UCG: *Report of Board of Visitors*, Appendix D (1) and (2).
56 *Report of the Board of Visitors – National University of Ireland, August 1959*, pp 12–13.
57 Appendix C in the *Report of the Board of Visitors* lists the 48 Professors and Lecturers who as a consequence of Statutes CV and CVII became members of the entire University's Faculty of Law.
58 *Report of Board of Visitors 1959*, Appendix D (2).
59 See above, p. 122.
60 UCD Statute XXXVII.
61 Governing Body minute book, 25 Mar. 1947–21 Nov. 1950, 24 June 1947.
62 Academic Council minute book, 7 Nov. 1946–1 Nov. 1951, 12 Dec. 1946.
63 Ibid.
64 Ibid.
65 Governing Body minute book, 29 June 1943–18 Mar. 1947, 17 Dec. 1946.
66 See Governing Body minute book, 25 Mar. 1947–21 Nov. 1950, 27 Jan. 1948.
67 Ibid., 25 May 1948.
68 Donnelly had had experience of teaching Constitutional Law for the Diploma in Public Administration; he was to become President of the District Court.
69 Later a judge of the High and Supreme Courts. He was to be appointed an Assistant in the Law School, and his actions precipitated the Visitation of 1959–1960: see p. 138.
70 See *King's Inns Barristers, 1868–2004*, p. 226.
71 Ibid., p. 279.
72 Governing Body minute book, 1947–1950, 14 Oct. 1948.
73 Ibid., 1 Feb. 1949.
74 Governing Body minute book, 25 Mar. 1947–21 Nov. 1950, 21 Nov. 1950.
75 Governing Body minute book, 19 Dec. 1950–20 Oct. 1953, 26 June 1951, 27 June 1952, 30 June 1953; Governing Body minute book, 1953–1956, 11 May 1954, 30 June 1955.
76 Governing Body minute book, 1950–1953, 14 Oct. 1952.
77 Ibid., 27 Jan. 1953.
78 Governing Body minute book, 1 Dec. 1953–26 June 1956, 11 May 1954.
79 Ibid., 15 Oct. 1954, 26 June 1956.
80 Governing Body minute book, 1953–1956, 15 Oct. 1954.
81 Governing Body minute book, 1953–1956, 15 Oct. 1954.
82 Ibid., 14 Dec. 1954.
83 Governing Body minute book, 1956–1959, 28 June 1957.
84 See above, p. 130.
85 Kelly had recently obtained his doctorate in Heidelberg. In his first book, *Princeps Iudex*, published in Weimar in 1957, he is described as an Assistant at UCD.
86 Governing Body minute book, 1956–1957, 28 June 1957.
87 Governing Body minute book, 1956–1959, 15 Oct. 1957.
88 Governing Body minute book, 1953–1956, 29 May 1956.
89 Governing Body minute book, 3 Mar. 1959–31 Jan. 1961, 24 June 1959.
90 Governing Body minute book, 1959–1961, 18 Oct. 1960.
91 Governing Body minute book, 14 Mar. 1961–22 Jan. 1963, 16 May 1961.
92 Governing Body minute book, 1959–1961, 24 June 1959.
93 Ibid.
94 Governing Body minute book, 1959–1961, 22 Oct. 1959.

95 Ibid.
96 Ibid.
97 Courts of Justice Act, 1924 (No. 10 of 1924), s.12. The retirement age in question has recently been set at 70: Courts and Court Officers Act 1995 (No. 31 of 1995), s.47.
98 Governing Body minute book, 1959–1961, 15 Dec. 1959.
99 *Report of Board of Visitors University College Dublin 1960*, Pr 5499, appendix.
100 Governing Body minute book, 1961–1963, 14 Mar. 1961.
101 Ibid., 16 May 1961.
102 See above, p. 30.
103 Governing Body minute book, 1961–1963, 16 May 1961.
104 Ibid.
105 Governing Body minute book, 1961–1963, 14 July 1961.
106 For the correspondence between J.P. MacHale and Wilmot on the issue, see ibid., 21 Nov. 1961.
107 Governing Body minute book, 1961–1963, 17 Apr. 1962.
108 Ibid.
109 Governing Body minute book, 1961–1963, 21 Nov. 1961.
110 Ibid.
111 Ibid.
112 Ibid.
113 See further Donal McCartney, 'University College Dublin', in Tom Dunne (ed.), *The National University of Ireland, 1908–2008, Centenary Essays* (Dublin, 2008), p. 87, where, however, this particular bone of contention is not rehearsed.
114 Above, p. 134.
115 Kenny to Tierney, 18 May 1959, in Governing Body minute book, 3 Mar. 1959–31 Jan. 1961, 24 June 1959.
116 Governing Body minute book, 16 Oct. 1956–12 Feb. 1959, 28 June 1957. For exchanges on the question in 1956, see McCartney, *UCD – A National Idea*, p. 281.
117 Governing Body minute book, 1956–1959, 28 June 1957.
118 MacHale to Kenny, 23 Mar. 1959: Governing Body minute book, 1959–1961, 24 June 1959. This letter is also reproduced in the *Report of the Board of Visitors* (below, n.125) at p. 5.
119 Ibid.
120 Kenny to MacHale, 23 May 1959: ibid.
121 In fact, this seems to have been a proposed UCC College lectureship in Russian language and literature: John A. Murphy, 'University College Cork', in Tom Dunne (ed.), *The National University of Ireland 1908–2008, Centenary Essays* (Dublin, 2008), p. 47 at p. 53 and at p. 339 n.32.
122 Governing Body minute book, 1959–1961, 24 June 1959.
123 Ibid.
124 Governing Body minute book, 1959–1961, 22 Oct. 1959. Henchy, McGilligan's colleague in the Law Faculty, at these hearings was to support Kenny's point of view.
125 *Report of the Board of Visitors to University College, 1960*, Pr. 5499.
126 University College Dublin Act 1960 (No.16 of 1960).
127 *Dáil Debates*, vol. 181, col. 1090–1118 (3 May 1960).
128 Ibid., at col. 1118.
129 Above, p. 138.
130 John Kenny, 'The Visitation in University College, Dublin', *Science and Freedom*, 17 (Dec. 1960), 7–15.
131 Kenny, 'Visitation', 7–8.
132 Ibid., 10.
133 Ibid., 11. The *Report of the Board of Visitors*, at p. 2, contains these statistics as well.
134 Kenny, 'Visitation', 12–13.
135 Ibid., p. 15. The records are not exactly clear that this did *not* take place, but such could well be the correct inference to draw.
136 Kenny, 'Visitation', 14.
137 Ibid., 15.
138 Séamus Henchy, 'The Visitor of the National University', *University Review*, 2 (1961), 16.
139 McCartney, *UCD – A National Idea*, ch. 8.
140 Ibid., p. 282.
141 McCartney, *UCD – A National Idea*, p. 282.
142 Ibid., p. 283.
143 Both Finlay and Kenny were paid extra as Assistants for teaching Property and Equity in the sessions 1960–1961 and 1961–1962.
144 Kelly was concurrently, from 1961, a Fellow of Trinity College, Oxford.
145 Governing Body minute book, 12 Mar. 1963–10 Mar. 1965, 25 June 1963.

146 Ibid., 16 Oct. 1963.
147 Ibid., 16 Oct. and 17 Dec. 1963.
148 Governing Body minute book, 8 June 1965–24 May 1966, 16 Nov. 1965.
149 Governing Body minute book, 1963–1965, 11 Mar. 1964.
150 Ibid., 10 Mar. 1965.
151 Governing Body minute book, 1965–1966, 8 June 1965.
152 Ibid., 24 May 1966.
153 Governing Body minute book, 28 June 1966–29 June 1967, 24 Jan. 1967.
154 Ibid., 14 Mar. 1967.
155 Governing Body minute book, 17 Oct. 1967–15 Oct. 1968, 17 Oct. 1967.
156 See my preface to the John Kelly commemorative volume of the *Irish Jurist*, 25–7 (1990–2), v–vi.
157 Governing Body minute book, 8 June 1965–24 May 1966, 24 Feb. 1966.
158 See *King's Inns Barristers, 1868–2004*, p. 274 (sub nom. Ó hInnse, Séamus).
159 *Miscellaneous Irish Annals, AD 1114–1437*, ed. with trans. and index Séamus Ó hInnse (Dublin, 1947).
160 Above, p. 133.
161 'The Communist theory of law', *Studies*, 46 (1957), 411. The choice of the topic could have been inspired by the controversy some years earlier over the L & H's debate on the motion, 'The ideals of the Communist Manifesto are worthy of humanity': see Governing Body minute book, 25 Mar. 1947–21 Nov. 1950, 1 Feb. 1949.
162 Séamus Henchy, 'The Visitor of the National University', *University Review*, 2:7 (Autumn 1961), 16.
163 *Modern Law Review*, 25 (1962), 544.
164 Governing Body minute book, 14 Mar. 1961–22 Jan. 1963, 16 Jan. 1962. Henchy's appointment to the Bench took effect on 15 Jan.
165 Governing Body minute book, 1 Dec. 1953–26 June 1956, 21 Feb. 1956.
166 Above, p. 130.
167 *Report of Board of Visitors – National University of Ireland, August 1959*.
168 Above, p. 138.
169 McCartney, *UCD, A National Idea*, p. 301.
170 *Irish Times*, 11 April 2009.
171 Gerard Hogan, 'The judicial thought and prose of Mr Justice Seamus Henchy', *Ir Jur*, 46 (2011), 96.
172 [1984] IR 36.
173 Criminal Law Amendment Act 1935 (No. 6 of 1935).
174 [1974] IR 284 at 325.
175 5 Geo. IV, c. 83.
176 The phrase is Mr Justice Hogan's: *Ir Jur*, 46 (2011), 96 at 99.
177 *King* v. *Attorney General* [1981] IR 233 at 257.
178 *Dillon* v. *Minister for Posts and Telegraphs*, Supreme Court, 3 June 1981.
179 S R & O 1939, no. 202, art. 6, 1 (2).
180 [1986] IR 13.
181 [1986] IR at 23–4.
182 *Ir Jur*, 46 (2011), 96.
183 Governing Body minute book, 25 Mar. 1947–21 Nov. 1950, 21 Nov. 1950; Governing Body minute book, 1 Dec. 1959–26 June 1956, 29 May 1956.
184 Governing Body minute book, 14 Mar. 1961–22 Jan. 1963, 17 Apr. 1962: above, p. 137.
185 London and Maryland, 1954.
186 Ibid., p.v.
187 S.Z. Ehler, *Twenty Centuries of Church and State* (Maryland, 1957); *President's Report, 1963–1964, Academic*, p. 23.
188 Ehler, *Twenty Centuries of Church and State*, p. 149.
189 *Capuchin Annual 1965*, p. 217.
190 *Capuchin Annual 1966*, p. 53.
191 *Irish Times*, 25 Oct. 1966.
192 'Millennium Poloniae; *Capuchin Annual 1967*, p. 314.
193 *Capuchin Annual 1971*, p. 183.
194 Ehler, *Twenty Centuries of Church and State*, p. 67.
195 Diarmaid MacCulloch, *Reformation: Europe's House Divided, 1490–1700* (London, 2003), p. 334.
196 Governing Body minute book, 14 Mar. 1961–22 Jan. 1963, 20 Mar. 1962.
197 Governing Body minute book, 12 Mar. 1963–10 Mar. 1965, 12 Mar. 1963.
198 *President's Report, 1958–1959, Academic*, p. 14.
199 'On applying the modern term "state" to the middle ages', in J.A. Watt, J.B. Morrall and F.X. Martin (eds), *Medieval Studies presented to Aubrey Gwynn SJ* (Dublin, 1961), p. 492.
200 *President's Report, 1959–1960, Academic*, p. 32; *President's Report, 1963–1964, Academic*, p. 23.

201 Governing Body minute book, 14 Mar. 1961–22 Jan. 1963, 18 Dec. 1962.
202 *President's Report, 1964–1965, Academic*, p. 21.
203 *President's Report, 1970–1971, Academic*, p. 27.
204 *Le Monde*, 9–10 May 1965.
205 See its obituary of Ehler in the autumn issue 1972, and see, too, *Irish Times*, 27 May 1972.
206 Governing Body minute book, 1961–1963, 29 June 1961.
207 Governing Body minute book, 1963–1965, 30 June 1964.
208 *King's Inns Barristers, 1868–2004*, p. 185.
209 Governing Body minute book, 8 June 1965–24 May 1966, 24 Feb. 1966.
210 See Governing Body minute book, 1966–1967, 14 Mar. 1967.
211 Finlay to Hogan, 15 June 1967: ibid., 24 June 1967.
212 Governing Body minute book, 17 Oct. 1967–15 Oct. 1968, 17 Oct. 1967.
213 Charles Lysaght, obituary of W. D. Finlay, *Sunday Independent*, 17 Oct. 2010.
214 *Report of President, 1985–1986*, p. 167.
215 In 1964 he was also to travel to Washington, DC for a meeting of the Canon Law Society of America: *President's Report, 1963–1964, Academic*, p. 24.
216 *The Jurist* (Washington DC, Catholic Univ. of America, 1960).
217 See *President's Report, 1963–1964, Academic*, p. 23.
218 Cahir Davitt, 'Some aspects of the Constitution and the law in relation to matrimony': *Studies*, 57 (1968), 6.
219 Ibid., at 29.
220 Ibid., at 30–1.
221 *King's Inns Barristers, 1868–2004*, p. 297.
222 *King's Inns Barristers, 1868–2004*, p. 218; *DIB*, v, 82.
223 Above, p. 143.
224 G.H., 'Obituary: Professor John M. Kelly: a personal recollection', *Irish Law Times* (n.s.), 9 (1991), 68.
225 See *Ir Jur*, 23 (1988), 1; *President's Report for 1990–1991*, p. 246.
226 Above, pp 161ff, 164ff.
227 *Dáil Debates*, vol. 311, col.1107: 14 Feb. 1979. See further E.G. Hall, *The Superior Courts of Law: 'Official' Law Reporting in Ireland, 1866–2006* (Dublin, 2007), p. 339.
228 See, for example, John O'Dowd, 'John Kelly, politician and scholar', *Studies*, 100 (2011), 455.
229 *The Independent*, 26 Jan. 1991.
230 *The Times*, 26 Jan. 1991.
231 Ibid.
232 *Ir Jur*, 2 (1967), 279.
233 *Ir Jur*, 18 (1983), 259.
234 *Dublin Univ LJ*, 10 (1988), 5.
235 Weimar, 1957. It is reviewed by J. Gaudemet in *Tijdschrift voor Rechtsgeschiedenis*, 27 (1959), 99.
236 *Princeps Iudex*, p. 1, n.1.
237 John Boyle, *Matters of Honour* (London, 1964); see above, p. 164.
238 London, 1966.
239 *Roman Litigation*, p. 29.
240 Ibid.
241 Ibid., p. 8, n.3.
242 Ibid., pp 56–61. Hardly a surprise of course to those familiar with Robert Harris's portrait of Cicero in his two novels, *Imperium* and *Lustrum*.
243 *Roman Litigation*, p. 86.
244 D.E.C. Yale, *LQR*, 83 (1967), 458.
245 P.W. Duff, 1967 *Camb LJ* 124.
246 D.A. Binchy, *Studies*, 55 (1966), 448 at 450.
247 Ibid.
248 For Binchy's views on his own role as a teacher of Roman law, see above, p. 96. There is a long 12-page review too by Giovanni Pugliese in *Tijdschrift voor Rechtsgeschiedenis*, 35 (1967), 291.
249 Wolfgang Kunkel, *Römische Rechtsgeschichte*, 6th ed. (Köln and Graz, 1971): idem, *An Introduction to Roman Legal and Constitutional History*, 2nd ed., trans. J.M. Kelly (London, 1973).
250 Oxford, 1976.
251 *Studies in the Civil Judicature of the Roman Republic*, p. 136.
252 Peter Stein, 1977 *Camb LJ* 390.
253 Alan Watson, *LQR*, 93 (1977), 149.
254 Dublin, 1961.
255 Dublin, 1967.
256 (1864) 17 ICLR 1.
257 (1883) 14 LR Ir 105.
258 [1898] 2 IR 167.
259 1937 Constitution, Article 40.6.1. ii.
260 *Studies*, 51 (1962), 201.
261 Dublin, 1980.
262 The 3rd and 4th editions (Dublin, 1994 and 2003 respectively).

263 Eoin Carolan, 'Irish constitutional scholarship in review: considering J.M. Kelly's *The Irish Constitution*', in Thomas Mohr and Jennifer Schwepppe (eds), *Thirty Years of Legal Scholarship* (Dublin, 2011), p. 321.
264 Ibid.
265 Ibid.
266 Ibid., p. 331.
267 Oxford, 1992.
268 Gerard Quinn, *Ir Jur*, 28–30 (1993–6), 408.
269 D.J. Ibbetson, *LQR*, 109 (1993), 320 at 321.
270 *Irish Times*, 16 May 1992.
271 John Boyle, *Matters of Honour* (London, 1964). Kelly's preference for a title had been *Heidelberg man*: Ronan Keane in his foreword to Kelly's *A Short History of Western Legal Theory* (Oxford, 1992), at viii.
272 Ibid., p. 44.
273 Ibid., p. 127. Patrick Leigh Fermor was a good deal more fortunate in his real-life choice of accommodation – the Red Ox Inn – run by Herr and Frau Spengel in the Heidelberg of 1933: See *A Time of Gifts* (London, 1977), pp 56–7, 60–1.
274 *Matters of Honour*, pp 61–3.
275 Ibid., p. 124.
276 Ibid., p. 177.
277 Ibid., ch. 33.
278 Ibid., p. 190.
279 Ibid., p. 42.
280 Ibid., p. 110.
281 Lalage and Phryne are two women idolised in the poems of Horace (*Carmina*, I. 22. 10, 23, II. 5. 16 (Lalage); *Ep*. 14. 16 (Phryne)). In his Sabine wood Horace would sing of 'his' Lalage, whilst roaming free; he loved her sweet laughter and sweet talk. Phryne, the courtesan, sounds somewhat different. Not content with one lover, she yet filled him with lustful yearnings: me libertina neque uno contenta Phryne macerat.
282 *Matters of Honour*, p. 192.
283 Ibid., p. 111.
284 Ibid., p. 122.
285 Ibid., p. 180.
286 Ibid., p. 206.
287 John Kelly, *The Polling of the Dead* (Dublin, 1993).
288 Ibid., p. 165.
289 Ibid., p. 2.
290 Ibid., p. 13.
291 Ibid., p. 1.
292 Ibid.
293 [1949] IR 45. For Goertz's dramatic suicide, see the *Irish Times*, 24 May 1947.
294 [1954] IR 319.
295 *The Polling of the Dead*, pp 152, 156.
296 Ibid., p. 162.
297 Ibid., p. 165.
298 Ibid., p. 156.
299 Matthew Cobb, *The Resistance: The French Fight against the Nazis* (London, 2009), ch.8.
300 *DIB*, v, 82 at 84.
301 *Belling the Cat: Selected Speeches and Articles of John Kelly*, ed. John Flanagan (Dublin, 1992).

5 MERGER TALK AND FURTHER GROWTH: THE LAW SCHOOL, 1967–2000

1 *Report of Commission on Higher Education 1960–67*, vol. I, p. 301.
2 Ibid., p. 308.
3 Ibid.
4 Ibid.
5 Ibid.
6 This short excursus on the importance of Constitutional Law is redolent of the views previously expressed by Binchy. See above, ch. 4.
7 Ibid., p. 304.
8 Ibid., p. 306.
9 The episode is excellently described by Donal McCartney: See his *UCD: a National Idea: the History of University College, Dublin* (Dublin, 1999), ch. 9.
10 *Report of Commission on Higher Education*, vol. 1, pp 415–17.
11 The broad outline of what was to transpire roughly follows McCartney's account: *UCD: a National Idea*, ch. 9.
12 Faculty of Law minute book, 1948–1970, 16 Oct. 1967.
13 The proposal that this should be done emanated from the then dean, John Kelly, and seconded by Professor Ehler.
14 Faculty of Law minute book, 1948–1970, 16 Oct. 1967.
15 Faculty of Law minute book, 1948–1970, 11 Mar. 1968. This was in the form of a resolution proposed by the Dean, John Kelly, and seconded by Dr Hand.

16 Faculty of Law minute book, 1948–1970, 23 July 1968.
17 Faculty of Law minute book, 1948–1970, 30 Apr. 1970.
18 Faculty of Law minute book, 1970–1986, 5 Dec. 1972.
19 For the gift of the Chief Baron Palles library, see above, Ch. 2 and Ch. 6.
20 Governing Body minute book, 30 May 1972–2 Mar. 1973, 30 Jan. 1973.
21 Governing Body minute book, 27 Mar. 1973–12 Feb. 1974, 16 Oct. 1973.
22 45 BCL degrees were conferred by UCD in 1965–6. That number had shot up to 113 for 1975–6.
23 McCartney, *UCD: a National Idea*, p. 341.
24 Ibid., p. 342.
25 Governing Body minute book, 17 Oct. 1967–15 Oct. 1968, 30 Jan. 1968.
26 Ibid., 19 Mar. 1968.
27 Governing Body minute book, 19 Nov. 1968–21 Oct. 1969, 19 Nov. 1968.
28 Ibid.
29 See, e.g., *Irish Times*, 11 Jan. 1969.
30 Governing Body minute book, 19 Nov. 1968–21 Oct. 1969, 11 Mar. 1969.
31 Governing Body minute book, 19 Nov. 1968–21 Oct. 1969, 1 Oct. 1969.
32 Faculty of Law minute book, 1948–1970, 31 Aug. 1967.
33 Ibid.
34 Governing Body minute book, 17 Oct. 1967–15 Oct. 1968, 30 Jan. 1968.
35 Above, p. 130.
36 See McCartney, *UCD: a National Idea*, pp 384–5.
37 McCartney, *UCD: a National Idea*, p. 385.
38 See, too, Governing Body minute book, 18 Oct. 1981–15 Dec. 1982, 29 June, 15 Oct. 1982.
39 Osborough and Niflis.
40 The shock the interruption occasioned to the Rt. Revd Monsignor John Horgan, the Professor of Metaphysics, who sat on the Faculty, left an indelible impression on one of the gate-crashers.
41 Faculty of Law minutes, 17 Oct. 1968.
42 Ibid., 6 Dec. 1968.
43 The need for reform, given the small size of the teaching team in Law, was regularly stressed: ibid., 25 May 1970.
44 Ibid., 1 June 1971.
45 Faculty of Law minutes, 14 Jan., 29 Feb., 11 June, 12 Oct., 2 Nov. 1972.
46 Faculty of Law minutes, 10 Apr. 1975. This was the meeting at which Osborough was elected dean.
47 Faculty of Law minutes, 6 Dec. 1968, 22 Apr. 1969.
48 McCartney, *UCD: a National Idea*, pp 348–9.
49 Faculty of Law minutes, 18 Oct. 1968.
50 Governing Body minute book, 30 May 1972–2 Mar. 1973, 30 May 1972.
51 Faculty of Law minute book, 26 Jan. 1971–14 Nov. 1986, 29 Feb. 1972.
52 Faculty of Law minute book, 1948–1971, 15 June, 7 Oct. 1963, 15 July 1965.
53 Governing Body minute book, 15 Oct. 1976–22 Nov. 1977, 19 May 1977.
54 Governing Body minute book, 13 May 1975–22 June 1976, 13 May, 21 Oct. 1975, 11 May 1976; minute book, 20 Dec. 1977 – 6 Feb. 1979, 27 June 1978.
55 That same year he was to take up a chair in the University of Birmingham on leaving Florence.
56 Governing Body minute book, 27 Mar. 1973–12 Feb. 1974, 27 Mar., 15 May 1973; minute book, 13 May 1975–22 June 1976, 18 Nov. 1975; minute book, 15 Oct. 1976 – 22 Nov. 1977, 28 June 1977.
57 Governing Body minute book, 19 Nov. 1968–21 Oct. 1969, 30 June 1969.
58 As in the case of Jim Dooge, Professor of Civil Engineering, who became Cathaoirleach of the Seanad in 1973: see Governing Body minute book, 27 Mar. 1973–12 Feb. 1974, 28 June 1973.
59 Governing Body minute book, 19 Nov. 1968–21 Oct. 1969, 20 June 1969, reporting the decision of the Committee on 11 June.
60 Governing Body minute book, 1965–1969, 20 June 1969.
61 Governing Body minute book, 25 Nov. 1969–20 Apr. 1971, 18 Dec. 1969.
62 See, e.g., Governing Body minute book, 20 Dec. 1977–6 Feb. 1979, 17 Oct. 1978.
63 UCD, Statute CXIV, Ch. I (1981).
64 UCD, Statute CXIV, Ch. I.
65 *The Origins of the English Legal Profession* (Oxford, 1992).
66 *The Making of the Common Law* (London and Rio Grande, 1992).
67 *The Earliest English Law Reports, vol. I* (1995), *vol. II* (1996), *vol. III* (2005), *vol. IV* (2007). These are, respectively, Selden Society volumes 111, 112, 122 and 123.

68 Faculty of Law minutes, 23 May 1991.
69 Faculty of Law minutes, 16 Oct. 1991.
70 Faculty of Law minutes, 20 Nov. 1991.
71 Faculty of Law minutes, 16 Oct. 1991.
72 Wilkie Collins, *Man and Wife* (Oxford, 2008), p. 297. *Man and Wife* was first published in 1870.
73 Faculty of Law minutes, 12 May 1999, 10 May 2000.
74 Governing Body minute book, 6 Mar. 1979–25 Mar. 1980, 13 Mar. 1979.
75 Governing Body minute book, 18 Oct. 1981–15 Dec. 1982, 29 June 1982.
76 Faculty of Law minutes, before minutes for 13 Feb. 1987.
77 Ibid.
78 Faculty of Law minutes, 23 May 1987.
79 Faculty of Law minutes, 17 Nov. 1989.
80 Faculty of Law minutes, 25 Nov. 1998, for the structure of the relevant degree programme. Year 3 would be spent at a French university law school; and two of the UCD subjects would be taught mainly in French.
81 Faculty of Law minutes, 25 Oct., 18 Dec. 1990.
82 See Law staff meeting minutes, 22 Feb. 1995.
83 Law staff meeting minutes, 27 Oct. 1999.
84 Law staff meeting minutes, 26 Jan. 2000.
85 Governing Body minute book, 15 May 1984–14 May 1985, 23 Oct., 18 Dec. 1984.
86 Governing Body minute book, 21 Oct. 1986–30 June 1987, 24 Nov. 1986.
87 The three letters were dated 14 Oct., 17 Oct. and 21 Oct. 1986.
88 Governing Body minute book, 1986–1987, 12 Feb. 1987.
89 J.B. Ames, *Lectures on Legal History and Miscellaneous Legal Essays* (Cambridge, MA, and London 1913), p. 361.
90 Ibid., p. 362.
91 Ibid., p. 361.
92 Statute I, Chap XV, para. 10.
93 Governing Body minute book, 25 Sept. 1987–20 Dec. 1988, 24 Nov. 1987.
94 Ibid.
95 Governing Body minute book, 1987–1988, 15 Oct. 1987.
96 The discussion itself had been precipitated by a report of 30 Jan. 1987 on the retirement age presented to the Finance Committee of the Governing Body: Governing Body minute book, 21 Oct. 1986–30 June 1987, 12 Feb., 31 Mar. 1987.
97 Governing Body minute book, 1987–1988, 18 Oct. 1988: Governing Body minute book, 14 Feb. 1988–13 Feb. 1989, 16 May 1988.
98 Conveniently recorded in Governing Body minute book, 13 Mar. 1990–19 Dec. 1990, 26 June 1990.
99 *Eogan* v. *University College Dublin* [1996] 1 IR 390, [1996] 2 ILRM 302.
100 Governing Body minute book, 1987–1988, 24 Nov. 1987.
101 Ibid., 22 Mar. 1988.
102 Governing Body minute book, 18 Oct. 1981–15 Dec. 1982, 18 May 1982.
103 Governing Body minute book, 25 Sept. 1987–20 Dec. 1988, 15 Oct. 1987.
104 Governing Body minute book, 11 Feb.–15 Dec. 1992, 15 Oct. 1992.
105 Professor Kenny kindly supplied me with a copy of the remarks he delivered on the occasion (12 Nov. 2011), which I have made use of for this paragraph.
106 *Irish Independent*, 20 Oct. 1991.
107 See, generally, John F. Buckley, 'Legal education; a steep curve of learning' in Eamonn G. Hall and Daire Hogan (eds), *The Law Society of Ireland, 1852–2002: Portrait of a Profession* (Dublin, 2002), 177.
108 *Bloomer* v. *Incorporated Law Society of Ireland* [1995] 3 IR 14.
109 Solicitors Acts, 1954 and 1960 (Apprenticeship and Education) Regulations, 1991 (S.I. no. 9 of 1991), art. 30.
110 [1996] 1 IR 403, [1996] 2 ILRM 481.
111 Solicitors Acts 1954 to 1994 (Apprenticeship and Education) Regulations, 1997 (S.I. no. 287 of 1997).
112 Buckley, 'Legal education: a steep curve of learning', at 183–84.
113 No. 24 of 1997.
114 London, 1979.
115 Hand's major articles for medieval Irish legal history are conveniently listed in the Bibliography accompanying vol. 2 of *A New History of Ireland* (Oxford, 1987), at p. 888.
116 'The common law in Ireland in the 13th

and 14th centuries: two cases involving Christ Church, Dublin', *JRSAI*, 97 (1967) 97.

117 *Radcliffe and Cross's The English Legal System*, 5th ed., ed. Lord Cross of Chelsea and G.J. Hand (London, 1971).

118 *Report of the President, 1981–1982*, p. 46.

119 *Report of the Irish Boundary Commission 1925*, introduction by G.J. Hand (Shannon, 1970).

120 G.J. Hand, 'MacNeill and the Boundary Commission' in F.X. Martin and F.J. Byrne (eds), *The Scholar Revolutionary: Eoin MacNeill and the Making of the New Ireland* (Shannon, 1970), p. 199.

121 'His Majesty's directions for ordering and settling the courts within the Kingdom of Ireland, 1622', *Analecta Hibernica*, no. 26 (1970), 177.

122 'Rules and orders to be observed in the proceedings of causes in the High Court of Chancery in Ireland, 1659', *Ir Jur*, 9 (1974), 110.

123 UCD Statute CXIV, Ch. I (1981). It had been established by UCD Statute LXX, Ch. V (of 1971), which had replaced the Lectureship set up by UCD Statute LIX.

124 Governing Body minute book, 25 Sept. 1987–20 Dec. 1988, 15 Oct. 1987.

125 'Republican courts in Ireland, 1919–22'; *Ir Jur*, 5 (1970), 321; 'The genesis of the Dáil courts', *Ir Jur*, 9 (1974), 326.

126 'The development of electoral law in the Republic of Ireland', *NILQ*, 28 (1977), 357.

127 'The first Labour government and the office of Lord Advocate', *NILQ*, 26 (1975), 18.

128 See *DULJ*, 18 (1996), 211.

129 J.P. Casey, *Constitutional Law in Ireland*, 3rd ed. (Dublin, 2000).

130 'The Spanish Constitutional Court', *Ir Jur*, 25–27 (1990–2), 26.

131 'The development of constitutional law under Chief Justice O'Higgins', *Ir Jur*, 21, (1986), 7.

132 'Interpretation of constitutional guarantees: an antipodean history lesson?', *Ir Jur*, 31 (1996), 102. See, too, Casey's 'Criminal justice and the Constitution in Ireland', in Deirdre Curtin and David O'Keeffe (eds), *Constitutional Adjudication in European and National Law: Essays for the Hon. Mr. Justice T.F. O'Higgins* (Dublin, 1993), p. 193.

133 'State and Church in Ireland' in Gerhard Robbers (ed.), *State and Church in the European Union* (Baden-Baden, 1996), p. 157; 'Church autonomy and religious liberty in Ireland' in Gerhard Robbers (ed.), *Church Autonomy: a Comparative Survey* (Frankfurt am Main, 2001), p. 87.

134 *President's Report for 2006–7*.

6 THE LAW COLLECTION IN THE COLLEGE LIBRARY

1 *St Stephen's*, 1: 8 (Nov. 1902).

2 Academic Council minute book, 1909–1915, 14 Dec. 1911; Governing Body minute book, 1911–1913, 29 Dec. 1911.

3 Governing Body minute book, 1929–1931, 12 Dec. 1929.

4 Governing Body minute book, 1911–1913, 29 Oct. 1912; Governing Body minute book, 1913 – 1915, 23 June 1914.

5 Governing Body minute book, 1917–1919, 23 July 1918.

6 V.T.H. Delany, *Christopher Palles, Lord Chief Baron of Her Majesty's Court of Exchequer in Ireland, 1874–1916: His Life and Times* (Dublin, 1960).

7 See above, p. 30.

8 For the NUI Senate's condolences see NUI Senate minutes, viii, 180 (5 Mar. 1920).

9 Dáire Keogh, 'William J. Walsh, 1908–21' in Tom Dunne (ed.), *The National University of Ireland 1908–2008 Centenary Essays* (Dublin, 2008), 121 at 124–5.

10 See p. 205.

11 Governing Body minute book, 1923–1925, 24 Feb. 1925; see above, p. 205.

12 See Governing Body minute book, 1919–1921, 21 Dec. 1920.

13 Governing Body minute book, 1910–1921, 21 Dec. 1920.

14 McCartney, *UCD – a National Idea*, p. 293.

15 Governing Body minute book, 1919–1921, 15 Feb. 1921.

16 NUI Senate minutes, viii (1921 – 1922), 31 (19 Apr. 1921).

17 Governing Body minute book, 1919–1921, 21 Apr. 1921.

18 Governing Body minute book, 1923–1925, 16 Dec. 1924.

19 R.I. Page, *Matthew Parker and his Books* (Kalamazoo, MI, 1993), p. 2. The quadripartite indenture laying down the salient arrangements was dated 1 Jan. 1574: ibid.
20 Mrs Alice Stopford Green to Dr Coffey, 23 Feb. 1925: Governing Body minute book, 1923–1925, 24 Feb. 1925.
21 Governing Body minute book, 1947–1950, 18 Nov. 1947.
22 Governing Body minute book, 1959–1961, 28 June 1960.
23 Governing Body minute book, 1959–1961, 28 June 1960.
24 Governing Body minute book, 1919–1921, 21 Dec. 1920.
25 She had been appointed in the spring of 1951 in succession to Mr James O'Neill: Governing Body minute book, 1950–1953, 8 May 1951.
26 Governing Body minute book, 1959–1961, 28 June 1960.
27 Ibid.
28 J.P. MacHale to Alexander MacDonald, 28 July 1960: Governing Body minute book, 1959–1961, 18 Oct. 1960.
29 J.P. MacHale to Alexander MacDonald, 2 Aug. 1960: Governing Body minute book, 1959–1961, 18 Oct. 1960.
30 Governing Body minute book, 1959–1961, 20 Dec. 1960.
31 Ibid.
32 McCartney, *UCD: a National Idea*, p. 293.
33 Ibid., p. 294. This was the campaign in the L & H to force Tierney to stand down as president of the society *ex officio*.
34 Peter Martin, 'The political career of Michael Tierney, 1920–44', *Irish Historical Studies*, 37 (2011), 412 at 426.
35 For Forbes and his actions in the Library at an earlier date, see above, p. 118.
36 In the late 1970s Esther Semple, then the Law Librarian, expressed the belief that no contemporaneous catalogue was ever made in 1921: E. Semple to N. Jessop, 8 March 1978, UCD, file in Law Librarian's office.
37 (1891) 28 LR Ir 69.
38 (1890) 26 LR Ir 428.
39 'Liability of railway companies as carriers of passengers – I', *ILT & SJ*, 26 (1892), 59 at 60.
40 UCD, Special Collections, MS 14, no. 34. See Appendix III.
41 Undelivered judgment of Palles C.B. in *Walker* v. *Great Northern Ry. Co.*, at p. 1.
42 For the full judgment, see Appendix III, p. 245.
43 Governing Body minute book, 30 May 1972–2 Mar. 1973, 30 Jan. 1973; above, p. 174.
44 See, e.g., Faculty of Law minutes, 29 Oct. 1974.
45 Pasted in to the Academic Council minute book, 1915–1931, at entry for 31 Jan. 1928.
46 Academic Council minute book, 1915–1931, 31 Jan. 1928.
47 See above, p. 118.
48 Governing Body minute book, 28 June 1966–29 June 1967, 24 Jan. 1967.
49 Above, p. 171.
50 The authorisation of expenditure of £2,250 on sundry law reports (unspecified) by the Governing Body in 1971 may relate to these purchases: Governing Body minute book, 24 Nov. 1969–20 April 1971, 24 Mar. 1971. For details on further purchases of law reports, see Governing Body minute book, 23 May 1972–2 Mar. 1973, 23 May 1972 (£500), 1 Dec. 1972 (£1,443); Governing Body minute book, 13 May 1975–22 June 1976 – Irish law reports (£,2841), *U.S. Supreme Court Reports* and *Digests* (£550), *Academie de Droit International de la Haye Recueil* (£230).
51 Eamonn G. Hall, *The Superior Courts of Law: 'Official' Law Reporting in Ireland, 1866–2006* (Dublin, 2009), p. 324. For delays in the issuance of Irish law reports, see ibid., chs. 9 and 10.
52 *President's Report, 1958–59*, p. 44.
53 Governing Body minute book, 1953–1956, 14 Dec. 1954.
54 In June 1975, the Governing Body had sanctioned the purchase of the 128 vols of CLR for £1,270, but the following month an entire set was presented by the then Australian ambassador, Mr. Vincent Gair: see the photograph of the presentation in the *President's Report for 1974–75*, opposite p. 12. See, too, Faculty of Law minutes, 12 Sept. 1975.
55 (1850) 89 RR 725. For acknowledgement of the gift see Faculty of Law minutes, 4 Mar. 1976.
56 The latter purchase is specifically highlighted in the Librarian's Report for 1980–81.
57 Heaney to McHale, 27 May 1975: UCD

Library, File dealing with the Law section of the Library (Librarian's Office).

58 'The Faculty of Law: a report, 1965–1973, prepared by members of the Teaching Staff', pp 9–11.

59 Ibid., p. 10.

60 Ibid., p. 11.

61 Casey to McHale, 29 April 1986: UCD Library, File dealing with the Law section of the Library.

62 *Caird* v. *Sime* (1887) 12 App Cas 326.

63 12 App Cas at 354.

64 The thought is that of Harriet Martineau, see her short poem 'On, on, Forever': E.C. Stedman (ed.), *A Victorian Anthology, 1837–1895* (New York, 1895), p. 125.

65 12 App Cas at 354.

66 'Faculty of Law: Submission on Library needs'.

67 Ibid., p. 4.

68 Ibid., p. 1.

69 (1949) 339 US 629.

70 399 US at 632–33, judgment of Vinson C. J. for the court.

71 Sean Phillips to Paul O'Connor, 9 Jan. 1995: UCD Library, File dealing with the Law section of the Library.

72 Brady to Phillips, 9 Feb. 1988: ibid.

73 Phillips to Brady, 1 June 1988: ibid.

74 Semple to Deputy Librarian, Dec. 1977: ibid.

75 Semple to Deputy Librarian, 16 Oct. 1984: ibid.

76 Ibid.

7 HOUSING THE LAW SCHOOL

1 Governing Body minute book, 1908–1911, 15 Jan. 1910.

2 Governing Body minute book, 1908–1911, 25 April 1911. UCD was to agree to pay part of the rent for the two houses in Merrion Square for five years. It was also to be involved in paying NUI's rates bill.

3 Governing Body minute book, 1908–1911, 22 Mar. 1910.

4 A blow-by-blow account of the development of the Earlsfort Terrace site remains to be constructed out of the very full entries in successive Governing Body minute books, 1908–1911, 1911–1913, 1913–1915, 1915–1917, 1917–1919.

5 Governing Body minute book, 1917–1919, 23 July 1918.

6 Governing Body minute book, 1911–1913, 15 July 1911. The illumination of the address cost the College £5 12*s.* 6*d.*: ibid. There had been some controversy over the question whether it should be presented at all. Governing Body minute book, 1908–1911, 25 April 1911 (Professors Kettle and Magennis seeking an adjournment of the matter's consideration).

7 Donal McCartney, *UCD – a National Idea – the History of University College Dublin* (Dublin, 1999), p. 92.

8 Academic Council minutes, 3 Oct. 1941–10 Oct. 1946, 11 Dec. 1945; Governing Body minute book, 29 June 1943–18 Mar. 1947, 18 Dec. 1945.

9 *President's Report 1964–1965, Academic*, p. 5.

10 Governing Body minute book, 1967–1968, 17 Oct. 1967.

11 Faculty of Law minutes, 12 June 1980.

12 Faculty of Law minutes, reporting staff meeting of 3 Oct. 1984.

13 Faculty of Law minutes, 4 Oct. 1985.

14 Faculty of Law minutes, 30 Oct. 1987.

15 Law staff meeting minutes, 10 Apr. 1991.

16 Faculty of Law minutes, 20 Nov. 1991; 14 Oct., 18 Nov. 1992; 17 Feb. 1993.

17 *Oxford DNB*, xvi, 797; *DIB*, iii, 435.

18 *Origins of the Belfield Campus and UCD's Period Houses: Map and Guide* (2012).

19 An Act to enable Commissioners fully to carry into effect several Conventions for liquidating Claims of British subjects and others, against the Government of France, 1819 : 59 Geo. III, c. 31.

20 This protracted litigation is summarised in the introduction to the report of one of the associated lawsuits, *Trimlestown* v. *O'Shea* (1855), in a rare volume consulted for present purposes in the Meath County Library in Navan.

21 [1934] IR 311.

22 *Roebuck Castle: Catalogue of the valuable and antique contents including more particularly important collections of silver, jewellery and ornamental china, and a unique collection of needlework pictures, to be sold by auction commencing Monday, 20th day of September, 1943* (Dublin, 1943).

23 Pearson, *Between the Mountains and the Sea* (Dublin, 1998), p. 353.

24 Valletta memoir, ch.7.

25 Alan Hollinghurst, *The Line of Beauty* (London, 2004), p. 199.

8 EPILOGUE: THE LAW SCHOOL SINCE 2000

1 *Daily Telegraph*, 9 July 2012.
2 Paul Brand, Kevin Costello and W.N. Osborough (eds), *Adventures of the Law: Proceedings of the Sixteenth British Legal History Conference, Dublin, 2003* (Dublin, 2005).
3 Thomas Mohr and Jennifer Schweppe (eds), *Thirty Years of Legal Scholarship* (Dublin, 2011).
4 Quoted, entry on Bowen in *Oxford DNB*, vi, at 898.
5 Universities Act 1997, s. 33.
6 Statute 6, of 14 June 2005.
7 Memorandum by Paul O'Connor, 1 Oct. 2004: 'University Structures: Faculty of Law, UCD'.
8 M. Cary, *A History of Rome down to the Reign of Constantine*, 2nd ed. (London, 1954), p. 532.
9 Governing Body minute book, 11 Feb.–15 Dec. 1992, 24 Nov. 1992.
10 *The Times*, 30 July 2012.
11 All helpfully set down in the *President's Report for 1981–1982*.
12 *The Economist*, 8 Dec. 2012, 2 Mar. 2013; *Irish Times*, 30 Nov. 2012, 22 Feb. 2013.
13 Above, pp 53, 79.
14 Sarah Campbell, 'New Nationalism? The SDLP and the creation of a socialist and labour party in Northern Ireland, 1969–75', *IHS*, 38 (2013), 422, at 429.
15 These were attractions advertised for the Law Ball held at the Crowne Plaza, Blanchardstown in February 2013.
16 Charles Fearne, *Essay on the Learning of Contingent Remainder and Executory Duties* (London, 1772).

APPENDIX II: NEWMAN AND THE LAW

1 *Analecta Hibernica*, 20 (1958), p. 226.
2 Above, Ch. 1.
3 James Joyce, *A Portrait of the Artist as a Young Man*, p. 175.
4 *Letters and Diaries of John Henry Newman*, ed. C.S. Dessain et al., 31 vols (Oxford and London, 1961–84), xiv, 431.
5 Eardley's *The Imprisonment and Deliverance of Dr Giacinto Achilli, with some account of his previous History and Labours* (London, 1850); *Brief Sketch of the Life of Dr Giacinto Achilli: including a Narrative of his Proceedings, etc.* (Dublin, n.d.).
6 *Dublin Review*, 28 (March and June 1850), 469.
7 Wilfrid Ward, *The Life and Times of Cardinal Wiseman*, 2 vols (London, 1897), ii, 39.
8 *Dublin Review*, 28 (1850), at 477.
9 Ibid.
10 Ibid., at 471.
11 Ibid., at 481–98.
12 *Dublin Review*, 28 (1850), at 510–11.
13 Ibid.
14 Juvenal, *Sat.*, i, 73–4.
15 6 & 7 Vict., c. 96, s. 6.
16 M.C. Minow, 'Roman Catholicism on trial in Victorian England: the libel case of John Henry Newman and Dr Achilli', *Catholic Lawyer*, 36 (1995–6), 401 at 413.
17 See W.F. Finlason, *Report of the Trial and Preliminary Proceedings in the case of the Queen on the Prosecution of G. Achilli* v. *Dr Newman* (London, 1852); Minow, 'Roman Catholicism on trial in Victorian England'.
18 And see as well *R.* v. *Newman*, 3 Car & K 252; 175 Eng Rep 541.
19 Minow, 'Roman Catholicism on trial in Victorian England', at 434.
20 3 Car & K at 268; 175 Eng Rep at 549–50.
21 *R.* v. *Newman*, Dears 85, 169 Eng Rep 647; 1 El & Bl 268, 118 Eng Rep 437.
22 Ian Ker, *John Henry Newman: a Biography* (Oxford, 1988), p. 397.
23 *R.* v. *Newman*, 1 El & Bl 558, 118 Eng Rep 544.
24 6 & 7 Vict., c. 96, s.6.
25 *R.* v. *Newman*, Dears 125f, 169 Eng Rep at 664f. Minow's account differs at this point: see 'Roman Catholicism on trial in Victorian England', at pp 438–9.
26 Quoted in an editorial footnote to a letter of Newman's written at the conclusion of the criminal libel trial: Newman to F.S. Bowles, 31 Jan. 1853, in *Letters and Diaries of Newman*, xv, 279 n.1. Newman identified as the theme of the lecture by Coleridge, a Tractarian and friend of Keble, 'the deterioration of converts': Newman to Sister M.I. Poole, 31 Jan. 1853, in *Letters and Diaries of Newman*, xv, 280.
27 *R.* v. *Newman*, Dears 131–2, 169 Eng Rep 666–7.

28 See Minow, 'Roman Catholicism on trial in Victorian England', at 414, n. 70.
29 Ibid., 400, n. 224.
30 Newman to Archbishop Cullen, 5 Feb. 1853: *Letters and Diaries of Newman*, xv, 286. Newman was acknowledging the receipt of sums forwarded by Cullen to help Newman defray his legal expenses.
31 Finalson, *Report*, p. 26.
32 Quoted, Finlason, *Report*, p. 208.
33 Finlason, *Report*, pp 25–6.
34 Ibid., pp 196–201.
35 Ibid., p. 194.
36 Ibid., p. 195.
37 Sheridan Gilley, *Newman and his Age* (London, 1990), p. 271.
38 Finlason, *Report*, p.v.
39 See above, p. 239.
40 E. Foss, *A Biographical Dictionary of the Judges of England, 1066–1870*, 9 vols (London, 1848–64), ix, 165.
41 *Oxford DNB*: Foss, Edward.
42 *Oxford DNB*: Finlason, W.F.
43 I wonder if 'vigour' should read 'rigour'.
44 *Oxford DNB*: Coleridge, John Taylor.
45 *Oxford DNB*: Coleridge, John Duke; A.W.B. Simpson (ed.), *Biographical Dictionary of the Common Law* (London, 1984), p. 122.
46 *Dizionario Biografico degli Italiani*, i (Rome, 1960), 144 (D. Cantimori).
47 Quoted, Finlason, *Report*, p. 206.
48 Ibid.
49 Minow, 'Roman Catholicism on trial in Victorian England', at p. 452.

APPENDIX III

1 (1891) 28 LR Ir 69.
2 Special Collections, MS 14.
3 See the conclusion of the judgment, below.
4 *Bell* v. *Great Northern Railway Co.* (1890) 26 LR Ir 428.
5 'Liability of railway companies as carriers of passengers – I', *ILT & SJ*, 26 (1892), 59 at 60.
6 See the High Court judgment: (1890) 28 LR Ir 69. In the margin of the typescript original there are MS notes in places inserting case citations. These have been checked, expanded where necessary, supplied where missing and inserted as footnotes by transcriber.
7 lf. 'In the body of its mother'.
8 (1740) Barn 272, 290; 2 Atk 114, 26 Eng Rep 472.
9 1 Jac. II, c. 17, 1685 (administration of estates).
10 (1727) 2 P. Wms 435; 24 Eng Rep 803 at 807 (respondent, citing *Wallis* v. *Hodson* (1740) Barn 272, 290, 2 Atk 114, 26 Eng Rep 472).
11 Lit, 'in the nature of things'; in a legal context, 'in existence'.
12 (1699) 12 Mod 278, 88 Eng Rep 1320; sub nom. *Scatterwood* v. *Edge* (1699) 1 Salk 229, 91 Eng Rep 203.
13 *Doe d. Lancashire* v. *Lancashire* (1792) 5 T.R. 49, 101 Eng Rep 28.
14 *Doe d. Clarke* v. *Clarke* (1795) 2 H. Bl 399; 126 Eng Rep 617.
15 End quotation mark in the MS is an error. Buller J's quotation ends at end of the paragraph.
16 Citation in original omitted in MS. (1792) 5 T. R. 49, 101 Eng Rep 28.
17 *Doe d. Lancashire* v. *Lancashire* (1792) 5 T.R. 49, 101 Eng Rep 28.
18 Ibid. 5 T. R. at 60, 101 Eng Rep at 35.
19 *Miller* v. *Turner* (1747–48) 1 Ves Sen 85, 27 Eng Rep 907.
20 (1771) 5 Burr 2703, 98 Eng Rep 419.
21 *Doe d. Lancashire* v. *Lancashire* (1792) 5 T.R. at 62, 101 Eng Rep at 36.
22 (1771) Dick 446, 21 Eng Rep 343.
23 (1798) 4 Ves Jun 227, 31 Eng Rep 117.
24 4 Ves Jun at 321, 31 Eng Rep at 163.
25 (1740) Barn 272, 290; 2 Atk 115, 26 Eng Rep 472.
26 *Doe d. Lancashire* v. *Lancashire* (1792) 5 T.R. 49, 101 Eng Rep 28.
27 *Doe d. Clarke* v. *Clarke* (1795) 2 H. Bl 399, 126 Eng Rep 617.
28 3 Co. *Inst* 50.
29 (1713) 1 P Wms 244, 24 Eng Rep 373.
30 *Sir Robert Burdet* v. *Hopegood* (1718) 1 P Wms 486, 24 Eng Rep 484.
31 Part of the body of the mother.
32 Bl Com iv.5.

Sources

NATIONAL ARCHIVES

Memoranda Roll, 9 & 10 Henry VIII (Ferguson MS 1a. 49. 136. f. 52)

NATIONAL UNIVERSITY OF IRELAND

Charter
Statutes
Calendars
Minutes of Meetings of NUI Senate, from 1909

UNIVERSITY COLLEGE DUBLIN

Charter
Statutes, both with Roman numerals and after 2005, with Arabic numerals
Calendars
Origins of the Belfield Campus and UCD's Period Houses: Map and Guide (2012)

I *President's Office*
Reports of the President, from 1909

II *Archives Department*
Minutes of Governing Body, from 1908
Academic Council Minute Books, from 1915
Memorandum on the Public Services (Temporary Economies) Bill, 1933 presented by Representatives of the Staff of the Three University Colleges [1933]

III *School of Law*
Minutes of Meetings of Faculty of Law (i) 1948–1971; (ii) 1971–1986; (iii) 1987–2000
Minutes of Law Staff Meetings, 1990–2002
The Faculty of Law: a Report 1965–1973, prepared by Members of the Teaching Staff
Faculty of Law Submission on Library Needs (Paul O'Connor, 1986)
University Structures: Faculty of Law, UCD (Paul O'Connor, 2004)
Law Alumni Journal, vol.1, no.1 (1999)

IV *James Joyce Library*
a) *Librarian's Office*
Files relating to the Law Collection in the Library
b) *Law Librarian's Office*
File relating to the Palles collection in the Law section of the Library
c) *Special Collections*
Collection of Judgments of Chief Baron Palles (MS 14)

Honorable Society of King's Inns
Benchers' minute books, 1856–1869, 1885–1901
Report of the Education Committee, 1876

Oratory of St. Philip Neri, Birmingham
Newman Dublin Papers

In Private Ownership, England
Memoir of Westby Family, prepared by Mrs Lois Valletta (Valletta memoir)

Bibliography

WORKS OF REFERENCE

Burke's Peerage, Baronetage and Knightage, 107th ed. 3 vols, Wilmington, Delaware, 2003
Burke, Bernard, *A Genealogical and Heraldic History of the Landed Gentry of Ireland,* 10th ed. London, 1904
Bence-Jones, Mark, *A Guide to Irish Country Houses,* revised ed. London, 1988
G.E.C., *The Complete Peerage,* 14 vols., various editors, London; Stroud, Glos., 1910–98
Dictionary of Irish Biography, 9 vols, Cambridge, 2009
Dictionary of National Biography, 21 vols, London, 1908–09
Dictionary of National Biography, 1922–1930, ed. J.R.H. Weaver, London 1937
Dictionary of National Biography, 1941–1950, ed. L.G. Wickham Legg and E.T. Williams, Oxford 1959
Dizionario Biografico degli Italiani, vol. 1, Rome, 1960
Dublin Almanac and General Register of Ireland for the Year of Our Lord 1848, Dublin, [1848]
Foss, E., *A Biographical Dictionary of the Judges of England, 1066–1870,* 9 vols, London, 1848–64
Johnston–Liik, E.M. *History of the Irish Parliament, 1692–1800*, 6 vols, Belfast, 2002
King's Inns Admission Papers, 1607–1867, ed. Edward Keane, P.B. Phair and T.U. Sadleir, Dublin, 1982
King's Inns Barristers, 1968–2004, ed. Kenneth Ferguson, Dublin, 2005
MacLysaght, Edward, *More Irish Families,* Galway and Dublin, 1960
O'Higgins, Paul, *A Bibliography of Irish Trials and Other Legal Proceedings,* Abingdon, Oxon, 1986.
Oxford Dictionary of National Biography, 60 vols, Oxford, 2004
Simpson, A.W.B., ed. *Biographical Dictionary of the Common Law,* London, 1984
Who was Who, 1916–1928, 4th ed. London, 1967

OFFICIAL PUBLICATIONS

Note: See too the Index to Legislation, etc. and the Index to Cases at Law

Lords' Journal, Ireland, from 1634
Calendar of Treasury Books, from 1660
Calendar State Papers, Ireland, 1666–9
Irish Parliamentary Register [1781–97] 17 vols, Dublin 1782–1801; repr. Bristol and Tokyo, 1999
Hansard, 3rd series
Hansard, 5th series
Royal Commission on University Education in Ireland (Robertson Commission)
First Report, 1901 (Cd. 825)
Appendix, 1901 (Cd. 826)

Second Report, 1901 (Cd. 899)
Appendix, 1902 (Cd. 900)
Third Report, 1902 (Cd. 1228)
Appendix, 1902 (Cd. 1229)
Final Report, 1903 (Cd. 1483)
Appendix, 1903 (Cd. 1484)

Royal Commission on Trinity College, Dublin and the University of Dublin (Fry Commission)
First Report, 1906 (Cd. 3174)
Appendix, 1906 (Cd. 3176)
Final Report, 1907 (Cd. 3311)
Appendix, 1907 (Cd. 3312)

Report of the President of Queen's College, Belfast, for 1908–09, 1909 HC, xx, 715

Report of the President of Queen's College, Cork, for 1908–09, 1909 HC, xx, 803

Report of the President of Queen's College, Galway, for 1908–09, 1909 HC, xx, 831

Twenty-seventh Report of the Royal University of Ireland for 1908, 1909 HC, xx, 869

Dublin Gazette, 1911

Dáil Eireann Debates

Documents on Irish Foreign Policy, vol. 3 – 1926–1932, ed. Ronan Fanning, Michael Kennedy, Dermot Keogh and Eunan O'Halpin, Dublin, 2002

Documents on Irish Foreign Policy, vol. 4 – 1932–36, ed. Catriona Crowe, Ronan Fanning, Michael Kennedy, Dermot Keogh and Eunan O'Halpin, Dublin, 2004

Report of the Board of Visitors – National University of Ireland, August 1959

Report of the Board of Visitors, University College, Dublin, 1960 (Pr. 5499)

Commission on Higher Education, 1960–1967, *II Report*, vol. 1, 1967 (Pr. 9389)

Report of the Irish Boundary Commission, 1925, intro. G. J. Hand, Shannon, 1970

GENERAL

Ames, J.B., *Lectures in Legal History and Miscellaneous Legal Essays,* Cambridge, MA and London, 1913

Annals of Ulster, vol. 3 – 1379–1541, ed. and transl. B. MacCarthy, Dublin, 1895

Anon., 'The Catholic University and legal education', *Dublin Review,* 41 (1856), 226

Anon., 'Liability of railway companies as carriers of passengers – I', *ILT & SJ,* 26 (1892), 59

Anon., 'Review of Eardley's books on Giacinto Achilli', *Dublin Review*, 28 (1850), 469

Andrews, C.S. *Man of No Property,* Dublin and Cork, 1982

Arkins, Thomas, 'The commercial aspect of the Irish Penal Code', *Studies*, 1 (1912), 257. 'The penal laws and Irish land', *Studies*, 1 (1912), 514

Baird, H.M., *History of the Rise of the Huguenots,* 2 vols, New York, 1879

Barnard, T.C., 'Lawyers and the law in later seventeenth-century Ireland', *IHS*, 28 (1991), 256

Barr, Colin, *Paul Cullen, John Henry Newman and the Catholic University, 1845–1865,* Leominster, 2003

Barrington, Donal, 'The Constitution in the Courts', *Administration*, 35 (1987), 110

Bewley, Charles, *Hermann Göring and the Third Reich: a Biography Based on Family and Official Records*, New York, 1962

Binchy, D.A., 'The old name of Charleville, Co. Cork', *Eigse,* 10, pt 3 (1962–3), 211
—— 'An Irish ambassador at the Spanish court, 1569–1574': *Studies,* 10 (1920), 353, 573; 11 (1921), 199; 12 (1922), 83, 461; 13 (1923), 115
—— 'The Irish Benedictine congregation in medieval Germany', *Studies,* 18 (1929), 194
—— 'Irish history and Irish law: I', *Studia Hibernica*, 15 (1975), 7; II, *Studia Hibernica,* 16, (1976), 7
—— *A Grammar of Old Irish*, Dublin, 1946
—— 'Heinrich Brüning', *Studies,* 21 (1932), 385
—— 'Paul von Hindenburg', *Studies*, 26 (1937), 223
—— 'Adolf Hitler', *Studies*, 22 (1933), 29
—— *Church and State in Fascist Italy*, Oxford, 1941; repr. 1970
—— *Críth Gablach*, Dublin, 1941, repr. 1970
—— 'The diplomacy of the Vatican', *The Bell,* 12 (1946), 99
—— 'Background of the Italian general election', *Studies,* 37 (1948), 257
—— 'Partition and a policy of national unity', *Studies,* 24 (1935), 20
—— 'Proposals for a new Senate', *Studies*, 25 (1936), 20
—— 'Two Blasket autobiographies', *Studies,* 23 (1934), 545
—— *Corpus Iuris Hibernici,* 6 vols, Dublin, 1978
—— 'The linguistic and historical value of the Irish Law tracts', *Proceedings of the British Academy*, 29 (1943), 195
—— 'Bretha Crólige', *Eriu,* 12 (1938), 1
—— 'Sick-maintenance in Irish law', *Eriu,* 12 (1938), 78
—— 'Secular institutions' in Myles Dillon (ed.), *Early Irish Society*, Dublin, 1954
—— 'Patrick and his biographers – ancient and modern', *Studia Hibernica,* 2 (1962), 7
—— *Celtic and Anglo-Saxon Kingship,* Oxford, 1970
—— 'The legal capacity of women in regard to contracts' in Myles Dillon and D.A. Binchy (eds), *Studies in Early Irish Law,* Dublin, 1936
—— 'MacNeill's Study of the ancient Irish laws' in F.X. Martin and F.J. Byrne (eds), *The Scholar Revolutionary: Eoin MacNeill, 1867–1945, and the Making of the New Ireland,* Shannon, 1973
—— 'Ancient Irish law', *Ir Jur,* 1 (1966), 84
—— 'Celtic suretyship, a fossilized Indo-European institution?' *Ir Jur*, 7 (1972), 360
—— 'Lawyers and chroniclers' in Brian Ó Cuiv (ed.), *Seven Centuries of Irish Learning, 1000–1700,* Cork, 1971, p. 50
—— 'The passing of the old order' in Brian Ó Cuiv (ed.), *The Impact of the Scandinavian Invasions on the Celtic-speaking Peoples, c.800–1100 AD,* Dublin, 1975
—— 'The law and the universities', *Studies,* 38 (1949), 257
Binchy, William, 'Values and policies in tort law: the emerging Irish debate' in Thomas Mohr and Jennifer Schweppe (eds), *Thirty Years of Legal Scholarship,* Dublin, 2011, p. 162
Bodkin, M. Mc D. *Recollections of an Irish Judge – Press, Bar and Parliament*, London, 1914
Boyle, John, *see* Kelly, John
Brady, James C., *Religion and the Law of Charities in Ireland*, Belfast, 1975; *Succession Law in Ireland*, 1st ed. Dublin, 1989; 2nd ed. Dublin, 1996
Brady, James C. and Anthony Kerr, *Limitation of Actions in the Republic of Ireland,* 1st ed. Dublin, 1984; 2nd ed. Dublin, 1994
Brand, Paul, *The Origins of the English Legal Profession*, Oxford, 1992
—— *The Making of the Common Law*, London and Rio Grande, 1992

—— *The Earliest English Law Reports* – I [Selden Society 111] London, 1995
—— Ditto – II [Selden Society 122] London, 1996
—— Ditto – III [Selden Society 122] London, 2005
—— Ditto – IV [Selden Society 123] London, 2007
—— 'Irish law students and lawyers in late medieval England', *IHS*, 32 (2000), 161
Brand, Paul, Kevin Costello and W.N. Osborough (eds), *Adventures of the Law: Proceedings of the Sixteenth British Legal History Conference Dublin, 2003*, Dublin, 2005
Breatnach, Liam, *A Companion to the Corpus Iuris Hibernici*, Dublin, 2005
Buckley, John F., 'Legal education: a steep curve of learning' in E.G. Hall and Daire Hogan (eds), *The Law Society of Ireland, 1852–2002: Portrait of a Profession*, Dublin, 2002
Bury, J.B., *The Science of History*, Cambridge, 1903
The Cambridge Companion to John Henry Newman. ed. Ian Ker and Terrence Merrigan, Cambridge, 2009
Campbell, Sarah, 'New Nationalism? The SDLP and the creation of a socialist and labour party in Northern Ireland, 1969–75', *IHS*, 28 (2013), 422
Carolan, Eoin, 'Irish constitutional scholarship in review: considering J.M. Kelly's *The Irish Constitution*' in Thomas Mohr and Jennifer Schweppe (eds), *Thirty Years of Legal Scholarship*, Dublin, 2011
Cary, M., *A History of Rome down to the Reign of Constantine*, 2nd ed., London, 1954
Casey, J.P., *Constitutional Law in Ireland*, 1st ed., London, 1987; 3rd ed., Dublin, 2000
—— *The Irish Law Officers: Rules and Responsibilities of the Attorney-general and the Director of Public Prosecutions*, Dublin, 1996
—— *The Office of the Attorney-general in Ireland*, Dublin, 1980
—— 'Church autonomy and religious liberty in Ireland' in Gerhard Robbers (ed.), *Church Autonomy: a Comparative Survey*, Frankfurt am Main, 2001
—— 'Criminal justice and the Constitution in Ireland' in Deirdre Curtin and David O'Keeffe (eds), *Constitutional Adjudication in European and National Law: Essays for the Hon. Mr. Justice T.F. O'Higgins*, Dublin, 1993
—— 'The development of constitutional law under Chief Justice O'Higgins', *Ir Jur*, 21 (1986), 7
—— 'The development of electoral law in the Republic of Ireland', *NILQ*, 28 (1977), 357
—— 'The first Labour government and the office of Lord Advocate', *NILQ*, 26 (1975), 18
—— 'The genesis of the Dáil courts', *Ir Jur*, 9 (1974), 326
—— 'Interpretation of constitutional guarantees: an antipodean history lesson?', *Ir Jur*, 31 (1996), 102
—— 'Republican courts in Ireland, 1919–22', *Ir Jur*, 5 (1970), 321
—— 'The Spanish Constitutional Court', *Ir Jur*, 25–27 (1990–92), 26
—— 'State and Church in Ireland' in Gerhard Robbers (ed.), *State and Church in the European Union*, Baden-Baden, 1996
'Chanel', *see* Clery, Arthur E.
Clery, Arthur E., pseud. 'Chanel', *The Idea of a Nation*, Dublin, 1907
Clery, Arthur E., pseud. Synan, Arthur, *The Coming of the King: a Jacobite Romance*, Dublin, 1909
Clery, Arthur E., *Dublin Essays*, Dublin and London, 1919
—— 'Accents: Dublin and otherwise', *Studies*, 10 (1921), 545
—— 'The philosophy of sanity: Chesterton and Belloc', *Studies*, 11 (1922), 571
—— 'The politics of "Macbeth"', *Studies*, 10 (1921), 19
—— 'Shakspere and Christianity', *Studies*, 10 (1921), 299

Clery, Arthur E., and J. McWalker, *The Public Health Acts Amendment Act 1907, with Explanation, Full Commentary upon the Sections and Summary of Recent Health Decisions*, Dublin, 1908

Clery, Arthur E., Hugh Kennedy and Michael Dawson, *The Town Tenants (Ireland) Act 1906, and the Rules and Forms made Thereunder,* Dublin, 1907

Cobb, Matthew, *The Resistance: the French Fight against the Nazis*, London, 2009

Coghlan, D., *The Ancient Land Tenures of Ireland*, Dublin, 1933

Cosgrove, Art (ed.), *A New History of Ireland, ii: Medieval Ireland, 1169–1534*, Oxford, 1987

Crawford, J.G., *A Star Chamber Court in Ireland: the Court of Castle Chamber, 1571–1641*, Dublin, 2005

Cregan, Donal, 'Daniel A. Binchy – obituary: the road to Emmaus', *Irish University Review*, 19 (1989), 310

Curran, C.P., *Under the Receding Wave,* Dublin, 1970

Curtin, Deirdre, and David O'Keeffe (eds), *Constitutional Adjudication in European and National Law: Essays for the Hon. Mr Justice T.F. O'Higgins*, Dublin, 1993

Davitt, Cahir, 'Some aspects of the Constitution and the law in relation to matrimony', *Studies*, 57 (1968), 6

Dawson, William, 'Arthur Clery', *Studies*, 22 (1933) 77

Delany, V.T.H., 'Legal studies in Trinity College, Dublin, since the Foundation', *Hermathena,* 89 (1957), 3

—— *Christopher Palles, Lord Chief Baron of Her Majesty's Court of Exchequer in Ireland, 1874–1916: his Life and Times,* Dublin, 1960

Dillon, Myles, and D.A. Binchy (eds), *Studies in Early Irish Law*, Dublin, 1936

Dunne, Tom (ed.), *The National University of Ireland, 1908–2008: Centenary Essays*, Dublin, 2008

Durrell, Laurence, *Justine*, London, 1963

Eardley, E., *The Imprisonment and Deliverance of Dr Giacinto Achilli, with some Account of his Previous History and Labours*, London, 1850

—— *Brief Sketch of the Life of Dr Giacinto Achilli, including a Narrative of his Proceedings, etc.*, Dublin, n.d.

Ebeling, F.W., *Archivalische Beiträge zur Geschichte Frankreichs unter Carl IX*, Leipzig, 1872

Ehler, Sydney Z., *Twenty Centuries of Church and State,* Maryland, 1957

—— 'On applying the modern term "state" to the middle ages' in J.A. Watt, J.B. Morrall and F.X. Martin (eds), *Medieval Studies presented to Aubrey Gwynn SJ*, Dublin, 1961

—— 'Decline of Communism', *Capuchin Annual* 1965, p. 217

—— 'Church and State in the present world', *Capuchin Annual* 1966, p. 53

—— 'Millennium Poloniae', *Capuchin Annual* 1967, p. 314

—— 'The question of the Holy Places in Palestine', *Capuchin Annual* 1971, p. 183

Ehler, Sydney, and John B. Morrall, *Church and State through the Centuries,* London and Maryland, 1954

Farrell, Brian, 'The drafting of the Irish Free State Constitution – I', *Ir Jur*, 5 (1970) 115; 'II', *Ir Jur*, 5 (1970), 343; 'III', *Ir Jur*, 6 (1971), 111; 'IV', *Ir Jur*, 6 (1971), 345

Fearne, Charles, *Essay on the Learning of Contingent Remainders and Executory Duties*, London, 1772

Fermor, Patrick Leigh, *A Time of Gifts*, London, 1977

Finlason, W.F., *Report of the Trial and Preliminary Proceedings in the Case of the Queen on the Prosecution of G. Achilli* v. *Dr Newman*, London, 1852

Finlay, Thomas, 'The class of "43"', *UCD: Law Alumni Journal,* i, no. 1 (1999), 17
FitzGibbon, John, *'A Volley of Execrations': the Letters and Papers of John FitzGibbon, Earl of Clare, 1772–1802*, ed. D.A. Fleming and A.P.W. Malcomson, Dublin, 2005
Froude, J.A., *The English in Ireland in the Eighteenth Century,* 3 vols, London, 1872–1874
Gilley, Sheridan, *Newman and his Age,* London, 1990
Gower, L.C.B., 'English legal training', *Modern L. Rev.*, 13 (1950), 137
Gurney, D. Frances, *Poems,* London, 1913
Gwynn, Denis, 'John E. Pigot and Thomas Davis', *Studies,* 38 (1949), 145
Hall, E.G., *The Superior Courts of Law: 'Official' Law Reporting in Ireland, 1866–2006*, Dublin, 2007
Hall, Eamonn G., and Daire Hogan (eds), *The Law Society of Ireland, 1852–2002: Portrait of a Profession,* Dublin, 2002
Hand, G.J., *English Law in Ireland, 1290–1324*, Cambridge, 1967
—— 'MacNeill and the Boundary Commission', in F. X. Martin and F. J. Byrne (eds), *The Scholar Revolutionary: Eoin MacNeill and the Making of the New Ireland,* Shannon, 1970
—— 'The common law in Ireland in the 13th and 14th centuries: two cases involving Christ Church Dublin', *JRSAI,* 97 (1967), 97
—— 'Rules and orders to be observed in the proceedings of causes in the High Court of Chancery in Ireland, 1659', *Ir Jur,* 9 (1974), 110
—— 'Obituary: Professor John M. Kelly', *Irish Law Times (ns),* 9 (1991), 68
Hand, G.J. et al. (eds), *European Electoral Systems Handbook*, London, 1979
Hand, G.J., and Victor Treadwell (eds), 'His Majesty's directions for ordering and settling the courts within the kingdom of Ireland, 1622', *Analecta Hibernica,* 26 (1970), 177
Healy, Maurice, *The Old Munster Circuit,* London, 1948
Henchy, Séamus, *Miscellaneous Irish Annals, A.D. 1114–1437,* Dublin, 1947
—— 'The Communist theory of law', *Studies,* 46 (1957), 411
—— 'Precedent in the Irish Supreme Court', *Modern L. Rev.,* 25 (1962), 544
—— 'Fosterage in early Irish law', PhD (NUI), 1943
—— 'The Visitor of the National University', *University Review*, 2 (1961), 16
Heron, D.C., *An Introduction to the History of Jurisprudence,* London, 1860
Hogan, Gerard, 'The judicial thought and prose of Mr Justice Seamus Henchy', *Ir Jur*, 46 (2011), 96
Hollinghurst, Alan, *The Line of Beauty*, London, 2004
Jaekel, Siegfried (ed.), *Menandri Sententiae,* Leipzig, 1960
Jenkins, Dafydd (ed.), *Celtic Law Papers,* Brussels, 1973
Johnston, William, 'The parliament of the Pale', *LQR,* 34 (1918), 291
—— 'The first adventure of the common law', *LQR*, 36 (1920), 9
—— 'Ireland in the medieval law courts', *Studies,* 12 (1923), 553
—— 'The English legislature and Irish courts' *LQR,* 40 (1924), 91
Joyce, James, *A Portrait of the Artist as a Young Man*, Harmondsworth, Middlesex, 1960
—— *Stephen Hero*, London, 1991
Justice, Jean, 'L'Egypte de 1914 á 1925', *Le Flambeau: Revue Belge des Questions Politiques et Littéraires* (1925)
—— 'Les premières relations entre la Belgique indépendante et l'Egypte, 1837–1838', *Revue Belge de Philologie et Histoire* (1928)
Kelly, J.M., *Princeps Iudex,* Weimar, 1957
—— *Fundamental Rights in the Irish Law and Constitution,* 1st ed., Dublin, 1961, 2nd ed., Dublin, 1967
—— 'The inner nature of the tort action', *Ir Jur*, 2 (1967), 279

—— 'Equality before the law in three European jurisdictions [Germany, Italy, Ireland]', *Ir Jur*, 18 (1983), 259
—— 'Hidden treasure and the Constitution', *Dublin Univ LJ*, 10 (1988), 5
—— *Studies in the Civil Judicature of the Roman Republic*, Oxford, 1976
—— *Roman Litigation*, Oxford, 1966
—— *A Short History of Western Legal Theory*, Oxford, 1992
—— *The Polling of the Dead*, Dublin, 1993
—— *Belling the Cat: Selected Speeches and Articles of John Kelly*, ed. John Flanagan, Dublin, 1992
—— *see, too*, Kunkel, Wolfgang and Carolan, Eoin.
—— *The Irish Constitution*, Dublin 1st ed., 1980
—— ditto, 3rd ed. Dublin, 1994, ed. Gerard Hogan and Gerry Whyte
—— 4th ed. Dublin, 2003
Kelly, John, pseud. Boyle, John, *Matters of Honour*, London, 1965
Kennedy, Michael, 'Our men in Berlin: some thoughts on Irish diplomats in Germany, 1929–1939', *Irish Studies in International Affairs*, 10 (1999), 57
Kenny, Colum, 'Adventures in training: the Irish genesis of the "remarkable and far-sighted", Select Committee on Legal Education, 1846' in Brand, Costello & Osborough (eds), *Adventures of the Law*
—— *King's Inns and the Kingdom of Ireland: the Irish 'Inn of Court', 1541–1806*, Dublin, 1992
—— *Tristram Kennedy and the Revival of Irish Legal Training, 1835–1885*, Dublin, 1996
Kenny, John, 'The Visitation in University College, Dublin', *Science and Freedom*, no. 17 (Dec. 1960), 7
Keogh, Daire, 'William J. Walsh, 1908–21' in Tom Dunne (ed.), *The National University of Ireland, 1908–2008, Centenary Essays*, Dublin, 2008
Ker, Ian, *John Henry Newman, a Biography*, Oxford, 1988
Kohn, Leo, *The Constitution of the Irish Free State*, London, 1932
Kotsonouris, Mary, *Retreat from Revolution: the Dáil Courts, 1920–24*, Dublin, 1994
—— *The Winding up of the Dáil Courts, 1922–1925: an Obvious Duty*, Dublin, 2004
Kunkel, Wolfgang, *Römische Rechtsgeschichte*, 6th ed., Köln and Graz, 1971
—— *An Introduction to Roman Legal and Constitutional History*, 2nd ed., trans. J.M. Kelly, London, 1973
Lawson, F. H., *The Oxford Law School, 1850–1965*, Oxford, 1968
Lecky, W.E.H., *History of England in the Eighteenth Century*, 8 vols, London, 1878–90
Longford, Elizabeth, *Victoria R.I.*, London, 1966
Liebermann, Felix, *Die Gestze der Angelsachsen*, 4 vols, Halle, 1898–1916
Lyall, Andrew, *Irish Exchequer Reports; Reports of Cases in the Courts of Exchequer and Chancery in Ireland, 1716–1734* [Selden Society 125], London, 2009
McCartney, Donal, *UCD – a National Idea: the History of University College, Dublin*, Dublin, 1999
—— 'University College Dublin' in Tom Dunne (ed.), *The National University of Ireland, 1908–2008, Centenary Essays*, Dublin, 2008
MacCulloch, Diarmaid, *Thomas Cranmer*, New Haven, CT and London, 1996
—— *Reformation: Europe's House Divided, 1490–1700*, London, 2003
McDonnell, A.D., *The Life of Sir Denis Henry, Catholic Unionist*, Belfast, 2000
McDowell, R.B., and D.A. Webb, *Trinity College Dublin 1592–1952, an Academic History*, Cambridge, 1982

McGilligan, Patrick, 'The railway problem: facts to be faced', *Studies*, 21 (1932), 360
MacKenna, Sir Brian, 'Discretion', *Ir Jur*, 9 (1974), 1
MacLiammóir, Michael, *All for Hecuba*, 2nd ed., Dublin, 1961
MacLysaght, Edward, 'The railway problem: facts to be faced', *Studies*, 21 (1932), 353
——, *Irish Families, their Names, Arms and Origins*, Dublin, 1957
MacNeil, Iain Roderick, *Bankruptcy Law in East Africa*, Nairobi, 1966
—— *Cases and Materials in Contracts: Exchange Transactions and Relationships*, Mineola, NY, 1971
—— *Contracts, Instruments for Social Cooporation – East Africa: Text, Cases, Materials*, South Hackensack, NJ, 1968; *see too*, Morison, Robert S.
MacNeill, Eoin, *Celtic Ireland*, Dublin, 1921
—— *Early Irish Law and Institutions*, Dublin, 1935
—— 'Prolegomena to a study of the ancient laws of Ireland', *Ir Jur*, 2 (1967) 106
MacNeill, J.G. Swift, *The Irish Parliament – What it Was and What it Did*, London, Paris, New York and Melbourne, 1885
—— *Titled Corruption: the Sordid Origin of Some Irish Peerages*, London, 1894
—— *English Interference with Irish Industries*, 2nd ed., London, Paris, New York and Melbourne, 1886
—— *Home Rule and Religious Intolerance: a Refutation of Unionist Charges in a Forgotten Speech of Mr Gladstone Recalled*, London, 1912
—— *W.E. Gladstone: Anecdotes and Reminiscences*, London, 1898
—— 'The Irish parliament and the mandate for Union', *Contemporary Review*, 105 (1914), 331
—— 'The breakdown of the Dublin Castle regime', *Contemporary Review*, 110 (1916), 22
—— 'The Prince's marriage and the Royal Marriage Act 1772: a plea for repeal', *Law Quarterly Review*, 38 (1922), 74
—— 'Thoughts on the Constitution of the Irish Free State', *Journal of Comparative Legislation and International Law*, 3rd series, 5 (1923), 52
—— *Studies in the Constitution of the Irish Free State*, Dublin, 1925
—— *What I Have Seen and Heard*, London, 1925
MacNeill, M.C.P., *A Blessed Life, being a Biographical Sketch of the Revd John Gordon Swift MacNeill, MA*, Dublin, 1891
Macnie, D.L., and Moray McLaren (eds), *New Shell Guide to Scotland*, London, 1977
Maitland, F.W., *Collected Papers*, Cambridge, 1911
Martin, F.X., and F.J. Byrne (eds), *The Scholar Revolutionary: Eoin MacNeill, 1867–1945, and the Making of the New Ireland*, Shannon, 1973
Martin, Peter, 'The political career of Michael Tierney: 1920–44', *IHS*, 37 (2011), 412
Maume, Patrick, 'Nationalism and partition: the political thought of Arthur Clery', *IHS*, 31 (1998), 222
Meenan, James (ed.), *Centenary History of the Literary and Historical Society of University College, Dublin, 1855–1955*, Dublin, 2005
Minow, M.C., 'Roman Catholicism on trial in Victorian England: the libel case of John Henry Newman and Dr Achilli', *Catholic Lawyer*, 36 (1995–96), 401
Mohr, Thomas, 'The Privy Council appeal as a minority safeguard for the Protestant community of the Irish Free State, 1922–1935', *NILQ*, 63 (2012), 365
Mohr, Thomas, and Jennifer Schweppe (eds), *Thirty Years of Legal Scholarship*, Dublin, 2011
Moody, T.W., and J.C. Beckett, *Queen's, Belfast, 1845–1949: the History of a University*, 2 vols, London, 1959

Morison, Robert S., *Students and Decision-making: a Report by Robert S. Morison, Chairman of Cornell's Commission on Student Involvement in Decision-making, and Comments by Iain MacNeil,* Washington, 1970

Morrissey, T.J., *Towards a National University: William Delany SJ (1835–1924),* Dublin, 1983

Moylan, Hannah, 'A plea for specialization', *St Stephen's,* 1: 2 (1901), 34

Murnaghan, James A. 'The Royal University and research', *St Stephen's,* 1: 3 (1901), 44

—— 'The development of supreme judicature in Ireland', *Studies,* 1 (1912), 130

—— 'The lordship of Ireland and the counties palatine', *Studies,* 2 (1913), 846

Murphy, H.L., *A History of Trinity College Dublin from its Foundation to 1702*, Dublin, 1951

Murphy, John A., 'University College Cork' in Tom Dunne (ed.), *The National University of Ireland 1908–2008 Centenary Essays,* Dublin, 2008, p. 47

Murray, Christopher, *Sean O'Casey: Writer at Work*, Dublin, 2004

Newman, J.H., *The Idea of a University,* ed. I.T. Ker, Oxford, 1976

—— *Letters and Diaries*, ed. C.S. Dessain et al., 31 vols, Oxford and London, 1965–1977

Ó Criomhthain, Tomás, *An t-Oileánach*, Dublin, 1929

Ó Cróhan, Tomás, *The Islandman* (trans. Robin Flower), Dublin, 1934

Ó Cróinín, Dáibhí, *Early Medieval Ireland, 400–1200*, London and New York, 1995

Ó Cuiv, Brian (ed.), *The Impact of the Scandinavian Invasions on the Celtic-speaking Peoples,* c.*800–1100 AD,* Dublin, 1975

O'Dowd, John, 'John Kelly, politician and scholar', *Studies,* 100 (2011), 455

O'Higgins, Paul, 'Arthur Browne', *NILQ,* 20 (1969), 255

O'Higgins, T.F., *A Double Life,* Dublin, 1996

Ó hInnse, Séamus, *see* Henchy, Séamus

O'Rahilly, Alfred, 'The Irish university question', *Studies,* 51 (1962), 209

Osborough, W.N., 'Preface', *Ir Jur*, 25–7 (1990–92), v

Ó Suileabhain, Muiris, *Fiche Blian ag Fás,* Dublin, 1933

O'Sullivan, Maurice, *Twenty Years A-Growing* (trans. Moya Llewellyn Davies and George Thomson), London, 1933

Ó Tuathaigh, Gearóid, 'The position of the Irish language' in Tom Dunne (ed.), *The National University of Ireland, 1908–2008, Centenary Essays,* Dublin, 2008

Owen, Morfydd E., 'D.A. Binchy', *Studia Celtica,* 24–5 (1989–90), 152

Page, R.I., *Matthew Parker and his Books,* Kalamazoo, MI, 1993

Pearson, Peter, *Between the Mountains and the Sea; Dun Laoghaire – Rathdown County,* Dublin, 1998

Plummer, Charles, *Vitae Sanctorum Hiberniae,* Oxford, 1910

Powell, Ashley, *A Manual of Egyptian Arabic*, Cairo, 1926

Quinn, A.P., *Wigs and Guns: Irish Barristers in the Great War*, Dublin, 2006

Radcliffe and Cross's The English Legal System, 5th ed., ed. Lord Cross of Chelsea and G.J. Hand, London, 1971

Rashdall, Hastings, *The Universities of Europe in the Middle Ages*, new ed. by F.M. Powicke and A.B. Emden, 3 vols., Oxford, 1936

Robbers, Gerhard (ed.), *Church Autonomy: a Comparative Survey*, Frankfurt am Main, 2001

—— *State and Church in the European Union,* Baden-Baden, 1996

Roebuck Castle: Catalogue of the Valuable and Antique Contents including more particularly Important Collections of Silver, Jewellery and Ornamental China, and a Unique Collection of Needlework Pictures, to be sold by Auction commencing Monday 20th day of September, 1943, Dublin, 1943

Scott, Sir Walter, *Scott: Poetical Works,* ed. J. Logie Robertson, London, 1904

Shaw, Francis, 'Post-mortem on the second Patrick', *Studies,* 51 (1962), 237
Sheehy, J.G., 'Male physical impotence in juridical proceedings', *The Jurist*, Washington DC, 1960
Society of Jesus, *A Page of Irish History: the Story of UCD, 1883–1909*, Dublin and Cork, 1930
Stedman, E.C. (ed.), *A Victorian Anthology, 1837–1885*, New York, 1895
Sullivan, F.S., *Lectures on the Constitution and Laws of England with a Commentary on Magna Carta*, ed. S.P. Donlan, Clark, N.J., 2003
Sweeney, J.M.G., 'Arthur Browne', *Journal of Maritime Law and Commerce*, 26 (1993), 58
Synan, Arthur, *see* Clery, Arthur E.
Thurneysen, Rudolf, *Handbuch des Alt-Irischen*, Heidelberg, 1909
Tierney, M., 'Daniel O'Connell and the Gaelic past', *Studies,* 27 (1938), 369
Ua Clerigh, Arthur, *The History of Ireland to the Coming of Henry II,* London, 1908
——, *The Franchises and the Registration of Parliamentary Voters in Ireland,* 3rd ed. Dublin, 1886.
—— *Some Thoughts on Reform in the High and County Courts in Ireland,* Dublin, 1885
—— *The Queen's Colleges in Ireland,* Dublin, 1868
Vinogradoff, Sir Paul, *Outlines of Historical Jurisprudence,* Oxford, 1920
Walsh, J.E., *Ireland Sixty Years Ago,* Dublin, 1847
Walsh, P.J., *William J. Walsh, Archbishop of Dublin,* Dublin, 1928
Walsh, William, *The Irish University Question,* Dublin, 1890
Ward, Wilfrid, *The Life and Times of Cardinal Wiseman,* 2 vols, London, 1897
Wasserschleben, F.W.H. (ed.), *Die Irische Kanonensammlung,* 2nd ed., Leipzig, 1885
Watt, J.A., J.B. Morrall and F.X. Martin (eds), *Medieval Studies Presented to Aubrey Gwynn SJ,* Dublin, 1961
Webb, John, *Municipal Government in Ireland, Medieval and Modern*, Dublin and London, 1918
—— *Industrial Dublin Since 1698, and the Silk Industry in Dublin: Two Essays*, Dublin, 1913
—— *The Guilds of Dublin,* Dublin and London, 1929
Wheeler-Bennett, J.W., *Hindenburg, The Wooden Titan,* London, 1936
White, Terence de Vere, *Kevin O'Higgins,* Tralee, 1966
Whitla, William, *The University Education Question in Ireland: its Difficulties and their Solution,* Belfast, 1899
Wordsworth, William, *Poetical Works*, ed. E. De Selincourt and Helen Darbishire, 2nd ed., Oxford, 1954

Index of Legislation Etc.

Index to Cases at Law

Note: the ensuing list does not include precedents cited by Palles C.B. in his judgment in the *Mabel Walker* case (Appendix III)

General Index